THE DIPLOMACY OF
THE RUSSO-JAPANESE WAR

The
Diplomacy of
the Russo-Japanese War

BY JOHN ALBERT WHITE

PRINCETON UNIVERSITY PRESS
PRINCETON, NEW JERSEY
1964

Printed in the United States of America
by The Maple Press Company, York, Pennsylvania

To Dorothy, Geoffrey, and Kenneth

Preface

THE YEAR 1905 appeared to be an eventful and significant year at the time and has increased in historical importance in the last six decades. The two world wars fought since 1905 have cast the Russo-Japanese War in the role of a prelude to even greater events unanticipated then in St. Petersburg or Tokyo or at the Portsmouth Conference. The Japanese loss in 1945 of her continental possessions also lends a retrospective meaning to the Russo-Japanese War; it was the beginning of a great but unsuccessful era of Japanese expansion due to the success of this first venture in contesting Russian dominance in Eastern Asia. For Soviet Russia, too, her victorious emergence from the Second World War has been impressive though her position has now been largely modified by the revival of China as a competitive Far Eastern power.

The reversal of roles which followed the Second World War was given due prominence in Premier Stalin's remarks regarding the consequences of the Yalta agreement. He noted then, according to *Pravda* on September 3, 1945, that Russia's defeat four decades before had remained a depressing memory for the Soviet people. He concluded: "Today, Japan has recognized her defeat and signed the act of unconditional surrender." It was, in his view, the end of a cycle that was signalized by the return of many Russian rights and interests in Manchuria that had been lost to Japan in 1905 and subsequently.

The year 1905 was also a time of revolution. Had a number of circumstances been different during the succeeding years, this might have remained for Russia merely an unhappy and unfortunate episode. The revolution, however, had important consequences and it too has since been associated in an unpredictable way with the major developments of the twentieth century. Both the war and the revolution have reverberated throughout Asia and the world, playing a major role in the "awakening of Asia" with all its consequences—a protracted period of transition to some new, but as yet undefined, era.

A reappraisal of the Russo-Japanese War has been in order for some time, not only because of the intrinsic importance of the subject but also because of the accumulation of new evidence. Both the Soviet and Japanese governments have issued valuable source materials. Other governments, notably those of France,

Germany, and Great Britain, have supplemented these with selections from their own archives. While Russian writers have contributed many secondary accounts over the decades, it is only recently that Japanese scholars have turned to a general reassessment of their own nation's role in the war. Other countries have done surprisingly little with this subject.

In the United States the last general account was Tyler Dennett's *Roosevelt and the Russo-Japanese War*, published in 1925 before most of the presently available documentary sources had appeared. This book was based largely on the papers of Theodore Roosevelt and has remained the standard account in English. Considering the limited sources available to the author, it is remarkable how valid most of his judgments remain. The materials now available and the passage of time have, however, added greatly to the understanding of the war as well as its setting and historical significance.

This study is concerned with the cosmopolitan rather than the national significance of the war. Two things in particular have encouraged this approach to the subject: the publication of documentary sources by various governments that provide an opportunity for an international view, as well as the first real chance to view these documents dispassionately and in perspective. To achieve this dual purpose, certain limitations have been consciously accepted: one, to emphasize the diplomatic, political, and economic aspects of the war rather than the military, and two, to aim at an objective appraisal, knowing that such a study will consequently fail to satisfy the partisan point of view that has continued to influence most thinking about the war.

The wide-ranging search for the materials used in this book has elicited valuable help from persons and institutions too numerous to mention. It is understood that no project of this scope could be carried out without the cooperation of many persons of good will and I wish to convey to all my sincere appreciation.

Three contributions in particular must nevertheless be mentioned. The Rockefeller Foundation generously made possible access to the indispensable archival and library resources of Japan. Professor Theodore H. von Laue of the University of California at Riverside allowed me to read the manuscript of his valuable book, *Count Witte and the Industrial Development of Russia*, since published by the Columbia University Press. Finally, Professor Byron Emory of East Michigan State College gave me the picture of the Naval Store House at Kittery Naval Yard, Portsmouth.

The mechanical problems encountered in the course of writing this book were not unusual. The systems of Romanization and transliteration used are, with some exceptions, the standard ones and will be left to speak for themselves. The use of Russian materials in close conjunction with other sources made it necessary to use the new style for all Russian dates and they are so given unless otherwise indicated.

JOHN ALBERT WHITE

Honolulu
July 1963

Contents

Preface   vii
Abbreviations   xiii

PREWAR DIPLOMACY

1. China and the Balance of Power   1
2. Witte's Manchurian Empire   11
3. The Opposition to Witte   31
4. Russia's "New Course"   50
5. The Isolation of Russia   76
6. The Opening of the Final Negotiations   95
7. Peace Comes to an End   112

WAR AND DIPLOMACY

8. A Decisive Military Thrust   135
9. Japan's Wartime Diplomacy   155
10. Russia's European Flank   170
11. An Impending Deadlock   185
12. A Return to Diplomacy   206

THE PORTSMOUTH CONFERENCE AND A NEW BALANCE OF POWER

13. Mediation and the Conference   227
14. The Peace Campaign   247
15. The Spoils of War   263
16. The Crisis: Sakhalin and Indemnity   282
17. "Balanced Antagonisms" in Action   310
18. China and the New Balance of Power   330

APPENDICES

1. Russo-Japanese Diplomatic Exchanges 1901–1904   349
2. Issues Discussed at the Portsmouth and Peking Conferences   359
3. Chronology   369

Bibliography   379
Index   405

ABBREVIATIONS

B.D.—George P. Gooch, *et al.*, *British Documents on the Origins of the War, 1898–1914*, 11 Vols., London, 1926–1938.

China No. 2 (1904)—Great Britain. Parliamentary Papers, "Blue Books," *China No. 2 (1904): Correspondence Respecting the Russian Occupation of Manchuria and Newchwang*, London, 1904.

Correspondence—Japan. Imperial Diet, *Correspondence regarding the Negotiations Between Japan and Russia (1903–1904)*, Presented to the Imperial Diet, March 1904, Washington, 1904.

D.D.F.—France. Ministry of Foreign Affairs, *Documents Diplomatiques Francais (1871–1941)*, 2ᵉ Serie (1901–1911), 14 Vols., Paris, 1930–1955.

Dnevnik—M.N. Pokrovsky, *Dnevnik A.N. Kuropatkina*, n.p., 1923.

F.R.—V.M. Vonliarliarsky (attributed to), "Why Russia Went to War with Japan: The Story of the Yalu Concession," *Fortnightly Review*, DXXI, New Series, May 2, 1910, pp. 816–831, DXXII, New Series, June 1, 1910, pp. 1030–1044.

G.P.—Johannes Lepsius, *et al.*, *Die Grosse Politik der Europaishen Kabinette 1871–1914, Sammlung der Diplomatischen Akten des Auswartigen Amptes*, 54 Vols., Berlin, 1922–1927.

J.F.O.—Japan. Foreign Office, "Diplomatic Correspondence," a file of manuscript documentary materials in the Japanese Foreign Office.

K.A.—Union of Soviet Socialist Republics. Central Archives, *Krasnyi Arkhiv* 106 issues in 73 Vols., Moscow, 1922–1941.

Kaneko, *Beikoku*—Kaneko Kentaro, *Beikoku Daitoryo Kaiken Shimatsu.*

Kaneko, *Nichiro*—Kaneko Kentaro, *Nichiro Seneki Beikoku Tairyuki.*

K.G.—Japan. Foreign Office, *Komura Gaikoshi*, 2 Vols., Tokyo, 1953.

K.I.—B. Romanov, "Kontsessiia na Ialu," *Russkoe Proshloe*, No. 1, Moscow, 1923, pp. 87–108.

MacMurray—John V.A. MacMurray, *Treaties and Agreements with and concerning China, 1894–1919*, 2 Vols., New York, 1921.

M.C.R.—United States. Department of Commerce, *Monthly Consular Reports, 1903–1905*, Washington, 1904–1906.

M.C.T.—Military Correspondent of the Times [Charles A'Court Repington], *The War in the Far East 1904–1905*, New York, 1905.

M.H.S.—Nagayama Yasumasa (ed.), *Shimbun Shusei Meiji Hennen Shi*, 15 Vols., Tokyo, 1934–1940.

M.K.N.K.D.H.—Japan. Foreign Office, *Manshu ni kansuru Nisshin Kosho Dampan Hikki.*

N.G.M.—Japan. Foreign Office, *Nihon Gaiko Monjo*, XXXIII-XL, Tokyo, 1956–1960.

N.G.N.—Japan. Foreign Office, *Nihon Gaiko Nempyo narabi Shuyo Monjo*, 2 Vols., Tokyo, 1955.

N.K.D.H.—Japan. Foreign Office, *Nichiro Kowa Dampan Hikki; tsuki Ryokoku Zenkenin Hiseishiki Kaiken Yoroku*, August–September, 1904.

N.K.S.—Japan. Foreign Office, *Nichiro Kosho Shi*, 2 Vols.

Obzor—Russia. Ministry of Foreign Affairs, *Obzor Snoshenii s Iaponieiu Koreiskom Delam s 1895 goda*, St. Petersburg, 1906.

Protocoles—Japan. Foreign Office, *Protocoles de la Conference de la Paix entre le Japon et la Russie.*

Protocols—Japan. Foreign Office, *Protocols of the Peace Conference between Japan and Russia.*

R.–I.V.—Union of Soviet Socialist Republics. Central Archives, *Russko-Iaponskaia Voina; iz Dnevnikov A.N. Kuropatkina i N.P. Linievicha* (Foreword by M.N. Pokrovsky), Leningrad, 1925.

Romanov, *Ocherki*—Boris A. Romanov, *Ocherki Diplomaticheskoi Istorii Russko-Iaponskoi Voiny*, Moscow, 1947.

Romanov, *Russia*—Boris A. Romanov, *Russia in Manchuria (1892–1906)*, Leningrad, 1928, Ann Arbor, 1952.

U.S.F.R.—United States. Department of State, *Papers Relating to the Foreign Relations of the United States*, 1903–1905, Washington, 1904–1906.

PREWAR DIPLOMACY

1. China and the Balance of Power

IN JUNE 1903, General Aleksei Nikolaevich Kuropatkin, the Russian minister of war, reached Japan for an official visit. He was enthusiastically welcomed and royally housed in the Shiba Detached Palace in Tokyo, the former city villa of the lord of Kii. In the course of his brief stay, he was received by the Imperial family as well as the prime minister and a host of other civilian and military officials. Dinners and military reviews were held in his honor. From all appearances even an observer fairly close to official circles might have wondered whether, contrary to rumors and reports, Russia and Japan might not after all compromise their differences and avoid a clash.

Yet, as the principals in this dramatic visit well knew, appearances were completely deceiving. They were all painfully aware that this was undoubtedly the last opportunity to halt the rapid deterioration of Russo-Japanese relations and to prevent the war which seemed to many an imminent danger. Behind the scenes of the pageantry, they sought in serious conversations for some leading string that might disentangle the seemingly hopeless snarl into which the relations of the two countries had fallen.

The effort, it must be said in retrospect, was superficial, particularly in proportion to the gravity of the problem. Even the realization that this was the eleventh hour failed to bring any notable flexibility into the negotiations. In fact, they appear to have done little more than review the principal issues and probe for the willingness of the other party to yield. In the end, the endeavor stopped far short of a genuine compromise that might have tempered the rigid demands of national interests. They used this occasion as though the frustrated attempts to compose their differences over the years had produced a rigidity in their attitudes that foredoomed any reasonable accommodation.

It is hardly surprising, therefore, that no mutually acceptable formula was found. Instead, all parties left the conference impressed with the deepening crisis. The Russian minister of war returned to St. Petersburg to stress the serious danger of war and the determination of the Japanese to defend their interests. Meanwhile, in Tokyo the government turned to the grim task of formulating the proposals which were to constitute both the basis for the final negotiations and the rationale for the war.

The issues as defined in these exchanges were expressed in the language of national interests. And indeed, against the backdrop of existing international chaos, this was a point of view that no contemporary statesman, whether Russian, Japanese, or any other, could be expected to disregard. The diplomatic exchanges contained only hints concerning the larger problems that had given national interests the prominence they had acquired by 1903. These larger problems scarcely needed reiterating for the leading statesmen of the time whose public careers spanned many of the tense years preceeding the crisis. Confronted by a situation so menacing to their own national interests, they had to seek such solutions as lay at hand rather than await a more ideal yet unrealizable outcome.

The Boxer Rebellion in the summer of 1900 had forced the issues into the open; almost immediately, this drew together the military forces of several nations. Each nation was drawn into participation out of fear of injury to its own national interests and as a means of warning its rivals against violation of those interests.

By the mid-1890's it had already become apparent that international rivalries would have to be taken more seriously if China were to sustain her political and territorial integrity. She had survived the intense orgy of seizures which reached a climax in 1898 largely because there was at that time a sufficient balance of effective strength among the rival powers to prevent serious consequences from monopoly of power. The commercial advantages enjoyed throughout China preserved the value of territorial integrity and acted as a political formula for blocking further Chinese dissolution.

By 1900 and the outbreak of the Boxer Rebellion, the situation was somewhat different. In the first place, the optimism inspired by the promising effort of China in 1898 to reform and strengthen her political structure had long since been completely dissipated. The Boxer Rebellion of 1900, therefore, acted as an alarm which sent all the powers scurrying once more to their diplomatic stations to insure their already considerable holdings and to guarantee their control over any future division of spoils. This attitude was given additional significance by the fact that Great Britain, the western nation with the greatest stake in China and in the preservation of its existing order, faced the new crisis with one hand tied down by the Boer War.

Russia acted boldly under these new circumstances and occupied Manchuria. Though the other powers had also sent military forces to China to guard their interests, the Russian situation was different. Russia had ready access to China across the frontier and had more troops already in China than any other power. Also, Chinese rights being violated by Russia were in the immediate sense more extensive and potentially more valuable than those of any other power.

The Russian occupation of Manchuria in 1900 paralleled the disturbing experiences of the past decades, especially the past five years. The Russian advance southward toward India and China had presented statesmen from London to Tokyo with serious problems. Was this not simply the most recent stage of a forward movement which included the advance in Persia? The Russian progress in Manchuria during the past five years seemed to indicate that it was. There was indeed reason to fear a prolonged if not permanent Russian occupation of Manchuria.

Among the widespread and often highly imaginative contemporary endeavors to understand and interpret this era of severe international tensions, some of the most cogent and generally accepted interpretations were directed specifically and with foreboding toward Russia and her unrelenting outward expansion.

In March 1900, a few weeks before the Russian troops entered Manchuria, Admiral Alfred T. Mahan, the American philosopher of naval power, published an article in *Harper's New Monthly Magazine* in which he expressed the following thoughts:

"Upon a glance at the map one enormous fact immediately obtrudes itself upon the attention—the vast, uninterrupted mass of the Russian Empire, stretching from the meridian of western Asia Minor, until to the eastward it overpasses Japan."[1] Admiral Mahan pointed out that the Russian land frontier presented no political obstacle to the exertion of concentrated strength and distance alone raised a communications problem. Furthermore, since the Russian southward advance was guarded by a mountainous center, "It is upon, and from the flanks of this great line that restraint, if needed, must come. . . ." Whether this restraint were exercised from the flanks or upon the center by way of India, he felt that Britain would have a major responsibility for making it a reality. Therefore, he suggested that "These concurrent facts—and factors—suggest, what will hereafter become

[1] A.T. Mahan, *The Problem of Asia*, Boston, 1900, pp. 24ff.

increasingly apparent, that we have here again a fresh instance of the multiform struggle between land power and sea power."

In the same month that Japan opened negotiations with Russia, August 1903, the French military attaché in London added another disconcerting view of Russia's expansion.[2] He portrayed the Russian advance as an attempt to blend her power and territories with those of China; this would ultimately form a solid block of power which could render obsolete all previous achievements in acquiring rights and interests in China whether through the "open door" or "spheres of influence." He saw Russia building her relationship with China on the unique foundation of a contiguous territory and projecting herself into China through jointly used railways, financial operations, roads, and rivers. He noted with particular interest the viceroyalty that Russia had just created in the Far East to join administratively the Russian Amur and Maritime regions with the new acquisitions in Manchuria; British interests indeed seemed threatened, as this French interpretation shows. Clearly, Russia's advance was viewed with alarm and interpreted as different from that of other nations.

Russia's geographical advantage, in fact, appeared so overwhelming that her competitors were hardly disposed to concern themselves with the menace which the Boxer Rebellion constituted for her interests. Yet throughout Manchuria her uncompleted railway network, and with it the foundation of her imperial plans, lay exposed to a hostile Chinese population. Domestic administrative antagonisms rather than a failure to appreciate the need for action account for Russia's delay in sending forces into Manchuria. These were not sent, in fact, until it became evident that the railway guards were insufficient to deal with the situation.[3]

Sergei Witte, the Russian minister of finance, under whom the guards were administered, sought to prevent if possible the entry of the regular military forces, representing a rival ministry, by increasing the guards from 4,500 to 11,000. He also urged Li Hung-chang, the governor-general of Chihli Province and plenipotentiary for dealing with the foreigners, to keep the situation under control as much as possible. By July 9th, however,

[2] d'Amade to Andre, Aug. 24, 1903, *D.D.F.*, III, 538. (Consult Abbreviations given on page xiii.)
[3] A. Malozemoff, *Russian Far Eastern Policy, 1881–1904*, Berkeley, 1958, pp. 142ff.; Romanov, *Russia*, p. 180; C.C. Tan, *The Boxer Catastrophe*, New York, 1955, pp. 159–161.

Witte was ready to acknowledge the inadequacy of these measures and to request the immediate dispatch of military forces to Manchuria. Troops already concentrated for such an eventuality at Khabarovsk were forthwith moved up the Sungari River to suppress the uprising. In less than three months most of Manchuria was under Russian occupation.

One aspect of the situation that confronted Russia has been described as follows by a British visitor:

"The Boxer movement was as violent in Southern Manchuria as anywhere in China, and the symptoms were identical: railways destroyed, foreign houses burned, and foreigners murdered. The only reason why fewer missionaries were killed is that the wave came later than in Chih-li, there was ample warning, and there were Russian troops on the spot."[4]

The disturbances in North Manchuria also invited Russian military intervention because they projected the menacing situation up to and even across the frontier into Russian territory. This was stimulated by a number of circumstances. There was the Russian uncertainty as to the attitude the large resident Chinese population would assume regarding the appeal of the anti-Russian movement in Manchuria. This was aggravated by the great distance between the Russian Far East and European Russia. The consequent isolation from military protection in itself aroused fear among the local Russians.

Two events occurred in the river town of Blagoveshchensk that ignited this explosive situation.[5] First, sporadic bombardment from the Chinese side of the river inspired rumors of a coming invasion and increased the tension among the unprotected population. On July 14, just five days after Russian military forces had crossed into Manchuria, some Russian ships moving along the river were stopped by the Chinese at Aigun, twenty miles downstream from Blagoveschchensk. Open hostilities immediately broke out. Second, the rounding up for deportation of all Chinese residents of the town was ordered. On July 17, as the unfortunate Chinese residents were being driven across the river, they were fired on by the Russians and many were killed.

[4] H.J. Whigham, *Manchuria and Korea*, London, 1904, p. 111.
[5] A. Malozemoff, *Russian Far Eastern Policy, 1881–1904*, Berkeley, 1958, pp. 140–42; L. Deutsch, *Sixteen Years in Siberia*, London, 1905, pp. 327–342; A. Hosie, *Manchuria: Its People, Resources and Recent History*, Boston, 1910, p. 281; *Obzor*, pp. 9ff.

Russia's participation in the intervention in China was qualified from its inception by an already established policy that had been outlined in a note of June 18 to Admiral Alekseiev, the Commander in chief at Port Arthur.[6] In it Foreign Minister M. N. Muraviev, a few days before his death, clearly defined a separate and different role for Russia in China. The assumption of Muraviev's note was that Russia's common frontier with China entitled her to a special position with respect to the other powers in China. The note made it clear that this required unqualified support for Russian nationals and property while at the same time maintaining an attitude of detachment toward the other allied powers. The point was also made that the activities of the other powers would be watched for any signs of possible menace to Russian interests. The note stated that the official attitude toward China would continue to be friendly and any Russian activity would involve only assistance to the Chinese government in stamping out rebellion. Beyond this Russia would avoid any leading role in the supression. This attitude became a cause of irritation, particularly between Russia and Germany, since the latter wished to retaliate vigorously for the murder of Baron Klemens von Ketteler, the German minister to China.

Russia's close tie with China, Muraviev's note further explained, would constitute a shield for her special interests and she would continue to protect her own rights and interests along with those of China. He stated that Russia would follow this advantageous policy and seek a separate settlement with China and he so informed the powers in a circular note on August 25th.[7] This note completed the estrangement between Russia and the other allies. It drew a clear distinction between the mission of the Russian military forces and those of the allied powers; the only legitimate function for the combined operation was, in the Russian view, the protection of foreign nationals and the rendering of assistance to the Chinese government in restoring order. It was made clear that no other excuse for not evacuating troops from the Peking region would be acceptable. Although Russia subsequently further clarified her views on her position in relation to the other powers, the note of August 25th clearly challenged the principle of equality of rights in China.

    [6] Muraviev to Alekseiev, June 18, 1900, I.I. Korostovets, *Rossiia no Dalnem Vostoke*, Peking, 1922, p. 20.
    [7] Lamsdorf to Urusov, Aug. 25, 1900, *D.D.F.* (1st Series), xvi, 414–416.

Russia's separate role in relation to China was forcefully exemplified by her conduct in the Peking-Tientsin area which served to increase further the fear of Russian objectives. The powers had agreed not to take advantage of existing conditions to acquire territory—a principle subscribed to by Great Britain, Germany, and even Russia herself. It was discovered, however, that in early October Russia had seized a concession area at Tientsin.[8] The Russian commander, General N.P. Linievich, made no attempt to excuse or disguise his act; he simply declared that the acquisition was Russia's by right of conquest.[9] The seizure initiated a chain reaction and within the next few weeks several other nations resorted to similar compensating action aimed at preserving the balance of power.

Russia soon began to force her policy on China in a more permanent way and sought a commitment from China through two separate documents. The governor-general of Mukden, Tseng Ch'i, finally approved the first of these, an agreement with Admiral Alekseiev signed on November 26, 1900, after three weeks of severe pressure.[10] The agreement, in effect, left Russia free to maintain control of Manchuria as long as she considered it necessary.

Meanwhile, the Russian conditions for withdrawal had been in preparation and were finally presented to China on February 8, 1901;[11] this document was really an ultimatum that applied to all of Manchuria and reflected no consultation with the Chinese government. Its provisions were largely unacceptable to China and its purport totally unacceptable to Japan. These conditions for withdrawal had been worked out in St. Petersburg by the ministers of foreign affairs, finance, and war, principally the latter two.

Russia was clearly determined to obtain concessions from China while the Boxer troubles were still effectively keeping the situation off balance. Accordingly, her demands contained two principles that China might be expected to accept more readily under these trying conditions: first, the separation of the question

---

[8] H.B. Morse, *International Relations of the Chinese Empire*, 3 vols., New York, 1918, III, 323–326; Lansdowne to Lascelles, Jan. 22, 1901, *B.D.*, II, 23.
[9] N. Poppe, "Russian Circular Announcing Occupation of the Left Bank of Peiho," Nov. 6, 1900, *U.S.F.R.*, 1901, p. 41.
[10] W.W. Rockhill, *Treaties with or concerning China and Korea, 1894–1904*, Washington, 1904, pp. 201–202; MacMurray, I, 298–320, 329.
[11] Romanov, *Russia*, pp. 187–212.

of the evacuation of military forces from that of continuing Russian domination in the whole border region; and second, the principle that the reimbursement that Russia was to receive as compensation for the Manchurian losses would be carefully differentiated from that contemplated by the allied powers.

The 14 articles of the demands presented in February 1901 may be divided into two general groups; the first 7 articles dealt with the immediate relations between Russian and China in Manchuria; the other 7 articles dealt with the problems of long-range tenure. The first 7 articles stipulated in part; Russia would restore formal political authority in Manchuria to China; Russia would maintain troops in Manchuria until peaceful conditions prevailed and compensation was paid; Russian forces would cooperate with the Chinese authorities; China was not to have any troops there until after the completion of the railway; the number of troops would be determined between the Chinese and Russian officials; and the importation of arms and ammunition was to be prohibited. These articles also provided: China would remove such higher administrative officials as were not acceptable to both governments; for areas outside the railway zone the Chinese under Russian supervision were to organize a foot and mounted police force under the direction of the local governors; China would accept no foreigners as advisors in her army or in the North China fleet; and the autonomous status of the city government of Chinchowting was to be abrogated.

Among the second 7 articles were provisions to the effect that China would grant no concessions for railway construction, mineral rights, or industrial enterprises without Russian consent in the border regions of Manchuria, Mongolia, Kansu, and Sinkiang; and that she would neither build railways without Russian consent nor grant to foreigners the right to use land in these regions, except Newchwang. It is notable that in September 1900, in a vain attempt to keep Russia out of Manchuria, the Chinese government had proposed special privileges in the other frontier areas.[12] Now Russia was proposing to accept this in addition to the monopoly position she wanted in Manchuria.

The rest of the articles dealt with the compensation for losses incurred by the Russians in the Boxer uprising. It was specified that this was to be paid to the Chinese Eastern Railway Company and the Russo-Chinese Bank—the two institutions through which

[12] Romanov, *Russia*, pp. 187ff.

the Russian minister of finance exercised control over Manchuria. Another provision covered the granting of "certain privileges, modification of existing concessions, or the issue of new concessions." Individual Russians were given the right to sue for damages.

Following the report of the Tseng-Alekseiev agreement in the London *Times* on January 3, 1901, Russia skillfully and convincingly set forth her aims in China during the next few months, both through diplomatic channels and the public press.[13] An officially inspired Russian article of early April 1901 stated that the situation required the restoration of normal relations between China and the other powers,[14] and this could be accomplished only by removing the foreign troops from the capital province and permitting the Chinese Imperial court to return to Peking, a point already made in the circular note of August 25, 1900. In addition to these shared problems, Russia again stressed her special problems with regard to China: the common frontier and the preservation of traditional good relations. On the question of evacuation, Russia's foreign minister stated that her special interests in Manchuria suffered from the same confused and chaotic conditions as those of the other powers. Reiterating the principle expressed in the Russian note of August 25, he continued:

"When it came to the final evacuation of Manchuria the Russian government would be obliged to obtain from the Central Government of China an effective guarantee against the recurrence of the recent attack on her frontier and the destruction of her railway, but had no intention of seeking this guarantee in any acquisition of territory or of an actual or virtual protectorate over Manchuria . . ."[15]

As a consequence of the signing of the Anglo-Japanese Alliance on January 30, 1902, Russian insistence on her special position in China seemed to abate temporarily. The first indication of a change of attitude came with the announcement of the Franco-Russian declarations of March 16 and 20, 1902, supporting the

[13] Lansdowne to MacDonald, Jan. 29, 1901 (encloses Lamsdorf note to Japanese minister in St. Petersburg), *B.D.*, II, 34; Tower to Hay, April 8, 1901, No. 412 (encloses article from *Journal de St. Petersburg* of April 6, 1901), *Despatches*, No. 35, Roll 56, Vol. 56.
[14] Tower to Hay, April 8, 1901, *op.cit.*
[15] Scott to Lansdowne, Feb. 6, 1901, *China No. 2 (1904)*, pp. 5–6.

independence of China and Korea and the freedom of trade and industrial enterprise within these countries for all nations, principles which Russia would shortly transgress and then deny.[16]

Russia nevertheless appeared to be putting these principles into practice when the Sino-Russian treaty of April 8, 1902 was announced.[17] At first glance the Sino-Russian treaty seemed to promise that Russia would evacuate her troops from Manchuria in three six-month stages within eighteen months of the date of the agreement. However, Article Two of the agreement contained a proviso to the effect that the withdrawal of troops would be carried out as stated "provided that no disturbances arise and that the action of other Powers should not prevent it." Both the Chinese and Russian negotiators recognized that the inclusion of this phrase would, if actually applied, nullify all the rest of the agreement.[18] Chinese objections are said to have been overcome by a bribe of over 40,000 rubles. The final effects of this proviso did not become apparent immediately since Russia fulfilled the first part of the agreement by withdrawing on schedule from the area west of the Liao River.[19] Russian intentions became clear, however, when her troops were not withdrawn from the second area as scheduled in April 1903; her troops remained until they were eventually forcibly removed by the Japanese armies in 1904–05.

Russia had responded to the Boxer Rebellion in 1900 by a systematic attempt to confirm the exceptional position in Manchuria at which she had been openly aiming since 1895. Following a practice well established among the powers in China and elsewhere, Russia relied on a crisis, on the weakness of China, and on the desire of the powers to localize and limit the disorder to enlarge her existing interests. Russia, however, had miscalculated the deep fear that her unilateral acts inspired and the determination of the Japanese not to be put off again. Consequently, Japan was able to take advantage of Russia's errors and press for a solution to a long-standing problem.

[16] *Obzor*, p. 77; G. Michon, *The Franco-Russian Alliance*, 1891–1917, New York 1929, pp. 116–121.

[17] Romanov, *Ocherki*, pp. 451–455; MacMurray, I, 326–329.

[18] Romanov, *Russia*, pp. 243–244.

[19] *K.G.*, I, 304; M. Hori, *Nichiro Senso Zengo*, Tokyo, 1940, pp. 111ff.; J. Otsu, *Dainihon Kenseishi*, 10 Vols., Tokyo, 1927, V, 638–639.

2. Witte's Manchurian Empire

THE RUSSIAN STAKE in Manchuria was a prize of unique importance and well worth a struggle. Unlike the competitive circumstances at the seaports through which the western powers and Japan had to seek entrance into China, Russia's access was over a land frontier subject to her exclusive control. It was over this frontier that her railway penetrated to the principal points in Manchuria, giving Russia domination over its present economic life as well as a potential monopoly of its future. To the east Russia could menace Japan's interests in Korea and block her further penetration westward. In Manchuria, Russia also had a base of operations of incomparable strategic value for economic and ultimately political penetration of intramural China.

Sergei Iulievich Witte was the individual who had been primarily responsible for fashioning Russia's sphere of interest in the Far East and whose official interests were therefore most directly brought into focus by the Japanese challenge. One of Russia's most distinguished statesmen of the late Imperial period, he was the minister of finance after 1892 and became the principal architect of the nation's new industrial structure. His dominating personality and his growing prestige had at first stimulated confidence in his plans; later they inspired fear of the consequences and of his personal ambitions.

Through inheritance and early environment, Witte had received both a taste for change and a sense of solidarity with the conservative elements in Russian society.[1] His father, Iulius Fedorovich Witte, was apparently a descendant of a Dutch family that had settled in the Baltic provinces under the Swedish regime. At the time of Sergei's birth in 1849, the family lived in Tiflis, where his father was head of the department of state lands under the governor general of the Caucasus. His father, while an official in Saratov Province, had been manager of a model state farm and, during his years in the Caucasus had been instrumental in the development of natural resources, including the manganese deposits at Chiaturi, now one of the largest manganese-mining centers in the world. When Sergei was 6 years old his father had acquired hereditary nobility. Sergei's mother, Ekaterina Andreevna Fadeeva, was the daughter of the governor of Saratov

---

[1] T.H. von Laue, "Sergei Witte and the Industrialization of Russia," Ms., n.d., Ch. IV; S.I. Witte, *Vospominaniia*, 3 Vols., Moscow, 1960, I, 5–6.

Province; through her, Sergei was related to the princely Dolgoruky family and to the well-known theosophist, Madame Elena Petrovna Blavatskaia.

While a student at Novorossiisk University, Witte developed his apparently considerable mathematical talents and had intended to pursue an academic career, but his mother's family considered this unsuitable for a nobleman. In 1871 he entered the government with the rank of titular councillor at the ninth rank in the office of the governor general of Odessa and Bessarabia.

In 1877 Witte left government service and entered railway work with which he was to remain identified to the end of his active career. For the next 12 years he pursued a successful and profitable career in railway administration for a private company. In 1889 the minister of finance, I.A. Vyshnegradsky, invited Witte to join him in St. Petersburg and take charge of the railway department created to supervise the new tariffs. In 1892 Witte became minister of finance, the position he held while carrying out the industrial transformation of the country, in the course of which he established his enormous power and prestige.

Witte brought to his career an impressive personality, which seems to have been conditioned by a striking physical appearance and an incisive mind. Even in his pictures one is struck by his massive physical bulk; he was tall, broad-shouldered, and large in frame to the extent of appearing somewhat ungainly. A.P. Izvolsky wrote of him that "his whole frame suggests something that might have been shaped by the rude blows of an axe. His features would have had character, were it not for a malformation, almost a fracture of the nose, which gave him a certain resemblance to the portraits of Michelangelo."[2] Below his high forehead, his large brown eyes caused Senator Albert Beveridge to say of them that they had "an expression of patience and weariness about them which reminds you of what you have read about the eyes of Lincoln."[3] Witte expressed himself in a low voice, looking directly at the person he was addressing. In spite of the simplicity, even the reticence, of his manner, the American minister found him "exceedingly forcible in the defense of his own opinions, which carry such weight in the Council of State and are so generally accepted by the other cabinet ministers that he is now looked

[2] C.L. Seegar, *The Memoirs of Alexander Iswolsky: Formerly Russian Minister of Foreign Affairs and Ambassador to France*, London, 1920, pp. 113–114.
[3] A.J. Beveridge, *The Russian Advance*, New York, 1904, p. 439.

upon as the paramount influence under the Emperor in shaping the policy of Russia, but he is not often inclined toward a merely agreeable interchange of ideas in conversation, and never likely to make a statement not intended to produce some specific result."[4]

As Witte rose to unbelievably high stature in the official world of St. Petersburg, it became clear that his gruff and sometimes impatient manner was only one of the weapons available to his enemies to bring him down; another weapon available to them took the form of anti-Semitism, then so prevalent in court and official circles. One aspect of anti-Semitism centered around his wife, Matilda Ivanovna Lisanevich, whom he had married after his arrival in St. Petersburg.[5] He apparently discovered Matilda first at the theater and soon began to frequent the circles which she sponsored. Although Matilda was the wife of a physician related and known in court circles, her name was linked with scandal. In spite of these social impediments, Witte was determined to marry her. He assisted her in getting a divorce, and they were married in 1892; the scandal, however, continued—remarriage apparently did not change her way of life. She was never accepted at court until Witte's triumphant return from Portsmouth in 1905. It remains unclear whether the most significant objection to Matilda was her ancestry or her unsavory reputation.

Witte also earned the ill-will of his anti-Semitic contemporaries in official circles. The number of Jews with whom Witte was associated both within his ministry and in the financial and business community in Russia and abroad was often a matter for comment by his enemies. In 1905, at the time the question arose as to whether the Jews should be permitted to stand for election to the proposed national legislative body, Witte found himself at odds with official views and advocated they be given this right.[6] When approval was granted, he was in America and received the news enthusiastically. In fact, the minister of finance, V.N. Kokovtsov, noted with obvious displeasure that this was the only one of his many communications which Witte answered.

Meanwhile, Witte's unpopular associations became one of the planks in the program to overthrow him. As in the case of his

[4] Tower to Hay, No. 404, Mar. 13, 1901, *Despatches. Russia,* Roll 58.
[5] Von Laue, *loc.cit.;* Witte, *op.cit.,* I, 272–275; S.R. Tompkins, "Witte as Minister of Finance, 1892–1903," *The Slavonic and East European Review,* XI, Apr., 1933, London, pp. 590–606.
[6] V.N. Kokovtsov, *Out of My Past,* Stanford, 1935, pp. 50ff.

marriage, it is difficult to determine with any precision to what extent anti-Semitism formed a bond among his enemies who already had sufficient reason to wish him out of the way. It is not impossible even to assume that his pro-Jewish attitude may have been among the reasons he was sent to America to negotiate the treaty of Portsmouth.

Witte's official career was characterized by his complete devotion to the service of the sovereign and of the state. The first steps in his rise to power were taken under Alexander III who reposed complete confidence in him and, therefore, gave him considerable freedom of action. With the accession of the young, inexperienced, vacillating, and insecure Nicholas II, the stage was set either for a completely dominant role by the powerful minister or for loss of favor arising from lack of Imperial support. Both predicaments unfortunately followed one another and, in the end, sovereign and minister cordially hated one another. Witte nevertheless retained his complete devotion to the principle of monarchy both at home and abroad.[7] In spite of his frustrating experiences with Nicholas he continued to feel that monarchy provided the best form of organization for building the more efficient Russian toward which he strove. Conversely, he opposed in principle and practice any dilution of the powers of monarchy by granting rights to the people, accepting such grants only to preserve the remaining monarchial prerogatives.

As a minister working under and for a monarch, Witte seems to have visualized himself as the manager of a vast business organization. Although he was aware of the importance of a general economic theory as a working principle at this level, it appears that he never succeeded in achieving one.[8] He seems to have thought too much of the purely material and too little of the imponderables of his vast new state. Although some of his projects were broadly conceived and vast in extent and significance, others were clearly an afterthought.

The administrative structure he developed was above all centered in himself as the architect-in-chief of the monarch. He grew very fond of power and, when he saw it slipping, made many compromises to save it. He exhibited no desire to share his own power with anyone—the monarch, his colleagues in the minis-

[7] Tompkins, op.cit., pp. 601–604; Prince Bernhard von Bülow, Memoirs, 4 Vols., London, 1931, II, 42–43.

[8] Von Laue, loc. cit.; Seegar, op.cit., pp. 131–135.

tries, or private business enterpreneurs. Ultimately he visualized his vast enterprises as developing under the control of a purged and efficient bureaucracy and had little taste for free enterprise or the political principles current in the Western world. For example, when dismissed from his ministerial position, he refused to become associated with any private enterprise; he chose rather to remain a part of the bureaucratic world where he felt the real fulcrum of power and authority lay.

From his relatively secure base as an Imperial minister of finance, Witte projected his plan of rapid industrial development. The projects which made up his "system" began to absorb a major portion of the state budget, the grasp of his power touched the lives of increasing numbers of people, and he became the master of what amounted to a state within a state. Izvolsky wrote that:

"In this way Count Witte had the control of an innumerable crowd of functionaries of all denominations and all ranks, a network of schools of lower and even higher grades, a vast territory—a veritable kingdom, in fact, of which he was the sole master—an army, a fleet, even a diplomatic service. Furthermore, on account of his constant tendency to extend indefinitely the power of the state to the detriment of personal initiative and activity which was still in its infancy in Russia, one may say that for some ten years he was the real master of the 160 million inhabitants of the Empire. Truth compels me to say that the greater part of the elements composing the system created by him were better organized, performed their function more perfectly, and were imbued with a broader and more modern spirit than the corresponding government services."[9]

Witte's vast empire reached out into the Asian regions of Russia and included relations with neighboring Asian states. He conceived of Russia's mission there as a projection of her unique spirit and organization.[10] Since her geographical location made her part of both East and West, her historical experience gave her a sympathetic appreciation of the people of the East, and her national spirit, lacking the rigid exclusiveness characteristic of some countries, had the capacity to accommodate diverse races and peoples. These qualities, while they rendered fusion with

[9] Von Laue, *op.cit.*, Ch. VI.
[10] *ibid.*, Ch. V, VII.

the West impossible, made Russia the natural bearer of cultural enlightenment to the East and it was her duty to guard the peoples of the East against the imperialistic ambitions of the western countries.

The success of some aspects of Witte's "system" was as striking as the failure in others. In purely industrial development he was able to count an impressive number of triumphs as the indices of production rose sharply in many industries. It was also characteristic of his program that there was a considerable influx of foreign capital, a concentration of industry in a limited number of large enterprises closely associated with the government, and a significant addition to the railway network.

Unquestionably the most fateful and in many ways the most significant of Witte's projects was the construction of the railway across Siberia and Manchuria to the Pacific. The project was a unique ensemble of objectives and purposes.[11] With his eye so firmly fixed on seeking every advantage for Russia, Witte could hardly have missed the significance of the Suez Canal and the trans-Canadian railway, both controlled by Russia's perennial competitor. A railway across Siberia could challenge the dominance of these routes over the Pacific, and particularly the Chinese, trade. With an effective transportation route, Russia could more easily defend her Pacific territories and rights and assert her claims to others as competition opened the door to further advances.

At the time Witte became minister of finance, the desire for expansion in Asia, particularly Eastern Asia, was strongly expressed among vocal groups in Russia.[12] The further growth of extensive British commerce as well as the strategic advantages of the British and French territorial acquisitions in Burma and Indochina respectively, were viewed with apprehension. This was especially true of those who held that if Russia were going to seek new commercial outlets it would have to be in Asia, where she could compete far more favorably than in the European market. Furthermore, the territorial gains of the Western powers had evoked the specter of a dangerously upset balance of world power to Russia's detriment. The solution to this problem, as many in

---

[11] J.A. White, *The Siberian Intervention*, Princeton, 1950, pp. 47–50; M.N. Pokrovsky, *Vneshniaia Politika Rossii v xx Veke*, Moscow, 1926, pp. 17–18; Romanov, *Russia*, pp. 43–44; *M.C.R.*, pp. 272–273; Romanov, *Ocherki*, pp. 22–24.

[12] B.H. Sumner, "Tsardom and Imperialism in the Far East and Middle East, 1880–1914," *Proceedings of the British Academy*, London, 1941, xxvii, 37–43.

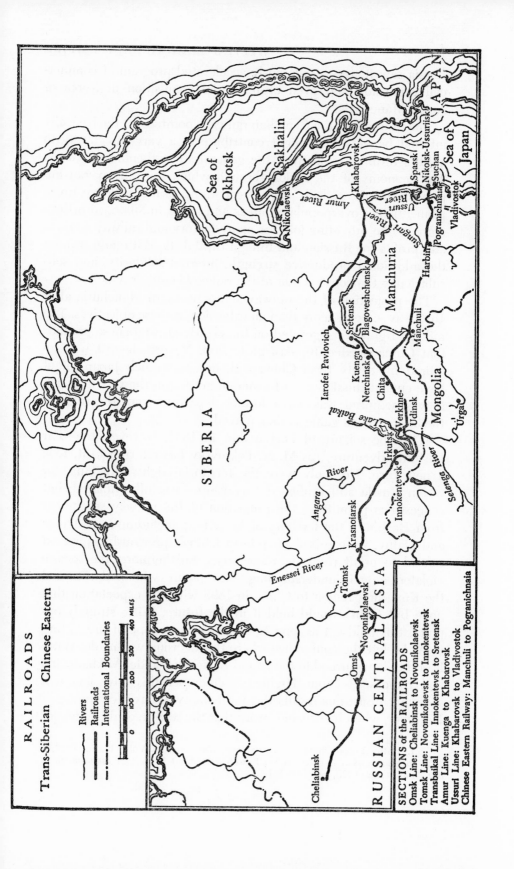

RAILROADS
Trans-Siberian   Chinese Eastern

—— Rivers
—— Railroads
·–·–· International Boundaries

0   100   200   300   400 MILES

SECTIONS of the RAILROADS
Omsk Line: Cheliabinsk to Novonikolaevsk
Tomsk Line: Novonikolaevsk to Innokentevsk
Transbaikal Line: Innokentevsk to Sretensk
Amur Line: Kuenga to Khabarovsk
Usuri Line: Khabarovsk to Vladivostok
Chinese Eastern Railway: Manchuli to Pogranichnaia

RUSSIAN CENTRAL ASIA

SIBERIA

Sea of
Okhotsk

Sakhalin

JAPAN

Sea of
Japan

Japan

Nikolaevsk

Amur River

Khabarovsk

Ussuri River

Spassk
Nikolsk-Ussuriisk
Suchan
Pogranichnaia
Vladivostok

Sungari River

Manchuria

Harbin

Manchuli

Mongolia

Urga

Iarofei Pavlovich

Sretensk
Blagoveshchensk

Kuenga
Nerchinsk

Chita

Verkhne-
Udinsk

Lake Baikal

Selenga River

Irkutsk

Innokentevsk

Angara   River

Enessei River

Krasnoiarsk

Tomsk

Omsk

Novonikolaevsk

Cheliabinsk

Russia saw it, was a vigorously accelerated program of commercial expansion and even of territorial acquisition in Korea or North Manchuria.

The example of the Canadian railways pointed out the basically internal benefits that might contribute in a very direct way to Witte's ultimate objective—the general strengthening of Russia. The economy of the region through which the railway ran improved and the railway encouraged the peasants to leave European Russia's overpopulated areas and move to Siberia. Furthermore, while providing jobs for many factory and railway workers and profits for Russian and foreign capitalists, Witte also wanted the additional productive strength, internal solidarity, and self-sufficiency the construction of the railway could provide.

The projection of the railway across northern Manchuria after 1896 was scarcely more than an extension of these objectives. The railway rights were granted on the clearly anti-Japanese grounds that China needed Russia's protection. Nevertheless, it was acquired by treaty from China and, however much Japan might have envied Russia's good fortune in getting it, the way in which it was acquired was not a formal departure from the rules of the international game as then played.

With the seizure of Port Arthur in 1897, however, the "Far Eastern adventure," as M. N. Pokrovsky has referred to it, took a new turn. Not only were the territorial rights of China, for whom Russia still professed friendship, forcefully violated, but concessions permitting the projection of the railway southward from Harbin to the territory of Kuantung, including Port Arthur and Dalny, were seized in spite of China's previously expressed refusal to grant rights in these areas. Furthermore, the seizure violated a tacit understanding with Japan, who had returned the Kuantung region to China in 1895 with the expectation that none but China would hold it in the future. Witte strongly opposed this bold act as long as there was any hope of preventing it. As he left the conference where this decision was made, Witte is said to have turned to the Grand Duke Aleksander Mikhailovich and remarked: "Your Highness, remember this day; you will see what disastrous results this fatal step will have for Russia."[13] However, when he became aware that the seizure could no longer

[13] S.I. Witte, *Vospominaniia. Tsarstvovanie Nikolaia* II, 2 Vols., Berlin, 1922, I, 123; another version is given in W. Korostowetz, *Graf Witte, der Steuermann in der Not,* Berlin, 1929, pp. 160–161.

be forestalled, he returned again to his plans and presented the demands that he hoped China would be urged to grant in order to carry them out.[14]

Why was Witte so disturbed about the acquisition of these new benefits? His ambitions in China remained as frankly economic, political, monopolistic, and long-range as they had been the year before when he had acquired the railway franchise in northern Manchuria. At that time he had been eager to acquire a concession in the very same region that the seizure now placed within his reach. Witte's opposition on this occasion clearly arose over procedural rather than substantive matters. His whole course of action in these and succeeding years leaves no doubt that he envisioned the continuing projection of his expansive enterprises as far into China as circumstances permitted. He thought his plans might be endangered by foreign or domestic opposition or rivalry. He foresaw the complications that the occupation of Port Arthur would unquestionably bring from both Peking and Tokyo as well as from the Russian military commander at Port Arthur with whom he would have to share the administration of the Russian stake in Manchuria.

The pivot and nucleus of Witte's Far Eastern enterprises were the Russo-Chinese Bank. This bank was established by charter, December 5, 1895, and signed by the representatives of the French banks and the Russian government—the French shares amounting to five-eighths and the Russians holding the rest of the shares in the institution.[15] Its first chairman was Prince Esper Esperevich Ukhtomsky, a close friend of the Russian Emperor and his traveling companion during his world tour only a few years before. The bank's charter gave it broad powers including the financing of commerce, the issuance of bank notes, the minting of local currency, and the acquisition of railway and telegraph concessions. It was intended to be the instrument for carrying out Witte's penetration of China and lands beyond since its branches were widely scattered. The bank was legally the parent organization of the Chinese Eastern Railway; through this fiction Witte was able to claim that the railway was a private company and thus overcome Li Hung-chang's objection to a Russian government railway in Manchuria.

[14] Romanov, *Russia*, p. 140.
[15] Witte, *op.cit.*, i, 40–41; C.F. Remer, *Foreign Investments in China*, New York, 1933, pp. 557–565; Malozemoff, *op.cit.*, pp. 44, 70–74.

By 1898 another fiction was being used to extend Russian railway interests into the very center of China; Belgium was represented as the financial leader in the proposed Peking-Hankow railway. In the end the scheme was frustrated when its actual intent became known. Meanwhile, the Russo-Chinese Bank was simultaneously promoting Russian business in various centers of China.

Manchuria, over which Russian control was in fact steadily increasing, was still legally a Chinese region. All but a small part of it was under the jurisdiction of the governor general at Mukden.[16] This official was also commander in chief of all military forces in his province as well as high commissioner in charge of the defenses of all Manchuria. The region as a whole was divided into three provinces with the following populations in 1894: Fengtien in the south with its capital at Mukden (4,725,000); Kirin in the east with its capital at Kirin (626,000); and Heilungchiang in the north with its capital at Tsitshihar (400,000). From the standpoint of Russia's freedom to act without local opposition, to encourage Russian settlement, and to develop the area economically along lines most suitable for her own objectives, the sparsely populated province of Heilungchiang in the north was the most attractive.

In the building of Witte's imperial structure in Chinese Manchuria, the town of Harbin was the key center.[17] Located on the right bank of the navigable Sungari River 350 miles west of Vladivostok and 600 miles north of Port Arthur, the town was ideally placed for an administrative center. In addition to the railway administration, it contained an imposing branch of the Russo-Chinese Bank. In the course of time the railway and the bank had made Harbin an important financial and commercial center, attracting increasing numbers of Russians and Chinese. In the chaotic currency situation of Manchuria, the bank had been able to produce considerable stability by making the ruble more and more the accepted medium of exchange as the Japanese were doing with the yen in Korea. Harbin was quickly becoming an impressive monument to Russian determination to dominate Manchuria. Both business and industry grew rapidly

[16] H.B. Morse, *The Trade and Administration of China*, London, 1921, pp. 228ff; Hosie, *op.cit.*, pp. 28–41.

[17] *M.C.R.*, LXXV, Apr., 1901, pp. 1–8; Whigham, *op.cit.*, pp. 75, 134–137; B.B. Glinsky, *Prolog Russko-Iaponskoi Voiny. Materialy iz Arkhiva Grafa S. Iu. Witte*, Petrograd, 1916, pp. 223–227.

and most of the new activity was in Russian or Chinese hands though there was a small amount of foreign business. The leading industry was flour milling, an industry which the Russians were expanding rapidly and continued to expand after the outbreak of war increased military need.

The general growth of the town is indicated by the increase of the population from 20,000 in the autumn of 1902 to 60,000 a year later. The American consul, Henry Miller, reflected this expansive mood when he wrote in December 1903: "It is in this city more than in all others combined that Russia is asserting her intention of becoming an active industrial force in the affairs of the Orient, and her people are already giving the place the title of the Moscow of Asia."[18]

About 150 miles south of Harbin, along the left bank of the Yitung River, a tributary of the Sungari, stood Kuanchengtze. Though it lay administratively within Kirin Province, it served the adjacent Mongol area as the tax-collecting center. It was the seat of a number of industries and was the commercial mart for the northern region with a population estimated in 1903 at about 250,000. The railway ran nearby, outside the mud-walled Chinese city. After 1905 Kuanchengtze declined in importance as the Japanese gave greater emphasis to the town of Changchun, 2 miles to the south.

At the southern end of the railway and in the southern part of the Liaotung Peninsula was the leased territory of Kuantung in which both Port Arthur and Dalny were located.[19] Port Arthur, formerly known as Lüshun, had before March 1898 been China's most important northern naval base, administered by the governor general of Chihli Province in his capacity of superintendent of trade for the northern ports. Its new name came from a Lieutenant William Arthur who had been associated with the plans to fortify the harbor. Under Russian administration Port Arthur grew rapidly both as a naval and a commercial port, though Dalny was intended for the latter role. Dalny lay 33 miles northeast of Port Arthur and was formerly known as Dalien and later, under Japan, as Dairen. According to Witte he had suggested this new name to the Russian Emperor after the

[18] Hosie, op.cit., p. 218; B.L.P. Weale, Manchu and Muscovite, London, 1907, pp. 443–446; Japan. Department of Railways, An Official Guide to Eastern Asia. I Chosen, Manchuria, Siberia, Tokyo, 1920, p. 274.

[19] Malozemoff, op.cit., pp. 23ff; Hosie, op.cit., pp. 48, 242, 250; M.C.R., LXXX, Apr., 1904, pp. 161–162.

first Russian soldiers had used it.[20] The new name seemed appropriate because it sounded like the Chinese name and because it meant "distant." Under Witte's control this port was rapidly transformed into an instrument of his policy of monopolizing Manchurian commerce. To this end he built feverishly and used his considerable prestige and power in St. Petersburg as well as his control over the merchant marine and other governmental agencies to channel trade to Dalny. He took steps to reduce the competition of Newchwang and to systematize the competition of Vladivostok. By the end of 1903, however, it became apparent that Port Arthur was the true competitor since shippers perferred it; thus Dalny was a failure.

Newchwang, or more accurately its port city of Yinkow about 30 miles to the south, became the subject of considerable concern and controversy as it appeared more and more as a hostage to fortune at Russia's mercy.[21] It was opened for commerce as a treaty port in 1861. Since it provided an international outlet at the mouth of the Liao, one of the most heavily settled river valleys in Manchuria, it grew rapidly. In the course of time it became a commercial center of international importance, particularly to Japan, Great Britain, and the United States, and later also to Russia. The wares on its docks came from all the producing regions of Manchuria as well as other parts of China and from abroad. The merchants who conducted this flourishing business were largely nonresident, coming from Manchuria, other parts of China, and from foreign countries. In due course, also, branches of the Imperial Maritime Customs Administration and of the Russo-Chinese Bank became a part of the financial and commercial life of Newchwang.

When the bubonic plague broke out in the town in July 1899, all these diverse peoples were drawn together to combat it. The Russians, through the Chinese Eastern Railway and the Russo-Chinese Bank, played a major part by providing money to establish the International Sanitary Board. It remained, nevertheless, an international undertaking with a British chairman, and doctors and sanitary engineers furnished by the Russians and the Japanese. Its work was vigorously advanced and by early December the plaque was said to be under control. By the

---

[20] Witte, op.cit., I, 133.
[21] Hosie, op.cit., pp. 35–62 passim; Whigham, op.cit., pp. 16–18.

summer of 1900, however, Newchwang was again experiencing trouble, this time with more serious consequences.[22] The Chinese anti-foreign organization, the Boxers, had begun to use it as an organization and recruitment center. The Russians, Japanese, and British watched the situation with alarm. With the possibility of intervention in everyone's mind, the tenseness grew and by the latter part of July the Russians were threatening to bombard the city and the British community had requested a gunboat from their Far Eastern naval commander. Meanwhile, the Japanese were standing by with gunboats and transports. In the midst of this explosive situation it was brought to Russian attention that the order had gone out from Mukden to kill all foreigners, the price on the head of a Western European being reportedly 25 Chinese lan, and on that of a Russian 50 lan.

The Russians took the initiative. With the support of a Japanese force, they occupied the town on August 4, 1900. The Chinese officials fled, leaving the way open for Russia to gather complete direction of affairs into her hands. By evening, General Fleischer was in control and had raised the Russian flag over the customs house and the forts. The Russian consul, Ostroverkhov, was made the civil governor of the town and selected a council representing the commandant, the consular corps, the foreign firms, the Chinese commercial houses, the customs administration, the sanitary board, and the police.

The customs commissioner, C. A. V. Bowra, carried on under the new regime as before. Later, however, Sir Henry Hart took the precaution or replacing him with a regular customs official of Russian nationality, N. A. Konovalov. With the departure of the Chinese officials, the Haikuan Bank in which the customs receipts were deposited was closed; at the suggestion of Russia the receipts were now deposited in the Russo-Chinese Bank.

From the beginning, the Russians made full use of the facilities of Newchwang in the construction of their railways in South Manchuria. Since their new ports at Port Arthur and Dalny were not yet completed, they expedited the construction of the main line of the railway by bringing the materials through Newchwang and thereby raised the prosperity of the port to the highest level it had yet attained. It was noted at the time that the bar in the

[22] Korostovets, op.cit., pp. 53–59; S.F. Wright, *Hart and Chinese Customs*, Belfast, 1950, pp. 798–800.

harbor limiting entry and the 4 months of solid ice each year would ease the task of the Russians in attracting trade to their new ports.[23]

By a combination of luck, alertness, and default, the Russians had fallen heir to the control of the busiest port in Manchuria and one on which all other commerce there depended. Mr. Whigham must have expressed a very general view when he wrote:

"For my part, having just come from Port Arthur and Dalny, and having seen what the effect of the Russian railway might become, . . . and seeing that they were making an excellent income for their officials out of the native customs at New-chwang, I could not see why they should retire from a position they had so easily acquired except under the strongest pressure."[24]

One can only admire the optimism and courage of Sir Robert Hart who, against these odds, tried to persuade the Russians to permit the opening of a station of the Maritime Customs Administration at Dalny.

In order to make the best use of Newchwang, the Russian plan called for a branch railway from there. Accordingly, a railway was started in the spring of 1898 and by May 1899 it was ready for use as far as Tashihchiao, the point where it joined the main line from Port Arthur to Mukden. By July 1901, a year after the occurrence of the Boxer Rebellion and the Russian occupation of Manchuria, the southern branch was joined at Kuanchengtze to the line projected from the north and through service was established in Manchuria.

The occupation of Port Arthur and the Kuantung region in late 1897 meant the introduction of military elements into Manchuria. This was not only a challenge to Witte's ministerial supremacy, but the introduction into Manchuria of all the evils of divided responsibility in policy and administration.[25] Witte, through his administrative functionaries carried on the affairs of Harbin, Dalny, and the railway with all its associated enterprises. By employing his own railway guards, popularly known as "Matilda's Guards" after Witte's wife, he kept his own sphere of activity as completely free of military influence as possible.

---

[23] Whigham, op.cit., pp. 17–18.
[24] ibid., p. 26.
[25] Korostovets, op.cit., pp. 4–5.

Sergei Iulievich Witte

Aleksander Mikhailovich Bezobrazov

Baron Komura Jutaro

Baron Kaneko Kentaro

Witte's competitor in Manchuria was Admiral Evgenii Ivanovich Alekseiev and behind him the ministers of war and navy. Alekseiev was commander in chief of the military and naval forces in the Far East and civilian administrator of Port Arthur and the Kuantung Leased Territory with the title of commander in chief. The ministry of foreign affairs was represented on Alekseiev's staff by I. I. Korostovets. In practice, however, Korostovets was overshadowed by the authority of the commander in chief whose administrative jurisdiction gave him actual control over foreign affairs. Meanwhile, Witte, with the tremendous advantage of his prestige and ready access to information through his efficient and numerous corps of agents abroad, managed to exercise an influence over other aspects of foreign affairs. The stage was clearly set for endless discord and misunderstanding, a situation doubly charged with danger in view of the hostile local context in which Russia had to carry on her Manchurian venture.

Pressed by his competitors on many sides and by the ominous international situation which followed in the wake of the Anglo-Japanese Alliance in 1902, Witte found it expedient to take stock of his endangered Far Eastern enterprises. In July 1902, he took what he intended to be an important step in strengthening his hold on Manchuria by organizing the Manchurian Mining Company, like the railway an arm of the Russo-Chinese Bank and ultimately of his ministry.[26] This was obviously an endeavor to counter his ambitious competitors in St. Petersburg who were seeking to acquire concessions in Manchuria as a means of undermining his control there and of steering a new course in Far Eastern affairs. The object of the Mining Company was to acquire concessions as widely as possible and to hold them until he was able to develop them. The shareholders were all officials of his ministry: A.I. Putilov, director of the chancellery of the ministry; L.F. Davydov, an official of the credit division; and A.I. Rothstein, a director of the Russo-Chinese Bank and closely associated with Witte in Manchuria. By the time Witte was dismissed from office in the summer of 1903, the Mining Company had acquired a number of concessions though none had yet been brought into operation.

In September and October 1902, Witte took another step in defense of his Manchurian interests. He went to the Far East

[26] Romanov, *Russia*, pp. 263–265.

on an inspection tour, surprisingly his first trip to a part of the world so important to him.[27] He visited Dalny, Port Arthur, Vladivostok, and other places of special interest. Upon his return he reported his findings to the Emperor and to some of his ministerial colleagues. His statements at that time constitute a strikingly forthright and even shrewd analysis of both the problem and the remedy as he saw them. They also served to bring about in the coming months a complete reconsideration in Russian official circles of the Manchurian problem.

The central problem, as Witte saw it, was Japan, both in her own right and as a spearhead for general foreign pressure on Russia. Addressing himself to the problem in terms characteristic of the concurrent discussions with Japan, he saw two main facets of the question: one, there was the expressed determination of Japan to bring Korea under her control if not domination, and, two, Russia's need for time to establish herself more firmly in the Far East. On the assumption that Japan must in some way be satisfied, he saw the uninviting possibility that Russia might face the choice of giving up all Korea or risking war. He saw a war as potentially disastrous because once hostilities had commenced, Russia could count on her other enemies menacing her not only in the Far East, but in the Middle East and the West as well. Even though it might become necessary to turn over all of Korea to Japan in order to avoid war, Witte did not regard this step as necessarily fatal to Russia's ultimate Far Eastern plans since it was not, in his view, an irrevocable act. For, with Japan in possession of Korea, she would have a common frontier with Russia and this would make it possible to keep the frontier inflamed and costly to defend. Meanwhile Russia would be preparing for the time when she could take over Korea.

This statement provides two interesting insights into Witte's view of the Far Eastern problem: first, he clearly saw Russia's stake in Manchuria as ultimately expanding in all directions to the frontier, well beyond the thin ribbon of the railway zone and the leased territory which then constituted the legal limits of her sphere; and second, his concept of frontier relationships with Japan was diametrically opposed to that of his critics who visualized Russia on the defensive in the event of Japan's occupying Korea.

[27] Witte, *op.cit.*, I, 202; Malozemoff, *op.cit.*, pp. 200–201; Glinsky, *op.cit.*, pp. 196–197, 208–219, 239–244.

Turning to the problem of Russia's relations with the foreign powers in the broader sense, Witte found the immediate situation equally menacing.[28] In this regard, he saw the construction of the southern branch of the Manchurian railway as a potential weakness. For as European and Japanese business increased in all parts of China, the new railway would only serve to open up new frontiers for it. In this way, he feared, foreign business, particularly British and Japanese, could flood both Manchuria and the Russian Far East. It was with this in mind that Witte had abolished the *porto franco* privileges at Vladivostok and Nikolaevsk on the Amur two years before. He was now proposing to go a considerable step further and protect Vladivostok and Manchuria by a tariff.

Witte was by no means alone in his anxiety about Russia's inability to compete economically with the other powers. About a year before his own inspection tour, an interested investor returning from a trip to Manchuria had warned Witte of the danger that British, Japanese, and German business held out for Russia's meager entrepreneurial capabilities.[29] Another contemporary Russian observer expressed himself even more bluntly. He wrote that Russian business could thrive only if tariffs excluded all foreign competitors. In short, outright annexation appeared to be the ultimate solution.[30]

This issue was brought into clear focus by the pressure of the other powers, particularly the United States and Japan, to open new commercial centers in Manchuria. Addressing himself specifically to this practical aspect of the problem, one official stated bluntly that "the fuss made by America, England and Japan would only make Russia sit tighter in Manchuria and never leave it, and this would only benefit Russia."[31]

During the Anglo-Russian negotiations in 1903, the Russian ambassador in London, Count A.K. Benkendorff, expressed the same thought more diplomatically and at the same time with greater relevance to Russia's dilemma. He said "that Manchuria should be discussed as a question where Russian interests predominate . . ." and that in the matter of opening new com-

[28] Glinsky, *op.cit.*, pp. 237–240.

[29] Report to Witte, Oct. 1, 1901, F.A. Lvov, *Likhodei Biurokraticheskago Samovlastia kak Neposredstvennye Vinovniki Pervoi Russko-Iaponskoi Voiny*, St. Petersburg, 1906, pp. 10–18.

[30] Malozemoff, *op.cit.*, p. 195.

[31] F. McCormick, *The Tragedy of Russia in Pacific Asia*, 2 Vols., New York, 1909, I, 49.

mercial centers there "he begged us not to press too hard on the subject of rates and tariffs, explaining that in every country where British and Russian trade competed, British goods drove Russian goods out of the market, and that we knew this to be the case."[32]

Another weakness which Witte's report brought to the attention of the Emperor was the sparse population of the Russian Far Eastern regions. He wrote:

"Your Imperial Majesty, in the meetings of the Siberian Railway Committee, has frequently pointed out the desirability of a rapid colonization of the Ussuri region and the unsettled coast of the Amur in order to strengthen there the Russian bulwark against the sea of the Yellow race. There is no doubt that both China and Japan suffer from over-population, and sooner or later this surplus will seek to settle among us. Therefore, in order to be the victors in a possible future struggle with the Yellow race, we must establish a bulwark of Russian population along our frontier with China which would have sufficient strength to protect their own interests as well as those of the Empire."[33]

Settlement was, therefore, one of Witte's essential methods of keeping Russia's Far Eastern territories in Russian hands.

With respect to the crucial problem of Russian relations with the Chinese administration in Manchuria, Witte concluded that the situation was chaotic and that the cause of it was the continuation of the military occupation. The occupation was not only making it impossible for the Chinese authorities to preserve even basic law and order but, what was even worse in the long run, was alienating the Chinese population throughout the occupied area. Furthermore, this question was too intimately associated with Russia's relations with Japan to be considered in isolation. Witte recommended as a solution to this problem that the agreement with China regarding the withdrawal of the forces be honored punctually.[34] He admitted that military protection was necessary for Russia's Far Eastern possessions, but he held that this could be satisfactorily taken care of by the railway guards who, by the time the evacuation was complete, would number 24,500, and by the available military forces in the ad-

[32] Hardinge to Lansdowne, Nov. 22, 1903, B.D., IV, 184.
[33] Glinsky, op.cit., pp. 196–197.
[34] ibid., p. 219.

jacent Maritime region who could be called in on short notice. Among those who agreed that this provided adequate security he named: Lieutenant General Dieterichs, chief of the Trans-Amur border guard; Lieutenant General Chichagov, military governor of the Maritime Territory; Major General Weimar, chief of staff of the border guard; and Major General Kholshchevnikov, chief of staff of the Maritime military district.

In weighing Russia's objectives in Manchuria, Witte's own motives are necessarily of the utmost importance. He seems to have expressed these most explicitly and precisely in a memorandum written some months after his Manchurian report.[35] By then the emphasis in the discussions of the Manchurian problem had shifted somewhat, but Witte had not visibly changed his views on fundamentals. He continued to depict the Manchurian question in his characteristically personal, practical, and long-range approach. He predicated his policy on the assumption that China would ultimately fall prey to the foreign powers and would be partitioned.

This fundamental assumption gave rise in Witte's thinking to a number of corollaries. One of these was that the problem of Manchuria was only a part of the more general problem of China and that in this larger context Russia's goals were by no means limited to Manchuria. Secondly, the annexation of Manchuria was clearly a necessary goal for Russia; in the competitive environment of the Far East, however, its successful realization would be possible only if Russia avoided any unseemly display of eagerness or urgency and, above all, if she patiently awaited the opportune moment. Thirdly, in the existing troubled state of the Far East, Russia should concentrate her efforts on inconspicuously engulfing areas already at her disposal, avoiding for the time being any outright annexation. Annexation now would be premature in that it would incite other powers to do the same and thus preempt areas of China which should in time also fall to Russia.

Witte considered premature annexation a positive danger to Russia's Far Eastern undertaking even from a purely internal point of view. With reference to economic development, Russia's ability to absorb and use effectively the natural wealth of Manchuria was limited and could not be carried out rapidly. If she had not yet been able to make use of the wealth of Central Asia

[35] *ibid., pp.* 338–340.

and the Caucasus during her long tenure there, how could she be expected in the immediate future to use the vast and, from the standpoint of transportation, far more inaccessible wealth of Manchuria. Finally, mindful of her already overwhelming nationality problems, Witte observed that if Russia were to try to absorb with undue haste the people of Manchuria, she would simply be adding a "Chinese problem" to her already complicated Finnish, Polish, Jewish, and Armenian population problems. He anticipated that failure in this respect would simply drive these people more decisively than ever into the arms of Japan and thus raise a permanent obstruction to Russia's future progress.

These reflections on Russia's Far Eastern interests and prospects provide ample evidence that Witte was not an opponent of expansion. On the contrary, he envisioned the Russian advance on a far grander and more meaningful scale than most of his critics. With characteristic self-confidence he felt that this great Russian advance could proceed most successfully under his sole direction; he alone could guarantee that it would be carried out peacefully and that, for Russia a least, it would be beneficial in character. Above all, in the troubled world of the Far East, only Witte could propel it onward at a rate compatible with the ability of Russia to support it and of the people of the region to accept it.

3. The Opposition to Witte

OPPOSITION to Witte was in a very direct sense a consequence of his considerable success in providing the substance of the dreams and hopes of the eighties and early nineties. To accomplish this he had found it necessary to develop the national economy, particularly the industrial sector. In time his interests became so widespread that they infringed upon ever new phases of the national life from agriculture to foreign affairs. Even the Imperial prerogatives were challenged.

At the turn of the century two new factors, both potentially inauspicious for Witte's system, came into being almost simultaneously. The seemingly robust economic expansion of the 1890's came to an end and a severe depression followed. This encouraged Witte's critics: those from various levels of national life, and those to whom his system was part and parcel of the Imperial structure which they hoped to destroy in any case.

At the same time, Russia's Far Eastern program, so vulnerable to criticism because it was so intimately associated with Witte, appeared to have become embroiled with the foreign powers in the Far East where Russia was least capable of defending herself. While opposition to Witte had been substantial since 1895, the continued upward trend of the economy and of Russia's political fortunes in the Far East had left him secure in his power for the time being. But the depression, followed by the Boxer Rebellion and its aftermath, gave the opposition new hope of unseating him.

This ominous turn of affairs inspired the easily predictable criticism as well as many volunteers armed with plans to improve the situation. It also brought to the fore those who hoped for a radical revision of the cherished objectives of only a decade before; in general this took the form of a re-evaluation of Russia's interests. In a vein characteristic of this change of attitude *Novoe Vremia* wrote in April 1901: "What we want is the good of Slavdom and the entrance to the Black Sea; no Port Arthur, no Shan-hai-kwan, no Pei-ho can take the place of the Bosphorus."[1] But it was too late to disown a program which many besides Witte had wanted and which by then had so irretrievably embroiled the nation with a whole cluster of competitors. The prob-

[1] Sumner *op.cit.*, pp. 42–43.

lem of the moment was to find a way out of the impasse to which this program had led.

The effective opposition to Witte's Far Eastern policies first took shape around alternative plans for exploiting the natural wealth made accessible by the Siberian and Manchurian railways.[2] It was feared by Witte as well as his opponents that if Russians failed to take advantage of these opportunities someone else would. Sharing as they did a keen awareness of Russia's financial and entrepreneurial inferiority, they feared that if something were not done the upshot would be an influx of foreign entrepreneurs; their current experience made these fears clearly justified.

The vehicle for the most forceful and successful challenge to Witte's power in the Far East was a concession granted by the Korean King on September 9, 1896, during the time he was taking refuge from the Japanese at the Russian legation in Seoul.[3] The recipient was a Vladivostok merchant of Swiss origin named Iulius Ivanovich Briner, a surname formerly spelled Brüner. Having reputedly lived in the Far East since 1868 Briner was something of a pioneer in the Russian import and export business there and his foreign commercial interests were widespread on the Pacific coast though concentrated for the most part in Japan and Korea.

Briner's official connections appear to have been close since he received the concession through Carl Weber, the Russian minister in Korea. Furthermore, at the time he received it he was serving on a border commission with Nikolai Gavrilovich Matiunin, a Russian diplomat of many years experience in the Far East and the first vigorous promoter of the project. It is apparent, therefore, that from the very first the concession was closely associated with official circles if not official policy.

The concession was granted to Briner and his heirs for a period of 5 years, later extended by agreement. He was authorized to solicit capital for the enterprise and to form a Korean timber company with headquarters at Vladivostok and branches at Seoul

[2] Lvov, *op.cit.*, pp. 10ff; V.M. Vonliarliarsky, *Moi Vospominaniia, 1852–1939 gg.*, Berlin, 1939, p. 125; *Dnevnik*, Apr. 2, 1903, p. 45.

[3] The concession agreement is given in A.I. Gippius, *O Prichinakh Nashei Voiny s Iaponiei. C Prilozheniiami (Dokumenty)*, St. Petersburg, 1905, pp. 52–55; Lvov, *op.cit.*, pp. 19–20; P.I. Torgashev, *Avantiura na Dalnem Vostoke*, Moscow, 1907, p. 217; Malozemoff, *op.cit.*, pp. 177–186; T. Baelz, *Awakening Japan; the Diary of a German Doctor, Erwin Baelz*, New York, 1932, pp. 230–231.

and Chemulpo. The company would have the exclusive right to exploit timber within the concession area, to explore beyond this area for other timber wealth, and to expand into "appropriate regions." In order to do this, the concessionaire had the right to build roads and horse-car routes, clear the river for floating timber, and build homes, workshops, and mills.

The location of the concession is itself the key to its strategic significance. It included, as the Russians defined it, an area of 1,800 square miles stretching across the northern frontier region of Korea from the mouth of the Yalu River on the west to the mouth of the Tiumen River on the east and including Dazhelet Island in the Sea of Japan. It encompassed, therefore, two of the three places in the Korea Peninsula which were of the greatest significance to Russia.[4] One was the Tiumen River region which borders the Maritime Territory of the Russian Far East and lies near the important but vulnerable city of Vladivostok.

The second of these places was the Yalu River lowlands in which the most controversial part of the concession lay. In the delta at the mouth of the river stood the town of Yongampo. Since this not only lay along the sea approaches to Port Arthur but constituted a natural shipping outlet for the lumber concession up-stream, it almost inevitably became a focal point in the Russo-Japanese controversy. Farther up the river were the two towns which lay along the ancient tributary route between Seoul and Peking. These were Uiju on the Korean side and Antung on the Manchurian side. Along with Yongampo, the controversy would shortly rescue the names of these towns from the obscurity of the forgotten past.

The third of these strategic places lies at the southern tip of the peninsula. It had an interest for Russia paralleling that of the other two and, because it lay along the sea route between them, was strategically associated with them. This is the Fusan-Naktong River basin which is located across the strait from the Japanese islands and athwart the sea route from Vladivostok to Port Arthur. Fusan had been in earlier centuries the point of contact between Japan and Korea and was more recently the terminus of a railway which Japan was building to Seoul. Clearly Japanese control of any of these places would inevitably be as distasteful to Russia as Russian control would be to Japan.

At the time the concession was granted there seems to have been no one in official circles sufficiently convinced of its political potentialities, either in domestic or foreign affairs, to support it beyond its original acquisition. It was a time when Russia was basking in the unearned goodwill made possible by Japan's unfortunate Korean adventure. Even in the autumn of 1897 when Briner went to St. Petersburg seeking financial aid, he found little encouragement.[5] A.I. Rothstein, a director of the Russo-Chinese Bank and chairman of the short-lived Russo-Korean Bank, showed no interest in spite of the fact that his Korean bank had no other investments at the time. Not until Briner turned again to his former benefactor, Matiunin, now chargé d'affaires in Seoul, did he have reason to expect any better success.

Matiunin, his knowledge of Far Eastern affairs setting him apart from almost all of his colleagues in the official world of St. Petersburg, was the first person other than Briner to show an active appreciation of the possibilities, economic as well as political, of the project. In particular, he visualized two potential uses for the concession, both soon to be espoused by the adventurer, Bezobrazov, and both ultimately to become firmly rooted in official policy. One of these was the prospect of using the concession to create a Russian sphere in North Korea. In his apologia, written some years later, Bezobrazov cited as a model the instance of the Bremen merchant, F.A. Lüderitz, who in 1883 had acquired a considerable sector of land in Africa.[6] The following year it was taken over by the German government to form the nucleus of German West Africa. The second point which Matiunin and Bezobrazov agreed was significant was that unless Russia operated the concession it might fall into other hands, such as English or Japanese.

Those to whom Matiunin broached the subject of the concession and who were soon to become its active sponsors were persons who were either close to the Imperial court themselves

    [5] Vonliarliarsky, op.cit., pp. 125ff; F.R., pp. 816–831, 1030–1044; Friedrich von Steinmann, Russlands Politik im Fernen Osten und der Staatssekretär Bezobrazov, Leipzig, 1931, pp. 35–56; K.I., pp. 87–108.
    [6] A.M. de Besobrassow, "Les Premieres Causes de l'Effondrement de la Russie. Le Conflit Russo-Japonais," Le Correspondent, ccxci, Paris, 1923, p. 585; compare M.E. Townsend and C.H. Peake, European Colonial Expansion since 1871, Chicago, 1941, pp. 166–167.

or had entrée to those who were close to it. The first of these was Aleksander Mikhailovich Vonliarliarsky, an ex-officer of the Chevalier Guards Regiment and a former ordnance officer under the Grand Duke Nikolai Nikolaievich during the Russo-Turkish war. Through these and other channels Vonliarliarsky found it easy to discuss his project with such official persons as the foreign minister, Count Muraviev, and the minister of finance, Sergei Witte.

His encounter with Witte was, from the very beginning, to cast a shadow of official disapproval on the project and the people associated with it and to make progress impossible for several years. Vonliarliarsky had in mind the formation of a company which could serve as a master organization for the whole region of Eastern Siberia, Mongolia, Manchuria, and Korea; subsidiary companies were to be brought into being for particular areas or purposes as needed.

Witte, on his part, already had such an organization in his Russo-Chinese Bank, which had in turn spawned the necessary specialized companies. With Witte's generally uncongenial outlook on competitive interests, he could hardly have been expected to encourage one of such magnitude or of such exalted sponsorship. Vonliarliarsky and his associates responded by regarding Witte as a competitor and, in time, as an enemy. Instead of accepting Witte's veto on his project, Vonliarliarsky sought help in other quarters and ultimately brought the problem to the attention of Aleksander Mikhailovich Bezobrazov, an acquaintance from the days of his military service. Bezobrazov must have seemed at the time a happy choice, particularly in view of his official connections, his enthusiasm and, above all, his availability for an adventurous scheme.

Bezobrazov was the son of a wealthy marshal of the nobility of St. Petersburg.[7] He had formerly served as an officer in the same guard regiment as Vonliarliarsky but had left the military service after an unhappy experience, patently with his honor and integrity untarnished by the incident. His judgment, however, was questioned and one of his associates attributed to him ". . . ill-balanced faculties—in which a strong imagination predominates—and a morbid hankering after fads."[8] Yet in the years immediately preceding his association with the Yalu con-

[7] Malozemoff, op.cit., p. 179, Seegar, op.cit., p. 268; Witte, op.cit., I, 165–166; R. Rosen, Forty Years of Diplomacy, 2 Vols., London, 1922, I, 210.
[8] F.R., p. 816.

cession he served, apparently with reasonable success, under the wealthy and well-known Count I.I. Vorontsov-Dashkov, formerly the commander of the guards regiment in which Bezobrazov had served and then the minister of the Imperial court, and with Count A.P. Ignatiev, the governor general of Western Siberia. The former esteemed him highly enough to introduce both him and his project into Imperial court circles.

The fact that it has in the past been commonly assumed that the Bezobrazov "clique" or "circle" was in some way responsible for the measures which led to the outbreak of the war renders the composition and nature of this group of considerable importance. In this respect two groups must be distinguished. The first was so closely associated with Bezobrazov that their interests were considered by contemporaries to have been practically identical. There seem to have been only three who qualified for such a role: Bezobrazov himself, his cousin, Admiral A.M. Abaza, and Abaza's wife.

The correspondence of these three, published in the Soviet *Krasny Arkhiv*, testifies to their special and close relationship. The letters exchanged after Bezobrazov had gone abroad were written in the belief that the activities described were in the best interest of the country, but needed to be kept secret from their political enemies—at one time they feared their enemies were reading their mail. In one case the precaution was taken of having Abaza's wife personally carry to Bezobrazov in Geneva a message about a conversation with the Emperor.[9] The enemy was referred to in the correspondence by code, using the term "mangy triumvirate" for the group and, for the individuals, such terms as "the nostril" (Witte), "the grouse" (Kuropatkin), and "the tadpole" (Lamsdorf).

The rise of Bezobrazov to a position of notability was made possible because his interests were shared by individuals of far greater consequence than the Abaza family. There was a considerable number of such persons from the Emperor down who were in one way or another associated with Bezobrazov and Abaza as evidenced by the letters and other proofs. These persons were brought together because they shared certain aims, principally the overthrow of Witte, though even this highly placed group were unsuccessful in this until the great minister was well past the zenith of his career. Their anti-Semitism

---

[9] Abaza to Bezobrazov, June 8, 1904, *K.A.*, xvii, 73.

served as a useful cohesive force, partly because it lay easily at hand as an accepted article of their social code and also because they thought it had a bearing on the struggle against the finance minister.

In addition to the Bezobrazov-Abaza "circle," the adherents of the anti-Witte party may be said to have consisted of two principal groups in addition to the Emperor. The first of these was the small number of individuals who were the primary promoters of the timber concession project. These included besides Bezobrazov, Abaza, Matiunin, and Vonliarliarsky, and a number of other persons such as Matvei Osipovich Albert, the director-manager of the Neva Shipbuilding Company.[10] Albert was also a railroad promoter and had qualified for membership in the anti-Witte group when the latter had thwarted him in getting a railway concession.

The other class of persons who were associated with the promotion of the concession were individuals of rank and prestige who must have seen it purely as a means of promoting their own aspirations with respect to Witte rather than for any value the timber concession might have had for them. Prominent among these was the Grand Duke Alexsander Mikhailovich, a brother-in-law of the Emperor and a bitter enemy of Witte, to whom, presumably, Count Vorontsov-Dashkov had introduced Bezobrazov. The Grand Duke, among other positions, held the sinecure office of chairman of the Volunteer Fleet, a function that was under Witte.

Bezobrazov planned to attract the Grand Duke to the project by detaching the Volunteer Fleet from Witte's administration and establishing him as head of a separate Chief Administration of the Volunteer Fleet. He would then have been able to circumvent the minister of finance entirely by establishing within this new Administration a Commercial Department which could have sponsored the timber concession as a government enterprise. But the plan failed because of the opposition of the Empress and the Emperor's uncle, General Admiral Grand Duke Aleksei Aleksandrovich.

Another ranking supporter of the project, V.K. Plehve, apparently needed far less encouragement. In April 1902, after the assassination of the minister of interior, Witte had blocked the candidacy of N.V. Muraviev, then minister of justice, only to

[10] Romanov, *Russia*, p. 271.

find that his bitter enemy, Plehve, had been appointed. He had thus acquired two formidable adversaries among the ministers. The differences between Witte and Plehve transcended mere bureaucratic rivalry; Plehve represented both the bureaucratic traditions and the interests of the land-owning nobility which he and others felt had fared badly in competition with Witte's system.[11] At a special conference in 1897 where the problem had been discussed, Witte had refused financial support for the nobility, withholding funds that might have detracted from the construction of the Manchurian railway.

Once in office, Plehve is said to have played a major part in the overthrow of Witte. The minister of finance returned the complement by assigning Plehve a major responsibility for bringing on the war with Japan. Witte undoubtedly intended a final blow at his opponent's reputation when he passed on the often-repeated words which Plehve reportedly addressed to Kuropatkin: "Aleksei Nikolaevich, you do not know the internal condition of Russia. We need a small, victorious war to stave off revolution."[12]

The sympathy of the Emperor for this project is not difficult to understand when his personality is compared with that of Witte.[13] If such characteristics as determination, sense of reality, ability to bring a plan into operation, and understanding of affairs are considered, the two men must be placed at opposite poles. Furthermore, Witte was an entrenched heritage from the Emperor's respected father, a fact which must have had a paralyzing effect on his will to oppose the determined minister, much less displace him. In short, the Emperor was hardly the man to stand up easily to the imperious Witte. It may very well be, therefore, as V.I. Gurko has suggested, that the so-called Bezobrazov scheme appeared to the Emperor as a plausible means of rallying support for blocking Witte.

In addition to commercial and personal motives, these people shared a number of ideas having to do with the strategic implications and potentialities of the Manchurian venture.[14] Bezobrazov and others began with the assumption, as Witte did, that Manchuria must be considered as prospectively Russian

[11] von Laue, op.cit., Ch. VII.

[12] Witte, op.cit., I, 262; repeated from another point of view in R.-I.V., p. IV.

[13] von Laue, op.cit., Ch. VI: V.I. Gurko, Features and Figures of the Past, Stanford, 1939, pp. 259–262; Korostovets, op.cit., p. 170.

[14] Steinmann, op.cit., pp. 39–63 passim; Besobrassow, op.cit., pp. 579–589; Gurko, op.cit., pp. 259–266.

territory. He expressed the view that the acquisition of Manchuria had been a mistake in the first place, though he seemed to attribute this more to the foreign minister at the time, Prince A.B. Lobanov-Rostovsky, than to Witte. However, once having taken this step, adequate defense measures were necessary to guard it from competitors such as Japan and it was on this vital question that their theoretical differences with Witte arose.

Witte's policies, Bezobrazov wrote, had given Russia a large and valuable stake in Manchuria. Not only had the enterprise been an extremely expensive one, but it had created a veritable Caucasian state within the Chinese state. Moreover, after creating this vast and costly venture which would be sure to invoke the envy of China as well as the other powers, Witte had failed to provide for its defense. Consequently, it now stood defenseless. Writing about this many years after, Bezobrazov felt that the one defense facility that had been provided, Port Arthur, had more than compensated for its cost. On this question, it must be said, Bezobrazov was by no means alone.[15]

Bezobrazov saw in the Briner concession a vehicle for providing for the defense of Manchuria which was so obviously lacking. For the holder of the concession was, at least for its legal duration, the potentially effective master of North Korea. It provided the means of making good the mistaken policy of retrenchment in North Korea represented by the Rosen-Nishi agreement of 1898; particularly since that time the Japanese menace to Korea had increased and was now vividly exemplified by the railway Japan was projecting northward from Fusan. It was against this obvious menace that Bezobrazov proposed to use the concession and thus provide a shield for Russia's Manchurian enterprises.

The whole diplomatic and military conception on which Witte had based his policy, Bezobrazov maintained, was mistaken. He had relied on good relations with China which was obviously too hostile and impotent to provide any practical support whatsoever. A more reliable basis of support had to be found to protect Russia's unique position in Manchuria. To Bezobrazov this could be provided by Germany in a Franco-Russo-German entente; this, along with the proposed military defenses in North Korea, provided his formula for vital security in the Far East.

[15] Gippius, *op.cit.*, pp. 22–24, where this point is more fully discussed.

The plan to realize these strategic objectives was written jointly by Vonliarliarsky and Bezobrazov at the time the latter first became associated with the project.[16] It was drawn up in the form of a memorial dated March 12, 1898 and presented to the Emperor by Count Vorontsov-Dashkov. In it the authors suggested that the Briner concession be put into operation by the organization of a semi-official "East Asia Company" modeled after the British East India Company. This company was to be so organized and managed that it would not be forced to concern itself about dividends, but rather was to concentrate on serving the Imperial interests. The company would control both local affairs and Russia's entire Far Eastern policy.

It was proposed that, with these large powers, the company would be in a position to seek, in two ways, the "peaceful possession of Korea" for Russia. On the one hand, it would enlist for Russia's effort the cooperation of both partners and competitors in Far Eastern enterprises. Hopefully, American and French capital might be attracted to help in the development of the concession and this would give these countries a stake in the Russian enterprise and thus a reason for cooperating in its defense. In addition, the company could be of service to Japan by seeking other material benefits for her in Korea. At the same time the authors visualized Russia's taking some definite steps in defense of the region by settling cossack reservists in North Korea, a proposal which undoubtedly had in mind the analogy of the Persian Cossack Regiment.

In a number of ways, all of them falling short of complete success, this project was favorably received and might have prospered but for Witte's opposition. With at least formal Imperial patronage, the group was able, on May 24, 1898, to acquire an option on the Briner concession for an initial payment of 20,000 rubles, the transaction to be completed after the formation of the proposed company.[17] The option was taken in the name of an official of the ministry of the Imperial court, Privy Councilor N.I. Neporozhnev.

Since the option would expire within a few months if no further action were taken, the group was eager to take immediate advantage of so favorable a requirement. By early July they were

[16] F.R., pp. 823–824; K.I., pp. 97–98.
[17] Steinmann, op.cit., p. 41; Romanov, Russia, p. 268; F.R., p. 825; Vonliarliarsky, op.cit., pp. 126–129.

able to send an expedition out to make a preliminary survey of the concession. In the course of the next few months the decision to project the railway southward from Harbin to Port Arthur temporarily turned Imperial interest away from the project; this group had urged the building of a railway from Port Arthur to Vladivostok through or near the concession area. Nevertheless, the project survived the lapse of interest. By June 1900 the proposed company, known as the East Asian Development Company, became at least a theoretical reality. This time, however, it was not only Witte but the preoccupation of the government with the Boxer Rebellion that frustrated further progress.

The post-Boxer period was in general far more congenial for the proponents of the Yalu concession and the East Asian Development Company largely as a consequence of the deterioration of Witte's power and prestige and the decline of his economic and political enterprises. Temporarily, however, the minister of finance appeared as able as ever to hold off his competitors and tried valiantly to do so. On February 2, 1902 he forced the dissolution of the East Asian Development Company and in July he seemed to have eliminated any reason to revive it by organizing his own Manchurian Mining Company. But in retrospect these measures appear even more defensive than his earlier ones. Furthermore, his more frequent readiness to compromise with the opposition raises the suspicion that he must have seen the realities of his predicament.

Meanwhile, his enemies were hopefully laying the groundwork for reconstituting the company they needed to operate their timber concession. One of the newer principals in the enterprise, Ivan Petrovich Balashev, master of the hunt at the Imperial court, was in the Far East in the spring of 1902 acting as the field manager for the project. From there he wrote to the Emperor on March 25, 1902 urging him to come personally to Manchuria to learn directly about the situation there. Making a very direct and emphatic appeal, Balashev wrote: "I urge you to come here now in order that you may be convinced of the necessity of allowing no further delay in annexing Manchuria to your dominions and of proclaiming the annexation right here on the spot."[18] He advocated immediate action for two reasons. One was that such a bold step would obviate any further questioning of Russia's rights and thus settle the issue once and for all. The

[18] Balashev to Emperor, Mar. 25, 1902, R.-I.V., pp. 133–135.

other reason was that, confronted by the activities of Britain in Persia and of Germany in Asia Minor, Russia urgently needed to free herself from the Manchurian problem and be prepared for action in other danger spots.

Another effort to take the fullest possible advantage of a favorable situation, again seemingly in response to Witte's own Far Eastern sojourn, was Bezobrazov's Far Eastern journey between November 1902 and April 1903.[19] Two aspects of this trip remain somewhat obscure. The first is the precise origin of the trip. It is clear, nevertheless, that the Emperor's wish that he make the trip was first expressed at the conference held at the Livadia palace in Yalta on November 9, 1902 when Witte reported his analysis of the Far Eastern problem. The Emperor's wish was further made clear when he ordered that a credit of 2 million rubles be made available to Bezobrazov at the Russo-Chinese Bank at Port Arthur. But whether this amount came entirely from an extra budgetary 10-million-ruble reserve fund or was in part made up by contributions from the Grand Duke Aleksander Mikhailovich and Count Aleksei Pavlovich Ignatiev is not known.

The answer to the other problem, that having to do with Bezobrazov's relationship with other members of the anti-Witte group during his tour in Manchuria, can be deduced from his activities there. Since it is known that the general management of the project at St. Petersburg was in the hands of Vonliarliarsky, that the field manager in Manchuria was Balashev, and that the larger interests being served were those of persons of far higher standing than his, it seems likely that Bezobrazov played a role that was of less importance than that of the others. On May 15, a few weeks after his return from Manchuria, Bezobrazov was awarded the rank of state secretary,[20] apparently to give him the standing he needed to carry out his duties in a society which valued status very highly.

It is safe to assume, therefore, that Bezobrazov was a promoter who found in the project an outlet for his energies and patriotic sentiments, the latter being a factor which should not be underrated, particularly in a retired officer of a guards regiment. He served the group in part by helping to supply a rationale for

[19] Malozemoff, op.cit., pp. 208–214; Glinsky, op.cit., pp. 260–268; Romanov, Russia, pp. 280ff; Kokovtsov, op.cit., pp. 21–22.

[20] Romanov, Russia, p. 285; A.A. Savinsky, Recollections of a Russian Dilpomat, London, 1928, p. 43.

its existence and a compelling idea for its working policy. He also made a practical contribution by showing the way to put into practice the ideas which held the group together exemplified in his trip to Manchuria.

During his tour in Manchuria, Bezobrazov occupied himself with the larger strategy of Russia's Far Eastern entanglements rather than confining himself to the narrower field of interests defined by a timber concession. In a report which he sent to the Emperor he stated that:

". . . close and immediate acquaintance with affairs in the Far East leads to the inevitable conclusion that our present position on this distant frontier must be considered very unfavorable. The unfavorable aspect of our position consists in the fact that after the expenditure of two billion rubles and after victorious action of our army, we have lost our prestige and self-confidence, considering ourselves weak, making concessions and finding ourselves on the verge of economic, and perhaps also military, defeat."[21]

Among the numerous projects with which Bezobrazov was occupied during his tour was of course the timber concession and the more general problem of the Yalu frontier. He planned to deal with both these issues by uniting under a single direction the Briner concession and two other concessions on the Manchurian side of the Yalu River.[22] One of these was held by Lieutenant Colonel A.S. Madritov, who had acquired it by questionable means while in command of the Mukden arsenal in 1900. The other one had been more recently acquired by F.A. Lvov, a private promoter who had come to the Far East in 1900 hoping to recoup his fortune. In order to escape from the requirements of the new Chinese concession regulations promulgated on March 17, 1902, Lvov had organized his company as a joint Sino-Russian venture both in personnel and financing. In the end these two Manchurian concessions were not realized, both having been merely preliminary agreements which were never approved. This weakened Bezobrazov's entire Yalu strategy since it left the Manchurian part without any legal foundation.

The failure to acquire the desired rights on the Manchurian side of the river thus had the effect of enlarging without Chinese

[21] Glinsky, op.cit., p. 263.
[22] Lvov, op.cit., pp. 21–23, 58–65.

approval the Russian zone of occupation in Manchuria. For, when Bezobrazov's plan was put into operation his defense establishments included both sides of the river, using as bases such points as Fenhuangcheng and Antung on the Manchurian side and Yongampo and Uiju on the Korean side.

Bezobrazov's first proposal to bring discharged reservists into the region ostensibly as workers in the lumber enterprise but primarily as the nucleus of a military force, found no support from the military authorities if it implied any official sponsorship of the project.[23] He turned next to a general recruitment of any available people including the discharged reservists on an unofficial basis and this turned out to be a group of varied origins: Russians, Koreans, and Chinese, the latter largely ex-Boxers, discharged soldiers, or bandits.

These activities were carefully and anxiously observed by the Japanese who followed them from the very beginning in April 1903 when Bezobrazov had put his plan into operation.[24] From early April the Russians were observed cutting timber in the Yalu region and concentrating military forces in the Antung area, the latter estimated by the Japanese at about 2,000 men. Then construction work was observed at Yongampo at the mouth of the Yalu River with Russians, Koreans, and Chinese occupied on the project.

Within a few weeks of the first appearance of this Russian activity, the Japanese began to learn some disturbing details which pointed to a permanent Russian operation at Yongampo.[25] They received reports that the Russians had bought some 490 acres of land in the town and were constructing houses and a garrison there. It was also learned about the same time that at least some of the persons seen there were in fact soldiers out of uniform. The conclusion was unavoidable that the Russians intended to entrench themselves in the Yalu region for an indefinite time.

This determined Russian advance into Korea, coming at a time when it already seemed abundantly clear that the Russian

---

[23] *Dnevnik*, Mar. 16, 1903, pp. 38–39; for somewhat contradictory evidence see S.I. Witte, *Vynuzhdennia Raziasneniia po Povodu Otcheta Gen. Ad. Kuropatkina o Voine s Iaponiei*, Moscow, 1911, pp. 84–85, 92, 99; compare Gurko, *op.cit.*, p. 262; K. Asakawa, *The Russo-Japanese Conflict; Its Causes and Issues*, Boston, 1904, pp. 292–294.

[24] Hayashi (Korea) to Komura, Apr. 2, Hayashi to Komura, Apr. 6, Major Nozu (Seoul) to Chief of General Staff Oyama, May 6, 1903, *N.G.M.*, xxxvi-i, 452ff.

[25] Mizuno to Komura, May 10, Hayashi to Komura, May 15, 1903, *N.G.M.*, xxxvi-i, 454–455.

forces would not be withdrawn from Manchuria in the immediate future, was an event of the greatest importance. The attitude
expressed at the time by the Japanese ambassador in Peking is
apparently representative of official opinion since it reflects the
new tactics shortly adopted by the government. He wrote concerning Russia that:

"Judging from her present acts no doubt can be entertained
as to her project to extend her aggressive policy to Korea by
taking all possible measures in the valley of the Yalu under
pretext of protecting forest which she may also claim to have duly
acquired. Prince Ching once told me that the Russian demand
for forestry concession at Yalu was considered to have some
ulterior design that could not be complied with. What the
Prince called ulterior design is nothing more than acquisition
in name of forestry concession of the base of operations against
Japan in Korea."[26]

Diplomatically, the Yalu affair served Japan's purpose by providing a rallying point for the support of the United States and
Britain in her intended showdown with Russia. An attitude
expressed by Whigham may well be representative of the spirit
in which these countries responded to Japan's cause. He wrote:

"This is inserting the thin edge of the wedge with a venge-
ance. The world at large is still exercising its mind over the
absorption of Manchuria when Russian troops appear on the
left bank of the Yalu, and the Russian Government, on the
strength of a concession . . . demands the right not only to cut
the timber, but to put up a telegraph-line and establish military
posts on Korean soil!"[27]

In addition to the Yalu project, Bezobrazov carried out several
other changes in Manchuria, all intended to enchance Russia's
prestige and security in the Far East: he promoted production
at the Fushun coal mines in order to lessen dependence on
Japanese coal; he encouraged steam navigation between the Yalu
and Port Arthur and on the lower course of the Liao River;
recognizing one of Russia's most serious drawbacks, he gave
35,000 rubles to the Port Arthur *Novyi Krai* newspaper to be
used to start an English language newspaper to help offset the

[26] Uchida to Komura, May 19, 1903, *N.G.M.*, xxxvi–i, 186.
[27] Whigham, *op.cit.*, p. 209.

anti-Russian attitudes of the existing English language journals in the Far East.[28] However one may appraise the ill-fated Yalu project, these measures at least appear well-conceived and appropriate.

While the group to which Bezobrazov belonged constituted the most spectacular and best organized rival of Witte's Manchurian enterprise, two other sources of opposition should be mentioned. One of these might be called his free enterprise competition and was, therefore, doomed to failure in a situation controlled by Witte.[29] The ambitions of this group were voiced by Fedor Aleksandrovich Lvov who had come to the Far East in 1900 hoping to recoup the fortune he had lost the year before in the financial crisis. In the end Witte blocked his way far more effectively than he did Bezobrazov's because Lvov lacked the latter's effective political support.

In addition to his own advantage, Lvov saw in his project two important benefits. One was the fact that it would have encouraged private enterprise in Manchuria and would, therefore, have developed the region much more effectively than the controlled bureaucratic enterprise was capable of doing. The other factor was the ability of private enterprise to carry out this development without arousing the suspicions of either China or Japan. To do this he proposed a genuinely cooperative venture to be called the Russo-Chinese Joint Stock Lumber Company in which Chinese and Russians would cooperate on an equal basis on the Board of Directors and throughout the entire enterprise. He tried to gain support for this venture by coordinating his efforts with Lt. Col. Madritov. But in the end the concessions they both received on the Manchurian side of the Yalu River came to nothing.

Another source of opposition to Witte was the minister of war, General A.N. Kuropatkin. His inclusion by the Bezobrazov group among the "mangy triumvirate" was not entirely a misunderstanding of his position; for he and Witte apparently remained outwardly on reasonably good terms. Nevertheless, his rivalry was real and important to understand for an accurate appraisal of the Far Eastern problem. While his outlook was undoubtedly affected by the usual ministerial jealousy, his expressed opposition is clearly a product of his professional solici-

[28] Malozemoff, op.cit., p. 209.
[29] Lvov, op.cit., pp. 21–23, 58–65.

tude for the defense of the country. Since he was, at the same time, no less interested in the expansion of Russia than either Witte or Bezobrazov, his views represent merely a more cautious version than theirs of the expansive thinking of the time.

Kuropatkin learned his early lessons in international and colonial politics during his military and administrative experience in Central Asia.[30] He had fought in the war with Turkey and in Central Asia, where he had served as chief of staff to General M.D. Skobelev. He became commandant of Transcaspia in 1890 and remained at this post until he was made minister of war in 1898.

During his service in Transcaspia, Kuropatkin had been intimately associated with Russia's vigorous expansion program in Persia. His career had shown him to be a courageous officer, an industrious and effective administrator, and a man whose honesty was everywhere recognized. At the same time, it was also true that his sense of duty had matured in an environment of competitive colonial politics and of the exercise of the palatine powers characteristic of a military command on an active frontier.

General Kuropatkin's reservations with respect to Manchuria had to do with the practical problem of defense which came within his jurisdiction as minister of war. He felt that the Manchurian affair had unnecessarily burdened the defense capabilities of the country beyond its capacity. In a pyramid on which he ranked the defense interests of the nation, he established the following priorities: at the base of the pyramid he placed the most significant factor, the security of the western frontier against the powers of Central Europe; next in descending order of importance came the maintenance of domestic peace and order throughout the military districts of the country; the security of the southern frontier toward Afghanistan, Persia, and the Ottoman Empire; the security of the Maritime region toward Japan and China; Russian interests in Manchuria; and, finally, Russian interests in Korea.[31]

From this schematic conception of the nation's available defense resources as well as the experience of the immediate past, Kuropatkin concluded that the military commitments in Manchuria must be reduced. In the first place, the basic fact

[30] Witte, op.cit., I, 134–141; R.-I.V. p. 6; R.A. Pierce, Russian Central Asia, 1867–1917, Berkeley, 1960, pp. 86–87.

[31] A.N. Kuropatkin, The Russian Army and the Japanese War, 2 Vols., New York, 1909, I, 185; R.-I.V., pp. 6–7; Glinsky, op.cit., p. 205.

of Russia's presence in Manchuria had to be completely reconsidered. Kuropatkin wrote that he would have advised against
building the railway across Chinese territory had he been
consulted. It was now, however, an accomplished fact and had to
be considered in this light. The Boxer Rebellion had fully revealed to what dangers the costly enterprise was exposed. Were
Russia now to withdraw her military forces entirely from Manchuria, this would simply invite China, encouraged by the other
powers, to make it impossible for Russia to enjoy her rights there.

Russia was, accordingly, forced to reconsider her tenure in
Manchuria in the light of her defense capability. This led him
to the further conclusion that the southern part of Manchuria
was too exposed to be defensible under existing conditions and,
hence, that only North Manchuria should be retained. He felt
that North Manchuria should be held under conditions which
would give Russia complete control over all questions bearing
on its defense. This meant either annexing it outright or placing
it under a protectorate.

Among the factors which, Kuropatkin asserted, had a vital
bearing on the defense was communications. The railway which
crossed North Manchuria was a link in Russia's communications
with Vladivostok. If it were endangered, Russia would have
to undertake the costly, difficult, and protracted task of constructing a railway to Vladivostok by way of the Amur region
of the Russian Far East. The railway problem was, in turn,
intimately associated with the population question; the railway
had thus far acted as a conductor, inviting large numbers of
Chinese settlers.[32] If this were not controlled, the Chinese would
come in increasing numbers and would in time convert not only
North Manchuria but also the Russian Maritime region into a
primarily Chinese area.

Other elements in Kuropatkin's argument outlined the desirable
benefits rather than the compelling reasons for following his
plan. In the first place, possession of North Manchuria might
actually be considered an asset to the national defense in this
region since Russia's boundary with China would actually be
shorter with a frontier running through the center of Manchuria.
Not only would the frontier in this way be reduced by half but
this would, in turn, reduce the defense needs proportionately.

[32] V.P. Petrov, "Manchuria as an Objective of Russian Foreign Policy," Washington, 1954, pp. 116–118 substantiates this view.

Finally, there was the question of Russia's financial stake in Manchuria: if Russia were to try to hold it all she might lose it all, but, by holding a part of it more securely, a substantial and vital portion of her enormous investment might be saved.

Whatever one may say about the theoretical correctness of the several formulas for dealing with the Manchurian problem, in retrospect Kuropatkin appears to have had the most reasonable and practicable plan and one which deserved more consideration than it received. One is constantly impressed throughout the final month of heated discussion preceding the outbreak of war, with the soundness of Kuropatkin's advice as a means of offering Japan an acceptable compromise.

It is apparent that his advice was disregarded, not because it was found to be inherently faulty, but because it was caught in the crossfire of warring factions. He relied on the merits of his arguments without the complete support of either of the principal partisan groups. Witte wrote this appropriate epigram to Kuropatkin at the time he also had fallen a victim in the political struggle: "Ours is a regime in which intrigue plays an unseemly role."[33]

[33] *K.A.*, xix, 71.

4. Russia's "New Course"

THE TASK which confronted the Russian government in the autumn of 1902 was indeed a complex one. It was an assignment that even a government more efficiently organized and better informed about the Far East would have found perplexing in the extreme. Under external pressure, harmonizing the domestic contentions seemed entirely possible. A policy did in fact evolve that could be considered a Russian national policy. The seemingly insoluble problem, however, was to bring either one of the dominant domestic views into focus with the requirements of the existing international situation.

Nevertheless, this is what the Russian government contemplated doing in a series of conferences held between November 1902 and the summer of 1903. A new policy was formulated at these conferences that has become known as the "new course" and Russia proposed to pursue this course in the Far East. The ultimate outcome of events, to be sure, testifies to the inadequacy of this policy in the light of conditions. In view of the proposals made by General Kuropatkin, the suspicion arises that this policy of the "new course" may not even have represented the maximum concessions compatible with the demands of national interest.

The first conference was held on November 9, 1902 at Yalta, where the Emperor was spending his winter vacation.[1] The ministers of war, foreign affairs, and interior attended and had an opportunity of hearing Witte's report on his Far Eastern tour. This conference was apparently preliminary and exploratory since most questions were intentionally left for future discussion even though General Kuropatkin pleaded for an immediate decision. Also, it was after this conference that Bezobrazov was sent to the Far East to gather new information. A broad and systematic attack on the problem was clearly intended, a reconsideration in keeping with the urgency disclosed in the concurrent negotiations with Japan.

In spite of its intentionally preliminary nature, the conference disclosed complete unanimity on at least one vital issue: a fact that in itself might have ruled out any sincerely conceived negotiations with Japan. This was the agreement on the part of all those present that ultimately Manchuria must either be annexed

[1] Malozemoff, op.cit., pp. 201–202; Glinsky, op.cit., pp. 268–269.

to Russia or, at least, be dependent upon her. The view was expressed and accepted by some that, until either of these conditions had been fulfilled, the colonization of even the railway zone should not be carried out. Even those who disapproved of this priority agreed that colonization and possession of Manchuria were interdependent and desirable. Clearly the Russian mission in Manchuria was understood by all members of the conference.

The most charitable conclusion one can draw from their reaffirmation at such a critical moment of this assumption as fundamental to the success of the new policy would be that they were actually unaware of the degree to which it narrowed down the negotiable area as far as Japan was concerned. In the light of all known official Russian views on the matter, it would be more realistic to see in this decision the thinking of a group concerned entirely with the minimum conditions by which its whole program could be realized, making little or no allowance for the Japanese determination not to retreat from the minimum of their own expansion program.

About a week before the next conference was to be held, General Kuropatkin took the initiative in discussing the evacuation question with various persons including A.I. Pavlov and P.M. Lessar, the Russian envoys to Korea and China respectively.[2] The objective of the conversations was apparently to sound out the possibility of gaining support for Kuropatkin's plan to forestall evacuation of North Manchuria. Pavlov assured Kuropatkin of his support. In the course of the conversation, Pavlov also emphasized his conviction that the problem then confronting Russia with respect to Korea was the political instability of that nation in the face of current international pressures. For, while Japan was losing no time in extending her control in Korea, the Koreans were politically and militarily incapable of any decisive action in their own behalf. Should the Japanese create an excuse for sending military forces to Korea, they would meet with no effective opposition.

Pavlov felt that the Bezobrazov scheme could only serve to aggravate this situation by limiting Russia's freedom of action. For, while Korea must, of course, eventually become Russian, he thought that the best tactics would be to allow Japan to take it over for the time being if necessary. When the occasion arose for a final showdown, Russia could most easily defeat Japan on

[2] *Dnevnik*, pp. 23–24.

Korean territory and therewith eliminate any effective opposition to Russian domination.

About a week after these conversations, on January 24, 1903, the second conference was held in St. Petersburg.[3] In addition to Pavlov, Lessar, the minister of foreign affairs and other foreign office officials, the Russian minister to Japan, Baron R.R. Rosen, was present. While it is not known whether all three Russian envoys to the Far Eastern countries were in St. Petersburg by design, this conference was in fact a gathering of foreign office officials to plan a concerted approach to the vital issue of evacuation.

In spite of Pavlov's assertion of only a few days before that he would support Kuropatkin's plan to leave forces in occupation of North Manchuria, this conference decided unanimously that the military occupation of Manchuria should be terminated. However, it was stipulated that this would not be carried out until adequate guarantees had been given by China for the safety of Russian interests in Manchuria, a stipulation already expressed in the circular note of August 25, 1900. A list of guarantees, classified as either essential or merely technically desirable, was agreed upon. While the precise guarantees were changed from time to time, the Russian government continued to insist that some guarantees were an indispensable prerequisite to withdrawal from Manchuria.

After these preliminary discussions, a special plenary conference was held on February 7, 1903 to consider the Manchurian question.[4] The conferees constituted the most authoritative policy-making body which, following Russian administrative practice, could be assembled to deliberate on Far Eastern policy. Furthermore, since the conclusions reached in spite of factional opinions and interests were approved by the Emperor, they must be assumed to represent the considered, official views of the Russian government.

The conference was presided over by Count V.N. Lamsdorf, the minister of foreign affairs, and, in addition, the seriousness of the issue was emphasized by the presence of other foreign office representatives, including Prince Obolensky, the ministers of

---

[3] Glinsky, op.cit., pp. 269–270; Romanov, Russia, p. 289; Makino to Foreign Office, No. 37, July 27, 1905, J.F.O.

[4] K.A., LII, 110–124; Glinsky, op.cit., pp. 271–275; Romanov, Russia, pp. 289–291; Malozemoff, op.cit., pp. 202–205.

war, navy, and finance, as well as the three Russian envoys in the Far East.

The conference directed its attention specifically to the issues raised by the Japanese proposals made some months before. Lamsdorf stated that, in view of the Russian "national interests" which unavoidably touched Korea, the Japanese proposals were unacceptable. This opened up a full discussion of the issues, both those concerning Korea as well as those dealing with Manchuria. The views expressed ranged from those of Admiral Tyrtov, who opposed any concessions to Japan which would restrict Russian access to the port of Masampo, to those of Baron Rosen, Russian envoy to Japan, who counseled against the acquisition of any Korean territory. Rosen felt that under present conditions it was unlikely that Japan would make an attempt to seize any part of Korea. It was better, therefore, not to stir up the waters.

Regarding the most immediate question, the conference decided that an agreement with Japan was desirable, but felt that Russia should await the Japanese initiative before pursuing the discussions any further. Meanwhile, in preparation for the anticipated Japanese negotiations, Russia should clarify her stand on all the vital issues. One of these, Korea, was considered vital but was postponed for future discussion.

The principal discussions at this conference centered on the Manchurian issue. A decision was reached ultimately to withdraw all military forces but with two severe and, as it turned out, fatal qualifications. One qualification was made in response to Kuropatkin's solicitude for the security of the region, particularly with respect to the problems which might arise with the increasing influx of Chinese settlers accompanying the completion of the railway and the further growth of the economy. His plan for the permanent retention of North Manchuria was fully explored but disapproved by the conference. Nevertheless, on the strength of Kuropatkin's plea for delay because of immediate dangers, such as the prevailing difficult weather conditions and the presence of bandits, the conference agreed to postpone the second stage of the military evacuations scheduled for completion by April 8, 1903. This was accepted against the strong opposition of the ministers of foreign affairs and finance and the envoy to China, all of whom felt that even a temporary delay would have adverse repercussions on relations with the powers.

The other qualification regarding Manchuria concerned relations with China after the Manchurian evacuation. The recommendations of the Jaunary 24 conference on this matter were unanimously adopted. These incorporated into official policy, formulated under the threat of growing foreign pressures, the requirement that certain guarantees must be received from China as a condition of final evacuation. Further, the terms intended to be presented to China which had been drawn up by Lessar were discussed and accepted with only minor alterations. The conditions for evacuation were looked upon as supplementary to the agreement of April 8, 1902. They were not actually presented to the Chinese government until April 18, 1903 but were promptly and categorically refused by the Chinese envoy in St. Petersburg on April 22, 1903. They were made known almost immediately to other foreign governments and had an extremely adverse diplomatic effect for Russia.

The Russian demands, whether reproduced in seven or eight articles, are substantially the same.[5] One set of articles would have forbidden China to alienate the territory evacuated by Russia to any other power, or to establish any new treaty ports in Manchuria without Russia's consent, or to appoint any foreigner to an administrative agency which carried jurisdiction over any Russian interests.

A second set of articles was intended to guarantee all existing Russian rights in Manchuria, give Russia special rights in Newchwang generally and to the telegraph line connecting this town with Port Arthur and Mukden in particular, and preserve the existing administrative structure in Mongolia. These demands might be considered a frank, overt, and official expression of Russia's long existing determination to monopolize Manchuria against all competitors.

The next conference met on April 8, 1903.[6] This was the first anniversary of the evacuation agreement with China and the date on which the second stage of the troop withdrawal was to have been completed. It was held at a time when the outcome of the previous conference could not have been known since the demands had not yet been submitted to China. Those attending included the Grand Duke General Admiral Aleksei

---

[5] Glinsky, op.cit., pp. 274–275; N.G.M., xxxvi–i, 70–81; Romanov, Russia, pp. 289–293; Malozemoff, op.cit., pp. 205–206.

[6] Glinsky, op.cit., pp. 277–286; Besobrassow, op.cit., pp. 597–602.

Aleksandrovich, the titular head of the navy, as well as the ministers of foreign affairs, war, finance, and interior. Although Bezobrazov had left Port Arthur on April 2, he had not yet returned to St. Petersburg and his interests were represented by his cousin, Admiral Abaza.

The subject of discussion was the Yalu or timber concession issue. In the absence of Bezobrazov, Abaza brought the subject before the conference by reading a memorandum which presumably contained the ideas of the "Bezobrazov group." He emphasized the value of the project both as an enterprise in itself and as a shield for the Manchurian frontier and the railway communications to Port Arthur. His assertion that it had already justified itself as a business venture, while apparently not susceptible of disproof at the time, was later shown to be totally misleading. The suggestion in Abaza's memorandum that a company should be formed is of considerable interest. It not only reflects an attempt to revive the Bezobrazov plans of some months before, but furnishes a clear idea of the current hopes entertained by the group. He proposed that the new company should encourage American and French capital to participate in the enterprise, thereby giving these nations a stake in the region which they would find it necessary to help defend. He added that Baron Ginsburg had already taken some steps in this direction by holding preliminary discussions with Americans interested in Korean concessions.

Abaza concluded his presentation by making some concrete proposals which were to form the subject of the deliberations of the conference. These proposals were: that the minister of foreign affairs take steps to affirm Russian rights in Manchuria and to support the concession in Korea; that the minister of finance plan the proposed company; that the minister of war plan all necessary measures for the defense of Russian enterprises in Manchuria and Korea; and, finally, that measures be considered for uniting all administrative functions in the Far East in order to obviate the existing interdepartmental chaos.

Needless to say, while these proposals raised some fundamental and even disturbing problems, they were by no means unacceptable to the members of the conference. Even Witte appears to have accepted the idea of some modification of his financial monopoly in Manchuria. For it was decided to entrust to the minister of foreign affairs the task of investigating the concession and, if he deemed it feasible, to proceed to work it out in legal form. He was also requested to try, with the assistance of the minister of finance, to secure from the Chinese government a parallel concession on the Manchurian side of the Yalu.

If these endeavors were successful, the minister of foreign affairs was to bring the two concessions together under a single joint-stock company, organized under Russian law and with its jurisdiction limited to the Yalu region; the company was to be purely private though limited government participation was permitted and capital might be solicited from the United States, France, and Belgium.

It is the last of the decisions of the conference which reflects most accurately the shifting focus of ministerial control in Manchuria. For this gave the commander of the Kuantung Leased Territory administrative control over both these concessions and the company through which they were to be operated. The effect of this was to commit into the hands of his most effective competitor a kind of enterprise heretofore under Witte's jurisdiction.

It seems clear in retrospect that official thinking had for some months been moving in the direction of an accommodation between the advocates of the Yalu project and the military authorities. In late December 1902, in the course of a discussion with the Emperor about the introduction of Russian troops into the Yalu area, Kuropatkin had referred again to a proposal he had made a year before when the negotiations with Ito were in progress.[7] This was the suggestion that, in the interest of avoiding a clash with Japan, a neutral zone be established on the Korean side of the Yalu as a buffer between the Russian and Japanese spheres of interest. In the end this device was indeed accepted as official policy, unhappily with consequences very different from those apparently contemplated by Kuropatkin.

In the weeks following this conference, actions appeared to be making the Russian intentions in Manchuria and Korea clear beyond question or doubt. In particular, the presentation of the Russian demands to China on April 18 furnished a rallying point for the diplomatic support Japan needed to give force to her own demands.

The very next day after their presentation a copy of the demands was in the hands of Foreign Minister Komura, then at Osaka.[8] His vigorous protest was immediately sent off to Prince

[7] K.A., II, 14.
[8] K.G., I, 304–307; Harmand to Delcasse, Apr. 16, 1903, D.D.F., III, 253–255.

The Naval Storehouse at Portsmouth, New Hampshire, used by
the conference—a modern view

President Theodore Roosevelt and the Portsmouth delegates

To
Baron Kentaro Kaneko
with the regards of his friend
Theodore Roosevelt
March 20th 1905

President Theodore Roosevelt

Ching to form the first support for China's refusal of the demands four days later. On his return to Tokyo Komura took the next step by initiating his search for concerted action with Great Britain and the United States. These protests included a very specific objection to closing the door of commercial opportunity and an expression of Japan's desire that certain cities such as Mukden and Tatung be officially opened to free access. This was the wedge expanded so dramatically by Japan and the United States when, on October 8, 1903, the scheduled date of the final evacuation of Manchuria, they signed parallel agreements with China. These treaties reiterated the demands for the opening of new commercial points and amounted almost to an alignment of the United States with the Anglo-Japanese Alliance.

Russian activities in Manchuria and North Korea also served to confirm widespread suspicion.[9] The central fact was that the date April 8 passed without the completion of the second stage of the evacuation. Taken in conjunction with the Yalu valley occurrences and ultimately the actual reoccupation of certain places in Manchuria, this seemed to present conclusive evidence of a Russian design for permanent tenure. Again the protests from Japan, Great Britain, and the United States furnished reminders of the solid wall of diplomatic opposition Russia's policies were inspiring.

It was in the midst of this trying situation that Russian prestige abroad suffered one of its worst setbacks. On Easter Sunday, April 19, 1903, the day after Russia had presented the demands to China, an outbreak of violence against the Jews in the city of Kishinev shocked the world.[10] Kishinev was a city which was about two-thirds Jewish. The destruction in the Jewish quarters was almost complete, the streets being reported lined with ruined homes and shops. Estimates of the number injured or killed varied greatly but it was apparently high. President Roosevelt not only protested this affair but continued into 1904 to protest both the conditions which encouraged these outbursts and the recurrent outbreaks of trouble.[11] Far from ending, similar violent attacks continued through 1904 until they tended to

[9] J. Otsu, op.cit., v, 580–581; Kuropatkin, op.cit., I, 169.
[10] Report of April 24 from Kishinev published in the London Standard on May 1, 1903, U.S.F.R., 1903, pp. 712–715; C. Adler, Jacob H. Schiff, 2 Vols., New York, 1928, II, 117–118.
[11] Schiff to Rothschild, Apr. 4, 1904, Adler, op.cit., II, 120–122; McCormick to Lamsdorf, Aug. 22, 1904, U.S.F.R., 1904 pp. 791–792; A. Kraus, Reminiscences and Comments, Chicago, 1925, pp. 155–160.

merge with the revolutionary events of 1905. Again Kishinev as well as Odessa, Simferopol, and other cities were the scenes of outbreaks through 1905.

Aware of the furor her policy was creating, Russia tried ineffectively to give it an unaggressive interpretation.[12] She had sent Baron R. R. Rosen to replace A. P. Izvolsky as the Russian minister to Japan. If this change was indeed as deliberately conceived to create a better Russian image abroad as some interpretations would have it, then it can only be said that Baron Rosen could not have been sent as the herald of a new policy but rather to present the existing policy in a more conciliatory and palliative light. The same must be said of Russia's denials that she had in fact presented any real demands to China as well as her repeated assurances of her intentions to evacuate Manchuria. The official correspondence shows clearly that, at least among the diplomats, these Russian efforts failed to modify the exisiting conception of her intentions. This was as true of her bitter opponents, the Japanese, as it was of her best friends, the French.

The condition of affairs in St. Petersburg during the weeks following the conference is ample evidence of the fact that, far from becoming more conciliatory, the Russian attitude had, if anything, become firmer. In the first place, it was at this time that Bezobrazov returned from the Far East to take a leading part in the formation of what came to be known as the "new course."[13] It was perhaps to make it easier for him to deal with the rank-conscious officials that he was given the largely honorary rank of state secretary and was appointed assistant to State Secretary Pokrovsky, the director of the Department of Industry, Science, and Commerce. These honors were apparently intended to prepare him for his next assignment; this time Bezobrazov was asked by the Emperor to act as coordinator for another conference to be held in a few days and to report its decisions to him.

The second notable occurrence of these weeks was the departure on April 28 of General Kuropatkin for the Far East on a dual mission having to do with the defense problem. The general subject of this mission had apparently first been broached by the Emperor in late February while Bezobrazov was in the

[12] Bompard to Delcasse, Feb. 27, Bompard to Delcasse, June 17, 1903, *D.D.F.*, iii, 139–140; 403–404; Japanese Foreign Minister to Hayashi, May 4, 1903, *B.D.*, ii, 203; Uchida to Komura, Apr. 28, 1903, *N.G.M.*, xxxvi-i, 88–89.
[13] Bezobrazov to Lamsdorf, May 21, 1903, *R.-I.V.*, p. 136; Romanov, *Russia*, p. 285; Malozemoff, *op.cit.*, pp. 217–218.

Far East;[14] he told Kuropatkin that he had sent a letter with Bezobrazov for Admiral Alekseiev on the subject of the proposed evacuation. The answer had just arrived, the Emperor continued, and stated Alekseiev's concern about the safety of Port Arthur in case of the evacuation of Mukden. Alekseiev suggested that, preparatory to evacuation, the Port Arthur garrison as well as the area of Manchuria along the Korean frontier should be strengthened. For Port Arthur, he suggested additional troops and provisions for a considerable period of time. As for the Korean frontier, he thought it could be held by the Chita Cossack regiment.

This conversation reveals an interesting concurrence of views on the vital question of defense of the Russian stake in Manchuria. Since Bezobrazov was then in the Far East and since Alekseiev has been thought of by some as one of the Bezobrazov circle, one might be tempted to conclude that Alekseiev was expressing Bezobrazov's ideas in his letter to the Emperor. In assessing this possibility, the fact that Admiral Abaza considered Alekseiev an untrustworthy associate of the group because he was always concerned about his own advantage must be taken into account.[15] Along with this must be considered the fact that Alekseiev had previously acted independently and with equal concern for the security of his jurisdiction and that he later had differences of opinion with Bezobrazov. It seems clearly indicated, therefore, that if Alekseiev's ideas in some way coincided with those of Bezobrazov, he may nevertheless have been exercising his independent judgment and may have felt that they constituted a reasonable approach to the solution of the problem.

The other significant aspect of Kuropatkin's conversation with the Emperor was his own reaction to Alekseiev's proposal. Far from disagreeing with it, he seems to have accepted it readily. In fact, he went on to suggest how, in very specific ways, the defenses in Manchuria could be brought up to a level consonant with the current military requirements.

In the light of this previous understanding with the two officials most concerned with the Far Eastern defenses and of the recent departure of General Kuropatkin on a defense mission, the Emperor's order to Admiral Alekseiev on May 15 seems to follow a natural sequence. It was in the form of a telegram sent, as

[14] *Dnevnik,* Mar. 1, 1903, pp. 36–37.
[15] A.M. Abaza to N.F. Abaza, June 21, 1904, *K.A.,* xvii, 36–37.

Romanov emphasizes, "without asking his ministers." In his telegram the Emperor ordered the commander in chief at Port
Arthur that "in minimal time and without balking at the necessary
expenditures, our fighting power in the Far East is to be placed
in complete equipoise with our politico-economic tasks, giving a
demonstration palpable to all of our determination to defend our
right to exclusive influence in Manchuria."[16] Witte's concurrence
when this telegram was disclosed to the conference held a few
days later testifies to the high degree of official sanction for this
policy and to the approval of its most natural opponent.

The third event which helps to elucidate the assumptions on
which Russia was then acting in the Far East was the conference held at Tsarskoe Selo on the evening of May 20, 1903.[17]
In keeping with the significance of a meeting where the "new
course" was to be officially launched, it was presided over by the
Emperor. Those in attendance included the ministers of foreign
affairs, finance, and the interior as well as Abaza, Bezobrazov,
Major General K.A. Vogak, a collaborator with the preceding
two, and General V.V. Sakharov, the army chief of staff, attending in the absence of General Kuropatkin.

This May conference was the last of those which dealt with the
formation of general policies concerning Manchuria. In formulating these, it brought into focus the previously established policies,
the findings of recent surveys respecting conditions in the Far
East, and the administrative measures taken up to the time it
met. Finally, it brought these strands together by formulating
a set of policy directives which came to be known as the "new
course." These were put into operation over the next three months
by a series of administrative measures which placed Russia in a
posture that convinced Japan no time could be lost in bringing
the issue to a showdown.

The fundamental issue to which the conference directed its
attention was the security of the Russian interests in Manchuria.
Action was taken on the assumption that the long, slender, exposed railway zone and the Kuantung Leased Territory at its
southern terminus were in a state of permanent siege by the
hostile Chinese of Manchuria and under a constant threat of
aggression from the Japanese who, it was further assumed, would
ultimately occupy Korea.

[16] Romanov, *Russia*, p. 284; Gurko, *op.cit.*, p. 275.
[17] *R.-I.V.*, pp. 9–25, 135–136; Besobrassow, *op.cit.*, pp. 603–608.

In a note written and distributed in advance of the conference by Bezobrazov, he expressed the situation in a formula: present Russian politico-economic interests outweighed her military preparedness. He proposed to correct this by bringing the two into better balance; in particular, he suggested that the defenses in the railway zone and the leased territory must be increased rather than reduced. While the action of the conference on this issue amounted to little more than approving a policy already partly put into practice, it is of considerable interest that it raised no significant protest from the participants in the conference. Witte, well informed through his agents of the course things were taking in Manchuria, seems to have prepared no counter-proposal. On the contrary, he stated categorically that he had no difference of opinion with the view proposed, a fact which Bezobrazov noted in the journal of the conference with considerable satisfaction. In this way the conference approved the fundamental tenet of the "new course": concessions could only lead to war and peace could be assured only by strength.

The other aspect of the defense question centered on the Yalu issue. While this was also approved along the line of a more aggressive policy, it elicited a more spirited discussion revolving around a matter of expediency rather than principle—the strategic significance of the region was generally conceded. The proponents of a positive approach argued that it was indispensable as a shield for both the Russian possessions in Manchuria and in Vladivostok. Furthermore, if Russia were to relinquish her hold on it, two fatal consequences would be sure to follow: it would be interpreted as a sign of weakness and Japan would seize both the concession and the strategic advantage it carried.

Witte questioned this on the grounds that, in the light of Japan's current attitude, it entailed serious risks. Bezobrazov reminded him that serious risks had been assumed in forcing the Japanese out of Kuantung in 1895 and in occupying it in 1897. Who could say that the third risk would necessarily lead to war? The emperor interposed his own view that the risk lay in not doing it rather than otherwise; with a complete disregard for the truth of the matter, he pointed out that the present state of things had in fact come about because one Russian concession had led to another. In the end a policy of defending the Yalu area was approved and became official policy. The precise conditions under which the defense was to be carried out was not made clear until the very eve of the war.

The remaining general issue brought before the conference was that of foreign competition in Manchuria. Assuming that the military preparations were completed, an acceptable guarantee ultimately received from China, and the withdrawal carried out, what protection would there be against foreign competition? Even before the conference met, one of its members, Vogak, had expressed his fear that the withdrawal of the military forces would only furnish an occasion for the powers to penetrate Manchuria.[18] Under cover of the open-door policy, these competitors would continue to make use of the railway and banking facilities to their own advantage and leave Russia no better off for all her efforts. With Russia's poorly developed commercial and industrial capabilities in Manchuria, the consequences could be highly undesirable for Russia. In fact, the solution to this problem was included in the Emperor's telegram of May 15 to Alekseiev dealing with the defenses of Port Arthur. This statement, read to the conference by Bezabrazov, made it clear that "the penetration of foreign influences into Manchuria is not to be permitted in any form whatsoever." Kuropatkin, who learned of the decision later, commented that such an order would be a source of considerable trouble since it would bring about a breach with all the countries having legitimate interests in Manchuria. Perhaps he was thinking specifically of the concurrent endeavors of Great Britain, the United States, and Japan in this respect when he concluded that this would complete Russia's isolation in the Far East. Nevertheless, the conference saw the matter as a question of balancing one drawback against another and this aspect of the "new course" was accepted with the rest.

The first of the decisions of the conference to be put into effect was the one concerning the Yalu concession. The concession was revived by the organization on June 13 of the Russian Lumber Company of the Far East, incorporating many of the features of the defunct East Asian Development Company.[19] It was to be a general development company with the right to acquire concessions of all kinds in Manchuria, Korea, and the Maritime Territory and to invite foreign capital investment, particularly American and French. In order to protect the conces-

[18] Vogak to Kuropatkin, Apr., 1903 R.-I.V., p. 13.

[19] Glinsky, op.cit., pp. 289–291; K.I., p. 87; Romanov, Russia, pp. 299–300.

sion, the company was permitted to use military detachments disguised as workers since the existing state of international tension forbade the overt use of military forces.

Several aspects of this policy are of special significance. One is that Plehve, the minister of interior and a strong partisan of the positive policy, not only supported the Yalu venture but actually took an active hand in the elaboration of the administrative organization. Secondly, at the time of the acceptance of the policy and apparently as a part of the same arrangement, Bezobrazov was able to have two additional brigades moved to the Far East.

It is apparent, therefore, that the Russian Lumber Company of the Far East, the final legal version of the Yalu enterprise, was a broad, all-inclusive organization such as its supporters had long envisioned. It was designed to give Russia the economic and legal foundations for a stake in this region which, it was hoped, would help to make a subsequent military conquest palatable to the powers. Furthermore, whatever the original concept of its promoters, the scheme was now of national significance and was firmly embedded in official policy.

The fact that Witte worked very closely with the new company is of great interest. An understanding was reached for general cooperation, including the joint operation of the Fushun mines, the latter belonging to Witte's Manchurian Mining Company. Witte had thus been maneuvered into coaction in this venture of Bezobrazov's that he believed was responsible for the war. His imputation of guilt to Bezobrazov, while not thereby wholly vitiated, nevertheless needs in this respect to be accepted with reservations. Furthermore, in retrospect the degree to which he was ready to cooperate can be seen as another milestone along Witte's downward path to political extinction.

At the time the May 20 conference was taking place, General Kuropatkin was in the Far East dealing with two closely related aspects of the defense problem. His mission had in fact been under consideration for several months. In late February, while Bezobrazov was in Manchuria, the Emperor had discussed the possibilities of some defense measures with Kuropatkin.[20] The conversation at that time was about the preparations for the defense of Port Arthur and the administrative difficulties which arose in Manchuria between the finance and war ministries.

[20] *Dnevnik*, Mar. 1, Mar. 29, 1903, pp. 35–36, 43; *R.-I.V.*, pp. 7–8.

These problems had been discussed and partially resolved at
the conference of April 8. From this came decisions to proceed
with the organization of the Yalu enterprise and to place it under
the jurisdiction of the commander in chief of the Kuantung
Leased Territory. It was also at this conference that the formal
decision was made to send Kuropatkin to the Far East. The
preparations for his journey occupied the next three weeks and
included conversations which must certainly have given consideration to the implications of the concurrent Chinese refusal
of the Russian demands.

The other purpose of General Kuropatkin's Far Eastern tour
was his visit to Japan.[21] Whatever may have been the source of
the ultimate inspiration for this visit, the actual initiative was
taken by Kuropatkin himself in a conversation with Kurino, the
Japanese minister in St. Petersburg. From the Japanese side,
however, the opportunity was immediately seized upon and
approval came from Tokyo the same day as the proposal. In due
course the project received the sanction of both Emperors, a
formal invitation was issued, and the details of the visit were
arranged. Before his departure from St. Petersburg, Kuropatkin
had several conversations with Kurino, who continued to hope
for a peaceful solution to the problem.

Kuropatkin's departure for the Far East on April 28 must have
been the subject of much speculation. Yet the reports of the
French ambassador to Paris reflect an accuracy in characterizing
the event that could hardly have been improved upon even by
the Russian foreign office.[22] Just before the general's departure
the ambassador wrote that Kuropatkin was going to Manchuria "to
organize Russian dominion there, or, if one prefers the official
terminology, to prepare the evacuation." The ambassador explained that this was by no means a contradiction of terms. For
Russia had no real intention of evacuating Manchuria. She
planned rather to concentrate her military forces in the railway
zone and at Port Arthur. He noted that his long experience in
Turkestan and Transcaspia had prepared Kuropatkin well for this
task. He felt sure that the minister of war would know how to
duplicate the experience in Khiva and Bukhara by observing a

[21] Bompard to Delcasse, Apr. 24, 1903, D.D.F., III, 266; Kurino to Komura,
Mar. 23, Komura to Kurino, Mar. 23, Kurino to Komura, Apr. 2, Kurino to
Komura, Apr. 3, 1903, N.G.M., xxxvi–I, 806–809; R.-I.V., p. 8.

[22] Bompard to Delcasse, Apr. 24, Bompard to Delcasse, June 17, 1903, D.D.F.,
III, 265–266, 403.

sufficient measure of respect for the local government while keeping the real authority securely in the hands of the Russian administration. Aware of the eastward movement of troops, he concluded that the present activities would leave Russia permanently established in Manchuria and, if anything, better prepared than before the "withdrawal" to defend it.

General Kuropatkin, according to his diary, left for the Far East in an optimistic mood because of the Emperor's commitment to finding a peaceful solution to the Far Eastern question.[23] However, by the time he had reached Harbin he had received the first of several telegrams from the Emperor which cast a shadow on this hopeful mood. The first one indicated that the Emperor had experienced a change of mind although Kuropatkin is very unclear as to how drastic the change was. However, he noted that it was significant enough to alter the understandings contained in the journal of the conference of April 8 which he had brought along for Admiral Alekseiev's inspection. The telegram also ordered him to take no steps to evacuate Mukden.

Telegrams which followed completed the image in Kuropatkin's mind of an altered outlook in St. Petersburg, at least so far as his own mission was concerned. One ordered him to await the arrival of Major General Konstantin Ippolitovich Vogak, the military agent in China and an adherent of the "Bezobrazov group," who was to accompany him to Japan. Another telegram directed him to discuss the findings of his tour in Japan with Bezobrazov at Port Arthur. The implication seems to be that this was his first notification that he would find Bezobrazov at Port Arthur on his return from Japan. In fact, a later telegram directed him to delay his departure from Japan, presumably to permit Bezobrazov to reach Port Arthur first.

Kuropatkin reached Tokyo on June 12.[24] His visit was under the personal sponsorship of the minister of war, General Terauchi Masatake, assisted by Lieutenant General Murata Atsushi and Colonel Tanaka Giichi, the latter a prime minister of a quarter of a century later closely associated with the "Memorial" and continental expansion. During his visit, Kuropatkin was received by the Emperor and met with elder statesmen, cabinet ministers, and others. He was given an opportunity to visit military in-

[23] R.-I.V., p. 8.

[24] K.G., i, 311; R.-I.V., pp. 25–26; Hori, op.cit., pp. 118–121; Harmand to Delcasse, June 16, 1903, D.D.F., iii, 400–401.

stallations and to review troops. In every formal and overt aspect of his tour, there was apparent a conscious effort to avoid any reminder of the tenseness inherent in the situation.

In private conversations with the prime minister, Katsura, and the foreign minister, Komura, the fundamental issues were broached though by no means solved.[25] In a discussion with Komura, Kuropatkin emphasized that he was speaking unofficially and for himself but that he wanted to see whether a way could not be found to reach a peaceful solution. He indicated that the problem of troop withdrawal was, from his point of view, inseparably associated with the security of the railway to Vladivostok and Port Arthur, an undertaking which represented to Russia an enormous investment.

Foreign Minister Komura, also carefully labeling his views unofficial, questioned the foundations of Kuropatkin's statements. He stated quite frankly that he was deeply disturbed by Russia's course in Manchuria. The withdrawal of the military forces and the security of the railway he regarded as two completely different questions. He objected to the presence of the military forces on two grounds: they constituted a potential menace to the security of Korea and their presence would become a first step in the partition of China. The latter he felt was inevitable since the other powers with interests in China would insist upon restoring the upset balance of power by demanding equivalent benefits. Such an outcome, he felt, would be equally disadvantageous to Russia and to Japan.

Kuropatkin's answer was drawn from the accepted official policies. He agreed that a partition of China was indeed undesirable, but he did not think that Russia's conduct in Manchuria would inspire this because her position in the Far East was exceptional in that her territory bordered on Manchuria and Korea. The railway into Manchuria was a Russian line and was, he implied, exceptional in the same way. Therefore, Russia's irreducible demands were those conditions which would insure the security of these special interests. An agreement with Japan would have to take this into account.

It is clear that Kuropatkin's mission to Japan had no influence on the general plans Russia was then putting into effect in the Far East. It was not, of course, intended that he consumate a

---

[25] Otsu, op.cit., v. 577–582; K.G., I, 311–313; I. Tokutomi, Koshaku Katsura Taro Den, 2 Vols., Tokyo, 1917, II, 123–127.

formal agreement of any kind with Japan. It was intended to be, at least from the Russian point of view, a reconnaissance mission in both the military and the political sense. Accordingly, Kuropatkin's reports to the Port Arthur conferences and later to the Emperor were looked to for supplementary information rather than as significant guidelines for a new policy.[26] A by-product of his mission, indeed an anticlimatic aspect, which served to dramatize the disappointing absence of results was the press report in the London *Standard* that a secret agreement had been concluded in which Russia had made some concessions. A firm denial from Komura ended this hope.

Kuropatkin was impressed with the determination and military readiness of Japan to support her national interests on the continent. Russia had to bear in mind, Kuropatkin reported, the existence in Japan of a group who were urging extreme measures and wanted the government to take a firmer stand on the Manchurian question. However, he felt that the group in power did not, for the present at least, constitute a danger as long as Russia confined herself to her legitimate interests in Manchuria. He emphasized, however, that interference in Korea would unquestionably cause an explosion. Furthermore, considering the Japanese determination with respect to Korea, Russia was in no position to prevent a Japanese landing there. It should be added that Baron Rosen, the Russian minister in Tokyo, supported this general appraisal of the determined Japanese posture.

The Port Arthur conferences, lasting from July 1 to 10, began the day after General Kuropatkin's return from Japan. Bezobrazov had already arrived to coordinate and report the conference.[27] The other participants included most of those concerned with Russian affairs in the Far East: Admiral Alekseiev; P.M. Lessar, the Russian minister at Peking; A.I. Pavlov, the Russian minister at Seoul; Major General K.I. Vogak, who had accompanied Kuropatkin to Japan; D.D. Pokotilov, the representative in China of the Russo-Chinese Bank and the Chinese Eastern Railway; Colonel D.L. Horvath, the director of the Chinese Eastern Railway and the commander of the railway guards; A.I. Iugovich, the chief engineer of the Chinese Eastern

[26] de Plancy to Delcasse, July 27, Bompard to Delcasse, Aug. 14, 1903, *D.D.F.*, III, 492, 535–536; M. Bompard, *Mon Ambassade en Russie* (1903–1908), Paris 1937, p. 43; Kuropatkin, *op.cit.*, I, 174–175; *R.-I.V.*, pp. 25–26; Kurino to Komura, July 28, Komura to Kurino, July 31, 1903, *N.G.M.*, XXXVI–I, 9–10.

[27] Glinsky, *op.cit.*, pp. 292–310; *R.-I.V.*, pp. 29–33; Gippius, *op.cit.*, pp. 48–51.

Railway; General A.M. Stessel, the commandant of the fort at Port Arthur; as well as local representatives of the ministries of finance, foreign affairs, and war.

Since the purpose of this conference was to put into practice the existing directives and decisions dealing with the security of Russian interests in Manchuria, its composition becomes of great interest. The identity of the participants clearly discloses that their selection was made from the departments of the government officially interested in Manchuria: foreign affairs, finance, war, and navy. It is also apparent that, from the standpoint of their being representative of either of the two major factions, the "Bezobrazov group" was considerably outnumbered by the others. Consequently, there was every reason to anticipate that the composition of this conference would make it a suitable forum for exploring a regional question dealing with national security.

There was, however, one significant item of information which the conference failed to receive, thanks to Bezobrazov. It was a directive telegraphed by Abaza to him while he was on his way to the Far East and was intended to have been forwarded both to Alekseiev and to all the Russian ministers in the Far East.[28] It stated that the Emperor had definitely decided to permit Japan to occupy Korea "perhaps even up to" the boundaries of the Russian concessions. While it left the precise delineation of the area conceded to Japan to be determined later, it clearly stipulated that this decision would be made by Russia. In order to avoid having this construed as a concession, the information was to be communicated to Japan only after the arrival in the Far East of the military reenforcements from European Russia. It concluded that the Emperor hoped this concession would avoid war.

One of the questions discussed at the conference was the withdrawal of troops from Manchuria. It was looked upon, as in previous discussions, as a necessary evil which Russia's hasty promises of the previous year, her present military unpreparedness, and the force of international opinion had rendered imperative. The conference made a straightforward, realistic attempt to carry out the promises made to China on April 8, 1902

---

[28] Abaza to Bezobrazov, June 24, 1903, V.L. Burtsev, *Tsar i Vneshniaia Politika*, Berlin, 1910, pp. 33, 43; Malozemoff, *op.cit.*, p. 220.

as reinterpreted in the Emperor's telegram of May 15, 1903, observing as much of the letter and as little of the spirit of the promise as circumstances permitted.

In dealing with the problem of security, the conference faced the task of framing a new set of conditions to be presented to China. At the same time, it had to be prepared to carry out alternative policies depending on whether or not China accepted the conditions. The question of specific demands to be made of China was brought before the conference in the form of 17 articles drawn up by General Kuropatkin. After discussing these the conference reduced them to 10. These conditions, in turn, were reconsidered by a conference called by the Emperor in St. Petersburg on August 14 and attended by the ministers of war, finance, and foreign affairs.[29] This group decided that, in view of the concurrent strengthening of the defenses in the railway zone and the Kuantung Leased Territory, some of the final 10 articles were unnecessary. Consequently, only 5 demands were presented to China on September 6, 1903. By this time, however, the Russo-Japanese negotiations were already in progress and the question had assumed a new gravity.

The articles discarded by the August 14 conference become of special interest because they were considered unnecessary and also because they were originally proposed by Kuropatkin, not Bezobrazov. One of these would have required China to promise that no foreign persons, other than Russian, would be employed in administrative positions in North Manchuria "where Russian interests predominate."[30] This article probably reflected an apprehension on Kuropatkin's part that the Chinese Imperial Maritime Customs Administration might be extended to North Manchuria. Its elimination may be seen as the final rejection at this unpropitious time of his plan to make this region wholly Russian. The other discarded demands dealt with the retention of certain telegraph lines in Russian hands, the requirement that China pay Russia for the construction of some telegraph lines, and the protection of Russian enterprises. At the Port Arthur meeting, Lessar had regarded the last condition as objectionable because it was unenforceable. Presumably, at the St. Petersburg conference it was considered too provocative toward other foreign

[29] Glinsky, op.cit., pp. 343–345.
[30] ibid., p. 306.

powers or, like the rest, unnecessary since reenforcements would presumably give Russia sufficient protection.

The demands presented to China on September 6 included the following:[31] a prohibition against the cession or lease by China to a foreign power of any part of Manchuria; a guarantee to Russia of the right to use and protect certain river and telegraph communications; a prohibition against the imposition of heavy duties on goods transported by railway; and the assurance that the Russo-Chinese Bank would be protected and the city of Newchwang kept under sanitary control.

Included with the demands was a schedule of Russian troop withdrawal in case they were accepted. This provided for the evacuation of Fengtien Province immediately, of Kirin Province within four months, and Heilungchiang Province in one year. This latter provision represented a radical revision of the Port Arthur proposals which would have delayed withdrawal for three years in order to allow time for strengthening the military establishment in Manchuria.

The reenforcement of Russia's military posture in the Far East was the second major aspect of the general security problem discussed at Port Arthur. Reenforcement was thought of as preparatory to evacuation. This seeming contradiction meant, on the one hand, that ultimately the troops would be removed from all points presently occupied outside the railway zone and the leased territory such as Fenghuangcheng, Liaoyang, Newchwang, and elsewhere. Strengthening the Russian position, on the other hand, meant that within the areas legally occupied the Russian military capability would actually be increased, decisive action then being possible at any time. Should China decline the demands, the Russian forces could simply remain where they were; should she accept them, the forces could be concentrated in the leased territory and the railway zone.

In determining the requirements for an adequate military posture in the Far East, the Port Arthur conference was able to profit by General Kuropatkin's experience in Japan. He informed them that Japan was better prepared for war than Russia. Apparently his advice that Russia should avoid all aggressive acts toward Korea and Japan was taken seriously by everyone but Bezobrazov, who reiterated his opinion that concessions would

[31] Uchida to Komura, Sept. 8, Uchida to Komura, Sept. 9, 1903, *N.G.M.*, xxxvi–i, 354–356.

be taken as a sign of weakness and would, therefore, only lead to disaster.[32]

The conference elaborated in some detail the plan for the increase in military strength.[33] It was estimated that the necessary changes would require an expenditure of 30 million rubles immediately as well as an annual outlay of 6 million rubles for several years. An additional 2½ million rubles was to be allotted to Admiral Alekseiev to place Port Arthur and other parts of Kuantung in a state of military readiness. It was further recommended that for defense purposes Port Arthur and Kuantung be constituted separate administrative areas; the Third Corps was allotted to Kuantung as a nucleus of its own defense preparations. Finally, it was urged that the transport capacity of all the Manchurian railways be increased, particularly for military use.

A third major subject of discussion at the Port Arthur conference dealt with Korea. Since this problem was most intimately associated with the interests of Japan it was recognized as an extremely sensitive one.[34] It had already been decided several months before that the Yalu enterprise would be, at least formerly, a private one. The conference acted on this decision but was apparently totally unaware of the Emperor's order to allow Japan a portion of Korea. It simply adopted the logical corollary of the earlier decision, that no person in official employment should be active in the company.

Acting on these assumptions, the conference established the following general policies to govern the relations with Korea: the occupation by Japan of all or even South Korea was disadvantageous to Russia; Russia must, nevertheless, be prepared for this occupation; Russia should protest without taking any corresponding measure such as the occupation of the North; the occupation by Russia of all or even of the northern part of Korea would be disadvantageous for Russia; Russian activity in Manchuria was unrelated to Korea; Russia had no aggressive intentions with respect to Korea and would support its independence; to make it impossible for Japan to see Russian activity on the Yalu as having any military-political character, Russia should take steps to give her activities there an exclusively commercial character with no military officers participating.

[32] Glinsky, op.cit., p. 308.
[33] ibid., p. 293; R.-I.V., pp. 30–32.
[34] Glinsky, op.cit., pp. 303–306; Gippius, op.cit., pp. 48–49.

Another aspect of the work of the Port Arthur conference was
an administrative reorganization centering in a newly created office of viceroy of the Far East. Although this has received only
the briefest mention in the reports of the conference, it is difficult to believe that it was not discussed, at least in private conversations. It is of course, possible that little discussion was
necessary since the decision carrying it out had been made at the
conference in St. Petersburg on May 20, 1903. Presumably all
that remained to be done was the elaboration of the details with
Admiral Alekseiev.

The need for a new organization was clearly apparent even
to foreigners who were aware of the competition of various
ministerial appointees in Manchuria. When Senator Beveridge
visited Manchuria in 1901 he received the impression that there
was a plan to make Admiral Alekseiev "the first and highest
representative of the Czar throughout Manchuria and the entire
Far East and even in Trans-Baikal Siberia."[35] As the situation
in the Far East became increasingly tense and the divided administration a corresponding burden in carrying out an effective
policy, it seemed inevitable that some better system would become necessary. By the summer of 1903 the loss of power and
prestige on the part of Witte seemed to open the way for a
unified administration in the hands of the military commander.

A decree of August 12, 1903 established the Viceroyalty of
the Far East.[36] Admiral Alekseiev was appointed to the new
office. With this exalted rank went not only such symbols of
dignity as a special flag and a twelve-gun salute, but the realities of prestige and power represented in an extensive jurisdiction. In area the viceroy's powers reached out from the center
at Port Arthur to include the Kuantung Leased Territory, the
railway zone, and the Transbaikal, Amur, and Maritime territories of the Russian Far East. Within these regions his jurisdiction extended to all Russians and all Russian rights. He commanded all military forces and transacted all foreign affairs that
affected his jurisdiction. The viceroy's powers were exercised
without any interference from local representatives. His chain
of command ran directly to a Special Committee for Far Eastern
Affairs, the president of which was the Emperor and the vice

[35] Beveridge, op.cit., p. 61.
[36] MacMurray, I, 122; North China Herald, Jan. 8, 1904; Gurko, op.cit., pp.
74–82.

president Plehve, the minister of interior. Since the committee never met, the viceroy had direct access to the Emperor through Abaza, the director of the secretariat.

Although this administrative reorganization was badly needed, it was brought about at the worst possible time. The decree instituting it was issued on the very day the negotiations with Japan were reopened. Not only did this create the impression in Tokyo that negotiations about this area were practically foredoomed, but it made their conduct laborious and almost necessarily protracted.[37] The viceregal system was far too new to function effectively, particularly in regard to foreign relations. As a consequence, a large share of the misunderstanding of Russian motives arising during the negotiations can be attributed to the inefficiencies of this new distribution of administrative responsibility.

The establishment of the new viceroyalty was an aspect of a more fundamental change in governmental policy which included also the dismissal of the renowned minister of finance. It would be a mistake to see in the sacking of Witte only the whim of Bezobrazov, the limitations of whose role are apparent enough. In fact, Witte had, in a host of ways, worn out his welcome as the occupant of a position so fraught with consequences for the entire country. He had, therefore, become an easy target for individuals who had their own reasons for wishing him out of the way. This was particularly true of persons such as the "Bezobrazov group" who were associated with a specific, alternative policy and who could, therefore, ride to success on a wave of general desire for an end to the prevailing uncertainty.

Witte, with his customary emphasis on his role as an imperial minister, was inclined to see his dismissal in a very personal light and to blame his relations with the Emperor.[38] He was well aware that Lamsdorf was not dismissed as foreign minister although associated with Witte's objectionable policies. He compared the relationship of the Emperor, Lamsdorf, and himself to that of a father who is about to divorce his wife and marry a younger woman. Both the children disapproved of this. The son let his disapproval be known in such a harsh and unkindly way that his father resented it and put his son out of the house. But the daughter expressed disapproval in a kindly and lovable

[37] Gurko, op.cit., pp. 281–284; Otsu, op.cit., v, 671.
[38] Witte, op.cit., i, 220–221.

manner, emphasizing her love for him, so that the father accepted her criticism. The Emperor's relief after he had disposed of his "harsh and unkindly" minister is reflected in an entry in his diary the day of Witte's dismissal: "Now I rule."[39]

Another version of the dismissal of Witte was brought out by General Kuropatkin.[40] He compared the situation to the explosion of three mines. The simile may have been inspired by Witte who told Kuropatkin that the rescript for the dismissal had been ready since early the previous January. The first mine, Kuropatkin wrote, had been laid by the Grand Duke Aleksander Mikhailovich who had long felt that Witte had too much power. The second and third mines were laid by Bezobrazov and Plehve respectively. The simile is an apt one in a way that probably did not cross Kuropatkin's mind. For in the enormous conflagration which followed, the foundations of the Grand Duke Alekseiev's social and political position were shaken, Bezobrazov was eliminated politically and completely discredited, while Plehve was assassinated.

The dismissal occurred on August 28, 1903, under circumstances which were dramatically lacking in ostentatiousness.[41] Witte had been asked by the Emperor to appear on that day to make a report. He was also asked to bring with him the assistant minister of finance and director of the State Bank, Eduard Dmitrievich Pleske. The latter was a puzzling request and left Witte to assume that the Emperor intended to ask about Pleske's forthcoming trip to Siberia.

The two men reached Peterhof at the appointed time. While Pleske waited in the reception room, Witte went in to give his report. This taken care of, the Emperor asked him for his opinion of Pleske. Witte replied by giving his assistant a good recommendation. Then the Emperor disclosed that he wished Witte to assume the office of chairman of the Committee of Ministers and had decided that Pleske should succeed him as minister of finance. Since Witte's new position was almost purely honorary in nature and function, the significance of this was clear. When Pleske came in, the Emperor said simply: "Sergei Iulievich has accepted the post of chairman of the Minister's Committee, for which I

[39] Malozemoff, op.cit., p. 226.
[40] Dnevnik, Sept. 1, 1903, pp. 59–60.
[41] Witte, op.cit., I, 218–219.

am very grateful to him, and I have decided to appoint you Minister of Finance."[42]

The conference at Port Arthur and later the conference at St. Petersburg had together developed an official administrative policy which would become the guideline for negotiations and then war. Because Bezobrazov had withheld vital information, the conference could not act in any final way with regard to Korea, this key problem remaining, therefore, unsolved at the Port Arthur conference. Like most policies, those formulated during the first half of 1903 were composed of many strands of opinion and national interests, most of them highly emotional in character. But it must be remembered that, however ill-conceived it might appear in the test to which it was soon subjected, it was a well-considered policy and not a product of hasty improvisation devised under pressure from a group of adventurers; it must be viewed, therefore, as a national policy.

[42] Kokovtsov, *op.cit.*, p. 6.

5. The Isolation of Russia

THE RUSSIAN OCCUPATION of Manchuria and intrusion into Korea were regarded by Japan as an infringement of her national interests. She was, therefore, determined to make the most of the occasion by forcing a showdown with Russia and ridding herself of a menace. A prerequisite, she was well aware from her unhappy experience in the Sino-Japanese war, would be an international opinion favorable to such an undertaking. This, in turn, would require acceptance of the view that Japan, by contrast to Russia, was fighting for the open door. Otherwise there would always exist the danger both of intervention by the other powers and of a resumption of the partition of China, either of which might easily annul any possible gains. On the other hand, if the existing fluid situation could be successfully transmuted into positive diplomatic leverage, Japan might be able to solve to her own advantage a long-standing and vital problem.

The source of danger to Japanese national interests and the central problem of the Far East was the existing weakness of China and Korea. Relative to the external pressures exerted upon them, these countries had in recent decades declined slowly and almost imperceptibly, but nevertheless impressively. Because Korea and Chinese Manchuria lay between Russia and Japan, there was always the danger that they might be influenced, politically or economically infiltrated, or seized by the rival nation, thus upsetting the balance of power.

As rumor and intrigue increasingly replaced the normal processes of international relations with respect to China and Korea, a sense of insecurity came to dominate the responses and acts of the governments concerned. The Russian foreign minister, N.K. Giers, was facing a problem of this kind when he wrote in the summer of 1894:

"Perfectly appreciating Li Hung-chang's confidence in us, we consider, however, inconvenient our direct interference in Korean reforms, for behind this proposition there is evidently hidden a desire to involve us in the Korean disorder and get our help."[1]

[1] Giers to Russian minister in Peking, July 7, 1894, B.G. Weber and S.R. Dimant (eds.), "Russian Documents Relating to the Sino-Japanese War, 1894–1895," *Chinese Social and Political Science Review*, Peking, XVII, No. 3, Oct. 1933, p. 510.

The Japanese prime minister, Katsura Taro, had this same inconvenient circumstance in mind when he wrote in the summer of 1905 that members of the Korean government were known to have intrigued not only with the Japanese and Russian governments against each other but also within the Japanese government itself.[2] Just recently, he said, a group of high Korean officials had secretly approached Ito Hirobumi, inviting him to accept a position as "governor general" or "dictator" of Korea.

Since the opening of Korea in the 1870's both Japan and Russia had shown themselves eager to forestall being outsmarted by seizing the prize first. During those years the strong hand of Li Hung-chang, whose viceroyalty included control over Chinese relations with Korea, had helped to hold the situation in check. But in the years immediately preceeding 1894, Japanese uneasiness over Russian intentions had tended increasingly to overbalance the cautious policy heretofore maintained. The situation had been explosive enough since the colossal Russian state had established a common frontier with Korea in 1860. But after 1890 the building of the Siberian railway promised to tip the balance even more favorably to Russia as the line reached completion.

By 1894 the Japanese government had reached the conclusion that the danger of war with China over Korea, even though it would expose both belligerents to pressures from Russia in the process, was overbalanced by the need for settling the question before it was too late. The Japanese armies boldly laid hold of Korea, drove the Chinese forces back through southern Manchuria, and seized the Kuantung peninsula with Port Arthur and Dairen. During the crisis of the succeeding months Japan conducted herself in a manner remarkably similar to the way Russia would in Manchuria after 1900. She prepared to exercise a protectorate over Korea and expressed her unwillingness to remove her troops until her requirements for security had been met.[3]

Japan's bold gamble foundered against growing and determined opposition from Russia just as Russia's venture would suffer defeat a decade later because of Japanese resistance. Russia soon came to see in Japan an even greater menace in the

[2] MacDonald to Lansdowne, July 31, 1905, *B.D.*, IV, 158–159.
[3] Cassini to Russian foreign minister, July 1, 1895, Weber and Dimant, *op.cit.*, p. 505.

Far East than Britain. In fact, after she had decided upon forcible intervention against Japan, Russia turned first to Britain for support. In the end, it was Germany and France which joined Russia in depriving Japan of her gains in the Kuantung peninsula. In Korea, Russia stood ready to offer help when Japan's overambitious plans for control alienated the Korean king and government. Russian prestige rose in the wake of Japan's defeat. But the diplomatic triumph by which Russia had turned two other European powers against Japan was not forgotten in Tokyo. Nor was the compensation they all received at China's expense.

When Japan began to repair the damage, she did not forget the value of the diplomatic weapon. Her first accomplishment was an accommodation with Russia regarding their respective interests in Korea. This was brought about in the Weber-Komura agreement signed at Seoul on May 14 and the Lobanov-Yamagata agreement signed at Moscow on June 9, 1896. The climax of Japan's pre-Boxer diplomatic rehabilitation was reached in the Rosen-Nishi agreement of April 25, 1898.[4] This recognized the residential, commercial, and industrial rights of Japanese in Korea. Coming as it did in the wake of Russia's acquisition of railway and lease rights in Manchuria, the treaty in effect accepted a balance of the respective interests of the two nations in Manchuria and Korea. As Russian pressure from Manchuria again mounted after 1900 the agreement came to be looked upon in Tokyo as a minimum guarantee from which there was to be no retreat.

The Rosen-Nishi agreement was favorable to Japan in two particular ways. Inasmuch as it signified a measure of Russian retreat, it gave the Japanese new stature and prestige. Also, by recognizing Japanese interests it encouraged the further growth of Japanese economic projects, a factor which had accompanied political efforts since the opening of Korea.[5] The Daiichi Bank had formed the core of economic development since its establishment in Korea in 1878. In the succeeding years its share in the economic life increased as it served in the role of a central bank

[4] Hori, op.cit., p. 32; Rosen, op.cit., I, 157–159; S. Shinobu and H. Nakayama, Nichiro Sensoshi no Kenkyu, Tokyo, 1959, pp. 161–162.

[5] Hori, op.cit., pp. 18–21; F.H. Harrington, God, Mammon and the Japanese, Dr. Horace N. Allen and Korean-American Relations, 1884–1905, Madison, 1944, p. 305; A.J. Brown, The Mastery of the Far East; The Story of Korea's Transformation and Japan's Rise to Supremacy in the Orient, New York, 1919, p. 151; Malozemoff, op.cit., p. 232; T. Hatada, Chosen Shi, Tokyo, 1952, pp. 175–178.

of Korea, exercising its extensive powers through the promotion of business, the issuing of bank notes, the regulation of the coinage, and the collection of customs receipts.

By the early years of the twentieth century, Japanese economic interests held a predominant place in Korea. More than three-quarters of Korea's foreign commerce was carried on with Japan. The principal import from Japan was cotton products while the principal export to Japan was foodstuffs, mainly rice. Japanese settlers outnumbered any other foreign group and lived largely in the towns where they served as advisors to the government and controlled most of the shipping and commerce as well as the fishing along the coast.

The aspect of Japan's pre-war Korean policy that most clearly exemplified the political significance of her role in the country, was the promotion of railway construction. The first link, connecting the port of Chemulpo (Inchon) with the capital at Seoul, was completed in 1900, opening up both politically and economically the center of the country to Japanese influences. The second installment, the Seoul-Fusan line, gave Japan the first half of a trans-Korean railway to Manchuria from the easily accessible port of Fusan (Pusan) which Japan dominated.[6] It was completed by January 1905.

The other sector of the mainline, running from Seoul to Uiju on the Manchurian frontier, was unavailable to Japan until the opening of the war gave her control of North Korea. The concession had been in the hands of a French company from 1896 until it was finally dropped in 1903. But in February 1904 the influx of Japanese troops finally cleared the way for construction to begin. The line was completed by April 1906, giving Japan dominance over this strategic route.

The long unsuccessful endeavor to acquire the concession to build the Seoul-Uiju line through North Korea was a venture into a region heretofore little touched either by Japanese or other economic interests. In addition to their untouched railway concession, the French had some mining and other interests.[7] The Russians held the Briner timber concession for years before strategic objectives dictated its fulfilment while it was still valid. In the long run, the Oriental Consolidated Mining Com-

---

[6] H. Conroy, *The Japanese Seizure of Korea, 1868–1905*, Philadelphia, 1960, pp. 478–479.

[7] Harrington, *op.cit.*, pp. 303–305; Whigham, *op.cit.*, pp. 189ff.

pany, an American venture centered in the Yalu River valley, was the most prosperous foreign holding in North Korea.

The entry of Japanese entrepreneurs into the timber industry in the Yalu River valley in the spring of 1903 was a primarily strategic venture. Had it been carried out under the assumption that the corresponding Russian operation was purely private and commercial in nature, it might have passed as merely competitive. However, the watchfulness which soon after revealed to the Japanese the official character of the Briner concession, establishes a strong probability that this had long been suspected. In this light the Japanese enterprises must be seen as both defensive and provocative. For it was clearly intended to serve as a means of holding the Russians at bay by discouraging their efforts to penetrate Korea.

The Japanese timber company apparently became the subject of active planning some time in March 1903.[8] The original grant was made by the Korean government to three Korean subjects on March 21, 1903. Within the next few days the concession went through two changes, first into Chinese hands and then into a Sino-Japanese company. The latter was formally established April 1, 1903 and approved the following day by the Japanese consul in Seoul. Although half the capital of the company was registered in the name of a Korean subject, there was no doubt as to where the direction was centered. The president was a Japanese merchant in Seoul, Abe Junsuke, and it was registered as a Japanese company under Japanese jurisdiction. The concession area was the same as that of the Russian timber company, a situation that almost predestined the conflict between the rival companies.

The significance of these Japanese attempts to expand into North Korea by means of railway and timber concessions was exemplified by the deliberations of an Imperial conference which met in June 1903.[9] Its purpose was to establish the policies which were to be followed in the forthcoming negotiations with Russia. Preliminary to this, the conference reviewed the entire range of Japan's continental interests. These, in turn, were seen as coming to a focus at two points on the mainland: Korea in the north and the Chinese province of Fukien in the south. While

[8] Hayashi to Komura (enclosure), May 2, 1903 *N.G.M.* xxxvi-i, 586–593.
[9] "Decision of the Imperial Conference," June 23, 1903, *N.G.M.*, xxxvi-1, 1–4; *K.G.*, i, 322–324; Otsu, *op.cit.*, v, 644–669.

the latter was for the time being recognized as second in priority, its ultimate significance could not, in the view of the conference, be disregarded. Geographically and politically, it was closely associated with Formosa on the one hand and with inland China on the other.

It was assumed that, as China lost control over her territory, partition of the country would emerge as a serious and even imminent possibility. For the time being Japan's policy rested upon her nonalienation agreement with China of April 26, 1898 by which Fukien was shielded from intrusion by any foreign nation other than Japan. However, should partition materialize, Japan would want a sphere of interest reaching not only into Fukien but considerably beyond.

With respect to Korea, it was noted at the conference that it constituted a sword pointed at the heart of Japan. Parallelling the official policy regarding Fukien Province, it was decided that under no circumstances must any other nation be permitted to establish control over Korea. Instead, Japan must obviate such a possibility by seeking control over it herself. To this end, the railway system must be completed as soon as possible.

After the completion of the Seoul-Fusan line, the right to build the Seoul-Uiju railway was to be acquired and the line built. This, in turn, must be connected with the Manchurian railway, including the route to Peking, a point which the Japanese would insist upon in the negotiations with Russia. The parallel between these plans and the projected railway in the south is striking. There it was hoped that a railway might sometime be built from Amoy into Kiangsi Province, with branch lines to Hangchow and Wuchang.

Japan's determination to defend these interests, plans, and prospects against Russian expansion, already demonstrated in 1894, was again expressed openly in early 1901. The occasion was the proposal of the Russian government on January 7, four days after the disclosure in the London *Times* of the Tseng-Alekseiev agreement regarding Manchuria, that Japan join in guaranteeing the neutrality of Korea.[10] Though this idea had come from the Koreans themselves, Russia saw the tremendous advantage it held for her both in blocking Japan and keeping her

[10] Lansdowne to MacDonald, Jan. 29, 1901, *B.D.*, ii, 34–35; Note from the Japanese minister in St. Petersburg, Jan. 22, 1901, *Obzor*, pp. 15–16, 66; Lamsdorf to Izvolsky, Jan. 30, 1901, *K.A.*, lxiii, 11.

at arms length and in giving her own strategy the appearance of a goodwill gesture toward Korea.

Japan's reply was an emphatic refusal. It stated flatly that Japan would not negotiate the question of Korea until the pre-Boxer situation had been restored in Manchuria. It drew a clear difference between the situation in 1898 and the present. At that time the Russians had just received the rights they had demanded in the Kuantung region of Manchuria. Having been granted by lease, these were necessarily temporary in nature. The present situation, however, was an occupation which had the appearance of permanence. Therefore, the Japanese government intended to postpone negotiations on the Korean question until the previous conditions had been restored in Manchuria. Meanwhile, the Rosen-Nishi agreement of 1898, which had recognized Russia's lease rights in Kuantung and the predominant interests of Japan in Korea, was assumed by Japan to constitute an adequate safeguard for both nations.

The Japanese reply might have been interpreted as a virtual ultimatum. It stated frankly and unequivocally her general views and laid down specific guidelines for future policy which she followed closely during the coming years: Japan would not tolerate Russia's continued occupation of Manchuria; the questions of Manchuria and Korea were inseparably associated in her view; the recognition of Japan's predominant interests in Korea would be a percondition to any further consideration of the Korean problem; Japan's interests in Korea had in her view already received Russian approval in the agreement of 1898; and, by implication at least, Japan was determined upon a limitation of the Russian interests in Manchuria.

The disclosure of the Tseng-Alekseiev agreement in early January 1901 also provided Japan with the opportunity to lay a firm foundation for her forceful Manchurian policy by commencing the diplomatic isolation of Russia. She did this at first by encouraging among the powers a sufficiently solid support to make it possible for China to refuse Russia's demands. A few days after the publication of the agreements, the Japanese minister in London, Baron Hayashi Tadasu, suggested that if the two countries were to make identical inquiries in St. Petersburg about the precise nature of the Sino-Russian arrangements, this could constitute an effective hint.[11] About two weeks later Hayashi again suggested

[11] Lansdowne to MacDonald, Jan. 12, 1901, *China No. 2 (1904)*, p. 4.

common action, this time in the form of identical protests to China regarding the signing of separate agreements with any single power. In due course not only Great Britain but Germany and the United States as well joined Japan in protesting separate agreements.[12]

The Chinese responded to this encouragement by an Imperial edict dated February 28, 1901. It stated the difficult and dangerous problem which Russia's demands posed for China. It invited further diplomatic support in these words: ". . . it is impossible for China alone to incur the displeasure of Russia by remaining firm. This is not only a question for China to study with all possible care, in order that it may be solved without any danger to her, but also a question in which the foreign governments interested should maintain the balance of power."[13] This response was encouraging in Tokyo and depressing in St. Petersburg. Along with the Chinese refusal on the same day of the Russian demands of February 8, it indicated that China had taken another self-assertive step.

Japan continued her search for diplomatic if not military support for dislodging the Russian armies from Manchuria. The concerted protests which she had inspired from Great Britain, Germany, and the United States had served their purpose. China had declined the demands and left Russia to ponder the next move. It was an opportune moment for Japan to seize the initiative. In early March 1901 she took the next step by announcing her determination to go to war with Russia if she could be assured that France could be restrained from joining in the conflict.[14] She added to the forcefulness of this statement by expressing her view that the Russian danger was advancing rapidly and must be dealt with before Russia had completed the railway and entrenched herself in Manchuria.

Japan's most effective diplomatic support, in view of the intended showdown with Russia, came from the Anglo-Japanese Alliance. The negotiations for this were begun in April 1901 when the Japanese minister in London, Baron Hayashi, made

[12] Lansdowne to MacDonald, Feb. 5, 1901, *ibid.,* p. 4, and notices of other declarations, *ibid.,* pp. 5–10.
[13] *ibid.,* p. 8.
[14] Lansdowne to Lascelles, Mar. 8, "Communications to Baron Hayashi," Mar. 9, Lascelles to Lansdowne, Mar. 10, 1901, *B.D.,* II, 41–42; Hayashi to Kato, Apr. 9, Hayashi to Kato, Apr. 11, Komura to Kato, Apr. 12, 1901, *N.G.M.,* XXXIV, 1–3; *K.G.,* I, 217–219; A. Galperin, *Anglo-Iaponskii Soiuz, 1902–1921,* Moscow, 1947, pp. 91–95.

some cautiously worded proposals in the form of personal suggestions to Lord Lansdowne, the British foreign minister.[15] Not
until June 1901, when the Ito cabinet was replaced by one headed
by Katsura and, more particularly, after September, when Komura
had assumed his post as foreign minister, was the coast clear to
discuss an alliance with a real prospect of success. By mid-October
Japan had made a definite and serious proposal which formed the
basis for discussing the actual terms for an alliance.

Parallel with the early evolution of the Anglo-Japanese alliance,
consideration continued to be given to following the pattern of
the Rosen-Nishi agreement by seeking a direct understanding
with Russia. Russia encouraged this by continuing to urge a
settlement which would include the neutralization of Korea.
The proposal to this effect was made in January 1901 and had
found Ito receptive.[16] Again in July, according to the German
chargé d'affaires in London, Baron Eckardstein, a similar though
somewhat more attractive offer was made.[17] This time the proposal was said to have come from Sergei Witte, the Russian
minister of finance, and held out as an inducement Russian help
in making a loan possible for Japan in Paris.

The following terms were suggested as a basis for discussion:
the neutralization of Korea; Japan to have administrative and
financial advisors in Korea; Japan to recognize officially Russia's
predominant position in Manchuria. Japan, Eckardstein wrote,
had turned down this proposal largely because it was not considered bona fide and because Japan was persuaded that it did
not take sufficiently into account the fact that Korea was not
capable of governing herself and would, therefore, only continue
to be a source of trouble even if she were neutralized. Japan
felt that Korea should bear the same relation to her as Egypt
bore to Britain. Nevertheless, Hayashi responded, the Katsura
cabinet would consider a proposal of this kind if it were bona fide.

Insofar as this may reflect an actual exchange of views, it helps
to explain the backdrop against which Ito Hirobumi conducted
discussions in Paris and St. Petersburg in the autumn of 1901.
For the alleged exchange of views in July is in any case an accurate reflection of the fact that while the Katsura cabinet
believed that an Anglo-Japanese alliance would provide the best

[15] Lansdowne to MacDonald, Apr. 17, 1901, B.D., ii, 89; Hayashi to Kato, Apr.
17, 1901, N.G.M., xxxiv, 7-9.
[16] Izvolsky to Lamsdorf, Jan. 17, 1901, K.A., lxiii, 8.
[17] Eckardstein to Foreign Office, July 19, July 26, 1901, G.P., xvii, 141-144.

leverage for forcing Russia to accede to the Japanese requirements regarding Manchuria, the possibility of a Russian agreement to attain the same objective was not ruled out. They agreed
with Ito that a settlement with Russia would ultimately be
necessary.

The difference between Ito and the Katsura cabinet was,
accordingly, a question of means rather than objectives. Ito saw
an Anglo-Japanese alliance as potentially provocative in its
effect on Russo-Japanese relations, and thus a possible cause of
war.[18] He also considered it, in any case, unattainable since Japan
lacked anything concrete to offer Britain while Britain had no
real interest in Korea, the focus of Japan's interest. Furthermore,
he saw no reason why an agreement with Britain could not also
be concluded in addition to an understanding with Russia, the
latter logically receiving first attention since it was the only
country which had as vital an interest in the problem as Japan.

It must be added that the Katsura government did in fact
try to come to an understanding with Russia both during and after
the negotiations with Britain. The reason, as partisans of either
view held, was that some support for Japan's endangered security
was conceded to be desperately needed; hence both approaches
were tried in the hope that one would accomplish the desired
result. The Katsura cabinet was clearly an active participant in
the negotiations which reached a negative climax in Ito's visit
to St. Petersburg.[19] Negotiations with Russia were further pursued
actively after the conclusion of the Anglo-Japanese Alliance,
and after July 1903 with renewed vigor. The real issues within
Japanese official circles had to do with timing and with obtainable
terms.

During Viscount Ito's visit to St. Petersburg, where he arrived
on November 25, 1901, the two antagonists, for the first time since
1898, came to grips with the fundamental issues that divided
them. Ito looked upon these issues as above all the exclusive concern of the two countries.[20] His own proposals were, in his view,

[18] K. Hamada, *Prince Ito*, Tokyo, 1936, pp. 138–141, 157–165; S. Kuroha,
Sekaishijo yori Mitaru Nichiro Senso, Tokyo, 1961, pp. 68–74.
[19] Izvolsky to Lamsdorf, Oct. 19, 1901, *K.A.*, LXIII, 37–40; A.M. Pooley, *The
Secret Memoirs of Count Tadasu Hayashi*, New York, 1915, pp. 140, 210.
[20] Pooley, *op.cit.*; Seeger, *op.cit.*, p. 21; A. Hiratsuka, *Ito Hirobumi Hiroku*,
2 Vols., Tokyo, 1929, I, 3, 19–20 (of special supplementary section entitled
"Nichiei Komei to Nichiro Kyosho [The Anglo-Japanese Alliance and Russo-
Japanese Understanding]"); Hamada, *op.cit.*, pp. 145–148; Glinsky, *op.cit.*,
pp. 187–189; Lamsdorf to Russian Emperor, Dec. 5, Lamsdorf to Izvolsky, Dec.
5, 1901, *K.A.*, LXIII, 44–47.

in the nature of amendments to the agreement of 1898 that had been predicated upon the temporary nature of the Russian tenure in Manchuria and the predominant rights of Japan in Korea.

Ito frankly informed his Russian hosts that even the tenure they held by agreement in Manchuria they owed to the Sino-Japanese war; therefore, he contended that the Russians could legitimately claim only the limited rights they had gained in 1898. Meanwhile, Japan was entitled to be guaranteed both the open door in Manchuria and preferential tariff rates on the Manchurian railways. It is a notable fact that Ito's formal proposals did not mention Manchuria, thus apparently by implication recognizing no change in Russia's position there since 1898.

With respect to Korea, Ito maintained, her inability to demonstrate control of her own affairs raised a problem that could not be disregarded and a clash would follow if both Russia and Japan undertook to deal with this situation. Since the fate of Korea was a matter of life and death to Japan, the only solution was to commit the protection of Korea into the hands of Japan. Ito offered assurances that this could be done without injury to the rights and interests of Russia. Japan would not use Korea as a strategic base menacing legitimate Russian interests in Manchuria or elsewhere. Nor would Japan fortify the southern coast of Korea or otherwise obstruct the free passage of shipping through the area of Tsushima.

In the conferences between Ito and Lamsdorf and the considerations of the issues among Lamsdorf and the ministers of finance and war, all these points were carefully studied. The concensus of the ministers of foreign affairs and war was that Ito's initial proposals were too highly favorable to Japan to be acceptable to Russia. Ito had in effect suggested placing Korea completely at the disposal of Japan, an act which would render entirely illusory Korea's independence.

Kuropatkin was, of course, greatly impressed with the military aspects of the proposals. He felt that the military advantages which would thereby accrue to Japan would render Korea a threat to Russian national interests and would be a sure prelude to a Russo-Japanese clash. Kuropatkin suggested that if Japanese troops were to be allowed in Korea, the northern part of the country should in any case remain unoccupied by them, a suggestion which two years later would help to render agreement between the two countries nearly out of the question.[21] In regard to Manchuria, to be sure, Ito's suggestions did not go nearly far enough to suit Russia.

Ito received the Russian counterproposal in Berlin and replied to Lamsdorf from there.[22] While the Russian proposal left the door open for further negotiations, Ito was clearly disappointed; he felt they had rejected proposals which were considered an irreducible minimum in Tokyo. He frankly told Lamsdorf that he did not see his way clear to recommend the Russian draft to his government. Nevertheless, Ito's conviction as to the necessity for an agreement with Russia remained unshaken. He felt that only in this way could Japan receive a guarantee covering Korea. As for guaranteeing the open door in Manchuria, the Anglo-Russian agreement of 1899 should have given him a hint that Britain might be no more eager than Russia to do this. In spite of these reservations, he gave his approval to the Anglo-Japanese Alliance.

Two aspects of the Ito-Lamsdorf proposals are of special significance; both underscore the basic nature of the divergence between the two nations. The first was the difference of views over the question of Japanese freedom of action in Korea. Point 5 of the Russian counterproposals illustrates this in two ways: the insistence on exercising control over the number of troops Japan might maintain in Korea and the stipulation that these troops must not penetrate into a zone along the Russian frontier.

The latter provision was a reflection of the Russian view that her position in Manchuria would be menaced by the presence of Japanese forces in Korea. It also became associated with the Russian Yalu timber concession, the desire to neutralize all of Korea, and the demand for a neutral zone in Korea to extend southward as far as the 39th parallel. This last requirement, more than any other, was to exemplify for the Japanese government the determined expansion policy of Russia and the frustration of their own projected control over Korea.

The other basic difference that separated the two nations was the Manchuria problem. Point 6 of the Russian counterproposals stated emphatically that Russian interests must be predominant throughout the border regions of the Chinese Empire. This was

---

[21] Kuropatkin to Lamsdorf, Dec. 23, 1901, *K.A.*, LXIII, 49.

[22] Ito to Lamsdorf, Dec. 23, 1901, *Obzor*, pp. 74–75; the notes are in Appendix 1, of this study.

clearly intended to correct the view Japan was known to hold
that Russian rights in Manchuria were limited rather than paramount, and this presumably held for the remaining border regions
as well. It foreshadowed a position taken by Russia during the
final negotiations; at that time it was to have the effect of preventing her from giving the guarantee of Chinese territorial
integrity which Japan demanded.

In the autumn of 1901, with a direct understanding with Russia
seemingly unattainable and with a sympathetic Japanese government in office, the discussions of the prospective Anglo-Japanese
alliance were finally undertaken in earnest. In late September,
Komura had assumed his position as foreign minister and by
mid-October Hayashi notified Lansdowne of his readiness to
proceed.[23] Within three weeks Lansdowne had a first draft
ready and on December 7, Katsura and Komura met with the
elder statesmen to discuss the alliance in very concrete terms.
By December 11 Hayashi was prepared to present the Japanese
counterproposal. With these two drafts in hand, the next few
weeks were occupied in elaborating the final draft which was
signed on January 30, 1902.[24]

The Anglo-Japanese Alliance in its completed form consisted
of 6 articles, essentially providing the following: recognition of
the independence of China and Korea and of the respective
interests of the allies in those countries; if either ally were to
become involved in war with another power in defense of those
interests, the other would remain neutral; if either became
involved in war with a second power in defense of these interests,
the other would join actively on the side of the partner; neither
party would enter into any other arrangement which would
prejudice these interests.

Japan returned immediately to the negotiations with Russia
which had been temporarily suspended by Ito in December
1901. In January 1902, even before the formal conclusion of
the Anglo-Japanese Alliance, Foreign Minister Komura instructed
the Japanese minister in St. Petersburg, Kurino Shinichiro, to
resume active discussions of the Korean question.[25] In conferences

[23] Lansdowne to Whitehead, Oct. 16, Lansdowne to MacDonald, Nov. 6, 1901,
B.D., II, 99–100; "Views Concerning the Anglo-Japanese Agreement Presented by
Foreign Minister Komura to the Genro Council." Dec. 7, Komura to Hayashi,
Dec. 8, Komura to Hayashi, Dec. 11, 1901, N.G.M., xxxiv, 66–75.
[24] B.D., II, 114–120.
[25] K.G., I, 297–300.

starting in late February, Kurino found Lamsdorf at least ostensibly amenable to working out an agreement. Lamsdorf did not appear to consider the Anglo-Japanese Alliance a bar to an agreement. Rather he still saw his exchange of views with Ito a few months before as the basis for resuming the discussions.

Before the end of 1902, two sets of proposals had been presented to Russia, one in early August and the other in early November.[26] Although the precise relationship between these proposals is not entirely clear, two things about them are abundantly evident: their relationship to the preceding Ito discussions and their incompatibility with the Russian objectives in the Far East. Nevertheless, the negotiations continued into 1903 though without any positive results except to serve notice on each party as to the sacrifices a compromise would require.

Compared with the well-defined commitment to Japan which Britain had made in the Alliance, the political role of the United States remained ambiguous, though friendly to Japan. Up to a certain point she was a supporting member of the Anglo-Japanese Alliance and was so recognized by Russia. Baron Rosen, Russian minister to Japan in 1903 and later to the United States, interpreted American activities in Manchuria as directed toward blocking a Russian monopoly there.[27] Writing about this period in later years, Baron Rosen also credited the United States with a major part in reinforcing Japanese opposition to Russia. He wrote in part:

"I personally saw the extent to which the influences of the assurances of moral and material support from America was decisive in the counsels of the Japanese government, for I sensed this very clearly during the conversations I conducted with the Japanese government just preceding the war."[28]

If by material support Baron Rosen implied the possibility of military cooperation, then he has overstated the case. It is, of course, true that Japan would have welcomed firm American support along with a definite commitment to that effect. But Baron Komura, the Japanese foreign minister, was well aware

[26] *ibid.*, pp. 298–299; Kurino to Russian Foreign Minister, Aug. 4, 1902, *Obzor*, p. 78.

[27] Rosen telegram, June 18, 1903, A. Kantorovich, *Amerika v Borbe za Kitai*, Moscow, 1935, p. 154; Barcley to Chinda, Apr. 26, Komura to Uchida, Apr. 26, Komura to Kurino, Apr. 30, 1903, *N.G.M.*, xxxvi-1, 82–83, 103–104.

[28] Rosen report, Mar. 19, 1910, Kantorovich, *op.cit.*, pp. 163–164.

that American backing, though of the greatest importance on any terms, was more likely to be moral than material.[29] For, as Secretary of State John Hay had already expressed the national policy, the United States had no intention of using force even to preserve the open door.

Unprepared to use force, the United States had to find other means of protecting what was clearly important to her. For, in spite of Russian assurances that American goods would suffer no discrimination, American commercial interests as well as the very principle of the open door appeared to be at stake. The American government responded by establishing diplomatic solidarity with Britain and Japan. On the occasion of the signing of the Anglo-Japanese Alliance, an American protest was lodged against Russia's scheme to force China to approve an economic monopoly in Manchuria in the name of the Russo-Chinese Bank.[30] In fact, however, the timing of this protest, presented to both China and Russia, suggested a degree of support for the Alliance which was somewhat misleading.

The United States also demonstrated her solidarity with the Anglo-Japanese Alliance by means of a plan elaborated by William W. Rockhill, a close friend and trusted advisor on Far Eastern policy to President Roosevelt.[31] Rockhill had observed at close range the Russian occupation of Manchuria and was convinced that the intention was to monopolize it. He was determined that the drive must be contained in Manchuria rather than allow it an opportunity to advance southward into other parts of China. He proposed to accomplish this by taking advantage of the opportunity provided by the Boxer Protocol of 1901 to reconsider commercial relations with China. By inserting in a new commercial treaty with China a provision for the opening to commerce of two additional cities in Manchuria, he hoped to bolster the Chinese will and capability to resist a Russian monopoly there. Further, by concerting this plan with the Japanese government to the extent that both would be making the same demand at the same time, the United States would appear to be establishing a united front with the Anglo-Japanese Alliance. Like the protest to Russia, this could be accomplished without any specific military commitment.

[29] Takahira to Komura, May 10, 1903, N.G.M., xxxvi-1, pp. 164–165.

[30] Romanov, op.cit., pp. 229–243; Cambon to Delcasse, Feb. 14, Porter to Delcasse, Feb. 17, 1902, D.D.F., pp. 103–104, 108–109.

[31] P.A. Varg, Open Door Diplomat; The Life of W.W. Rockhill, Urbana, 1952, pp. 51–56.

The American treaty with China was signed on the same date as the Japanese, October 8, 1903.[32] This date was the anniversary of the Sino-Russian agreement of April 8, 1902, by which Russia had promised to evacuate her military forces in three stages within eighteen months. It was Article XII of the American agreement which opened up the Manchurian cities of Mukden and Antung to international residence and trade.

In these ways the United States and Japan brought their plans to some extent into focus, thereby intensifying the hostile atmosphere in which Russia was forced to solve her Far Eastern problems. The signing of the treaties with China was followed, in both Manchuria and Korea, by a policy which favored a continuation of American-Japanese cooperation throughout the war. The American policy with respect to Korea, like that regarding Manchuria, had been formulated by 1903. It conceded to Japan the right to annex Korea in the interest of the welfare of the people of Korea and of the peace of the Far East.[33]

Even before these treaties had been signed, Russia was aware of the significance to her of the relationship they helped to formalize. In a report written a few months before their final conclusion, Baron Rosen characterized this situation as follows:

"The opening to foreign commerce of one or another region of China expresses not merely permission for the penetration into that region of foreign merchants and traders, but opens by treaty the stipulated places for the settlement of foreigners, places which will then be centers of foreign commerce and influence, and consequently of foreign jurisdictions. Points thus placed under the protection of foreign treaties could not any longer be considered the possession of any single power without clearly encroaching on the treaty rights of others. . . . Hence, it is clear that in the presentation to China of demands concerning the opening of new points in Manchuria for foreign commerce, the powers will have in view the establishment of an effective bar to the absorption of Manchuria by Russia."[34]

Turning to another aspect of the problem, Rosen reported that in his view the United States had been invited to join the Anglo-Japanese front against Russia. To him this appeared as a maneuver to use the "open door" for political purposes. He con-

---

[32] *U.S.F.R., 1903*, pp. 91–118.
[33] Harrington, *op.cit.*, pp. 323–324.
[34] Rosen telegram, June 18, 1903, Kantorovich, *op.cit.*, pp. 154–155.

cluded: "Accordingly, it is entirely clear that there exists in fact between America, Britain, and Japan complete mutual political understanding and cooperation."

These words express vividly the two ideas that lay at the root of the Far Eastern issue in 1903. One was the monopolistic objectives of Russia and Japan in Manchuria and Korea which had become a source of such widespread alarm as to inspire the formation of an anti-Russian front. The other was the differing conceptions of the open door. There was on the one hand the view that the door should be kept open for the free transaction of commercial and financial enterprise by all nations on an equal basis. The opposing view, so eloquently expressed by Baron Rosen, was that the door should be kept open for the purpose of simplifying Russia's plan to monopolize the available areas of China as circumstances permitted. Clearly, it was the same conception that was held in Tokyo with respect to Korea.

The international position of Japan was greatly enhanced by the Anglo-Japanese Alliance which had helped to bring about the identification of a group of nations either definitely opposed to Russian expansion or prepared to observe a neutral stance while others endeavored to curb it. At a single stroke France, the partner of Russia, had been neutralized under the watchful eye of Britain, and the United States had been encouraged to adhere to the Alliance in nonmilitary commitments. Long before the conclusion of the Alliance, it was apparent that Germany had no intention of joining any hostile group. In the early weeks of 1901 when the Russian occupation of Manchuria had brought the issue into the open, the German government had assured Britain and Japan simultaneously that in case of a Russo-Japanese conflict she would observe the strictest neutrality.[35]

Within three weeks after the signing of the Anglo-Japanese Alliance, Russia herself brought the question of Germany's intentions into clear focus. Count Lamsdorf, the Russian minister of foreign affairs, raised it in the form of a proposal that a joint Franco-Russo-German response be made to the Alliance.[36] He expressed the view that the Alliance would be a menace to Russian interests in China. It would encourage China to be less agreeable in discussing the guarantees Russia wanted in Man-

[35] Hatzfeldt to Foreign Office, Feb. 28, Emperor William to Foreign Office, Mar. 5, 1901, G.P., xvi, 327, 334.
[36] Alvensleben to Foreign Office, Feb. 19, 1902, Bülow to Alvensleben, Feb. 22, 1902, G.P., xvii, 156–160.

churia as a condition for withdrawing her troops. As a counter-measure he favored a revival of the Three Power group of 1895, to which he suggested adding Austria-Hungary and Italy. This would provide a formidable continental bulwark against British and Japanese ambitions.

The German government responded to this and succeeding Russian requests for assurances with a clear and frank statement of its policies.[37] While taking account of the fruitful Russo-German cooperation of the past, having in mind, perhaps, such correlated events as the occupation by Germany and Russia respectively of Tsingtao and Port Arthur, this policy nevertheless hewed strictly to the line of current national interests. The view was expressed that a revival at that time of the Three Power group appeared entirely detrimental to the interests of Germany which, it was emphasized, were purely commercial.

The German answer then turned to the hazards to which her commercial interests were exposed. With British sea power obviously in mind, it was stated that one of the principal consequences of reviving this combination would be an unnecessary exposure of German shipping lanes which even under existing conditions were inadequately defended. In addition, there was the undesirable prospect of alienating Japan, and of giving her added incentive to oppose Germany in China. In fact, the evidence from these years makes it apparent that Japan was already a significant commercial competitor and that Germany was well aware of it.[38] Finally, a return to the Three Power group would encourage the United States to associate herself with the Anglo-Japanese Alliance, thus producing a dangerous international combination. Hence, it would be German policy to observe strict neutrality in case of a Russo-Japanese conflict.

The considerable benefits which were likely to accrue to Germany, both in Europe and the Far East, from Russia's Far Eastern entanglement would be a consequence of the dispersal of Russian military strength eastward. In the West it would not only lighten the burden of military defense but, potentially at least, could make it immeasurably easier for Germany to press her expansion in the Balkans and the Ottoman Empire unhampered by effective

[37] Bülow Memorandum, Feb. 25, 1902, Bülow to Alvensleben, Mar. 7, 1902, G.P., xvii, 160–162, 170–172; Holstein Memorandum, July 12, 1902, Mühlenberg Memorandum, July 15, 1903, G.P., xix-1, 5–7, 10–12.

[38] M.C.R., Sept. 1904, pp. 41–43; Inouye to Komura, No. 464, Nov. 26, 1904, J.F.O.

Russian opposition. Even more intriguing, however, was the prospect it offered to weaken the Franco-Russian Alliance as the Russian ability to support France declined. For this promised the long-awaited opportunity for dealing separately with France and, even beyond this, the expectation of a complete reshuffling of the diplomatic pieces in Europe with an anti-British combination in mind.

In the Far East the shift of Russian strength could serve German interests in an even more direct fashion. The Anglo-Japanese Alliance offered assurances not only that these nations would keep a close check on Russia but also that Russia for her own reasons would necessarily maintain a constant watch on Germany's two rivals. Furthermore, having been alerted by the Boxer Rebellion and the Manchurian crisis to the dangers confronting her own Far Eastern interests, the United States would add another dimension to Russia's need for vigilance. As long as Russia did not collapse and therefore lose her usefulness as a bulwark, it would be to German advantage to leave her facing the Far Eastern friction as directly and as inescapably as she was now doing.

The new diplomatic alignment was patently a triumph of the greatest significance for Japan, a fact which is underscored by a comparison with the situation which pertained in 1895. Instead of a noncommital attitude toward Japan on the part of Great Britain and the United States and a hostile coalition of Russia, Germany, and France, it was Russia which now stood alone. The new disposition of power found its center of gravity in the Anglo-Japanese Alliance which represented a sufficiently firm commitment to attract the United States as a quasi alliance partner. It also kept France effectively neutralized under the watchful eye of Britain. Even German neutrality, though well suited to serve her own international plans and prospects, would find entirely congenial the idea of an alliance that kept Russia in check without any overtly hostile commitment by Germany. As long as it could be kept intact, this configuration of national interests would leave Russia effectively isolated.

6. The Opening of the Final Negotiations

THE SITUATION which had developed by the spring of 1903 presented Japan with the opportunity to test her diplomatic achievements. First, negotiations started by Ito in St. Petersburg over a year before had finally ended in futility early in 1903. Second, intelligence reports disclosed not only the true significance of the Yalu or timber concession venture, but also the fact that Russia was reenforcing her Far Eastern military strength as rapidly as possible. While some time would manifestly be required to complete these preparations, it was obvious that time was running out on such military advantage as Japan now had. At the same time, as Japan's own carefully planned program of military preparedness reached completion, she was approaching a point of maximum striking capacity. Finally, the factor which acted as a catalytic agent upon these developments was the refusal of Russia in April to carry out the second stage of the promised military evacuation of Manchuria, thereby reenforcing the current image of Russia as a violator of both Chinese and foreign rights while underscoring Japan's role in preserving both.

Japan's watchful sensitivity to events in Manchuria was dramatically emphasized by a public gathering held on April 8 in Ueno Park in Tokyo.[1] This was sponsored by the Anti-Russian League (Tairo Doshikai) to mark the day on which Russia had failed to carry out the second stage of the troop withdrawal. The League had recently been formed by patriotic groups from the Black Dragon Society (Kokuryukai) and the Black Ocean Society (Genyosha). Its purpose, like that of its parent organizations, was to emphasize one specific aspect of national policy, in this case to urge the chastisement of Russia for her conduct in Manchuria.

At the public meeting, the League endeavored to bring pressure to bear on official opinion by the adoption of a resolution calling for a more positive policy toward Russia. Specifically, it stated that since Russia was clearly not serious about the promised withdrawal from Manchuria, Japan and Britain ought to take steps to see to it that Manchuria was returned to China. This was followed by the presentation of similar proposals to both Katsura and Komura and a visit to the latter to give deliberate emphasis

[1] Otsu, *op.cit.*, v, 637–648; *K.G.*, i, 343; Conroy, *op.cit.*, p. 412.

to the demands. Throughout the negotiations and the war that followed, the patriotic groups watched events carefully, frequently voicing their displeasure when official policy appeared too compromising.

Having determined that the time had come for action, Japan faced two preliminary tasks: to discover whether the international environment was favorable for action, and to decide on a precise course to follow.[2] Bearing in mind at all times the humiliating Three Power intervention of 1895, Komura was well aware of how carefully the international situation had to be watched and sought to avoid the recurrence of such a defeat by a policy of constant close association with the United States and Great Britain, and by a firm insistence upon dealing directly with Russia in all matters without any third-power intervention. The foundation of his success lay in keeping the United States and Great Britain closely aligned with Japan by informing them at all times of his own intentions and by constantly sounding out their views.

Accordingly, in April Baron Komura began to test the reliability of the Anglo-Japanese Alliance in the event of some decisive action. Referring to the Russian failure to withdraw her troops as well as her presentation of new demands to China, he expressed his views to the British ambassador as follows:

"This would, of course, mean an absolute breach of their Convention with China, and a disregard of all assurances given to the various Powers. A permanent occupation of Manchuria by Russia would, in due course, mean a permanent occupation of Corea by the same Power, which would threaten the very existence of Japan. Consequently, said his Excellency, it behoved Japan to consider whether the time had not come to speak, for if she remained silent now and allowed Russia to remain in possession, the occasion for speaking might never occur again, and Japan's silence at this juncture would certainly impair her rights to assert herself later."[3]

With a favorable British response to these soundings and the clarification of her own course of action toward Russia, Japan called upon Britain for support with an increasing self-assurance. In early July, Komura reminded the British that: "The unre-

[2] K.G., I, 365–366.
[3] Komura to Hayashi, Apr. 26, 1903, N.G.M., xxxvi-i, 84; MacDonald to Lansdowne, Apr. 27, 1903, B.D., ii, 199.

strained permanent occupation of that territory [Manchuria] by Russia would create a condition of things prejudicial to those interests the defense of which was the object of the Anglo-Japanese Alliance."[4] In a conversation with Lord Lansdowne, Baron Hayashi, responding to the British foreign minister's specific request for more definite information, took one further step when he directly associated the Alliance with the specific terms of Japan's proposal to Russia. He stated that "the Imperial Government intend to ask from Russia recognition of Japan's special interests in Corea, as alluded to in the Anglo-Japanese Alliance, and, on their part, they propose to offer their recognition of Russia's special interests in railway enterprises in Manchuria."[5]

The dangerous waters into which the Alliance was heading could hardly have been pointed out with more complete candor. This statement brought into juxtaposition with the Alliance the very terms that had been at the center of discord between Japan and Russia ever since Ito's visit to St. Petersburg. As in previous exchanges, Britain approved this also.[6]

The alignment of Japan's policies with those of the United States proved a far more complex task than was the case with Britain. It was clear from past experience that, at most, the United States could be expected to take a firm stand on the Manchurian issue only if her commercial interests were endangered. Even the American protest in February 1902 against Russia's attempt to secure an economic monopoly in Manchuria for the Russo-Chinese Bank, however timely it may have been with respect to supporting the Anglo-Japanese Alliance, was no exception to this practice. This meant that American cooperation with Japan at this crucial moment would depend upon American interpretation of Russia's intentions in Manchuria.

Fortunately for Japan, Russia seemed to have provided a clear statement of her policy in the third article of the new demands she made of China in April 1903. This would have required that: "The Chinese Government shall not, without previous notice to the Russian Government, open of their own will new ports or towns in Manchuria nor shall permit foreign consuls to reside in these ports or towns."[7]

[4] Komura to Hayashi, July 1, 1903, *N.G.M.*, xxxvi-i, 4.
[5] Hayashi to Komura, July 8, 1903, *N.G.M.*, xxxvi-i, 7; Lansdowne to Mac-Donald, July 13, 1903, *B.D.*, ii, 208.
[6] British Foreign Office Memorandum to Hayashi, July 16, 1903, *B.D.*, ii, 209.
[7] Uchida to Komura, Apr. 26, 1903, *N.G.M.*, xxxvi-i, 78 and 80.

Although this statement appeared unambiguous, the matter was viewed somewhat differently in Washington. For the Russian and Japanese ambassadors there found themselves locked in a desperate battle of conflicting interpretations calculated to inspire a favorable response in American policy.[8] As long as possible the Russian government even denied the existence of the demands. Following this, Cassini, the Russian ambassador, argued that American interests would remain unaffected even if China were to accept the demands and gave assurances of special and favorable treatment.

In the long run, this protracted trialogue redounded to the advantage of Japan. For it was during these discussions that Japan and the United States began to consider means of exerting some joint pressure aimed at relaxing Russia's grip on Manchuria. Ultimately this was done by the conclusion of parallel treaties with China opening up certain new commercial points in Manchuria. The agreements were pointedly signed on October 8, 1903, the anniversary of the Sino-Russian agreement regarding the evacuation of Manchuria within eighteen months.

In building the international support required for her approaching showdown with Russia, Japan prudently rested her cause on foundations broad enough to support other rights and interests. Had she openly and obviously aimed at restoring the gains in southern Manchuria of which the Three Power intervention of 1895 had deprived her, it would have appeared as a war of revenge and she might have been left to face Russia alone.

Instead, Japan chose to emphasize a single, broadly appealing objective: the liquidation of the Russian menace to all established rights in Manchuria and Korea and, because of her own geographical relationship to Korea, to her national security in particular. In this way she sought for herself the very role of friend and protector of China to which Russia had aspired since 1895. In addition, it seemed reasonable that she would be able to rally to herself the foreign interests and ambitions which, however temporarily or illogically, saw their salvation in the open-door doctrine. For her initial establishment on the Asian mainland would only be possible with at least the tacit approval of the

[8] Takahira to Komura, May 3, May 5, May 6, May 9, May 28, June 6, July 17, 1903, *N.G.M.*, xxxvi-i, 132, 148–149, 152–153, 159–162, 210–212, 225–226, 293–294.

THE OPENING OF THE FINAL NEGOTIATIONS

THE OPENING OF THE FINAL NEGOTIATIONS 99

western powers and, consequently, under the auspices of the open door.

Just below the surface of Japan's common diplomatic front with the other powers were her special plans regarding Korea. These plans were well known to Britain and easily discernible to others. Moreover, the assumption on which they were based was one which Japan held in common with Russia and which was sympathetically regarded both in London and Washington. This was that, in view of her traditional political structure and sensitivity to pressures from powerful neighbors, Korea was incapable of maintaining an independent political posture under existing world conditions. It was assumed, therefore, that she would ultimately succumb to one or another of these pressures. Under these circumstances, Japan would require, as a fundamental condition of her own national security, that Korea must be under her protection if not complete control.

These diplomatic alignments, important as they were, could at best do no more than provide a congenial international climate for solving the problem. They could potentially alleviate Japan's fear of intervention and leave her free to face Russia alone. But, above all, Japan felt that she must face the Russian challenge now, either aggressively or in retreat. Baron Hayashi stated categorically to Lord Lansdowne that: "The Imperial Government believed that the policy of forebearance which they had hitherto pursued was a wise one, but they could not but come to the conclusion that the time had arrived for a change in that policy."[9]

This required an evaluation, first of Russia's determination to follow her present course of action and, secondly, of her capability to defend it if opposed. By mid-1903, there appeared to be ample evidence of Russian determination: the opening of through traffic on the railway to Vladivostok and Port Arthur, the continuing reenforcement of her military strength in the Far East, the unrelenting pressure on China, and, perhaps most alarming of all, her permanent civilian and military establishment in North Korea.

British military intelligence reports reveal not only the closeness with which Japan's alliance partner observed the situation. but also the common outlook which the partners shared with respect to the nature of the menace. A British report of late July

[9] Lansdowne to MacDonald, July, 3, 1903, *B.D.*, II, 207.

disclosed the following situation: that the Russians were clearly making another Kronstadt out of Port Arthur, and:

1. That the Russians have obtained a stronger hold over the country than is generally supposed.
2. That they are perfectly in earnest in their intention to gradually obtain the mastery over the country until it shall have, by force of circumstances, become a Russian province.
3. That nothing will cause them to withdraw in any way except force.
4. That they are anxious to avoid a conflict, but that they will accept a challenge sooner than give way . . . .[10]

It was with these obvious facts in mind that Prime Minister Katsura and Foreign Minister Komura contemplated the next move.[11] They saw in the existing situation a deadlock which one of the two antagonists must seek to break. The root of the problem lay in the fact that neither could allow either Korea or Manchuria to fall into the hands of the other.

From the Russian side, it was felt that the immediate problem was the security of the railway link between Harbin and Port Arthur and the sea communications between Vladivostok and Port Arthur. In the past Russia had sought unsuccessfully to protect the latter by controlling Masampo, near Fusan (Pusan) in South Korea. Similarly, the Russians considered the railway potentially menaced from Korea and could be expected to seize that country themselves rather than face the prospect of its falling into the hands of Japan.

From Japan's point of view, since her own national security was so intimately related to that of Korea, the only acceptable policy seemed to be the removal of the menace to Korea. This could be accomplished in part by demanding that Russia concede Korea to Japan. Along with this, however, must go the actual removal from Manchuria of Russia's offensive military capability. Finally, since this force was maintained there to support Russia's monopolistic pretensions, the latter must also be terminated and her recognized claims reduced to those she had legally acquired by 1898, the date of the last Russo-Japanese agreement on the matter.

---

[10] Report of Lt. Col. Wingate, July 29, 1903, *B.D.*, II, 211.
[11] *K.G.*, I, 324; Otsu, *op.cit.*, V, 665–668; Tokutomi, *op.cit.*, II, 157ff.

Under the circumstances, in the opinion of Katsura and Komura, raising the issue at that time could only be regarded by Russia as an open challenge. Therefore, even though this were done by means of a proposal to reopen diplomatic negotiations, Japan would face the alternative of either surrendering once and for all to Russia's requirements or pressing her adversary to the brink of war and beyond. In this sense, a decision to reopen negotiations was recognized as almost tantamount to a decision for war. In effect, it was not treated as such by the Japanese government since the actual decision to go to war was too important to link with a preliminary and probationary act. It would have to be arrived at later after the course of the negotiations had been observed, when all relevant factors could be carefully weighed.

General Kuropatkin had scarcely left Tokyo on June 16, 1903, when the government turned to the grim task of formulating its policy and procedure for dealing more decisively with Russia. The first step was taken at an Imperial Conference which met on June 23 and reached a decision on an acceptable policy after several hours of discussion.[12] This was attended by the following elder statesmen and cabinet ministers: Ito Hirobumi, Yamagata Aritomo, Oyama Iwao, Matsukata Masayoshi, Inouye Kaoru, Prime Minister Katsura Taro, War Minister Terauchi Masatake, Navy Minister Yamamoto Gonnohyoei, and Foreign Minister Komura Jutaro.

Because of the vital nature of the policy adopted and the possibility that its execution might be impaired by the difference of views between Katsura and Ito, steps were taken to obviate this by a cabinet reorganization that strengthened Katsura's position.

At the conference the policy with respect to Russia was discussed in the context of the entire spectrum of Japan's continental interests; these included both the Taiwan-Fukien and the Korea-Manchuria regions, though the main discussion centered on the problem of releasing Korea and Manchuria from the Russian grip. If Japan were to disregard the Russian occupation, it was feared that it would continue and ultimately become a permanent menace to the national security. Therefore, direct negotiations would be undertaken in the hope of reaching a settlement. The negotiations would aim at insuring the security of Korea by limit-

[12] "Decision of the Imperial Conference," June 23, 1903, N.G.M., xxxvi-i, 1-4; K.G., i, 322–324; Otsu, op.cit., v, 664–669.

ing the Russian activities in both Korea and Manchuria. It was fully recognized that this might, in fact, be difficult to achieve and that Japan must, therefore, be prepared to seek the desired solution at any cost.

The principles which the conference approved as guidelines for the negotiations were: to guarantee the independence and territorial integrity of China and Korea and the equality of commercial and industrial opportunity for foreigners within those countries; a mutual recognition by Japan and Russia of their existing legal rights in Korea and Manchuria and of the necessity of taking all measures required to guarantee them; a mutual recognition that, should these rights become menaced by potential or actual internal disturbances, Japan and Russia would be free to send military forces to protect them, but that such forces should be withdrawn as soon as the emergency was over; and that Japan must have the exclusive right, through advice and assistance, to bring about the necessary reforms in the Korean government. In addition to these general principles, such specific matters as the railways and Japanese interests in Korea were discussed as a guide to the negotiations.

On July 28, 1903 the next step was taken by sounding out the Russian government as to its willingness to undertake negotiations.[13] Within a few days the plan was fully accepted in St. Petersburg and the proposals were prepared for submission to the Russian government. Between this time and the opening of war in February 1904 there were four formal exchanges of views between the two governments. The first consisted of the Japanese proposals of August 12 and the first Russian counterproposals of October 3.[14]

During the fifty-two days which intervened before the Russian response was received, three significant episodes cast a cloud over the negotiations. The first was the transfer of the negotiations, at the request of the Russian government, from St. Petersburg to Tokyo.[15] Count Lamsdorf first broached this question to Kurino

[13] Komura to Kurino, July 28, Kurino to Komura, July 31, Komura to Kurino, Aug. 3, Kurino to Komura, Aug. 5, 1903. N.G.M., xxxvi-1, 8–13; also the same in Correspondence, pp. 1–10.

[14] Appendix 1, of this study.

[15] Kurino to Komura, Aug. 24, Komura to Kurino, Aug. 26, Kurino to Komura, Aug. 27, Komura to Kurino, Aug. 29, Kurino to Komura, Aug. 31, Komura to Kurino, Sept. 2, Kurino to Komura, Sept. 5, Komura to Kurino, Sept. 9, 1903, Correspondence, pp. 11–21, and N.G.M., xxxvi-i, 15–21; Bompard, op.cit., pp. 41–43.

Shinichiro, the Japanese minister, on August 23, a date by which, in the opinion of Komura, Russia should have had a counter-proposal ready. Lamsdorf explained the proposed change of venue in two ways. The first was that he would shortly accompany the Emperor on an extended trip to western Europe. The Emperor departed for the west in early September and, because of the illness of the Empress en route, did not return until early December. However, the seriousness of this as an obstacle to retaining in his own hands the conduct of the negotiations is open to serious question. This is suggested by Lamsdorf's assurances to Kurino that, wherever he happened to be in Europe, he would remain in close telegraphic communications with the negotiations.

It would appear that the second reason was more meaningful. This was the assertion that the work of the negotiations, including the preparation of the counterproposals, would in fact be committed to the viceroy at Port Arthur. Consequently, transferring the negotiations would, in the opinion of Lamsdorf, actually expedite them.

Realizing the portentous nature of this proposal, Foreign Minister Komura opposed it as forcefully as diplomacy permitted. He tried to claim for the negotiations the fullest commitment on the part of the Russian government by asserting that they had to do with "principles and not details." In several exchanges of views with Foreign Minister Lamsdorf he argued that they ought to be conducted at the highest level and should not be relegated to Port Arthur. But the Russians were unmoved and the Japanese had either to give up the negotiations or accept their first defeat. After seventeen days of pressing the issue, Komura consented on September 9 to the transfer.

Asked a few weeks after the war had begun when he first saw a break in Russo-Japanese relations in prospect, Kurino, the Japanese minister in St. Petersburg, singled out the point at which the negotiations were transferred from diplomatic into military hands.[16] There were other factors associated with the transfer that were almost as serious as the new and perhaps less sympathetic auspices under which they were conducted. One was the dual handling of each stage of the negotiations, in St. Petersburg and Port Arthur, that must in itself have accounted for considerable delay. Another was the inexperience of all the Rus-

[16] A. Tardieu, *Questions Diplomatiques de l'Anneé 1904,* Paris, 1905, pp. 240–241.

sian officials in dealing with these newly established channels for foreign relations. For the viceroyalty had just been formally established when the negotiations were undertaken.

Simultaneously, Russian pressures on both China and Korea made it impossible for Japan to forget the systematic, relentless nature of the expansion program with which she was dealing.[17] On September 6, three days before Komura finally accepted the transfer of the negotiations, Russia presented to China the five revised conditions for the withdrawal of troops. These had been drawn up at the Port Arthur conference in July and revised in August in St. Petersburg. While these presumably would have provided for the removal of troops within one year, they also contained, among other provisions, an unacceptable prohibition against foreign concessions that implied a violation of the freedom of commerce and enterprise.

With strong foreign support, China refused these demands on September 15. Furthermore, since the final stage of the evacuation was due to be completed by October 8, China also gave Russia instructions for the retrocession of Manchuria to the Chinese governor general. The Russian answer to this was that Manchuria was under the jurisdiction of Viceroy Alekseiev and that the matter would be left to him.

Russian pressure on Korea was in some respects even more effective than in the case of China. From her command post at Fenghuangcheng, on the Manchurian side of the boundary, Russia was reenforcing her position in Korea with arms and men. Meanwhile she continued to build a permanent stronghold at Yongampo. At Seoul, Pavlov was exerting every effort to gain from the Korean government a lease to the town. Even the counterpressure exerted by Britain and Japan to resolve the issue by opening the town as a commercial port, or just to stem the Russian deluge, was unavailing. Russia concluded the lease agreement for Yongampo on August 23; later the Russian proprietorship was emphasized by renaming it Port Nikolai.[18]

It is understandable that, with the passage of weeks during which Russia's only responses had been negative, the Japanese could begin to see the prospects for the negotiations as unpromising if not hopeless. Indeed this outlook was reflected in the highest

[17] K.G., I, 316–320; MacDonald to Lansdowne, Oct. 1, 1903, B.D., II, 216; Dubail to Delcasse, Sept. 16, Moulin to Andre, Oct. 3, 1903, D.D.F., III, 573, 594.

[18] Hayashi to Komura, Nov. 6, 1903, N.G.M., xxxvi-1, 573.

government circles, including Baron Komura himself. In late September, Komura, referring to the negotiations, said to the American minister: "They are making no progress at all. The only desire of the Russian Government seems to be to delay matters."[19]

Two days after this observation was made, Japan's fears as to the role the viceroy would play in the negotiations were confirmed. Baron Rosen, the recently appointed Russian minister, left Tokyo on September 23 for conferences at Port Arthur which were to delay the negotiations until his return to Tokyo with the Russian counterproposals on October 3.[20] Nevertheless, there might have been some comfort in the fact that, with experience in Japan dating back to 1875, Rosen was one of the best informed among Russia's senior diplomats in matters relating to Japan. It was presumably in recognition of this that he had been sent back to Japan at this crucial time and that later he was to be appointed Witte's colleague in conducting the peace negotiations at Portsmouth.

In past discussions of the Russo-Japanese issue, including those with Ito, Rosen had already disclosed his acceptance of the Russian expansion plans, and there had been general agreement to assign Manchuria to Russia and Korea to Japan. The forestry concession issue was thought of as forming the subject of a compromise—the Yalu area to go to Japan and the Tiumen sector to Russia. While this arrangement was never put into practice, it disclosed a willingness on Rosen's part to take all possible advantage of the concession. Also, the expression of his views here and elsewhere renders untenable the conception that Rosen had come to Tokyo as the spokesman of a "soft" policy.

Rosen faced the negotiations of 1903 in the same spirit, showing a pragmatic preference for the attainable. In his conversations with Admiral Alekseiev he stressed the determination and preparedness of the Japanese to back up their claims to Korea. Therefore, with regard to the newly established viceroyalty, it was not with its aggressive implications that he found fault, but rather with the failure of the Russian government to support these implications with force. He thought Alekseiev should have demanded reenforcements of about 300,000 troops and a substantial

[19] Baelz, op. cit., p. 229 (entry for Sept. 15, 1903); MacDonald to Lansdowne, Sept. 4, 1903, B.D., ii, 214; Griscom to Hay, Sept. 21, 1903, F.R., 1903, p. 618; L.C. Griscom, Diplomatically Speaking, Boston, 1940, p. 234.

[20] Rosen, op. cit., i, 222–228; Gurko, op. cit., pp. 268–271; G. Trubetzkoi, Russland als Grossmacht, Stuttgart, 1913, pp. 63–64; K.G., I, 333.

augmentation of the Pacific fleet with units from the Baltic. These conclusions about the balance of power were translated, apparently by Alekseiev and Rosen, into the terms of a counterproposal in a very simple formula: Russia would have to concede Korea to Japan, retaining Manchuria for herself. If this made it appear that he was inclined to write off the Yalu concession, it cannot be assumed that he opposed it in principle or necessarily opposed it at all.

The weeks following Rosen's presentation of the Russian counterproposals on October 3 were hardly conducive to the negotiation of peace. October 8, the day set for termination of the Russian occupation, brought new demonstrations of hostility: Alekseiev held a massive and spectacular military review at Port Arthur. An observer wrote: "I can still see the serried ranks of thousands upon thousands of white-bloused soldiers in the brilliant autumn sunshine. It was a review of defiance. Defiance of China, defiance of Japan, defiance of the world's public opinion."[21]

The response to this defiance, though diplomatic in nature, was almost as defiant and even more dramatic. It was a demonstration of American solidarity with the Anglo-Japanese Alliance. It took the form of parallel treaties signed by the United States and Japan with China on October 8, between them opening Mukden, Tatungko, and Antung to commerce.[22] When it is realized that the last two towns are located in the area of the Yalu, the force of this diplomatic thrust can be seen. Had either side considered retreat, this exchange would, for different reasons, have given them ample excuse to reconsider.

It is, therefore, not surprising that the Russians responded again with force, this time by the reestablishment of their grip on Manchurian where it had to some extent been relaxed. Mukden itself was reoccupied toward the end of the month.[23] Asked the reason, Alekseiev said that the measure was made necessary by the systematic opposition of the Chinese authorities to his directions. Some days before he had ordered the punishment of

[21] Weale, op.cit., p. 304 (picture); W.J. Oudendyk, "Russia and China," Journal of the Royal Central Asian Society, xxii, 3, July, 1935, p. 389.

[22] Wright, op.cit., p. 801; Romanov, Russia, p. 15; MacMurray, op.cit., i, 411–433.

[23] Uchida to Komura, Oct. 23, Uchida to Komura, Oct. 30, 1903, N.G.M., xxxvi-i, 408, 414; Boutiron to Delcasse, Nov. 14, and Nov. 25, 1903, D.D.F., iii, 134; R.-I.V., p. 35.

certain Chinese officials who had allegedly interfered with Russia's activities, stipulating that unless his demands were complied with he would reoccupy Mukden.

The precise reason Russia actually carried out this aggressive act is not wholly clear. Several concurrent events, nevertheless, leave the impression that it may have been inspired at that time by fear of the Chinese people and administration. Certainly the viceroy's order to the Chinese officials gives the reoccupation the semblance of a disciplinary gesture. This inference is reenforced by the fact that his statement appeared to hold out the promise that a change in the Chinese attitude might have some bearing on the duration of the reoccupation.

Other occurrences at this time underscore the Russian preoccupation with the Chinese restiveness under her control. In a report to the minister of war a few weeks before, Alekseiev had mentioned his fear of an imminent Japanese landing in Korea. This would give the reoccupation of Mukden the appearance of a precautionary warning against either Chinese collaboration with the Japanese or any act of defiance in response to their landing. The recent conclusion of the American and Japanese treaties with China opening Mukden for commerce also held the prospect of some Chinese response, at least to the extent of complying with the provisions of the treaties.

As both antagonists assumed increasingly rigorous and hostile postures, the likelihood of war became a subject of widespread speculation.[24] Even Komura admitted that he thought Russia would fight rather than be turned out of Manchuria. A possible Japanese landing in North Korea was talked about as the place the war might start. Because of the widespread fear of war, Lloyds of London were reported to have doubled their premiums on ships bound for the Far East. News of large coal orders at Cardiff for Japan, Russia, and the British Far Eastern Fleet was also reported. On hearing these rumors, the Russian Emperor demonstrated his unique detachment from the furor he had sanctioned by telegraphing to Viceroy Alekseiev, "I want no war."

The negotiations which Komura and Rosen carried on after the latter's return from Port Arthur on October 3 must indeed

[24] MacDonald to Lansdowne, Oct. 29, 1903, B.D., II, 220; Moulin to Andre, Oct. 3, 1903, D.D.F., III, 595; Boutiron to Delcasse, Oct. 9, Harmand to Delcasse, Oct., 21, 1903, ibid., IV, 10–11, 39; Bülow to Arco, Oct. 25, 1903, G.P., XIX-I, 14–15; Baelz, op.cit., pp. 233–234.

have seemed futile. After presenting the Russian counterproposals on the day of his return, Rosen met with Komura on four occasions, October 6, 8, 14, and 26, to seek some understanding of the premises on which their negotiations could proceed. It was out of these conversations that the next official Russo-Japanese exchanges emerged. In fact, the first exchange disclosed a difference of views that had been well known since the Ito negotiations in 1901.[25] In precise wording, however, they differed markedly from the earlier discussions and, in this respect, were closer to the Japanese proposals of 1902. One of the points of difference was the Japanese requirement that Russia guarantee the integrity, not only of Korea as had been asked in 1901, but also of China, a feature Japan had introduced in the course of the negotiations of 1902. Russia not only refused such a guarantee but added her refusal to guarantee for China the closely associated principle of equal opportunity. In a more positive vein, Russia demanded that Japan declare Manchuria outside her sphere of interest.

The portions of the proposals dealing with Korea were in most respects a restatement of the views exchanged between Ito and Lamsdorf nearly two years before. There was the same Japanese desire for practically complete freedom of action along with the Russian demand for the limitations which her own interests required. One notable addition was the Russian requirement that North Korea be preserved as a neutral zone. To an even greater extent than the monopolization of Manchuria, this was an issue about which Japan could hardly have been expected to compromise.

In the course of their negotiations during October, Komura and Rosen had quickly come to grips with the central problem which divided their governments—the refusal of both parties either to accept any limitations on their own side of the Manchuria-Korea frontier or to allow the opponent a completely free hand on the other side. Japan had entered the negotiations acting on the assumption that Russia's only legitimate rights were those she had acquired by 1898. Rosen had from the first considered this view unrealistic and insisted that the final agreement must take account of the changes of the past five years. Hence, in her counterproposals of December 11, Russia still refused to guarantee the integrity of the Chinese Empire.

[25] K.G., I, 334–340.

In the light of this attitude, Russia's action with respect to article 7 of her first counterproposal must be considered her nearest approach to a concession. This article which would have required Japan to declare Manchuria outside of her sphere of interest was discussed by Komura and Rosen. Komura suggested a compromise embodied in articles 7, 8, and 9 of Japan's proposals of October 30.[26] The Russian response of December 11 ignored the issue entirely, and presumably this meant that Russia had decided either to forego recognition of her monopoly in Manchuria or to ignore Japan's Manchurian claims under the treaty of 1898.

Russia also appears to have made a concession on the proposed railway connection between Korea and China. When the Imperial conference in Tokyo had decided on June 23 to undertake negotiations, it was assumed by those present as almost axiomatic that the railways would have to be linked through Manchuria. Accordingly, this demand was included in the original Japanese proposal. In her first counterproposal Russia had ignored this article; in her second response on December 11, however, Russia appeared to have acknowledged this request, but with the understanding that the railways would be linked "when the railways shall have been extended to the Yalu."

This apparent concession must, therefore, be evaluated in the light of Russia's continued insistence on a neutral zone in North Korea. It should be remembered that the insertion of this article was no accident growing out of hasty, last-minute decision. On the contrary it was a deliberate policy that was foreshadowed in Russia's successful effort in 1896, to persuade the French concessionaires to build the Seoul-Uiju railway with a Russian gauge. Russia's plan to control part or all of Korea was not only implicit in Witte's plans before the Boxer Rebellion, but explicitly stated more than once by official persons.

The first specific mention of a neutral zone in North Korea appears to have been made during the negotiations with Ito in December 1901 when General Kuropatkin suggested this as a means of avoiding friction with Japan. A year later he revived the suggestion, again with the objective of lessening tension with Japan but this time with special reference to the protection of the Yalu timber concession. The same idea was clearly implied in the Emperor's order to Bezobrazov in June 1903, as the latter was

[26] Appendix 1, of this study.

enroute to the conference at Port Arthur. This established the policy of excluding the Japanese from the Russian concession area in case they were to occupy Korea. In the early weeks of the negotiations Russian thinking about the elimination of Japanese influence from North Korea went beyond the neutrality of North Korea;[27] it was suggested that Japan be prohibited from building or operating railways north of Seoul and complete absorption of the region by Russia might be the best solution to the problem.

So obviously was Russia's insistence on a neutral zone foreshadowed in her established and expressed policies that Japan must have faced the prospect that it would become an issue. In any case, the Japanese counterproposal, that a neutral zone be established on both sides of the Yalu-Tiumen rivers, was not only a shrewd recognition of a seemingly unavoidable obstacle to a settlement, but, in the light of the determination Japan had exhibited in the struggle for the Yalu, an almost magnanimous gesture. While the negotiations proceeded as before, the neutral zone issue was unquestionably recognized as an impasse. Even before the negotiations began, it had been the fixed policy of the Japanese government to accept no compromise where Korea was concerned. The Russian refusal on December 11 to accept this compromise must have been, for the Japanese government, a very disturbing turn of events. One is left to wonder whether Russia intended to exchange her demand for a Japanese declaration excluding Manchuria from her sphere of interest for agreement on the neutral zone issue.

One of the aspects of the negotiations which the Japanese found particularly exasperating, and even humiliating, was the Russian delay in responding to their proposals—Russia's reply on December 11 came after a six-weeks' delay. This was a consequence in part of the cumbersome and dispersed administrative processes through which the negotiations had to pass before a reply could be formulated—the Emperor in Europe, Lamsdorf in St. Petersburg, Alekseiev in Port Arthur, and Rosen in Tokyo, all had a hand in formulating a plan. The significant delaying factor, however, was the inability of these people to consult together on the formation of a plan of action.

The negotiations themselves raised other perplexing problems. For the Russians were as convinced as the Japanese that the security of their interests depended upon holding their opponent at

[27] R.-I.V., p. 40.

arms length. The Russians had a tremendous advantage since they already occupied Manchuria. The Japanese could not match this with a parallel occupation of Korea without precipitating a major, and perhaps fatal incident.

This left the Russians to ponder the readiness and willingness of the Japanese to grasp the initiative and, having created an incident, to calculate how far they would be prepared to go in settling it to their own advantage.[28] Would they merely land troops in Korea or would they go beyond this? As the weeks passed Alekseiev, on whom the responsibility for the negotiations mainly rested, felt the situation was becoming desperate. It was impossible for Russia to retreat with dignity under the pressures now being concentrated on her by Japan, Great Britain, and the United States; the deadlock could only be broken by coming to an agreement with either Japan or China. Since this, in turn, assumed concessions from either Japan or China, the foreign support they enjoyed would probably render such an alternative out of the question. Consequently, Viceroy Alekseiev suggested that the negotiations be prolonged, if possible, to allow Russia time to reenforce Manchuria.

[28] Alekseiev to Emperor, Nov. 25, Nov. 28, Dec. 3, Dec. 8, 1903, Burtsev, *op.cit.*, pp. 48–53 *passim;* Alekseiev to Lamsdorf, Dec. 1, 1903, *Obzor,* p. 80; Lansdowne to Spring Rice, Nov. 25, 1903, *B.D.*, IV, 187; Boutiron to Delcasse, Nov. 25, Bompard to Delcasse, Dec. 4, 1903, *D.D.F.*, IV, 135, 161; *K.G.*, I, 344.

7. Peace Comes to an End

THE RUSSO-JAPANESE NEGOTIATIONS continued into the third round of discussions largely because the Japanese government was committed to follow them through. In the first place, the Japanese proposals were a conscious expression of the national aspirations and there could be neither compromise nor retreat if these goals were to be realized. Russia, already a great power with the enormous advantage of location on the Asian mainland, had shown herself equally adamant in pursuing her own interests. Russia would continue to refuse to compromise with a maverick that she considered incapable of anything more than delaying temporarily her own progress toward unchallenged dominance in Eastern Asia.

Japan had also to bear in mind the significance of her self-created role as the leader of a movement. Moral and diplomatic support had been given her by other nations because they saw in Japan the antidote to Russian ambitions. This coalition had been brought together with difficulty and could easily fall apart if Japan were to appear half-hearted in pursuing the common goal. Furthermore, should she turn back she might never again enjoy this unique opportunity of winning the coveted role of leadership in Eastern Asia and the status of a great power.

Consequently, the Japanese proposals of December 21 reflected in Tokyo and stimulated in St. Petersburg a mood of deep pessimism as to the possibility of avoiding war.[1] These two nations, as well as the powers watching eagerly from the side-lines, had hoped that some concession might miraculously save the situation. By this time, it was becoming apparent that war might come at any time. Among the principals this pessimism was a consequence, not of some wholly irresistible fate, but rather of the frustration each felt because the other refused to make the required compromise.

A pessimistic Russian view of the new Japanese proposals appeared in a communication which Admiral Alekseiev addressed to the Emperor on December 26, 1903 in these words:

"The new Japanese proposals, transmitted to me by telegram from Baron Rosen on December 22, are tantamount to a demand for formal recognition by the Russian government of a protec-

[1] Appendix 1 of this study.

torate of Japan over Korea. Meanwhile, even with such sacrifices we are not achieving our major objective—the removal of the existing indefinite state of affairs, for the Japanese government, while demanding concessions, not only will not promise to be satisfied with them but, on the contrary, openly gives warning that the grounds for misunderstanding continue to exist and that for their removal it is necessary, moreover, to include in an agreement all those regions of the Far East where the interests of the Empires converge . . ."[2]

He concluded that the demands would of necessity be considered unacceptable, that any further concessions would only lead to a break, and that Japan should, if necessary, be left to fulfill her aims in Korea without Russian approval.

The principal questions raised by the new Japanese proposals and by Admiral Alekseiev's telegram were those dealing with the continuation of the negotiations and the inclusion of Manchuria in the proposed agreement. To discuss them, the Emperor called a conference at Tsarskoe Selo on December 28.[3] Except for the absence of the ministers of interior (Plehve) and finance (Pleske, who was ill), the conference was as significant a gathering as the circumstances required. Foreign affairs was represented by Lamsdorf, the navy by the Grand Duke Aleksei Aleksandrovich, and the army by Kuropatkin. The presence of Admiral Abaza raises the possibility that this may have been looked upon as a meeting of the Special Committee for Far Eastern Affairs, particularly since he was selected to report its proceedings.

Although the conference ultimately approved both the continuation of the negotiations and the reintroduction into the proposals of a statement about Manchuria, there were serious doubts expressed about Russia's defiant posture. About three weeks before the conference, Kuropatkin had revived his suggestion of giving up South Manchuria and concentrating on the northern area.[4] Essentially, he asserted that Russia's stake in the Far East at the present time was insignificant politically, economically, and militarily and consequently was not worth the cost of defense; he suggested returning South Manchuria, the least defensible part, to China. Although both Witte and Plehve

[2] Burtsev, op.cit., p. 55.
[3] Malozemoff, op.cit., pp. 244–245; K.A., ii, Dec. 28, 1903, pp. 95–97; R.-I.V., pp. 43–44 (gives a variant date for the conference as does Burtsev, op.cit., pp. 57–59).
[4] K.A., ii, 79, 83, 87–89; Kuropatkin, op.cit., i, 188–93.

had agreed with him privately, neither were at the conference where he tried unsuccessfully to have the idea adopted.

Another aspect of the problem raised at the conference had to do specifically with Russia's capacity to make use of her new acquisitions. Lamsdorf noted that in all the conferences of earlier months Russia's purpose and aims in Manchuria had never been defined. The Grand Duke added that Russia was acting like a dog in the manger, unable to use Manchuria adequately herself yet denying it to others. Such an outcropping of doubt at this point in the proceedings affirms the persistence of the defensive component in Russia's Far Eastern policy, though it did not influence the outcome of the conference.

The agreement to continue the negotiations and to include in the proposals a statement about Manchuria may have been facilitated by a formula expressed at the conference by the Emperor. He said that, for the present, peace was desirable; as for the future, time was on the side of Russia and each year found her position strengthened. While this allowed the negotiations to continue, it ignored both Russia's existing weaknesses and Japan's insistence upon an immediate decision and followed the accepted view that Russia would ultimately occupy a dominant position in the Far East.

The Russian willingness to permit a statement about Manchuria was qualified in two important ways. In the first place, it was conditioned upon Japanese acceptance of the restrictions under which she might enjoy her asserted rights in Korea (including the recognition of a neutral zone in the north), and secondly, the enjoyment of any rights by other nations in Manchuria would be "exclusive of the establishment of settlements." How incongruous these conditions were in the settling of an allegedly conciliatory program the events of the past few months must have made abundantly clear. Nevertheless, with these limitations Russia was ready to recognize other treaty rights and privileges in Manchuria.

In Tokyo, the situation was viewed as extremely grave. A cabinet council was called on December 28 to reconsider the national policy and to make decisions dealing with final preparations for war, including the organization of the military establishment.[5] In particular, it dealt with the establishment of the Imperial Headquarters, the Supreme War Council, the

[5] K.G., I, 359.

completion of the Seoul-Fusan railway, the mobilization of Taiwan, the completion of two cruisers in London, and other relevant matters.

A restatement of Japanese aims with respect to the imminent possibility of war also came out of this December 28 meeting. This document was entitled "Japanese policy with respect to China and Korea in case of the collapse of the negotiations with Russia," dated December 30, 1903.[6] The first and most basic question with respect to China was the role of China herself in case of war. It was reaffirmed that a neutral rather than a belligerent role was the only acceptable one for China from the Japanese standpoint.

The Japanese felt that all foreseeable contingencies of war conditions justified this decision. The first of these was the security of the two principal elements of Japan's continental policy: the guarantee of Korean independence in the north and the projection of a Japanese sphere of interest inland from Fukien in the south. Although the former was clearly of greater importance for the moment, an erroneous policy with respect to China might place all continental interests in jeopardy. If, for example, China were to become a belligerent on the side of Japan against Russia, it was entirely conceivable that she might broaden the struggle to include all westerners. This could deteriorate into a Boxer-type antiforeign uprising which might, in turn, inspire foreign intervention and lead to the loss of Japan's southern interests while she was occupied in the north with Russia.

A corollary policy included limiting the war geographically to the specific area of China; this would have the double benefit of preserving the stability of the region and thus the sympathy of the other powers and, at the same time, of avoiding intervention. Again, it was important to limit the war to Russia and Japan, avoiding if possible those conditions which would bring in the alliance partners. Once the partners had entered the war, China could easily be swept in and the predicted chaos might ensue.

A third consideration was that if China were to become involved in the war, her financial burden would increase and with it all her internal troubles. And the fourth consideration was that a war with China and Japan allied against the western powers would inevitably revive the fear of the "Yellow Peril" and

[6] *N. G. M.*, xxxvi-i, 41–45; *N.G.N.*, i, 217–219.

lead to intervention. Finally, a Japanese victory, if she were un-
allied with China, would leave Japan immeasurably greater
freedom of action than otherwise. For Japan's success in her continental program was clearly dependent to a considerable extent
upon the nature of her relations with China. These had to be
close enough to provide the advantages of good rapport but
distant enough to leave Japan sufficiently free to exert necessary
and timely pressure.

Following her established policy, Japan kept Great Britain
and the United States informed of the current situation. On the
very day that her new proposals had gone to Russia, Hayashi had
notified Lansdowne of the seriousness of the relations with
Russia. Hayashi wrote that the situation "had reached an extremely grave stage and that a peaceful solution of the pending
questions seemed to have become improbable, if not impossible."[7]
He stated that it had become clear that Russia's demands could
not be met by Japan and concluded with an ominous note by
summarizing the existing balance of military power of the prospective belligerents.

From diplomatic channels, the Japanese press, and other
sources, Britain also faced the fact that war appeared almost
inevitable. The cabinet discussed the situation and all its implications for the nation. In a memorandum to the King, Arthur
Balfour, the prime minister, summarized the British view as
follows: "The interest of this country is now and always *peace*.
But a war between Japan and Russia, in which we were not
actively concerned, and in which Japan did not suffer serious
defeat, would not be an unmixed curse. Russia . . . would have
created for herself an implacable and unsleeping enemy."[8] This,
he continued, would make Russia easier to deal with both in
Asia and Europe.

It would be a serious mistake to see in Balfour's memorandum
a concealed British eagerness to see Russia and Japan embroiled
in war. The sensitivity of the British with respect to the European
balance of power, soon to be given concrete form in the Anglo-

---

[7] Eckardstein Memorandum, Jan. 17, 1904 (enclosing Hayashi's memorandum
of Dec. 21, 1903), *G.P.*, XIX-I, 39–40.

[8] Barrere to Delcasse, Dec. 25, 1903, *D.D.F.*, IV, 200; Griscom to Hay, Dec. 31,
1903, *U.S.F.R.*, 1903, p. 622: Balfour Memorandum to Lansdowne, Dec. 22,
Balfour Memorandum to King, Dec. 28, Balfour Memorandum, Dec. 29, 1903,
B.E.C. Dugdale, *Arthur James Balfour; First Earl to Balfour*, 2 Vols., New York,
1937, I, 280–285.

French Entente, would preclude any such view. On the contrary, Britain had long been and remained vitally interested in some workable and dependable agreement with Russia and was, therefore, eager to have Russia become tractable enough to achieve this. Carrying it to the point, however, where German power would be left dominant in Europe, an entirely probable consequence of the outbreak of war, was not in the British interest.

Insofar as the Japanese side of the issue was concerned, Britain could do little more than accept whatever came since war was unquestionably one of the contingencies she had assumed when the alliance was signed, but two important questions remained. First, should Britain at this crucial moment seek to influence Japan for or against war? Balfour and the cabinet agreed that she could not do so without at the same time shifting to herself a portion of the blame for the outcome. The decision must be left entirely with Japan. This policy was adhered to throughout the war, much to the chagrin of President Roosevelt who at times would have liked to see pressures exerted on both belligerents.

The other question had to do with Britain's obligation in case Japan should face a humiliating defeat. Lansdowne felt that there might be a moral obligation on Britain's part to go to her rescue with military force. Balfour, however, disagreed; he felt that the alliance meant exactly what it said and that no such obligation was implied. To assume otherwise would be a serious matter for it would, as Balfour expressed it, leave Japan the arbiter "of peace and war for half the civilized world."

Britain's commitment to the Japanese cause was even then being tested over Japan's effort to obtain a loan from London.[9] Japan associated the loan directly with her military preparations which, in turn, could support either the preservation of peace or a more effective war, both alternatives being presumably of the utmost importance to Britain. The loan, however, was not permitted. This seems to have been in part because the amount desired, 20 million pounds, was too large, but also more importantly, because it was felt it would constitute an act of war. Whatever the actual reason, it was ultimately overlooked and Japan later received the desired loan. Meanwhile, however, since the Russian

[9] Balfour to Lansdowne, Dec. 31, 1903, Dugdale, op.cit., i, 283; Hayashi to Komura, Jan. 1, Komura to Hayashi, Jan. 3, 1904, N.G.M., xxxvii-i, 2, 6–7; Delcasse to Bompard, Dec. 21, 1903, D.D.F., iv, 194.

government succeeded in learning about it, the incident must have cost the Japanese some prestige in St. Petersburg.

Nevertheless, Britain and Japan succeeded in achieving a clear understanding of their respective roles in the event of war. In the very midst of the discussion of the proposed loan, Komura gave due emphasis to this by expressing his appreciation for the assurances Britain had given as the crisis approached.[10] He specifically approved a genuinely neutral British policy which by this time was the accepted national policy of both countries. In his message Komura added a strong plea for financial support on the ground that, if the war came, it was defensible in the broad sense as a means of maintaining the principle of treaty rights and commercial opportunity in Manchuria.

The propensity of Russia to violate accepted rights and interests was also stressed in notifying the United States of the course things were taking. Komura instructed the Japanese minister in Washington, Takahira, to convey the message in these terms:

"To Russia, who recognized the large development of commercial and industrial enterprises of Japan in Korea by an international compact as far back as 1898, this state of affairs must be better known than to any other power, and it cannot be a matter of surprise to her that Japan finds it impossible to acquiesce in an exceedingly abnormal and precarious condition which would inevitably result from Russia's remaining indefinitely in the flank of Korea, which is an important outpost of Japan's line of defense, and from the neutralization of a considerable territory of Korea comprising about one-third of the whole peninsula . . . ."[11]

Takahira was further instructed to emphasize that Japan was contending with a determined opponent of all except Russia's own rights and interests in China and Korea. The measure of his success in conveying a sense of Russia's unyielding determination is found in an entry in John Hay's diary for January 5, 1904:

". . . it is evident that no attempt at mediation will do any good. Russia is clearly determined to make no concessions to Japan. They think that now is the time to strike, to crush Japan

---

[10] Komura to Hayashi, Dec. 31, 1903, *N.G.M.*, xxxvi-i, 46.
[11] Komura to Takahira, Dec. 21, Dec. 23, 1903, *U.S.F.R.*, 1903, p. 621.

and to eliminate her from her position of influence in the Far East."[12]

The crisis which Russo-Japanese relations had reached was also known to the public through the press.[13] The *Neue Freie Presse* published a startlingly pessimistic opinion held by the German minister to China, Max von Brandt: if Russia were to insist upon important rights in North Korea or at Masampo, war with Japan would be inevitable. The *New York Times* and the London *Times* conveyed essentially the same message to their readers; they both described the facts effectively enough to leave the impression, as the end of December approached, that the situation in the Far East was menacing. In fact, even as early as December 10 a headline in the *New York Times* read: "Russia Menaces Korea." Attention was being focused on the North Korean problem and Japan and Britain were portrayed as engaged in urging Korea to open Yongampo as a commercial port while Russia was forcefully resisting this. By late December, both newspapers indicated clearly that a climax was near. On December 28 the *New York Times* announced the "Peril of General War," expressing fear that the war might engulf Britain, France, and China and thus become general. On the same day the London *Times,* in a modest understatement, admitted the possibility that, should the Russian answer be unfavorable, the situation might pass beyond the realm of diplomacy.

A frank portrayal of the diplomatic leadership consciously entrusted to Japan was conveyed in the *North China Herald* on January 8, 1904 in an article which stated that:

"The division of Corea as Russia proposes is impossible because . . . Russia is precluded by the Port Hamilton agreement from taking any territory whatever in Corea, and Japan is bound with us to do her best to vindicate in all circumstances the independence and integrity of Corea."

One striking fact about all these press reports was their apparently unconscious assumption that Russia's aims were aggressive and Japan's defensive in character. An article in the *New York Times* on December 18, 1903 exemplified this attitude.

[12] W.R. Thayer, *The Life and Letters of John Hay,* 2 Vols., Boston, 1919, II, 370.
[13] Makino to Komura, Dec. 29, Kurino to Komura, Dec. 29, 1903, *N.G.M.,* XXXVI-I, 39–40; Inouye to Komura, Jan. 6, 1904, *N.G.M.,* XXXVII-I, 12.

Entitled "Japan About to Act," without any hint that the reverse might be equally true, it simply noted that the situation was considered grave in Tokyo because of Russia's unwillingness to put the solution to the Manchurian and Korean questions on the same footing.

This very thought must have crossed Baron Komura's mind as he read the Russian counterproposals which Baron Rosen handed him on January 6, 1904. The Japanese government, indeed, found it impossible to accept the severe limitations that they would have imposed on her rights and interests in either Manchuria or Korea.[14] Perhaps the most difficult to accept was the insistence on the neutral zone. For, during their negotiations, Rosen had accepted, with the understanding that the matter would have to be referred to his government for approval, Komura's proposal to substitute a neutral zone on both sides of the frontier. The French ambassador in St. Petersburg reported that while it was Admiral Alekseiev who had refused to accept this, the Emperor had approved his stand.

In Tokyo there now seemed little reason to continue the negotiations since thus far they demonstrated only a hardening of the Russian attitude toward the vital issues. Komura saw little likelihood that this would actually change or that Russia could be expected to concede an acceptable formula on which an agreement could be based.[15]

Why did Japan, under these circumstances, continue the negotiations? One obvious reason was the natural reluctance to become embroiled with a potentially formidable adversary and another was the equally natural reluctance to be considered an aggressor. The prospect of leading Japan into the trap of breaking the peace was indeed frequently mentioned by Russian officials.[16]

Still another reason was the Japanese desire to prove herself a worthy and acceptable member of the society of nations. One important and difficult aspect of this problem was expressed by Ito Miyoji in answer to a question from a German physician living in Japan as to why Japan was so long-suffering as to continue the negotiations under existing conditions. Ito answered:

[14] *K.G.*, I, 349–350; Delcasse to Cogordan, Jan. 6, Bompard to Delcasse, Jan. 7, 1904, *D.D.F.*, IV, 220–223.
[15] *K.G.*, I, 351.
[16] Abaza to Alekseiev, Jan. 12, 1904, Burtsev, *op.cit.*, p. 67.

". . . Of course, what is really wrong with us is that we have yellow skins. If our skins were as white as yours, the whole world would rejoice at our calling a halt to Russia's inexorable aggressions."[17]

Ito's words were very timely indeed. For, only a few days before, Japan had officially divested herself of her "Asia for the Asians" leadership in favor of a neutral China, a policy which was intended to avoid the appearance of a racial war. Furthermore, at the very time Ito expressed his views, Russia was propagating in the West the image of herself as the defender of Europe against the dangers of pan-Mongolism.[18] Paralleling Japan's assumed role as defender of western rights in Eastern Asia, Russia was appealing for sympathy and support as the defender of an entire race. As the war proceeded and her prospects grew dimmer, Russia used this increasingly to rally both her own morale and her waning prestige abroad.

To plan the strategy under which new proposals would be made, an Imperial council was held in Tokyo on January 12, 1904.[19] Among senior officials scheduled to attend, the prime minister was most conspicuously absent because of illness. From this meeting there emerged a document ominously labeled "The Final Japanese Proposals for the Russo-Japanese Negotiations regarding Manchuria and Korea." While it was decided to urge Russia to reconsider, Japan would continue to insist upon her essential requirements. The slight chance of success was recognized, however, in the statement: "in the event that the Russian reply to the communication [of the proposals] should prove unsatisfactory or should be unreasonably delayed," the Imperial government should at once decide what measures they deemed necessary to defend their menaced position and to protect their rights and interests.

In conducting this last round of negotiations, Komura acted under a charge from the Imperial council that limited his freedom of action. He was directed to adhere strictly to the condition that there must be complete harmony between diplomatic action and planned military operations. This may be the reason that Komura showed such surprising irritation when Rosen

[17] Baelz, *op.cit.*, Jan. 19, 1904, p. 243.
[18] Kurino to Komura, No. 52, Jan. 20, Kurino to Komura, No. 55, Jan. 21, 1904, *J.F.O.*; Scott to Lansdowne, Jan. 21, 1904, *B.D.*, II, 239.
[19] Komura to Kurino, No. 23, Jan. 14, 1904, *J.F.O.*

remarked to him that Russia might not accept the proposals, replying excitedly and emphatically, "But we might compel you."[20] It is most certainly the reason Komura instructed Kurino so precisely on how to present the proposals to Lamsdorf. He wrote:

". . . you will be careful not to make any remark or to express any opinion even in your personal capacity. If he seeks explanation on any point you will ask for instructions. After you have made the communication you will not press for a reply until you receive express instructions to do so. In the meantime you will continue to watch carefully the attitude of the Russian Government and to use your best endeavours to ascertain what action they may possibly take in the present crisis."[21]

The Japanese proposals of January 13 are significant in relation to the war which followed three weeks later.[22] In the first place they constitute the last full statement of the issues on which Japan went to war, the next expression of views being the conditions on which she was ready to negotiate peace. Secondly, they were said by Russia to be in fact an ultimatum, expressed in such provocative language as to inhibit any further concessions. The phrase singled out in this way is the one which urged early action "since further delay in the solution of the question will be extremely disadvantageous to the two countries." There is no doubt that in a diplomatic context these words are highly provocative. On the other hand, they also reflect the embittered Russo-Japanese relations reached because of Russia's desire to delay and Japan's eagerness to hasten a solution, and furthermore, no real concession had been made to encourage any hope of success.

Japan's rigid stance was exemplified in these final proposals. They specified, it should be noted, that the following changes in the Russian terms must be made: elimination of the restriction on her strategic use of Korean territory; suppression of the article dealing with the neutral zone; a recognition of the territorial integrity of both China and Korea; the acknowledgment that Korea was outside the Russian sphere of interest; and the recognition of Japanese rights and privileges in Manchuria. In

[20] *K.G.*, I, 352.
[21] Komura to Kurino, Jan. 14, 1904, *N.G.M.*, xxxvii-i, 34.
[22] Appendix 1 of this study.

support of her demand for settlement rights in Manchuria, Japan maintained that without these she would not enjoy equality of rights with the other powers in China. These proposals clearly underscored the absence of progress that characterized the negotiations.

As the climax appeared to be approaching, several capitals, particularly Paris, became the centers of determined efforts to bring the principals together. France played an active role since she earnestly desired peace and because of the general conviction that her Russian alliance partner was the principal aggressor. Russia sought to use the good offices of Delcasse only with the hope of reducing the Japanese demands.

Since her own territory was a prospective battlefield, China also had a strong incentive for seeking the support of the powers.[23] While marshaling the general approval of the powers for the support of her neutrality in case war should actually break out, she also made every possible direct effort to prevent the war itself. Her efforts in London and Washington were unpromising largely because both countries were inclined to leave the important decisions up to Japan. Furthermore, both countries were regarded by Russia as officially so partisan to Japan that it was questionable how effective their good offices would have been in any case.

Korea having served as the issue on which Russia and Japan had brought their hostility into focus in early 1901, the question of the neutralization of Korea was revived during the negotiations.[24] In late August 1903, Korea was reported to be sending a court official to Paris to appeal for support in realizing this plan; and similar appeals were made to Russia and Japan to support a neutral policy. By January 1904, the position of Korea appeared to be desperate.[25] At Seoul the Russians were intriguing to neutralize the country as a bulwark against Japanese aspirations

[23] Uchida to Komura, Jan. 15, Jan. 16, Jan. 25, 1904, N.G.M., xxxvii-i, 47–50, 68; Dubail to Delcasse, Jan. 25, 1904, D.D.F., iv, 292; Cassini to Lamsdorf, Jan. 27, 1904, A. Dobrov, Dalnevostochnaia Politika S. Sh. A. v Period Russko-Iaponskoi Voiny, Moscow, 1952, pp. 312–313.

[24] Hayashi to Komura, Aug. 18, Aug. 27, Komura to Hayashi, Oct. 6, 1903, N.G.M., xxxvi-i, 718, 720–722, 725–726; Boutiron to Delcasse, Nov. 7, 1903, D.D.F., iv, 90.

[25] de Fontenay to Delcasse, Jan. 30, Feb. 2, 1904; D.D.F., iv, 306, 314–316; K.G., ii, 254; Kato to Komura, Jan. 11, Korean Minister of Foreign Affairs, Yi Tchi Yong, to Komura, Jan. 21, Komura to Hayashi (Seoul), Jan. 21, Hayashi to Komura, Jan. 24, 1904, N.G.M., xxxvii-i, 310–312, 314–316; D.G. Tewksbury, Source Materials on Korean Politics and Ideologies, New York, 1950, pp. 20–21.

and encouraging Korea to seek international acceptance for such a policy. Simultaneously, the Japanese were trying desperately to achieve a treaty foundation for the special position they claimed in Korea, an endeavor in which they were successful only after the war had begun. Meanwhile, guards were reaching Seoul to protect foreign nationals and interests and a Japanese descent on the Korean coast was expected at any time. It was in these circumstances that Korea made a last desperate appeal for support of her projected neutralization. The appeal was dated January 21 and was transmitted to Japan as well as the western powers. Transmitting messages to the West was difficult since the Japanese controlled the telegraph lines within the country and it was assumed unwise to use the Russian telegraph at Port Arthur. The problem was resolved by operating through the French minister who transmitted the messages from Chefoo in China. The response from the western powers was encouraging but indecisive; the French were aware of their role in frustrating an anticipated Japanese diplomatic success in Seoul.

The hope of using the good offices of France to moderate the rigid demands of the two antagonists apparently began to be considered seriously at the time of Lamsdorf's visit to Paris at the end of October 1903.[26] The responsibility was assumed by Delcasse at the expressed desire of both Britain and Japan and with the approval of Russia. Although it did not prevent the war, it did provide a forum for the discussion of some of the most difficult issues. Delcasse's conciliatory role was inhibited from the start by the official antipathy of both principals toward even the use of the terms "good offices" or "mediation," lest the decision be taken out of their hands. Furthermore, the Japanese were convinced that any delay would only serve Russia's interests.

From January 13, the day Komura handed Japan's final proposals to Rosen, serious discussions of all the outstanding issues were carried on, largely in Paris between Delcasse and Motono.[27] The latter wrote to Komura that, because of France's enormous

[26] Cambon to Delcasse, Oct. 27, Harmand to Delcasse, Oct. 29, Delcasse to Boutiron, Nov. 4, Cambon to Delcasse, Nov. 11, 1903, D.D.F., IV, 80, 103; Komura to Motono, No. 8, Jan. 14, 1904, J.F.O.

[27] Delcasse to Bompard, Jan. 13, Bompard to Delcasse, Jan. 16, Delcasse to Bompard, Jan. 17, Delcasse to Bompard, Jan. 21, 1904, D.D.F., IV, 242, 259–262, 264–266, 279; Motono to Komura, No. 11, Jan. 13, No. 13, Jan. 16, No. 16, Jan. 17, 1904, J.F.O.; Motono to Komura, Jan. 21, 1904, N.G.M., XXXVII-I, 62; Bompard, op.cit., pp. 46–48; G.M. Paleologue, Un Grand Tournant de la Politique Mondiale (1904–1906), Paris, 1934, pp. 5ff.

financial stake in Russia and her commitment to the preservation of peace, Delcasse's sincerity in preventing a rupture could be assumed. There ensued a series of exchanges which, by comparison with the course of the negotiations up to that point, are remarkable for their frankness and the apparent willingness of both parties to discuss fundamental issues. It may have been these moderating influences that account for the concessions which Russia appeared to be willing to make in her last counterproposals.

Although Japan had from the first exhibited far more enthusiasm for the French good offices than Russia, she had throughout maintained the same substratum of reserve and retained a firm theoretical opposition to mediation in any form while cooperating with the French. Komura decided by January 22 that a firmer approach was necessary;[28] the value of further negotiations was questionable for Japan since Russia insisted, even under French mediation, on holding a restraining hand over Japan in the use of Korea for strategic purposes, a clearly unacceptable condition unless Russia accepted a similar one regarding Manchuria.

Outside the negotiations themselves, there were premonitory signs that must have made further reliance on Japan's diplomatic advantage seem unwise. France had just been discovered in the act of helping to frustrate Japan's plan to establish her predominance in Seoul. If France were encouraged to continue to aid Russia in her scheme to pluck Korea out of the international controversy by neutralizing her, where would the erosion of the Anglo-Japanese Alliance stop? It could eventually obscure the most convincing issue; furthermore if France were to become committed to active partition, the Alliance would no longer serve either to neutralize France or localize the war, thus turning the clock back two years.

Meanwhile the Japanese operating principle that time was on the side of Russia, was receiving constant substantiation as Russia was observed rapidly building up her armed strength in the Far East.[29] Finally, at the very time Komura let his impatience be known to the Japanese minister in Paris, an ominous message was received from London to the effect that certain prominent and influential persons were suggesting that Russia and Japan

[28] Delcasse to Bompard, Jan. 21, 1904, D.D.F., IV, 279; Komura to Motono, No. 17, Jan. 22, 1904, J.F.O.; Hayashi to Komura, Jan. 22, 1904, N.G.M., XXXVII-1, 64.

[29] Romanov, Ocherki, p. 241.

submit their differences to arbitration.[30] This would have been
the ultimate in mediation.

Japanese fears were confirmed by an article from the *Journal
de St. Pertersbourg*, considered to reflect official views, reported in
a Swiss newspaper as follows:

"An article which may be considered as officially inspired
states that, in consequence of the ratification of the commercial
treaties between China on the one side and Japan and the United
States on the other, there now remains nothing else for Russia
but to annex Manchuria. The United States will not wage war on
that account and the position in regard to Japan will not be
changed thereby. No protest whatever is expected on the part of
the other great powers."[31]

An article which appeared in the *North China Herald* on
January 22, 1904, carried information that also served as a
reminder that the negotiations had changed nothing and must
have influenced Japan's course during the succeeding week. It
described a recent memorandum of the Russian viceroy at Port
Arthur, suggesting a temporary settlement by diplomatic means:

". . . arguing that Russia's geographical position and military
strength must in the course of time secure for her the status
she claims.

"No artificial barriers, he says, can long prevent this, but
her land forces, which are Russia's main strength, are at the
present moment insufficiently represented in the Far East.

"This once remedied, the question will gradually solve itself
in Russia's favor, whereas a campaign now would seriously
check the natural course of things."

An editorial comment pointed out that:

". . . nothing could be better calculated to determine Japan
not to let slip the present opportunity. Japan's first object is to
'seriously check the natural course of things' . . ."

Perhaps because he was not in possession of all the facts,
the Japanese minister in Paris was surprised when he received
Komura's announcement on January 22 that the recent Japanese

---

[30] Hayashi to Komura, Jan. 22, 1904, *N.G.M.*, xxxvii-i, 64.
[31] Inouye to Komura, No. 30, Jan. 20, 1904, *J.F.O.*

proposals were to be considered an irreducible minimum. He wrote:

"In reference to your telegram 17, I feel it my duty to submit the following for your consideration. . . . Detailed progress of the present negotiations induce me to the positive conviction that the Imperial government, while prepared to meet any contingency, were desirous of arriving at a peaceful understanding with Russia in as conciliatory a spirit as is compatible with an honorable solution. In no telegram or communication from you, inclusive your telegram 9, could I find any hint or indication to make me understand that our last proposals were an irreducible minimum, admitting no amendment . . ."[32]

Baron Komura's reply amounted to an apology insofar as the abruptness of his note was concerned,[33] but it clearly informed Motono that Russia must be disabused of any reason for assuming "that the Japanese government could be induced without serious difficulty to make further concessions." Neither side made any further concessions beyond those already discussed through the personal good offices of Delcasse. Nevertheless, the Japanese diplomatic representatives continued to search for some clue that would lead to a peaceful, though satisfying solution. In St. Petersburg the Japanese minister kept probing to the bitter end. In looking for the alleged "war party," he discussed the issues with Abaza, Bezobrazov, and Witte. By the end of the month he came to the unsatisfying conclusion that there was no specific "war party." Instead, he found a widespread opinion which he characterized as follows:

"In view of several difficult circumstances, I do not think Russia desires war in the Far East; on the contrary, she wishes for a peaceful solution but seems to be laboring under a tremendous conceit which leads to the opinion that an agreement regarding Manchuria would be looked upon as a great humiliation . . . Meanwhile the foreign press is making agreement increasingly difficult by emphasizing this factor."[34]

[32] Motono to Komura, No. 23, Jan. 24, 1904, *J.F.O.*
[33] Komura to Motono, No. 18, Jan. 25, 1904, *J.F.O.*
[34] Inouye to Komura, Nos. 27, 28 (numbers refer to Kurino's communications transmitted via Berlin), Jan. 14, 1904, *N.G.M.*, xxxvii-i, 39–42; Kurino to Komura, No. 70, Jan. 30, 1904, *J.F.O.*

These were some of the factors that helped to create a sense of complete hopelessness in Tokyo, along with an increasing commitment to war and even a sense of urgency in precipitating a break in relations before the opportunity for a favorable decision should be forever lost.

The Japanese severance of relations with Russia, at least in its initial stages, was still done on a note of reluctance. During the last week of January, the Japanese minister in St. Petersburg, acting in each case under specific instructions from Tokyo, made a series of urgent, though unrewarding, requests that Russia respond to Japan's proposals of January 13.[35] The beginning of this series coincided with the abrupt note to Motono in Paris; it ended with the laconic directive on February 3:

"You are instructed to make no further attempt to obtain the reply of the Russian government or to ascertain its nature until you receive express instructions to do so."

The final steps leading to the open break in Russo-Japanese relations came in rapid succession. The break was formally and officially approved at an Imperial council in Tokyo on February 4, 1904 and at 2:00 P.M. the next day, a message announcing this to the Russian government was dispatched from Tokyo. The message began with words which stated accurately and concisely the Japanese view of the difficulty:

"Further prolongation of the present situation being inadmissible the Imperial Government have decided to terminate the pending negotiations and to take such independent action as they may deem necessary to defend their menaced position and to protect their rights and interests. . . ."[36]

The document continued with a recital of the causes of the break as Tokyo saw them: the importance to Japanese security of the preservation of Korean integrity; the repeated refusal of Russia either to permit Japan the means of assuring this integrity or to guarantee the integrity of China; the continuing occupation of Manchuria; the Russian naval and military reinforcement of her Far Eastern position; and the general hopelessness of an

[35] Komura to Kurino, No. 35, Jan. 23, No. 38, Jan. 26, No. 41, Jan. 28, No. 44, Jan. 30, No. 49, Feb. 3, 1904, *J.F.O.*
[36] Imperial Conference, Feb. 4, 1904, Komura to Kurino, Nos., 50, 51, 52, 53, Feb. 5, 1904, *N.G.M.*, xxxvii-i, 92–95, 97–101.

enduring peace under these conditions. It concluded with the announcement that Japan would take appropriate action and that the Japanese minister planned to depart from St. Petersburg.

Simultaneously in St. Petersburg, equally fateful decisions were being made.[37] On January 28 a conference was held by the persons officially concerned to consider an answer to the Japanese proposals of two weeks before. The findings of the conference were made the basis of new counterproposals which were approved by the Emperor on February 2 and transmitted to Admiral Alekseiev the next day. It has been estimated that, at the earliest, this document might have reached Port Arthur by February 3 or 4 and Tokyo by February 4 or 5; in fact it has been alleged that the message was purposely delayed by the Japanese telegraph and only reached Rosen on February 7.

The question which this parallel sequence raises is of considerable importance: did the Japanese government sever relations under such conditions as to lay them open to the charge either of acting with undue haste or of being deliberately unreceptive to the Russian counterproposals? It is significant that the Japanese government was informed before the break that she might face this charge.[38] It was learned at this time that the substance of the Russian counterproposals had already been transmitted to the governments of France, Great Britain, and the United States and that the view was current that war could be avoided. The report continued:

"The conviction is now prevalent that Japan will have to bear the whole responsibility and find herself morally isolated if the crisis should result in any other issue than peace; for Russia has done the utmost in her power in giving satisfaction to Japan."

Was this message the last straw that helped the Imperial council the next day to decide to bring the issue to a head? Or was the whole matter immaterial to the action Japan took?

In the perspective of the Russo-Japanese problem as it had developed over the preceding years, these questions can only have meaning in the light of a further question: on the assumption that Japan did not receive the counterproposals, how would she have been expected to act? In answering this, there is information

[37] Malozemoff, op.cit., pp. 248–249; K.A., ıı, 103–105, 106; Romanov, Ocherki, pp. 275–277.
[38] Inouye to Komura, No. 39, Feb. 3, 1904, J.F.O.

from a few days before the time in question and from the very
day relations were broken.[39] Even considering these sources, it is
apparent that Japan would have had to assume that Russia still
insisted upon two conditions which Japan had long defined as
unacceptable: the restriction on her strategic use of Korea and
the neutral zone. In addition, since it was mentioned in the
earlier report and not mentioned in the last, she might reasonably
have assumed also that Russia remained unwilling to guarantee
the integrity of China. It was substantially under this impression,
the earlier information being even more positively objectionable
than the last, that the Imperial council acted on February 4 to
sever relations.

As a next step, it must be asked: if Japan had received the
counterproposals, would the difference have been likely to change
the decision of the Imperial council? Since the only difference
this would have made was the elimination of the demand for a
neutral zone, the answer must be negative. In fact, in the light of
the decision to eliminate the neutral zone by the Russian conference of January 28, Kurino's report had, in this respect,
created a mistaken impression. Still there remained two vitally
objectionable features: the restriction on the strategic use of
Korea and the refusal to give a general guarantee of the integrity
of China. These violated what Japan had defined as an acceptable
reciprocal relationship and would seem to be fatal insofar as
Japanese acceptance of the Russian terms was concerned. It
must be concluded that even the final Russian counterproposals
were unacceptable and that, in this sense, the question of timing
would have made no difference.

The departure of the two envoys from the capitals to which
they had been respectively accredited was for both a matter of
some consequence. Both had, within the limits of their national
loyalties, been outstandingly devoted to the preservation of
peace. Baron Rosen is said to have accepted the turn of events
with a sense of personal tragedy.[40] He had gained a reputation as
a sincere friend of Japan. The American minister later expressed
admiration for the way Rosen carried off the farewell calls after
the long, trying war of nerves. The Baroness, he added, broke
down under the strain and accused her friends of insincerity.

[39] Kurino to Komura, No. 62, Jan. 25, No. 79, Feb. 5, 1904, *J.F.O.*; Lansdowne
to Scott, Feb. 8, 1904 (two communications of the same date), *B.D.*, II, 247–249.
[40] Rosen, *op.cit.*, I, 231–233; Griscom, *op.cit.*, p. 242; Baelz, *op.cit.*, p. 245.

The Rosens departed on February 11, leaving Russian affairs in the hands of the Austrian minister. In a few months, Rosen would meet Komura again at the Portsmouth Conference.

In the case of Kurino, his departure from St. Petersburg was described as follows by a member of the British embassy:

"It was a curious sight. The station was full of people, most of them with the special edition of the newspaper in their hands, announcing a great naval victory of the Russians. The crowd stared at the carriage containing the Japanese but made no sign of approval or disapproval. The train moved off. When it was well out of hearing a very slight sound of whistling was audible and a slight cheer. Then the crowd went off quietly."[41]

Kurino and some of his staff were bound for Stockholm where he had already been accredited on a supplementary assignment— the diplomatic post at Stockholm was to play a significant role in Japan's wartime policy in Europe.

[41] Spring Rice to Roosevelt, Feb. 11, 1904, S. Gwynn, *The Letters and Friendships of Sir Cecil Spring Rice*, 2 Vols., Boston, 1929, I, 393.

WAR AND DIPLOMACY

8. A Decisive Military Thrust

THE JAPANESE CHALLENGE immediately disclosed the complete inadequacy of Russia's military preparedness. A whole generation, grown accustomed to the image of Russia as a vast and powerful nation moving outward upon her Asian neighbors with a distressing inevitability, was understandably surprised. Often, as the climax approached in Russo-Japanese relations, there had been speculation as to which was bluffing. Russia's early performance in the war on both land and sea seemed at least a temporary answer to this question.

At the same time, the prevailing conception of Japan had to be altered with equally dramatic suddenness. To a generation, both east and west, which had toyed with racial theories as a means of clarifying or distorting international relations, the new turn of affairs must have confirmed or refuted established opinions with startling suddenness. However, the statesmen who dealt with the realities of international affairs could hardly have missed the most significant fact of all—the emergence of a new, effective, and competitive world power.

Both antagonists made military preparations for war paralleling their political maneuvers to obviate it. Their endeavors, in this respect, appear to have been in direct proportion to the seriousness with which they viewed the prospect of war. Japan, realizing that to regain what the Three Power intervention of 1895 had taken away would require her full effort, prepared for the ordeal carefully and systematically.

Japan's preparation for war was carried forward as though it had been inspired by an article written by Baron Hayashi for the *Jiji Shimpo* in the summer of 1895. He wrote that Japan must lay the foundation for strengthening her army and navy by promoting commerce and industry and by enduring heavier taxes. Only in this way could she assert her position successfully. He continued:

"What Japan has now to do is to keep perfectly quiet, to lull the suspicions that have arisen against her, and to wait, meanwhile strengthening the foundations of her national power, watching and waiting for the opportunity which must one day surely come in the Orient."[1]

[1] Pooley, *op.cit.*, pp. 110–113.

The plan to realize this policy was in fact elaborated during late 1895.[2] Although temporarily frustrated by parliamentary opposition, the program was successfully put into practice in the course of the next few months. The financial foundation upon which it rested was the indemnity from China, the amount of which was half again as large as the entire military cost of the Sino-Japanese war. Since the latter expense was almost entirely covered by accumulated funds and by the budget, most of the indemnity could be directly applied to the rearmament program.

The rearmament program was very broad in scope, providing for the promotion of commerce and industry as well as a suitable adjustment of the tax base. The military budgets from 1896 on, show how this systematic increase in national military power was reflected in the rising expenditure. If the index number 100 were assigned to the ordinary military outlay for 1893, the equivalent figure for 1903 would be 328.

A planned increase in both branches of the military services was provided. The increasing tension between Russia and Japan and the growing certainty of war kept the preparations going at a forced pace. In the end both service programs were highly successful and the outbreak of war found the original plan substantially realized in guns, ships, trained men, and other tangible military requirements.

A ten-year plan, scheduled for completion in 1905, was worked out for the army. This effected the term of service of the men, the structure of the reserve system, the peace and war strength of the army, and the expansion of arsenals and other military facilities. There were actually two separate naval programs. One was completed by 1903 and the other was still in progress in February 1904.

When the moment for action came, Japan faced her adversary with a well-trained, spirited, and logistically manageable military force.[3] Her army could call upon a trained manpower of about 850,000. Of these, 180,000 were in the active forces, 200,000 in

[2] U. Kobayashi, War and Armament Taxes of Japan, New York, 1923, pp. 23ff; G. Ono, War and Armament Expenditures of Japan, New York, 1922, pp. 61–70, 142–144, 282–285; T. Shitei, Sensoshi Gaikan, Tokyo, 1943, pp. 426–427; Romanov, Ocherki, pp. 34–39.

[3] F.B. Maurice, "The Russo-Japanese War," The Cambridge Modern History, Cambridge, 1910, xii, 578; A.L. Sidorov, Russko-Iaponskaia, Voina, 1904–1905 gg., Moscow, 1939, p. 13; Kuropatkin, op.cit., i, 166; Aubert, Der Russisch-Japanische Krieg, 1904–1905, Berlin, 1909, 2 Vols. i, 12; G. Ogawa, Expenditures of the Russo-Japanese War, New York, 1923, pp. 28–29.

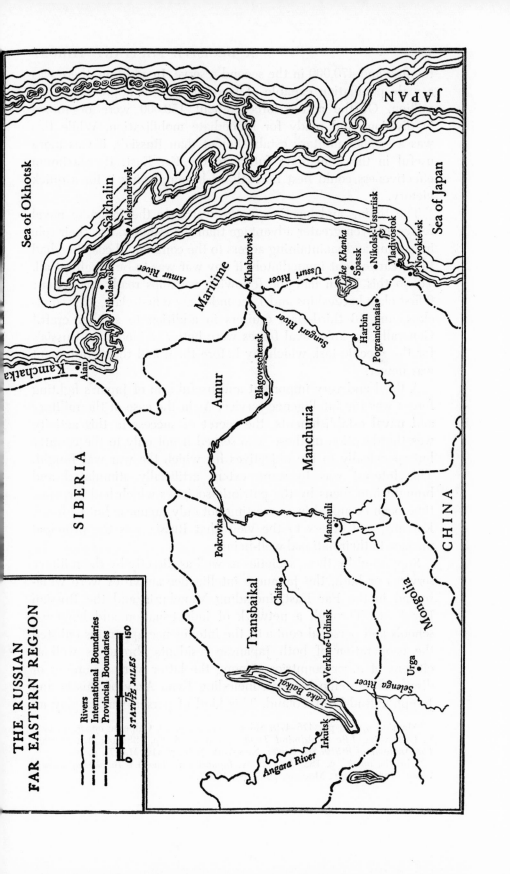

THE RUSSIAN
FAR EASTERN REGION

Rivers
International Boundaries
Provincial Boundaries

STATUTE MILES
0   75   150

Sea of Okhotsk

JAPAN

Sea of Japan

Kamchatka

Aian

Sakhalin

Aleksandrovsk

Nikolaevsk

Amur River

Maritime

Khabarovsk

Ussuri River

Lake Khanka

Spassk

Nikolsk-Ussuriisk

Vladivostok

Novokievsk

SIBERIA

Amur

Blagoveschensk

Sungari River

Harbin

Pogranichnaia

Manchuria

CHINA

Pokrovka

Manchuli

Transbaikal

Chita

Verkhné-Udinsk

Mongolia

Urga

Selenga River

Lake Baikal

Irkutsk

Angara River

the first and 470,000 in the second reserve. In addition, there was a male population capable of bearing arms of approximately 4 million. Of the active forces, about 150,000 were organized in divisions and ready for immediate mobilization. While this was a smaller military establishment than Russia's, it was more useful in the immediate future in the Far East. Its maximum effectiveness could best be realized by employing it for a quick victory.

The timing and location of the war gave the Japanese naval forces an even greater advantage than the military. For their role in gaining and maintaining access to the continental coastline had to be carried out immediately if any war was to be fought at all. To do this Japan had the following warships ready for action: 6 first-class battleships and 1 second-class; 6 first-class, 12 second-class, and 13 third-class cruisers in addition to smaller craft.[4] Generally, Japan's naval forces were better trained than Russia's for the specific task which lay before them and their equipment was newer.

A third and very important and useful arm of Japan's fighting forces was the intelligence service. As in the case of the military and naval establishments, the secret of success in this activity was the devotion of those who served it not only to the country but specifically to the objectives for which the war was fought. This interest was to some extent artificially stimulated and brought into focus by the patriotic societies which had for some time been occupied in converting not only Japanese but Chinese, Koreans, and others to the view that Russia was the principal menace to their national well-being.

Supported by these societies as well as directly by the military services or both, the Japanese intelligence activities were widespread in the Far East, including Manchuria and the Russian Far East.[5] Through a network of indoctrination and language schools and personal contacts, the intelligence apparatus enlisted the cooperation of both Japanese residents abroad as well as citizens of other countries. Among the latter were a number of disaffected foreign persons, including Evno Azev of Russia and Joseph Pilsudski of Poland. This kind of person was to play an

[4] Maurice, op.cit., pp. 478–479; Sidorov, op.cit., p. 13; Galperin, op.cit., p. 223; N. Ogasawara, Life of Admiral Togo, Tokyo, 1934, pp. 198–202; A.J. Marder, The Anatomy of British Sea Power, New York, 1940, p. 419; M.C.T., p. 16.

[5] Christie, op.cit., p. 182; A. Votinov, Iaponskii shpionazh v Russko-Iaponskuiu Voiny 1904–1905 gg., Moscow, 1939, pp. 10–57.

even more important part in the intelligence activities after the opening of the war.

Divided only by an often indistinct and even misleading line from those who contributed from their overt and unofficial observations, there were the active spies. These blanketed the areas of special interest in a variety of disguises and in uncounted numbers. Sometimes they were Japanese completely costumed as Chinese with appropriate queues; or they might be assigned as barbers or houseboys in private homes or even with the Russian army itself. One of these is strikingly portrayed in Aleksander Kuprin's "Captain Rybnikov." The Japanese hero, masquerading as a Russian officer, survived for a while the disconcerting experience of knowing that he was under suspicion only to disclose his identity by calling out "banzai" in his sleep.

Through the endeavors of these devoted investigators the Japanese government apparently faced the war with a far more accurate conception of their task than their enemy had. Through reports and photographs they had been taking the measure of their enemy for years before the war. General Fukushima Yasumasa, who had traveled through Siberia as a captain in 1893 and had become acquainted with Russia to some extent, was able to turn this understanding of the Russian people to account during the war as a troop commander at the original seige of Port Arthur. It is said that the initial naval strike at Port Arthur was able to use the thorough knowledge of the target gleaned from direct and recent reports of observers.

The years of careful probing had disclosed many of the weak spots in Russia's political, social, and economic structure. It was against these that the Japanese government directed an enormously expanded intelligence campaign during the war. Every endeavor was made, through revolutionaries and other dissatisfied groups, to reduce Russia's capacity to carry on the war and to undermine the government both at home and abroad.

If the program had been completely successful it would have incapacitated Russia for war by slowing down if not halting altogether railways and factory production of the country, reducing the morale of the fighting forces, and generally rendering ineffective Russia's military effort. Meanwhile, the program did not base its success entirely on these far-ranging objectives. It also provided throughout the war a steady flow of valuable information.

The chief person in this venturesome undertaking was Colonel Akashi Motojiro, the Japanese military attaché in St. Petersburg at the time of his appointment.[6] When the Japanese legation moved to Stockholm, Kurino, the minister, assigned Akizuki Satobu to carry on the regular diplomatic affairs there while he undertook the responsibility of coordinating intelligence operations in Stockholm, Berlin, and elsewhere. Meanwhile, Akashi received his orders from General Kodama Gentaro, the vice chief of general staff, to make his headquarters at Stockholm, near the Russian frontier, and to establish liaison with the disaffected groups inside and outside the country, reporting to him daily. Akashi was assisted by Lieutenant Colonel Enda and a staff and worked closely with Colonel Utsunomiya Taro in London.

The division of authority in intelligence activities appears in practice to have given the military representatives the leading role in trying to assist or even influence the revolutionaries. Komura stated clearly that while foreign office funds were available for espionage, they would not be used for the promotion of the revolutionary programs or internal disturbances.[7] The reason, he explained, was that the latter would not be approved by the emperors of Germany and Austria. Komura may also have been actuated by a reason which Ito gave in response to a question regarding this policy.[8] He stated that "a thorough-going revolution in Russia would be undesirable, for the Japanese would have no one with whom to negotiate peace."

Nevertheless, the spheres of civilian and military interest clearly overlapped to a considerable degree. The stated, as contrasted with the special, mission of the military intelligence officials, to discover the plans of the revolutionaries with respect to the war and to report on the Russian internal situation, was in fact shared by both the military and diplomatic representatives. The available reports would lead one to assume not only that the diplomatic officials played a major role in both these pursuits but that they also participated to a considerable extent in the liaison established with the revolutionaries. Furthermore, at least some of the military reports reached Tokyo through diplomatic channels.

[6] M. Akashi, "Rakka Ryusui," a manuscript in the Japanese Foreign office dated May 1938; T. Komori, *Akashi Motojiro*, Tokyo, 1928, 2 Vols., I, 151ff.
[7] Komura to Akizuki, No. 2, Jan. 7, No. 3, Jan. 26, 1905, *J.F.O.*
[8] Baelz, *op.cit.*, p. 340.

Akashi's organization included a broad network of direct and indirect associations. One of the principal persons through whom he operated appears to have been a student then in St. Petersburg, Nakada Shintaro, whose name seems to be given sometimes as Ueda Sentaro. He and his agents were posted in the cities of Russia and elsewhere in Europe. Through these Akashi reached an amazing number of persons then engaged in promoting liberal or radical programs aimed at the Russian monarchy. They included Prince P.A. Kropotkin, N.V. Chaikovsky, Catherine (Ekaterina Konstantinovna) Breshko-Breshkovskaia, V.I. Lenin, P.N. Miliukov, Maxim Gorky (A.M. Peshkov), and Father George (Georgii Apollonovich) Gapon of Russia; Konni Zilliacus and Kastoren of Finland; Roman Dmovski of Poland, and many others including an American named Morton.

The military mission was carried out through the gathering of information, the encouragement of programs which promised to create friction or subversion in Russia, and the support of such programs through the disbursing of funds and the supplying of arms.[9] While the available records establish the fact that funds and arms were contributed to these purposes, they do not provide any means of estimating the precise amounts in either case. They also establish the fact that the Japanese participated in the organization of the conference of opposition groups held in Paris from September 30 to October 8, 1904. Again, however, the precise kind and degree of participation is uncertain.

It is also difficult if not impossible to document the most vital question of all—the actual degree of participation of the Japanese in the internal chaos which ensued in Russia. Edward Dillon, a close observer of the Russian scene whose sources were undisclosed, did not hesitate to give the Japanese activities a large share of the credit for the breakdown in Russia. He wrote:

"The strikes, the demonstrations, the subterranean agitation, the spread of revolutionary leaflets, and the brisk, illegal traffic between Finland and Russia, were in varying degrees evidences of Japanese propaganda . . ."

[9] Utsunomiya to Chief of General Staff (via Hayashi), No. 6, Apr. 14, No. 200, July 16, No. 202, July 18, No. 208, July 20, 1904, Akizuki to Komura, No. 94, Nov. 21, 1904 and No. 25, Mar. 3, 1905, Tachibana to Komura, July 31, 1905, J.F.O.; A. Bullard, The Russian Pendulum: Autocracy-Democracy-Bolshevism, New York, 1919, pp. 97–98; E.J. Dillon, The Eclipse of Russia, New York, 1918, pp. 184, 291–293.

Among the non-Russians of the Russian Empire, the Finns and Poles were very responsive to the Japanese invitation to help undermine Russia.[10] The Poles were divided into political parties which reflected varying approaches to the question of dealing with Russia and, consequently, differing opinions about cooperating with Japan. While the Socialists and Social Democrats both desired Russian defeat, the former seem to have participated more actively in helping to bring it about.

Soon after the start of the war, Dr. Witold Jodko, a member of the executive committee of the Socialist Party, presented to Minister Hayashi in London a plan for giving direct assistance to Japan against Russia. He suggested: the recruitment of a Polish legion from Polish exiles to fight beside the Japanese army; the distribution of revolutionary pamphlets among Polish soldiers who were said to make up a substantial proportion of the Russian armies in Manchuria; encouragement to Polish soldiers to desert to the Japanese; and the destruction of railways and railway bridges through Russia and Siberia. All but the first of these were officially acceptable to Japan.

While the entire outcome of this collaboration is not known, some of the steps taken indicate that a serious purpose lay behind the proposals.[11] A few days after the original exchange of notes, a declaration was handed to Hayashi which denounced the war and expressed the hope of a Japanese victory and which was said to have been circulated among Poles. In the summer of 1904, representatives of the Socialist Party, including Joseph Pilsudski, were sent to Tokyo to enlist cooperation for a revolt in Russian Poland. To counteract this, Roman Dmowski of the more conservative Democratic Party was also sent to Tokyo though he was not received by Komura.

Russia's preparation for war, however menacing it may have appeared from Tokyo, was neither as carefully planned, as consistently executed, nor as complete in its final form as that of Japan. This was in part because Russia lacked the incentive which impelled Japan. The scornful attitude many Russians felt was

---

[10] M.K. Dziewanowski, "The Revolution of 1905 in Poland," *Journal of Central European Affairs*, xii, No. 3, Oct., 1952, pp. 259ff; Hayashi to Komura, No. 103, Mar. 16, Komura to Hayashi, No. 194, Mar. 28, 1904, Makino to Komura, No. 52, Feb. 3, 1905, *J.F.O.*

[11] Dziewanowski, *op.cit.*, p. 260; Hayashi to Komura, No. 110, Mar. 21, No. 173, June 9, From Roman Dmowski, Tokyo, July 20, Chinda to Makino, July 21, 1904, *J.F.O.*

expressed by Colonel Artemiev, the editor of the Port Arthur *Novyi Krai*. He remarked that: "Japan is not a country that can give an ultimatum to Russia, and Russia should not receive an ultimatum from a country like Japan."[12] This attitude was especially widespread in St. Petersburg.

The deficiencies of Russian striking power in the Far East were also due in part to the greater technical problems she faced in matching Japan, the fact that they were not easily resolved in a short time, and the tremendous outlay of money they required. In addition to the difficulties of defending Manchuria and Korea which Kuropatkin had frequently mentioned, there had also to be considered the tremendous distance to the center of trouble. Furthermore, it was impossible either to recruit a defense force locally in the Far East or to support it from there logistically.

There is reason to believe that, in spite of the expanded and far-flung Russian commitments, the defense ministries were not given adequate funds to correct these shortcomings. Several years after the war, with all the advantages of time and leisure to plan his answer carefully, Witte wrote a defense against Kuropatkin's charges which in this respect seems to support the general's assertions.[13] It leaves the distinct impression that the military requirements were satisfied on the basis of the finance minister's judgment in apportioning the budget rather than of an objective appraisal of the need.

If this was the case, it finds some justification in the nature of the problem Russia faced. There was first of all the vast distance between the European and Far Eastern centers of Russia as well as a complete absence of guidelines by which to form a policy to suit the new and changing situation. To make this worse, there was an almost unbelievable ignorance of Far Eastern developments and their significance. Even Witte, who was the driving force in the Far Eastern adventure, was a stranger to the area until 1902. These facts give some meaning to Gippius' early endeavor to interpret the Far Eastern events. He wrote:

"If we have been able to maintain ourselves on the shores of the Pacific Ocean, it is only because our own weakness there is matched by the weakness of our neighbors.

[12] McCormick, *op.cit.*, i, 45–46.
[13] Witte, *Vynuzhdenniia*, pp. 9–15.

"The rapid conversion of Japan into a strong military state similar to the contemporary great powers disturbed in the Far East the longstanding equilibrium of weakness which was so fortunate for us, and placed before us after the Sino-Japanese war the difficult problem: how to restore the lost equilibrium?"[14]

There was, nevertheless, no lack of direct appraisals of the situation and of the needs it engendered. Soon after the Sino-Japanese war, the governor general of the Maritime region, Lieutenant General S. M. Dukhovskoy, analyzed the situation and suggested appropriate action. He wrote:

"Scarcely thirty years have passed since the opening of the Suez Canal, yet the Pacific shores have already been transformed from an unknown and legendary land into a vital international arena. Before the eyes of a single living generation there have been strengthened and developed: Western Canada, California, Japan, the French colonies and other nations, and the vast trade interests of England and Germany. As a consequence of the Sino-Japanese war, and with the construction of the Siberian railway, the position occupied by Russia has further stimulated the development of the life of that region."[15]

After this candid appraisal of the situation, he indicated the steps Russia should take to meet the new challenges, particularly those arising from the growth of Japanese power and the competition of Britain, France, and Germany. He felt that Russia needed to promote colonization and to build new railways, one along the Amur River to Vladivostok supplementing the Chinese Eastern Railway and one connecting the latter with the Gulf of Chihli through South Manchuria. Although the Amur line was recommended because the Chinese Eastern crossed foreign soil, he still hoped that the control of Manchuria would be an eventual objective of Russian policy. To meet the situation in the coming years, he recommended increases in both army and navy in the Far East.

In the same year, 1896, the Grand Duke Aleksander Mikhailovich, the chairman of the Volunteer Fleet and a strong opponent of Witte, supported the demand for increased military preparedness. In a report, he outlined the new situation and included a

[14] Gippius, op.cit., p. 20.
[15] Report, Jan. 23, 1896, K.A., LII, 85.

specific program of rearmament to meet it.[16] In particular, he took note of the new ten-year rearmament program being developed in Japan and urged that Russia meet the challenge. His interests being specifically in the navy, his plan called for an increase in the naval establishment during the next ten years corresponding to that of Japan.

Though Russia did, in fact, prepare in some ways for the coming ordeal, her measures were inadequate. And, above all, these efforts failed to live up to the promise of these early proposals. Even though the issues were thoroughly rehearsed in the discussions of 1903, by contrast with Japan, Russia still failed to bring her military and political commitments into focus and to concentrate her strength where Far Eastern events clearly demanded. She seemed unable to rethink her traditional military requirements in the light of a new, distant, and menaced frontier. Consequently, the Russians appeared, paradoxically, to be less sensitive to the new situation than was even France or Germany.

While Japan's basic logistic problems were at all times dependent upon her navy, Russia had to look to both the navy and the railways. Though her navy was numerically much larger than Japan's, important sectors of it were antiquated and all of it was divided and dispersed. The Baltic fleet had its own regional mission and, in addition, was a long way from the Yellow Sea. The Black Sea fleet was unable, without risking British intervention, to pass through the Turkish strait.

Even in the Far East the fleet was dispersed and its facilities incompletely developed.[17] The main base at Port Arthur was 900 miles from the secondary base at Vladivostock. The main center itself had not been fully developed when the war broke out, lacking even the necessary docking and repair facilities which were available in this region only at the undefended commercial port of Dalny.

At the outbreak of war, Russia had in the Far East the following naval strength: 6 first-class battleships and 1 second-class battleship; 9 first-class and 2 second-class cruisers; as well as smaller craft. All of the battleships and the second-class cruisers and 4 of the first-class cruisers were at Port Arthur while 4 of the

[16] "Considerations about the necessity of strengthening the Russian fleet in the Pacific Ocean," Gippius, op.cit., pp. 43–47; F.R., p. 819.

[17] Maurice, op.cit., pp. 578–579; M.C.T., p. 16; Aubert, op.cit., I, 11; E.B. Potter, The United States and World Sea Power, Englewood Cliffs, 1955, p. 433; Malozemoff, op.cit., p. 245.

latter were at Vladivostock and 1 at Chemulpo. It was intended that the concentration at Port Arthur would block the Japanese attempt to gain control of the sea while the cruisers at Vladivostok would raid shipping along the Japanese coast. In preparing and timing the first strike it was undoubtedly true that the Japanese took into consideration the new battleship and the 2 first-class cruisers then in Red Sea waters on their way to reenforce the Russian fleet.

The Russian army in Manchuria relied for support mainly on the railway which extended for over 5000 miles from Moscow to Port Arthur. It is, therefore, a factor of the greatest military significance that this railway was then unfinished and single-tracked, and that its services were still inefficiently organized. The comparison has been made with the circumstances of the Crimean war period when Russia's overland transportation was extremely poor while her enemy was able to reenforce and supply an expeditionary force more easily by sea than Russia could supply her own forces. The parallel is also valid in respect to the impact of this situation on the final outcome. Kuropatkin's own appraisal was that:

"Next to the absence of a Russian fleet, the most important factor to assist the Japanese in their offensive strategy and to impede us was the condition of the Siberian and Chinese Eastern Railways."[18]

One of the principal difficulties was that at the time the war broke out the section of the railway which skirted Lake Baikal had not been completed. This meant that troops and supplies had to be conveyed across the lake when this was possible. The passage was made by ferry during the most favorable season, the steamers even acting as ice-breakers in the early stages of the formation of the ice cover.

The war broke out a few days after the end of the sailing season, a further tribute to the careful Japanese planning. For the next few weeks the army in Manchuria could only be reenforced by the slow and tortuous process of marching the troops across the ice. They were brought by train to Baikal station on the

[18] Maurice, op.cit., p. 578; Kuropatkin, op.cit., I, 242–268 passim; Kokovtsov, op.cit., pp. 24–25; E.A. Pratt, The Rise of Rail-Power in War and Conquest, 1833–1914, London, 1915, pp., 260–272; M.C.R., Nov., 1904, p. 69, 135; Romanov, Ocherki, p. 241; A.I. Sorokin, Russko-Iaponskaia Voina, 1904–1905 gg., Moscow, 1956, p. 30.

western bank and marched 25 miles across to Tankhoi station on the other side, a small sledge being used to carry the gear for every 4 men. When the ice had reached a thickness of 4 and one-half inches, tracks could be laid on exceptionally long sleepers to begin a more rapid rate of transport. This would be possible by middle or late March.

By September 25, 1904, the sector around Lake Baikal was finally completed. Instead of building this section farther south where the terrain was easier, it had been projected through the most rugged area, thus increasing the time and expense and requiring the construction of 41 tunnels. Meanwhile, the con-centration of forces in Manchuria, which in the more favorable season before the war had been proceding at the rate of about 7,000 men each month, had first been slowed to a trickle and then had been carried on at a very slow rate. The frustrating effect of this delay at a time when Russia was already suffering defeat is easy to imagine.

The war also underscored the technical shortcomings of the railway for military purposes. The most glaring difficulty was that the line was single-tracked and even lacked enough sidings to permit passing and thus increase the traffic. The repair facilities were poorly equipped for the increased demand. The fuel supply in the Far East was generally inadequate. Because of the depth to which the rivers were frozen and the high salt content of some of them, even water supply was difficult. In Manchuria, the number of spurs from the mainline was inadequate for military purposes. About 250 miles of these had to be built, most of them apparently after March 1905.

At the outbreak of war, Russia had east of Lake Baikal an estimated 135,000 troops, significantly less than in October 1900.[19] As in the case of the navy, the military forces were scattered, in part because of the traditional points to which they were as-signed. Their placement was also a consequence of the fact that, in contrast to her political program, Russia's military strategy was defensive and, therefore, had to anticipate the many possible variations in the enemy's plan of attack.

By April when the first significant land battle was taking shape, the distribution of Russia's major units was about as follows:

[19] Malozemoff, op.cit., p. 166; Maurice, op.cit., pp. 577–578, 583; Galperin, op.cit., p. 223; Sorokin, op.cit., p. 20; M.C.T., p. 34; Bompard to Delcasse, Aug. 1, 1903, D.D.F., III, 508.

45,000 were scattered along the railways with a concentration around Liaoyang under the direct command of General Kuropatkin; 19,000 were in and around Port Arthur under the command of Lieutenant General Stessel; 16,000 around Vladivostok under Lieutenant General Linievich; and 19,000 along the southern coast of Manchuria and the Korean frontier under Lieutenant General M.I. Zasulich.

The supreme command of the Russian armed forces in the Far East was held by three officers through the 19 months of the war.[20] The first was Admiral Alekseiev, the viceroy, whose tenure as commander in chief lasted until the end of the first major phase of the war, in October 1904. Soon after the opening of the war as the Japanese concentrated at Port Arthur, he moved his headquarters from the naval base to Mukden.

General Kuropatkin, the minister of war, was at first the commander-in-chief of the army in the Far East, a position to which he was appointed in late February. In October he succeeded Alekseiev as the commander in chief of all Far Eastern operations. He continued in this position until March 1905 when he, in turn, was replaced by Lieutenant General Linievich. At about the same time that Kuropatkin was selected as army commander, Vice Admiral S.O. Makarov was appointed commander in chief of the naval forces to replace Vice Admiral O.A. Stark under whom the navy had suffered frustrating reverses.

The war was opened by an attack of the Japanese Combined Fleet which departed from the naval base at Sasebo on February 6, 1904 under the command of Vice Admiral Togo Heihachiro.[21] Before leaving, he called his commanders together on his flagship, the "Mikasa," and read them the Imperial Order which stated their mission: "The Combined Fleet, according to the plan already made, intends to destroy the Russian Pacific Fleet and command the sea."

In the late afternoon of February 7, at a point off the southwestern coast of Korea, the signal was given for the Fourth Division to separate from the fleet and to head for Chemulpo. The division was under the command of Rear Admiral Uriu Sotokichi and convoyed the transports bearing units of what would

[20] Witte, op.cit., I, 262–266; Sidorov, op.cit., pp. 18–20; K.A., XLI-XLII, 168, 173.
[21] K.G., I, 379–380; K. Togo, The Naval Battles of the Russo-Japanese War, Tokyo, 1907, pp. 1ff; N. Ogasawara, op.cit., pp. 189–218; M. Ito, Kokubo Shi, Tokyo, 1941, pp. 229–240; Sorokin, op.cit., pp. 67–76; Maurice, op.cit., pp. 580–581.

become the First Army under General Kuroki Tamemoto. The next afternoon it was met outside the harbor by the Russian gunboat "Koreets" which acquired the distinction of starting the war in the formal sense when it opened fire on some of Uriu's scouts. With very little opposition, the troops were landed, Seoul was taken and the forces moved northward toward the Yalu where the first major land engagement was to take place.

The main fleet proceeded toward Port Arthur where its advance units began to arrive late in the night of February 8. The next morning the first of a series of successful attacks on Port Arthur was opened, the signal flags announcing to the fleet the famous message: "Victory or defeat depend upon this battle, you will do your utmost."

Within the next few weeks part of the Russian fleet was severely damaged and the rest contained. After the third unsuccessful naval encounter, the Russian commander, Vice Admiral Stark, was replaced by Vice Admiral Makarov. In mid-April, however, the Russians suffered a further crippling blow when this capable and respected officer sank with over 600 men aboard the battleship "Petropavlovsk" after it had been struck by a mine. He was succeeded in turn by Vice Admiral N.I. Skrydlov, former commander of the Black Sea fleet.

In spite of their own losses, the Japanese had gained the vital command of the sea. This enabled them to proceed with the establishment of the blockade of Port Arthur and the landing of forces in Manchuria. Using Chinampo in Korea as a point of rendezvous, they carried out landing operations by May 5 in the northern part of the Kuantung peninsula.

By landing their forces only 60 miles from Port Arthur, the Japanese were able to speed up their preparations for the next phase of the war, the seige of the naval base itself. Starting with units of the Second Army to be commanded by General Oku Yasukata, they went on to build up the Third Army under General Nogi Maresuke and the Fourth Army under General Nozu Michitsura. By June a united command in Manchuria was established with Field Marshal Oyama Iwao as commander in chief and General Kodama as chief of staff.

The first major land engagement of the war was fought at the Yalu.[22] The First Army under General Kuroki, ultimately sup-

[22] Maurice, op.cit., p. 583–585; F. Palmer, With Kuroki in Manchuria, New York, 1906, pp. 45–100; E. von Tettau, Achtzehn Monate mit Russlands Heeren in der Mandschurei, 2 Vols., Berlin, 1907, I, 85–105.

plemented with additional units to give it a strength of over 40,000 men, was concentrated on the left bank of the river near Uiju. The first units arrived in early April and the preparations for action began immediately. On the other side, the forces of General Zasulich, while dispersed over a considerable area, were concentrated around Antung, across from Uiju and somewhat southward. According to General Kuropatkin's plan, this force was intended merely to delay Kuroki's progress into Manchuria but was not to engage in any decisive actions.

While Kuroki's force was more than twice the size of his opponent's, he faced the problem of crossing the river. He solved this by keeping his adversary busy in the south while he sent his forces across from a point north of Uiju. By April 30 this operation had been completed and the First Army was ready to face the Russian force on the Manchurian side. The engagement ensued at Kuliencheng on May 1. It was followed 5 days later by the occupation of the Russian headquarters at Fenghuangcheng.

The Yalu victory was the first great achievement of the Japanese armies. Its most obvious consequence was the exclusion of Russia from Korea. At the same time, it brought into being precisely the situation which the Yalu plans associated with Bezobrazov were devised to obviate—the penetration of Japan into Manchuria. Instead of either retreating as he had been ordered to do and thereby prolonging his usefulness as a shield for Russian communications between Port Arthur and Mukden, or of committing his whole force against Kuroki, Zasulich did neither. He threw in only part of his force, lost the gamble and succeeded only in exposing the left flank of the Russian army concentrated at Liaoyang. When the Japanese followed this up within a few days by landing forces both at Takushan near the Korean frontier and at Port Arthur, the initiative was completely in their hands and the vacillating Russian strategy was exposed.

The moral victory and defeat and its impact on the morale of both sides was a factor of the greatest significance in the long run. As for the Japanese side, their successful crossing of the Yalu, retracing the footsteps their predecessors had followed in the frustrated victories of a decade before, was comparable in emotional impact only to the landing at Port Arthur a few days later. For these steps were taken on the retreating heels of the Russians, representatives of the might of one of the great world powers. As they moved forward, the Japanese soldiers are said to have sung:

"Comrades, can we live forgetting Comrades—gallant comrades —slain Ten years since? Oh! Powers ancestral, Did your life blood flow in vain? There must be some end to evil even in our life's short span; Now is the hour—for we are marching. Down with Russia! On, Japan!"[23]

The significance of the Yalu victory was not missed in Europe, the nerve center of world power, where the balance of power was at all times the subject of an earnest and penetrating scrutiny. Russian confidence must have been severely shaken by the article in the *Allgemeine Zeitung* which stressed the moral impact of the battle in these words:

"For the first time regiments of the Island Empire have measured themselves in a serious battle with a European army and have decorated their colors with bloody laurels . . . . The first battles of a campaign have an extraordinary moral importance which considerably exceeds the tactical advantage."[24]

The article compared the effect of this on Japan with the effect on Germany of the French defeat at Weissenburg in 1870.

With the victory on the Yalu and the landing of Japanese forces on the Manchurian coast, including the Kuantung Peninsula, the Japanese began the preparations for the next step—the isolation of Port Arthur. By this time the advantages and shortcomings of the opposing forces had become effectively apparent. The areas of Japanese superiority which appeared to be significant were: their ability to conceal from the Russians initially the debarkation points of their forces and, after their landing, their number and distribution; and the Japanese retention of the initiative to the extent that, in many cases, they were able to conceal completely even their immediate intentions.

On the other hand, the fundamental disagreements between Admiral Alekseiev and General Kuropatkin over major questions of strategy did nothing to bridge the gap in efficiency between the two forces. Instead, it wasted precious time, kept the Russians uncertain and off guard and blunted the Russian drive in the vital early stages of the war.

[23] I.S.M. Hamilton, *A Staff Officer's Scrap Book during the Russo-Japanese War*, 2 Vols., London, 1906, I, 170.
[24] M. Pavlovich, "Vneshniaia Politikai Russko-Iaponskaia Voina," L. Martov, etc., *Obshchestvennoe Dvizhenie v Rossii v Nachale XXgo Veka*, 4 Vols., St. Petersburg, 1910, II, 20; Inouye to Komura, No. 188, May 8, 1904, *J.F.O.*

The divergent views on strategy, in effect, projected into the conduct of the war the pre-existing attitudes toward Russia's Far Eastern problem. The views of Witte and Bezobrazov, each in his own way unmindful or disregardful of the real significance of Japan's determination, were focused in the strategy of Admiral Alekseiev, the commander in chief. He insisted that Japan be challenged from the first and at every possible point.

Kuropatkin, on the other hand, based his strategy on his own earlier estimate of the capacity of Russia, in the early stages of the war, to make an effective showing. His plan was to conserve Russian strength initially, and to carry out an offensive only after Russia had reenforced herself and prepared carefully. Meanwhile, the defeats to which the Russian soldier was subjected, in part because of indecision and indecisiveness, helped to provide fertile ground for the subversive and revolutionary propaganda which soon followed.

The second major blow to the Russian forces in Manchuria, the maneuver preparatory to the isolation of Port Arthur, came on May 5, the day before the Japanese army on the Yalu had occupied Fenghuangcheng. On that day the forces of General Oku's Second Army reached the northern coast of the Kuantung peninsula. With the close cooperation of the naval forces, the troops landed unopposed and by the 14th had effectively isolated Port Arthur.

Control of the approaches to the naval base was secured by the fighting which began on May 26 around Nanshan and ended 3 days later with the occupation of the port of Dalny. Although the cost to the Japanese forces was considerable, including the loss of two battleships, the results were impressive. Control of the region was secured and the seige, under General Nogi and the Third Army, could begin.

As the weeks passed without any decisive outcome, the grim prospects of the showdown became apparent. By August the Russians were becoming desperately concerned about their considerable naval power which lay bottled up and exposed to the artillery General Nogi was moving up for the seige. On the 10th, with the permission of their Emperor, they tried to escape with 6 battleships, 4 cruisers, and other craft. Some of these escaped to foreign ports, others were destroyed, but most of the large ships were driven back into the naval base. By August 20 Nogi's artillery was ready and the first general assault began.

The protracted seige at Port Arthur presented equally dangerous possibilities for Japan. At Liaoyang to the north General Kuropatkin had, by August, been concentrating and supplementing his main forces for months. His intention of going to the relief of the Russian forces at Port Arthur had already been demonstrated by the sending of Lieutenant General G.K. Stackelberg with some 26,000 men. This attempt had been blocked by General Oku who interposed a larger force and defeated General Stackelberg in mid-June at Telissu.

Meanwhile, Kuropatkin's forces at Liaoyang had continued to increase and by August the strength of the forces under his immediate command had passed 140,000 with more continuing to arrive. This meant that, even after assembling the major units of the 3 armies then available to him, Field Marshal Oyama was already outnumbered. Without waiting any longer and running the risk of losing the initiative and perhaps more, Oyama decided to strike.

The battle around Liaoyang was launched on August 24. It was opened by an attack on the right from Kuroki's First Army. The 12-day battle which followed was in several ways a Japanese victory though the outcome was indecisive. On the one hand, the Japanese, already outnumbered, suffered several thousand more casualties than the Russians. On the other hand, though the Russians retired first, they did so in good order and carried out their withdrawal just before the Japanese were considering the same thing.

The difference between the two antagonists which was most indicative of the future course of the war was the superiority of the Japanese in their conduct of the battle. Even at times when Russia's numerical superiority should have counted, the opportunity was lost. An observer with the Japanese armies noted on September 4, the day the Russian retirement was clearly in progress:

"Beyond all doubt the Russians have had twelve or thirteen divisions available to crush us had they felt fully determined to do so. But they have shown a great deal of vacillation, and until now our good luck has certainly been almost past belief."[25]

The battle at Shaho to the north where Kuropatkin had halted his withdrawal from Liaoyang was hardly more than a con-

[25] Hamilton, op.cit., II, 123.

tinuation of the battle of Liaoyang and, at the same time, a repetition of its major characteristics. The discrepancy in the conduct of the war was even more vividly displayed. For Kuropatkin had received reenforcements since the action at Liaoyang and more decisively outnumbered Oyama's forces than before. It was perhaps a consequence of his overreliance on superior numbers that he launched his first attack on October 4. It lost its momentum almost immediately, however, and 10 days later the front was once more relatively quiet.

The battles at Liaoyang and Shaho seem to have inspired among the Russians genuine hopes of future victory.[26] By the time operations in this area were resumed 5 months later, however, the relations between these powers and with the other powers had been altered by events in the West and at Port Arthur.

[26] W. Weressajew, *Meine Erlebnisse im Russisch-Japanischen Krieg,* Stuttgart, 1909, pp. 130–131.

9. Japan's Wartime Diplomacy

THE INTENSIVE Japanese military drive in Korea and Manchuria was accompanied by an equally determined diplomatic campaign, the objectives being to support the military effort and to insure the maximum political rewards. Since the success of the diplomatic campaign depended upon the fortunes of war, this offensive was focused on three stages of achievement.

The first stage was embodied in a plan to provide the conditions which could insure a military victory and its success was dependent upon the continued support of the United States and Great Britain. In a positive sense, one of these interested nations might be relied upon to provide the means of making a timely exit from the war in case the military effort should fail. Negatively, these two nations might be able to prevent the rise of a hostile coalition aimed at mediating the struggle to the detriment of Japan. Hopefully, these nations might also provide the financial support the war would require.

The second stage in Japan's diplomatic strategy would seek to guarantee the political objectives for which she had gone to war. The need to preserve a balance of power and so prevent one single nation from gaining a preponderance of interests, had in recent years given Far Eastern international relations a collective aspect. Consequently, Japan faced a threefold task with respect to the other powers: to preserve carefully the image of herself as the defender of foreign rights and interests in China; to portray her demands for compensation as no more than just rewards for defending these rights; and to maintain the fiction inherited from Russia that she was acting in defense of Chinese sovereignty.

As a third objective, Japan sought to create a new image of herself as a great power and a leading member of the world family of nations since this might entitle her to spoils of war over and above the modest prewar demands she had made of Russia. The best guarantee for success in such a program of aggrandizement was to achieve it as covertly as possible; premature disclosure of such a plan might only serve to bring about the final partition of China and close the door to future aggrandizement. The best rationalization for such a program would be that it was necessary for her national security.

The first measure taken to insure the continuity, under the

stresses of war, of good relations with Great Britain and the United States was the sending of two distinguished statesmen to these countries.[1] On the evening of February 4, 1904, a few minutes after he had left the Imperial conference where the decision had been made to go to war, Ito Hirobumi, president of the Privy Council, invited Baron Kaneko Kentaro to his residence to inform him of the decisions of the conference. Upon Kaneko's arrival, Ito told him that it had been concluded that Japan's objectives could not be achieved by peaceful means and that, consequently, the decision had been made that they must be achieved by war. For reasons closely associated with this decision, the conference had determined to send Baron Suematsu Kencho to Great Britain and Baron Kaneko to the United States.

Ito prefaced his remarks about Kaneko's specific mission with some general observations about the precedents and problems it suggested. Among them he noted the assistance Russia had given the United States during the civil war. He also pointed out that the present Russian ambassador to the United States, Count Cassini, had been associated with Russia's policy in China during 1894–1895 and specifically with the project which had forced Japan to retrocede to China the Kuantung Peninsula. Consequently a determined anti-Japanese attitude had to be expected from him. Ito also reminded Kaneko of the considerable American business interests in Russia as well as the intermarriages linking prominent Russian and American families, and advised careful observation and counteraction of these influences if necessary.

Kaneko's mission was first and foremost to combat all obstacles to the maintenance of American goodwill. In the first place, he was instructed to emphasize that the war had come in spite of all Japan's endeavors to avoid it until it was forced upon her by Russia. Secondly, he was to explain the "yellow peril" problem to the American people since it was foreseen that Russia would make use of this idea to the detriment of Japan. It must be made clear that Japan intended to play no part in emphasizing the racial division of mankind and had taken the positive precaution of advising China to observe a neutral attitude, thus hoping to avoid all misleading appearances of a coordinated Sino-Japanese plan aimed at the West. Ito also specified the direct relationship of Kaneko's mission to Japan's strategic war plans; undoubtedly

[1] K. Kaneko, *Beikoku;* K. Kaneko, *Nichiro;* K. Kaneko, *Nichro Seneki Hiroku,* Tokyo, 1930, pp. 1–10.

reflecting a view just expressed at the Imperial conference, he disclosed apprehension that the war might be difficult to terminate unless some country offered to mediate. As allies of the belligerents, he felt that Great Britain and France were not qualified for this role; Germany also was disqualified due to her unfortunate attitude toward Japan and the suspicion she had helped provoke war.

The United States appeared to be the only candidate for a mediatory role. Indeed, President Theodore Roosevelt, Ito felt, did occupy an impartial position between the belligerents and was well qualified to take measures toward the restoration of peace. Since Kaneko was an old acquaintance of the President's, both being Harvard alumnae, who knew America well, he would be able to make an appeal to the sympathies of the American people; his role in Japan's larger strategy was clear. Once the military and political objectives had been achieved, Japan would look to American good offices if necessary to extricate her from the war.

The mission of these special envoys may be further elucidated by noting their relationship to Viscount Ito and recalling the latter's imposing stature as well as the fact that he had long been identified with the opposition to the Katsura policies. Both Suematsu and Kaneko were closely identified with Ito, having been members of his cabinet and of the political party he had sponsored, the Seiyukai. Furthermore, Suematsu was Ito's son-in-law while Kaneko had been a member both of the Iwakura mission to the United States in 1872 and of the constitutional commission over which Ito had presided. Both men may have been specifically selected to serve as Ito's representatives, either to bolster his independent role or to lend unity to the national effort, or both.

Baron Kaneko's own version of his relations with President Roosevelt, a record of which was always transmitted to Baron Komura in Tokyo, gives the impression that they were very cordial and sympathetic. The first meeting was in every way typical; it took place at the White House at noon on March 26, 1904 and though ten or more persons were waiting, as soon as President Roosevelt received his card, he came right out and ushered him into his office and told Kaneko he had been awaiting his visit.

On the occasion of this first visit and the many which followed,

Roosevelt appeared to be frankly and sincerely committed to the justice of Japan's cause and to its ultimate triumph in the test of battle. He displayed a considerable knowledge of Japan and stated that the courageous course she had followed during recent years had aroused his complete admiration. Japan's performance as a rising power also inspired confidence in the President that she was suited to be the cultural and political leader in Eastern Asia and he heartily approved her assumption of this role.

Kaneko and Roosevelt, sometimes with Japanese Minister Takahira present, often discussed books or articles of mutual interest. Indeed on his first visit, Kaneko presented Roosevelt with a copy of an article he had published a year before entitled: "Japan and the United States: A Proposed Economic Alliance." At another meeting Roosevelt mentioned a book by Eastlake and Yamada dealing with the Sino-Japanese war from which he had learned about the organization and performance of the Japanese army.[2]

It was at Kaneko's suggestion that the President read the renowned study of the code of the warrior class, *Bushido*, by Nitobe Inazo; he later told Kaneko that he had ordered thirty copies for distribution among interested friends and felt the book had given him a new insight into the moral character of the Japanese people. It was the bold and undaunted yet refined, controlled, and directed spirit of the Japanese people which was the touchstone of his admiration for them. Unquestionably, it was also the source of his apprehension as to what their rise as a modern nation might portend for the United States.

In his discussions with President Roosevelt, and to some extent with Secretary Hay as well, Kaneko sought to clarify the issues which Ito had stressed. The discussions included: the "Yellow Peril" problem; the question of a victorious Japan's respect for western rights in China; the attitude of the European powers toward a victorious Japan; the prospects for ending the war; and the consideration of peace terms. In the discussion of these issues President Roosevelt demonstrated his strong partisanship toward Japan as well as his frank acceptance of a major role in the Far East for a victorious Japan.

Through their exchanges of views on these topics, Kaneko and Roosevelt established the cordial realtionship necessary for discussing the issues of crucial importance to each. For, while Kaneko

[2] F.W. Eastlake and Y. Yamada, *Heroic Japan; A History of the War Between China and Japan,* London, 1897.

wanted for Japan the assured support necessary to achieve the objectives of the war as well as a timely and advantageous exit from the war Roosevelt had to be as certain as possible that this would not be done to the detriment of American interests. Consequently, the President used every occasion to sow the seeds of a good relationship with a nation whose future he felt would be so important to the United States and left Kaneko with a clear concept of what the Far Eastern situation required to satisfy American interests.

The Far Eastern order which President Roosevelt envisioned was a segment of a more general conception of international relations.[3] He conceded economic factors a significant role in human affairs, but not the principal role. This was reserved for political factors which accounted for the fundamental contours of the world order. Such peace as the world enjoyed was made possible by a very precarious political equilibrium which was dependent for its stability on a multitude of forces constantly being exerted upon it.

In the early years of the 20th century, Roosevelt felt that the world balance of power was in the process of shifting: British influence, friendly to the United States, was waning while Russian influence, unfriendly to the United States, was rising. Russia, because of her size, location, and potential power, loomed as a factor of the greatest importance for the future and Roosevelt scarcely needed Mahan's assistance to see in this troubled situation a conflict of sea power against land power. Nor did he need any prompting to observe world developments with the hope of discovering some means of redressing the balance in a way favorable to the preservation of a stable world order in which the United States could live and prosper. Since the President saw the balance of power as the only available way of preserving peace, he sought every means of maintaining the balance. One of these was military preparedness and, particularly for the United States, a strong navy. Secondly, he promoted arbitration and other means of settling disputes. Finally,

[3] H.K. Beale, *Theodore Roosevelt and the Rise of America to World Power*, Baltimore, 1956, pp. 38, 99–100, 256–257, 276, 312, 336, 354, 393, 404, 407, 449–455; R. Hofstader, *Social Darwinism in American Thought (1860–1915)*. Philadelphia, 1945, 156; L.J. Hall, "A Partnership in Peacemaking: Theodore Roosevelt and Wilhelm II," *Pacific Historical Review*, xiii, 4, Dec. 1944, p. 391; G.E. Mowry, *The Era of Theodore Roosevelt, 1900–1912*, New York, 1958, pp. 181–185; J.M. Blum, *The Republican Roosevelt*, Cambridge, 1954, pp. 134–136.

he tried to use every opportunity to anticipate difficulties by bringing nations together and removing distrust that might lead to war. In 1905 he found himself the mediator in two major disputes, Morocco and the Far East.

In the Far East, with the help of Admiral Mahan, Brooks Adams, and W.W. Rockhill, Roosevelt saw China as the focal point of international rivalries.[4] Because of China's incapacity to control her own destiny, he assumed that competition for the domination of her territory would continue to constitute an unstable factor in Far Eastern politics. Should this operate to place too much control in the hands of any one of the contenders, it would have a profound effect on the balance of power both in the Far East and the world in general.

It was, therefore, of the greatest significance that should the partition of China occur, a proper balance should be observed. Among the guidelines for such an eventuality, he found the following to be important: a victory for Japan sufficient to balance Russia's existing advantage in Eastern Asia; no overwhelming victory for either party lest neither be in a position to constitute a check on the other; a preference for the mutual exhaustion of both belligerents, thereby reducing to the minimum the danger to the interests of the other powers; the avoidance of any close rapprochement of the belligerents, particularly in the form of a Russo-Japanese understanding, lest such a bloc endanger the interests of other powers. It is an interesting commentary on the similarity of American and German interests in this last point that in Sternberg's report on Roosevelt's feeling about a Russo-Japanese understanding the German Emperor wrote, "bravo!"

President Roosevelt's views of the Russians characteristically changed as they moved into the orbit of his established outlook on Far Eastern affairs. Before 1900 his feelings toward them ranged from disregard to a positive approval of them as bearers of civilization to the Asian people of the empire. After that time he began to see them in an increasingly less favorable light as they appeared to menace the more important civilizing influence of British-American interests. When the Russians refused to honor

---

[4] Beale, op.cit., p. 274; Varg, op.cit., p. 57; Mowry, op.cit., pp. 182–185; D.C. Baker, "Germany and the Far East, 1895–1908," Ph.D. dissertation, Berkeley, 1927, pp. 278–281; Bülow to Emperor, Aug. 31 and Dec. 24, 1904, Sternberg to Foreign Office, Feb. 3, 1905, G.P., xix-2, 535–540, 547–551, 567–568; Roosevelt to Spring Rice, Dec. 27, 1904, E.E. Morison and J.M. Blum, The Letters of Theodore Roosevelt, 8 Vols., Cambridge, 1951–1954, iv, 1089.

their pledge to withdraw their troops from Manchuria, his opposition to them rose sharply and he remained committed against them throughout the war.

Roosevelt's opinion of the Russians reflected some of the views then current about the hierarchical grouping of mankind by race and culture with the Caucasian Anglo-Saxon at the top. For Roosevelt this was a general guide for understanding little-known people rather than a rigid formula and he favored the Russians as long as he could see them as bearers of western culture. But when they came into conflict with Anglo-American interests and values, his favorable view of them changed. He wrote in March, 1904:

"There is much about the Russians which I admire, and I believe in the future of the Slavs if they can only take the right turn. But I do not believe in the future of any race while it is under a crushing despotism."[5]

Roosevelt also felt, and Secretary Hay agreed with him, that the Russians were untrustworthy and this produced a very unfortunate relationship in view of his future role as peace-maker. The Russian ambassador, Count Cassini, reported evidences of these poor relations to St. Petersburg. Secretary Hay expressed this view in his diary on March 1, 1904:

"Cassini came at three and stayed till five. His object was to hand me a memorandum from Russia which, like everything from that country has 'false bottom.' He talked for an hour about American unfriendliness. I told him that the Japs were cleverer—they talked of our friendliness."[6]

Roosevelt also showed his ability to let facts override an accepted article of belief where racial theories were concerned:[7] he had read with interest the racial concepts popular in his day and had been a student of John Burgess at Columbia. He had traced the conquest of the white man over the Indian in his *Winning of the West*. Starting with the flattering logic of Anglo-Saxon superiority found in the primitive German forests, he had pointed out the culmination of this grand tradition in the conquest of the American continent. Roosevelt's original view of the Japanese

[5] Roosevelt to Spring Rice, Mar. 19, 1904, Gwynn, *op.cit.*, I, 397.
[6] Thayer, *op.cit.*, II, 374.
[7] Hofstader, *op.cit.*, pp. 149–153.

retained traces of these assumptions but he changed these views as he learned more about them. The qualities he found in the Japanese—courage, determination, loyalty, and others—aroused his admiration and he accepted them personally and as a nation. He even feared them for these very qualities. It is a tribute to his early education and to the broadening of his horizon that he looked back again to the German forests for an illustration of his new and expanded outlook. He wrote of the Japanese in June 1905:

"As for their having yellow skin, if we go back two thousand years we will find that to the Greek and the Roman the most dreaded and yet in a sense the most despised barbarian was the white-skinned, blue-eyed and red or yellow-haired barbarian of the North—the men from whom you and I in a large part derive our blood."[8]

The immediate significance of the Japanese victory to President Roosevelt lay in its bearing on the security of American interests in the Pacific area. American commerce in the Far East as well as possession of the Philippines, were at stake and almost certainly in danger and his solution was found in maintaining a strong navy and in cultivating the good will of Japan. It was with these needs in mind that he pleaded for a more reasonable attitude in dealing with the problem of Oriental immigration in California. He wrote to Senator Henry Cabot Lodge with reference to the new California legislation on the subject:

"These Pacific Coast people wish grossly to insult the Japanese and to keep out the Japanese immigrants on the ground that they are an immoral, degraded, and worthless race; and at the same time that they desire to do this for the Japanese and are already doing it for the Chinese they expect to be given advantages in Oriental markets; and with besotted folly are indifferent to building up the navy while provoking this formidable new power—a power jealous, sensitive and war-like, and which if irritated could at once take both the Philippines and Hawaii from us if she obtained the upper hand on the seas. . . ."[9]

During their informal sessions, Kaneko and Roosevelt discussed the implications of the expected Japanese victory and the outlines of a new role for Japan in the Far East; they faced realisti-

[8] Roosevelt to Schneder, June 19, 1905, Morison and Blum, *op.cit.*, IV, 1240.
[9] Roosevelt to Lodge, June 5, 1905, *ibid.*, IV, 1205.

cally the fact that a triumphant Japan would expect some of the spoils of victory, particularly in view of their frustrating loss of these in 1895. Roosevelt confided his own fears to friends that a victorious Japan might adopt an arrogant posture toward the other powers and that a hostile clash was by no means impossible. He wrote to Spring Rice in June 1904: "I am perfectly well aware that if they win out it may possibly mean a struggle between them and us in the future; but I hope and believe not . . ."[10]

It was in view of these misgivings, and perhaps also to obviate the necessity for Japan to seek support from Russia for realizing her aims, that Roosevelt made certain positive gestures toward recognizing Japan's new stature. Among these was his suggestion that Japan adopt a policy with respect to Asia similar to the Monroe Doctrine. He seems to have broached this idea for the first time in a conversation with Kaneko on July 7, 1905.[11] Roosevelt did not intend that this should be construed as approval for domination of Asia but had in mind, rather, that Japan would be left to exercise a constructive guidance over affairs in Asia, curbing when necessary the aggressions of other foreign powers and performing a leading role among Asian countries. Roosevelt's words were not forgotten. At a farewell luncheon on September 10, 1905, Kaneko recalled the conversation of two months before and said that he wished to bring this to the attention of his government. Roosevelt replied that he did not want this idea made public during his term of office since it would only invite suspicion among the powers. The idea became well-known in later years both through the press and through its use as a justification for Japan's expansion policy.[12] Ex-President Roosevelt referred to it in an article in the *Kansas City Star* on January 13, 1919 while Kaneko significantly discussed its origin in an article written in 1932.

In addition to the sending of Kaneko and Suematsu, Japan made other goodwill gestures during the war.[13] Prince Fushimi

---

[10] Roosevelt to Spring Rice, June 13, 1904, Gwynn, *op.cit.*, I, 419.

[11] Kaneko, *Beikoku*.

[12] G. Blakeslee, "The Japanese Monroe Doctrine," *Foreign Affairs*, XI, 4, July 1933, p. 672; R. Fujisawa, "Roosevelt and Manchuria," *Contemporary Japan*, I, 3, Dec. 1932, p. 363; K. Kaneko, "A 'Japanese Monroe Doctrine,' and Manchuria," *Contemporary Japan*, I,2, Sept. 1932, pp. 175–184.

[13] Baelz, *op.cit.*, p. 358; *Japan Times*, June 6, 1905; Takahira to Hay, Oct. 12, 1904, *U.S.F.R.*, 1904, p. 448; Inouye to Komura, Nos. 224 and 227, June 3, No. 228, June 5, 1904, *J.F.O.*; Japan. Imperial Japanese Commission to the Louisiana Purchase Exposition, *Japan in the Beginning of the 20th Century*, Tokyo, 1904.

Sadanaru, a member of the Imperial family, visited the United States. He conveyed a special message of goodwill and friendship from the Emperor to the President and he visited the Louisiana Purchase Exposition in St. Louis in 1904.

Prince and Princess Arisugawa, also members of the Imperial family, carried out a goodwill mission when they attended the wedding of the German crown prince to Princess Christina of Denmark and a good deal was said about the political significance of this visit in both the Japanese and German press. Germany returned this courtesy with a visit of Prince Karl Anton von Hohenzollern and later Prince Karl went to the Japanese military headquarters in Manchuria as a military observer.[14] In view of the suspicion of increasing Russo-German cooperation, the relations with Germany were held to be of great importance in Tokyo.

Immediately after the outbreak of war, the Japanese government found it necessary to defend the way they had opened the war. The note severing diplomatic relations, despatched on February 5, stated that the government "reserve the right to take such independent action as they may deem best to consolidate and defend their menaced position, as well as to protect their established rights and legitimate interests." This was all the formal warning there was before the first blow was struck on February 8 and the actual declaration of war was not issued until February 10. In a manifesto issued on February 18 and a declaration to the powers on February 22, the Russian government vigorously protested this procedure:[15] the Japanese attack was labeled "treacherous" and, because it was delivered without a previous declaration of war, it was said to have been an "open violation of all customary laws governing the mutual declarations of civilized nations." This was followed by a list of specific offenses which were a consequence of the attack such as the violation of Korean neutrality and the capture of Russian merchant ships in the neutral ports of Korea.

The Japanese government defended their action on three grounds.[16] The first defense brought out that at the time war was

[14] Prince Karl von Hohenzollern, *Meine Erlebnisse während des Russisch-Japanischen Krieges, 1904–1905,* Berlin, 1912.
[15] S. Takahashi, *International Law Applied to the Russo-Japanese War,* New York, 1908, pp. 8–10.
[16] Takahashi, *op.cit.,* pp. 10–14; K.G., I, 379–384; L.F. Oppenheim, *International Law: A Treatise,* 2 Vols., London, 1952, II, 291–292; W.E. Hall, *A Treatise on International Law,* London, 1938, p. 451; Dillon, *op.cit.,* p. 288; Emperor to Alexeiev, Feb. 8, 1904, Burtsev, *op.cit.,* p. 76.

started, Russia's own intentions were clearly hostile and the Japanese notes of February 22 and March 2 recounted the notes exchanged during negotiations and alleged that these had shown no disposition to compromise on Russia's part; the movement of Russian military and naval forces into the Far East and the fortification of strongpoints there were also pointed out. Finally, they recalled the issuing of orders placing specific Russian military establishments in a state of war readiness.

The second Japanese defense, only alluded to in their reply because supporting facts were presumably not available then, alleged that, far from being surprised by the Japanese act, the Russians had in fact anticipated it. It is now abundantly clear that during the weeks preceding the war the Russians had expected a Japanese landing in Korea and had even conceded that such a landing would not in itself be considered an act of war—only the precise amount of Korea to be conceded to Japan without going to war had been left undetermined. Then, on February 8, Admiral Alekseiev received the Imperial order defining this point. It read:

"It it desirable that the Japanese, and not we, shall commence military action. Therefore, if they do not start action against us, you must not hinder their landing in southern Korea or on the eastern shore up to and including Genzan. But if on the western side of Korea their fleet carries out a landing, or without this passes to the north across the thirty-eighth parallel, then you may attack them without awaiting the first shot from their side. I have confidence in you. God help you!"

While there is no reason to assume that the Japanese government knew about this message, their intelligence could well have apprized them of every other element of Russia's preparation for hostilities.

Thirdly, in view of these specific circumstances the Japanese government maintained that the attack was not an "open violation of all customary laws," but on the contrary, was an acceptable act under the existing rules of international law; the conditions which justified this were, however, inadequately set forth in the Japanese statements. A breach of the peace without any provocation whatever has indeed been held to be contrary to international law. On the other hand, where there has been a controversy and negotiations have been carried on without success, an attack by one of the parties without a declaration had not been considered a treacherous act. The rules dealing with this matter were later clarified at the Second Hague Conference of 1907 largely as a response to the controversy raised in 1904.

The Japanese government also encouraged all nonbelligerent nations to maintain the strictest neutrality since localization of the war was viewed as absolutely essential if her objectives were to be realized. The example of 1895 was a stern warning against the intrusion of other interests into the struggle, either through mediation or participation. In addition to the fact that the war was being fought on Chinese soil, the task of maintaining strict neutrality was further complicated by the objectives of the two belligerents. Not only were there many cases in which Russian interests seemed opposed to it, but Japan herself engaged in acts that seemed to contradict one of her own basic conditions for success.

The powers readily declared their neutrality toward the belligerents early in the war,[17] but the difficulty lay in observing neutral conduct. As a near ally, the United States appeared least likely to place obstacles in Japan's path and at the outbreak of war had assumed the protection of Japanese interests in Russia and at Newchwang; later, she had extended her good offices to help several hundred Japanese leave Russia. American sentiment toward Japan was demonstrated in ways other than official acts and pronouncements and the Japanese responded to the obviously pro-Japanese Americans in Japan with enthusiasm—Americans entering Japanese gatherings were sometimes reportedly greeted by the "Star-Spangled Banner." Americans were also prominently represented among the military observers and war correspondents: General Arthur MacArthur, Captain Payton C. March, Captain John J. Pershing, the military attaché, and Richard Harding Davis.

It was the European powers with their considerable interests in China which seemed to need the most careful watching. The merest hint that these interests were in danger might bring on a wave of seizures which would eclipse those of 1898 and limit the gains available for Japan. The entente between

[17] Motono to Komura, No. 49, Feb. 2, Takahira to Komura, No. 36, Feb. 13, Inouye to Komura, No. 61, Feb. 14, Makino to Komura, No. 28, Feb. 17, 1904, J.F.O.; Loomis to Conger, Feb. 9, Komura to Hay, Feb. 7, Hay to Takahira, Feb. 9, Takahira to Hay, Oct. 11, 1904, U.S.F.R., 1904, pp. 146, 430, 436; Griscom, op.cit., pp. 243–249.

Britain and France in April 1904, seemed to obviate the danger of military intervention from their side, but Germany, although she had given firm assurances of neutrality, was carefully watched.[18] German policy toward Russia might encourage the latter to move forces from her western frontier to Manchuria and furthermore, Germany's interest in enlarging her stake in China was suspected from her prewar conduct.

The neutrality of China was a precarious matter at best and was undoubtedly the most hazardous aspect of Japan's diplomatic struggle. China issued a declaration of neutrality on February 12 and followed it with appeals to the powers for support.[19] The task of observing such a policy, difficult even south of the wall and along China's coast, was, however, almost impossible in Manchuria. Russia had from the first expressed grave doubts about even trying to observe it in an area which was a theater of war and she continued to be lukewarm toward the idea.

Russia's view of Chinese neutrality had some similarities with that of Japan.[20] To both, for different reasons, it had a tactical use. Russia could not assume that the Chinese would be friendly if they were to become belligerents, and indeed, Admiral Alekseiev felt that they might well declare themselves openly for Japan if provoked. Hence, in spite of the military inconvenience neutrality entailed, Russia was ready to bear it until she had established her military superiority. Meanwhile, she contented herself with the hope that China or Japan might conveniently commit a breach of neutrality.

One of Japan's major triumphs, paralleling in significance those on the sea and the battlefield, was her negotiations for loans to make her military effort possible.[21] The importance of these to

[18] Inouye to Komura, No. 160, Apr. 13, 1904, *J.F.O.*

[19] Conger to Hay, Feb. 13, Chinese Minister in Japan to Komura, Feb. 13, 1904, *U.S.F.R.*, 1904, pp. 120, 421–422.

[20] Alekseiev to Lamsdorf, Feb. 15, 1904, *K.A.*, XLI-XLII, 168; Abaza to Alekseiev, Sept. 22, Alekseiev to Abaza, Oct. 20, 1904, Romanov, *Russia*, p. 474; Conger to Hay, Mar. 4, 1904, *U.S.F.R.*, 1904, p. 128; Foreign Ministery of China to Chinese Minister in Washington, Jan. 21, 1905, *U.S.F.R.*, 1905, p. 136.

[21] Ogawa, *op.cit.*, pp. 65–71, 94; "Jacob H. Schiff the Pioneer of American Foreign Financing," *The Annalist*, XVI, 404, Oct. 11, 1920, pp. 452–454; Alfred Vagts, *Deutschland und die Vereinigten Staaten in der Welt-politik*, 2 Vols., New York, 1935, II, 1190, 1209; Kantorovich, *op.cit.*, pp. 165–166; A.M. Michelson, etc., *Russian Public Finance during the War*, New Haven, 1928, p. 235; E.H. Zabriskie, *American-Russian Rivalry in the Far East*, Philadelphia, 1946, p. 109; Adler, *op.cit.*, II, 120–122, 213–230; Witte to Lamsdorf, Aug. 15, 1905, *K.A.*, VI, 33; Cambon to Delcasse, May 14, 1904, *D.D.F.*, V, 148–149; Bernstorff to Bülow, May 17, 1904, *G.P.*, XIX-2, 648–649; Galperin, *op.cit.*, pp. 219–220.

the prosecution of the war is shown by the fact that these loans constituted over half of all her war loans and a significant portion of the total cost of the war. These loans were, to a large extent, won on the battlefield. For Japan had failed as recently as January 1904 to get British approval for a loan, but by the following May the Japanese loan was far oversubscribed in both London and New York. While her dramatic military victories unquestionably won for Japan her right to claim a loan from her well-wishers, it was specifically the leadership of Jacob H. Schiff of Kuhn, Loeb, and Company and other cooperating bankers that made it a reality. The sums desired by Japan were large for their day and Japan had not yet established herself as a good risk for such amounts at acceptable interests rates.

All these things considered, it is not difficult to understand why both members of the Anglo-Japanese Alliance showed their appreciation to Schiff so conspicuously. King Edward decorated Schiff for his cooperation with the Alliance and the Japanese government decorated him on two occasions—in 1905, with the Order of the Sacred Treasure and in 1906, during a visit to Japan with Mrs. Schiff, the Emperor gave him the Order of the Rising Sun.

It has been said that Schiff's financial leadership in this case was influenced by his desire to see Russia defeated. It is a fact that the world had only recently been shocked by the anti-Jewish pogroms in Russia, starting with the outburst at Kishinev. Influential Jews of the United States and Europe had tried unsuccessfully to persuade the Russian government to remedy the conditions which encouraged such acts. They had informed Witte's agent, Rothstein, that they would do their best to deny the money market of the United States to Russia until some concrete steps had been taken to better the lot of Russian Jews. Thus, it is not surprising that once they had decided that Japan was an acceptable financial risk, they gave her such help as they could.

The Japanese loan was arranged directly with Schiff by Viscount Takahashi Korekiyo, then the vice governor of the Bank of Japan. During the war, Takahashi was the financial commissioner for the Japanese government in London and New York. He later reported that he had met Schiff quite by accident in late April 1904, at a dinner given by Arthur Hill where he started a conversation with Schiff without knowing who he was. Having found little interest in a loan in New York he was naturally struck by the fact that his new acquaintance seemed "uncommonly interested in the war and in the affairs of Japan.[22]

The next day, Takahashi wrote, he learned who Schiff was and of his interest in the loan and within a few days the loan was concluded. In the course of his conversations with Schiff, he also learned something of his motivation. He expressed his strong feelings about the treatment of the Russian Jews and, as though in parallel, about Russia's responsibility for throwing Japan out of Manchuria in 1895. He felt that a defeat for Russia was the best corrective and perhaps the only means of bringing about better conditions within Russia. For these reasons he wanted to help throw the weight of American financial resources behind the Japanese effort. The loan negotiations were started just before the crucial battle of the Yalu and concluded a few days after—the bonds were placed on the market in London and New York on May 11 and 12 respectively. The loan of May 1904 was for 10 million pounds at 6 per cent for 7 years, secured on the Japanese customs receipts. It was floated in equal amounts by banks in New York and London. The following November another loan, for 12 million pounds was floated under the same conditions as the first. Both were a reflection of Japan's rising prestige in these two countries since each was far oversubscribed.

[22] Adler, *op.cit.*, I, 215.

10. Russia's European Flank

THE OUTBREAK of war between Russia and Japan relaxed the feeble controls which preserved a precarious stability in the international community. Russia had for months retained some of her best military forces near her western frontier; nevertheless, a countervailing influence had been removed from the European scene when the Russo-Japanese War broke out. While the largest and most strategically located of the great powers was forced to defend herself on a distant frontier, her rivals could stand by militarily uncommitted. Moreover, they would be eager to take advantage both of her weakness in the West and her victories in the East. This situation had long been anticipated by General Kuropatkin who had assigned the highest defense priority to the western frontier. Once Russia had become entangled with a hostile Far Eastern nation, he visualized the defense requirements as being permanently increased. If the military forces were not increased proportionately to the need, Russia's position as a European power would suffer.

From the European point of view the important fact was that the Eurasian giant had been challenged. It was believed by many that, barring the complete collapse and neutralization of Japan, Russia's frontier in the Far East would require permanent vigilance. Opportunities were offered for new diplomatic alignments in Europe and even the world, a prospect feared in France and welcomed in Germany. Consequently, Germany was largely responsible for the revisionist policies that were attempted in Europe during the war and seized the opportunity of the reduced tension on her eastern frontier to try repairing the already damaged Triple Alliance and to lay the ghost of new hostile combinations.

The German course of action during the war may be characterized as an aggressive defense aimed at strengthening her own position at the expense of the Franco-Russian Alliance. While Russia was financially, militarily, and diplomatically cast in a defensive role with respect to Europe, Germany was left to play an aggressive and revisionist role. The early developments of the war did not openly undermine Franco-Russian solidarity; nevertheless they furnished Germany both the clue and the opportunity for weakening it.

The failure of Germany's aggressive campaign is attributable to a number of factors including: the crudeness of her strategy; the general suspicion of her motives; the British determination not to countenance the excessive growth of German power if it could be avoided; the fact that the Franco-Russian Alliance had far greater durability than Germany had imagined; the miscalculation of Germany as to the degree to which Russia had been weakened; and, finally, the timeliness of the American proffer of good offices which helped to deal the final blow to the German effort.

In contrast with Japan, Russia's access to the money markets of Europe was well established by 1904.[1] About 46 per cent of her government debt was held abroad and her credit was such that she was able to obtain loans at less than 5 per cent, whereas a Japanese loan negotiation in 1902 had failed because American bankers had wanted 10 per cent. In the early stages of the war, Russia's credit was sustained by the widespread assumption that she would ultimately win. Consequently, her first loan of 350 million rubles, negotiated in Paris at about the same time Takahashi and Schiff were negotiating the Japanese loan in New York, was obtained at 5 per cent without difficulty. From a purely financial point of view, it was estimated that this would sustain the Russian war effort until early 1905, but this was not considered a sufficient guarantee for the future. Throughout the war, therefore, Russian financial needs remained an issue of the first importance, and were inconveniently dependent on the changes in the world situation. In addition to her constant defeats in the Far East and her declining internal cohesion, indeed largely because of them, Russia faced the shifting balance of power in Europe with increasingly less capacity to accept the consequences as far as her declining prestige and credit were concerned.

By the summer of 1904 the military and consequently the financial position of Russia had deteriorated noticeably. Both government and financial circles in Paris were becoming disturbed about the course of the war and increasingly reluctant even to consider further Russian loans. It was under these unfavorable conditions that Russia faced the renewal of her com-

[1] Romanov, *Russia*, pp. 17, 340–343; Kokovtsov, *op.cit.*, p. 17, H. Feis, *Europe the World's Banker, 1870–1914*, New Haven, 1930, pp. 210–219; Kantorovich, *op.cit.*, p. 165.

mercial treaty with Germany.[2] Although the German government
suggested the renewal and Russia was able to make it conditional
on the approval of a loan, the new treaty was a disappointment in
St. Petersburg.

Since he had concluded the original agreement, Witte was
asked to undertake the negotiations for the renewal. The outbreak of war and then the formation of the Entente had introduced new and complicating factors during the preliminary
discussions and the difficulties Russia faced were soon apparent.
Against the backdrop of these events the German Emperor's
lavish assurances regarding Russia's western frontier had to be
viewed as costly immunities for Russia and indeed the Emperor
indicated clearly that he wished a more favorable tariff arrangement for Germany. In addition, the Russian need for a loan
was bound to give Germany a considerable bargaining advantage.
Witte and Chancellor Bernhard von Bülow spent two weeks at
Norderney discussing the terms of the final agreement and Witte
let it be known that Russia was interested in permission to acquire
a loan in Berlin. Since he found Bülow at first opposed to this,
Witte made it a condition of signing the agreement and ultimately this condition was met and, in addition, Russia retained a
favorable tariff balance.

The agreement was signed inauspiciously on July 28, the
same day Plehve, the Russian minister of interior, was assassinated. While it contained some concessions to Germany on the
tariff question, the desired Russian access to the loan market
of Berlin was assured. This provision was followed up the next
October by the visit to St. Petersburg of the German banker,
Ernst von Mendelssohn-Bartoldi, to discuss a loan.

The first obvious alteration in the balance of power occurred
with the signing of the Anglo-French Entente in April 1904, just
before the Russian defeat on the Yalu and the acquisition of
loans by both belligerents.[3] The interest of Britain and France in

[2] Witte, op.cit., I, 269–286; Feis, op.cit., pp. 227–228; Romanov, Ocherki, pp.
343–344; Bülow memorandum, Nov. 2, 1904, G.P., XIX-2, 387–388.

[3] L. Albertini, The Origins of the War of 1914, 3 Vols., London, 1952, I, 145–
151; E.N. Anderson, The First Moroccan Crisis, 1904–1906, Chicago, 1930, pp.
82–86, 93, 105–106; D.D.F., IV, 533–543; E.W. Edwards, "The Japanese Alliance
and the Anglo-French Agreement of 1904," History, XLII, No. 144, Feb. 1957,
pp. 19–24; O.J. Hale, Publicity and Diplomacy; with Special Reference to England
and Germany, 1890–1914, New York, 1940, pp. 266–292; G.P. Gooch, Recent
Revelations of European Diplomacy, London, 1940, pp. 337–348; R.J. Sontag,
"German Foreign Policy, 1904–1906," American Historical Review, XXXIII-2, Jan.

composing their differences had by April 1903 brought them to the point of actively thinking about some understanding, serious discussions were under way by July, and on April 8, 1904, these discussions culminated in a series of agreements. The Anglo-French Entente dealt with a widely scattered collection of geographical localities representing points of existing and potential discord between the signatories. In the interest of liquidating all colonial differences, rights conceded to France in Newfoundland by the Treaty of Utrecht in 1713 were renounced; the definition of their respective spheres of interest in Thailand was projected from their agreement of 1896. The main focus of the agreement, however, was in North Africa. Britain's primary interest in Egypt and France's in Morocco were clearly defined and recognized; a recognition of the general interest in the Suez Canal and, in particularly, of Spain in Morocco was also included.

The significance of the Entente for its two partners lies in their respective needs for security. In the case of Britain this had been forcibly brought to her attention during the Boer War. At the moment there seemed to be two general directions in which her search might lead her. The first was toward an association with Russia or France, already united in an entente and opposing her interests over a broad front, especially in Asia and Africa. The second was toward an accommodation with either Germany or Japan on both. The latter alternative offered a partnership with relatively new and expanding world powers interested in checking the further expansion of the established powers.

Great Britain's first major venture in ending her diplomatic isolation, the Anglo-Japanese Alliance, came about through a process of elimination rather than choice. This Japanese venture was accomplished under the shadow of Ito's visit to Moscow late in 1901—a reminder that Japan, like Britain herself, might more logically seek a direct accomodation with her principal rival. Nevertheless, for the time being at least, both Britain and Japan had to do with half a loaf.

By the spring of 1903 it was clear that the Anglo-Japanese Alliance had not halted Russia's forward movement in the Far East. Britain was, therefore, again brought face to face with the need to seek security in another alliance that might not

1928, p. 280; O. Franke, *Die Grossmächte in Ostasien von 1894 bis 1914*, Braunschweig, 1923, pp. 242–243; R. Albrecht-Carrié, *A Diplomatic History of Europe Since the Congress of Vienna*, New York, 1958, pp. 240–243.

halt the Russian advance but might at least give her some guarantees against its consequences. To pursue further a partnership in a German-Japanese understanding as Britain had done in 1901 would have led to an alliance with Germany, an unrealizable objective as experience had already shown. On the contrary, relations with Germany were becoming distinctly hostile and since prospective withdrawals of Russian strength from the German frontier would further strengthen Germany, this seemed uninviting.

The only practical alternative for Britain was France with whom negotiations were accordingly undertaken in the spring of 1903. During the months the discussions were being carried on, the renewal of Russo-Japanese negotiations added new incentives for Britain's commitment to an agreement with France. Like the earlier Ito endeavor, the success of the Russo-Japanese negotiations might end the discord between these nations and leave Britain with even less leverage than before in St. Petersburg.

The fact that the Russo-Japanese negotiations terminated in war presented, if anything, an even more disturbing outlook. For in the early stages of the war there was at least a reasonable doubt that Japan would win. Britain might, therefore, be forced to intervene, if not out of a sense of moral responsibility, certainly to prevent the deterioration of her entire Far Eastern position. From this point of view, France loomed as a moderating influence against a vindictive Russia. Even barring such an outcome, a vital role remained for France; she might be expected to help moderate Russia's demands and, above all, she could to a considerable extent guarantee that neither partner of the belligerents would be drawn into the struggle.

France's interest in an entente had its roots in Delcasse's policy of counterbalancing the menace of the Triple Alliance and of promoting the nation's external expansion, particularly in Morocco. In pursuit of these objectives, Delcasse had exchanged assurances with Italy, uneasily associated with Germany and Austria-Hungary in the Triple Alliance, and had made his first approaches to Britain, the latter still unprepared to discuss the vital Mediterranean questions which stood between them.

By spring of 1903 the careful spade work of Paul Cambon, the French ambassador in London, as well as the dangerous Far Eastern situation, had succeeded in bringing the two parties together. Like Britain, France wanted to avoid being drawn into a possible war and was seeking guarantees against both the weakening and strengthening of Russia. Germany, of course, was an even more immediate menace in the French than in the British outlook.

The significance of the Anglo-French Entente was vividly exemplified by the unmistakable chagrin shown in Berlin.[4] Some contemporary observers were inclined to think this reaction could have been avoided if Delcasse had announced the Entente in April 1904 to Germany through diplomatic rather than public channels. But since Delcasse was seeking to strengthen France in a way that deliberately struck a blow at Germany's diplomatic and strategic defenses, it could hardly have been expected that this announcement would be accepted with good grace regardless of how it was managed.

Though the real impact in Berlin came somewhat later, the first bristling response was a true forecast of the general tenor. The German press, with an eye on the central issue, speculated on the consequences of the Entente for the Triple Alliance. Government spokesmen, unable to believe that the Egyptian-Moroccan issues had been so readily and cleanly resolved between the partners, exerted every effort to keep them alive and useful as a devisive expedient. The executive committee of the Navy League assembled at Dresden to demand an expanded naval building program. Far from any mere tilting with windmills, these were genuine expressions of the insecurity the Anglo-French Entente inspired in some German circles.[5] The formation of the Entente was the most recent of a continuing series of blows to Germany's security system. For example, on June 30, 1902, two days after the renewal of the Triple Alliance, Delcasse had helped to deal a severe blow to the Alliance: the Franco-Italian understanding of that date, resting as it did on a recognition of the Mediterranean interests of both, glaringly exposed the weakness of the Triple Alliance.

Before many months had passed the weakness of the Austro-Hungarian link with the Alliance was also sharply outlined against the background of Balkan unrest. Out of the clash of

---

[4] Inouye to Komura, No. 155, Apr. 10, No. 167, Apr. 21, 1904, *J.F.O.*; E.M. Carroll, *Germany and the Great Powers, 1866–1914*, New York, 1938, p. 501; F. de Pressense, "The Collapse of Russia. II, The Fall of M. Delcasse and the Anglo-French 'Entente,'" A.F. Harrison, "The Collapse of Russia. III Germany and Morocco," *The Nineteenth Century and After*, LVIII, 341, London, July 1905, pp. 31, 36–38; C.W. Porter, *The Career of Theophile Delcasse*, Philadelphia, 1936, pp. 38, 193.

[5] Albertini, *op.cit.*, I, 127–138; F.A. Ogg, "European Alliances and the War," *The American Monthly Review of Reviews*, XXXII, 3, Sept. 1905, pp. 297–301.

Austro-Italian interests in this area there emerged the Austro-Russian reapprochement focused on the preservation of the status quo in the Balkans. The Austro-Russian agreements of October 4, 1903 and October 15, 1904 appeared to be milestones along the path to Austrian independence of Germany and decline of the Alliance. To what extent this, like the Italian parallel, was encouraged by Delcasse's long, patient efforts in Vienna would be difficult to guess.

These occurrences had canceled out to a great extent the advantages to Germany of having Russia at war in the Far East. Somehow, it was felt, Germany would have to find solid footing again. Since her quest for security contemplated the prospect of using force, Germany looked first to her military power. Consequently, a few days after the conclusion of the Anglo-French Entente, the chief of general staff, Count Alfred von Schlieffen, was consulted as to the possibility of success in case of war with France.[6] The later well-known Schlieffen plan had, by this time, been in preparation for many years and was to be completed in 1905; it was essentially a scheme for a rapid and decisive war against France. This would be carried out by using Belgium as a route to Paris to deal a knockout blow before the defenses could be prepared. However, the element of surprise had already been extracted since the French government had learned about the plan indirectly from a member of the German general staff. Nevertheless the Schlieffen plan remained the foundation of the German defense system and of her aggressive attitude toward western Europe until the First World War.

With Russia temporarily tied down in the East and military plans for the West well under way, Germany felt ready to turn with a freer hand to the rebuilding of her political and diplomatic security system. Belgium and Holland comprised those parts of her intended system lying closest at hand and her strategic interest in them was already known even to those who were ignorant of the Schlieffen plan.[7] The same was true of her interest in Denmark and the control of the Danish straits.[8] This question became of special importance after the departure in October

[6] Paleologue, op.cit., pp. 63–64; Anderson, op.cit., p. 148; W. Goerlitz, History of the German General Staff, New York, 1954, pp. 131–134.

[7] Spring Rice to Roosevelt, n.d. (but probably Feb. 1905), Gwynn, op.cit., I, 396; D.C. Boulger, "The Collapse of Russia. IV Germany and Belgium," The Nineteenth Century and After, LVIII, 341, London, July 1905, pp. 44–46.

[8] Seegar, op.cit., pp. 73–78; K. Bornhak, Die Kriegschuld: Deutschlands Weltpolitik, 1890–1914, Berlin, 1929, p. 283.

1904 of the Russian Baltic Fleet left Germany even greater freedom of action in that region. Later in the year 1904 expression was even given to a fear that Germany might be contemplating a military occupation of Poland.[9]

Along with these forceful and desperate plans, Germany was interested in improving her diplomatic stature and in maintaining her world prestige and power. The formula under which she appeared to be operating was familiar to imperialistic encounters from Manchuria to Morocco. It had been expressed with reference to Morocco in the *Alldeutsche Blätter* of June 3, 1900 to the effect that Germany wanted to become a world power and, accordingly, wished a share in any reapportionments that were to be made.[10]

In pursuit of this objective she tried to build diplomatic goodwill in both the United States and Japan.[11] Germans were generally poorly regarded in Japan, sometimes even being looked upon as Russian spies. In a dramatic attempt to remedy this attitude, the German Emperor had telegraphed Japan early in the war that he was placing the unoccupied beds in the German naval hospital at Yokohama at the disposal of Japan for the wounded. Dr. Erwin Baelz, a German doctor residing in Japan, commented on the parallel between this act and the Emperor's conduct during the Boer War, first outraging British feelings with the Kruger telegram and then attempting to atone for it by lavish friendliness. In the present instant he apparently decided to cover up his yellow peril views with a new amiability.

German relations with Britain were almost beyond salvaging and after the formation of the Entente, relations with Great Britain cooled rapidly.[12] An article in *Vanity Fair* appeared to be calling attention to a time fuse when it suggested that the fall of Port Arthur would raise the question of Britain's right to Weihaiwei, concluding that such an issue could only be settled by fleets, a clear reference to the unfinished German naval construction program. In the larger arena of world politics in general, it seemed that Germany had come too late, pursued her objectives too abruptly, considered the feelings of others too half-heartedly, and, not surprisingly, had suffered some notable failures.

[9] Inouye to Katsura, No. 484, Nov. 17, 1904, *J.F.O.*
[10] Carroll, *op.cit.*, p. 486.
[11] Hall, *op.cit.*, pp. 393–394; Baelz, *op.cit.*, pp. 252, 254–256.
[12] Shebenko to Russian Emperor, Nov. 16, 1904, Sergeev, *op.cit.*, p. 59; Coerper report, Nov. 17, Schulenberg to Bülow, Dec. 13, 1904, *G.P.*, xix-2, 353–356, 360–365.

The principal German efforts were, for the time being, concentrated on the building of an enlarged security system founded on an understanding with Russia. Such a return to the reinsurance arrangement might have been suggested in any case by the renewed opportunities opened by Russia's preoccupation in Manchuria. The development of the Entente raised in Berlin the well-founded assumption that both Paris and London saw it as a link between the existing Franco-Russian Entente and a future Anglo-Russian understanding, a prospect which understandably caused nightmares in Berlin. Furthermore, Germany was fully aware of British hostility and its aggressive implications for her. While Franco-Russian relations were temporarily cooled over the Anglo-French Entente and before King Edward's persistence had had time to succeed in St. Petersburg, the time seemed to be ripe to seek a closer tie with Russia.

The foundation of the plan was an understanding with Russia to which, hopefully, France could be attracted. This would, in fact, be a revival of the Three-Power intervention group of 1895, a combination so recently proposed by Russia and so cavalierly refused by the German government, and would constitute the basic framework of a "continental alliance." This could be instrumental not only in preventing the dissolution of the Triple Alliance but also in blocking the further progress of an Anglo-Franco-Russian combination. Furthermore, such a formidable partnership, under German leadership, would give Britain reason to reconsider her attitude toward Germany. For she would then face a choice of association with the new alliance or complete isolation.

The opportunity for which Emperor William sought so eagerly to "soften up" Russia for a closer tie with Germany came with the sailing of the Russian Baltic fleet for the Far Eastern war theater. This was a measure which had been suggested by Admiral Makarov when he was appointed commander in chief of the Russian naval forces in the Far East.[13] Action, however, was slow, perhaps because of the known inadequacies of the fleet. In any case a decision was deferred until after the isolation of Port Arthur.

In time the least unservicable units of the Russian Baltic fleet were brought together to form the Second Pacific Fleet. Although

---

[13] Sorokin, *op.cit.*, pp. 288ff; Paleologue, *op.cit.*, pp. 127–146; P. Sykes, *The Right Honorable Sir Mortimer Durand*, London, 1926, p. 284.

the decision was made in June, the final plans for the movement of the fleet were developed at an Imperial conference at Peterhof on August 24, 1904. The fleet departed from Libau on October 15 ill-prepared, not only for the role it was intended to play in the war, but even for the passage to the war front. Many of the ships were antiquated, poorly constructed, and deficient in equipment, and the crews were poorly trained. Its commander in chief, however, was an outstanding naval officer, Rear Admiral Zinovii Petrovich Rozhdestvensky who was promoted to vice admiral en route to the Far East. As the following current rhyme indicates the pronunciation of the name of this new celebrity caused some difficulty:

> "And after all this an Admiral came,
> A terrible man with a terrible name,
> A name which we all of us know very well
> But no one can speak and no one can spell."

On the night of October 21–22, as the fleet was en route in the vicinity of the fishing grounds at Dogger Bank near Hull, England, it unwittingly and unintentionally ran into serious international complications. Some small British fishing craft were sighted, taken for Japanese torpedo boats and fired upon; without stopping to make any inquiries or investigate the damage, the fleet moved on. It headed southward through the Straits of Dover and finally halted at Vigo in Spain where it remained temporarily on government orders.

The fishing trawlers of the unfortunate Gamecock Fleet returned to their home port at Hull to count their losses.[14] The next day they brought their findings dramatically to the attention of the government and the British public in London; Sir Henry Seymour King, local member of Parliament, took a deputation of fishermen to London and the foreign office to tell their story. The owners of the Gamecock Fleet also brought an appeal directly to the foreign minister; two trawlers had been sunk and two damaged and a number of lives lost. The King wrote on the report: "A most dastardly outrage."

---

[14] Messrs. Jackson and Co. to Lansdowne, Oct. 23, 1904, B.D., IV, 5–6; Cambon to Delcasse, Nov. 6, 1904, D.D.F., v, 509–512; Hayashi to Komura, No. 331, Oct. 24 and No. 336, Oct. 26, 1904, J.F.O.; R. Hough, The Fleet that Had to Die, New York, 1958, pp. 48ff; S. Lee, King Edward VII—a Biography, 2 Vols., London, 1925–1927, II, 301–303; T. Itakura, Kokusai Funso Shiko, Tokyo, 1929, pp. 120–124.

The King's horrified reflection on the incident was shared by
the whole nation. From the senior statesmen and the London
press to the protesting crowds in Trafalgar Square and the people
throughout the country came an expression of indignation at the
apparent crudeness of the attack and the calloused attitude
toward the helpless fishermen; the inhumane aspect of the affair
was discussed over and over. If the admiral had sailed away from
the scene of the encounter to insure the security of his command,
why at least hadn't he conveyed some word to the authorities as
he passed the Straits of Dover?

The popular indignation was also reflected in the bristling
military and diplomatic stance of the government. As the crowds
echoed the certainty that Admiral "Jackie" Fisher, the First
Sea Lord, would "teach 'em," the Mediterranean, Channel,
and Home Fleets were alerted. Diplomatic notes began to take
the measure of the crisis on the official level. Count Benckendorff,
the Russian ambassador, hurried back from the continent to
offer his apologies, and the Russian Emperor, at first acting on
very little information, offered his regrets and gave assurances
of reparations to those who had suffered. It was soon evident that
the Russian measures were taking insufficient account of British
feelings on the matter. As the question of actual responsibility
seemed to fall from the shoulders of the Russian government, it
descended squarely on those of the unfortunate Admiral Rozhdestvensky. By October 26 his fleet was in fact bottled up by the
British fleet in Vigo harbor, a situation which could hardly avoid
leading either to war or to a sacrifice of prestige on one side or
the other. On the very day this naval confrontation occurred,
Lord Lansdowne wrote to the Russian ambassador with reference
to Russia's willingness to compensate for the incident:

"You will, however, pardon me for saying that this is not
enough. As I mentioned to you yesterday it is absolutely necessary that the Russian Gov[ernmen]t should ascertain who are the
persons responsible for this unprovoked attack on British fishermen and . . . that the guilty persons will receive exemplary
punishment."[15]

It seems likely that the delicacy, the tragedy, and the possible
consequences of this situation only gradually dawned upon the
two nations. A war would almost certainly have involved three

[15] Lansdowne to Benckendorff, Oct. 26, 1904, B.D., IV, 13.

of the major fleets in European waters: the Russian and the British as principals, and the French as an ally of Russia. It was unthinkable that France could avoid supporting her older ally and this would bring about the destruction of the Anglo-French Entente. The advantages to Germany of breaking up this annoying combination were exceeded in significance only by the power which would accrue to her from the neutralization or destruction of all effective naval competition near her home waters.

The crisis passed by October 28. Delcasse, and to some extent President Roosevelt, took an active part in helping the parties to avoid a struggle which would clearly have violated the interests of both. Britain and Russia agreed that the issue would be settled by an international commission: a commission made up of professional naval officers in addition to such legal and political advisors as each required. The following officers were appointed for this duty: Britain, Vice Admiral Beaumont; Russia, Vice Admiral Dubasov; France, Admiral Fournier; and the United States, Rear Admiral Davis. As a fifth member, Austria nominated Vice Admiral Baron von Spaun. The commission met in Paris on December 22, 1904, under the presidency of the French member and completed its work by February 25, 1905.

The commission accepted an interpretation of the incident unfavorable to Russia.[16] In the first place, the vessels on which Rozhdestvensky had fired were found to be unquestionably British fishing trawlers. Furthermore, all evidence pointed to the fact that these ships had committed no hostile act toward the Russian fleet. The commission also took account of the failure of the admiral to endeavor in any way to make any amends for his act either by helping the sufferers or even by bringing the incident to public attention. On these grounds, the commission approved the payment by Russia of a money indemnity.

The commission also took cognizance of the conditions that Admiral Rozhdestvensky alleged in explanation of his having mistaken the ships for Japanese torpedo boats. It was understandably to the advantage of Japan to prevent the Russian ships from reaching the Far East or to hinder and delay their progress in every way possible. It was learned that rumors of Japanese activi-

---

[16] Hay to Durand, Dec. 1, 1904, Choate to Hay, Mar. 1, 1905, *U.S.F.R.*, pp. 473–476; A.S. Hershey, *The International Law and Diplomacy of the Russo-Japanese War*, New York, 1906, pp. 235–245.

ties, perhaps themselves Japanese inspired, had come to the admiral's attention through both official and unofficial channels and that he had reasonably acted with extreme caution and had alerted his command accordingly. It was shown in evidence that this information had made the command nervous and extremely cautious and had spread fear among the crew. The passage through the Danish straits, which all suspected might be sown with mines, had been a terrifying experience and every vessel sighted was looked upon as a possible enemy ship. On the very day of the incident, there had been reports of torpedo boats in the vicinity of the fleet. In view of all these circumstances, the commission found Rozhdestvensky's caution justifiable and the fear which inspired the mistake understandable. These factors did not, however, lead them to condone the act.

The decision of the commission has been viewed as a commendable achievement since it drew a distinction between guilt and intent and gave each party a partial victory. The commissioners found that the act had indeed been committed and pronounced it unjustified. In recognition of this, the Russian ambassador officially closed the incident on March 9, 1905 when he handed Lord Lansdowne 65,000 pounds as a compensation for the losses suffered by the fishermen. At the same time, the commissioners recognized that it was not Admiral Rozhdestvensky's intent to commit this act since he was acting only to protect his fleet and he was not subjected to discipline. The decision unfortunately left untouched the vital problem of the security of merchant ships exposed on the high seas during wartime to vessels of war.

While the German press had maintained a correct attitude toward the Dogger Bank embroilment, Emperor William fanned the flames of resentment which the Russian Emperor felt toward the British.[17] Building on a voluminous correspondence intended to encourage Nicholas' receptivity to closer relations, William chose the moment of the height of the crisis to send a copy of a completed proposal for a formal understanding. He also made it clear that such a Russo-German alliance would be considered the

[17] Prinet to Delcasse, Oct. 30, 1904, D.D.F., v, 487–488; Franke, op.cit., pp. 242–243; William to Nicholas, Oct. 30, 1904, G.P., xix-1, 308; M. de Taube, La Politique Russe d'avant Guerre et la Fin de l'Empire des Tsars (1904–1906), Paris, 1928, pp. 47–49; E.M. Rozental, Diplomaticheskaia Istoriia Russko-Frantsuzkogo Soiuza v Nachale XX Veka, Moscow, 1960, pp. 63ff; E.S. Politovsky, From Libau to Tsushima, London, 1906, pp. 3–14.

foundation for a Franco-Russo-German understanding. German pressure on St. Petersburg for an alliance did not end with the assignment of the Dogger Bank issue to an international commission,[18] and the two rulers continued to discuss it. In spite of the depressing performance on the battlefield, the German Emperor encouraged Nicholas to anticipate victory in the war, particularly with reference to the unpromising prospects for Russia with regard to the siege of Port Arthur. The Dogger Bank incident lent itself ideally to the portrayal of Britain as an obstacle to the progress of the fleet toward its destination and the relief of Port Arthur. It was hardly a step beyond this to portraying Britain as an active ally with Japan against Russia.

The need to furnish coal for the eastbound fleet provided the German Emperor with a unique means of urging the alliance, enabling him to cast Britain in the role of Russia's enemy and Germany as Russia's friend.[19] The Dogger Bank affair had vividly shown Britain as apparently a cooperating ally of Japan, acting to delay the progress of the fleet. Germany, on the other hand, had shown her goodwill by permitting the Hamburg-American Line to supply coal to the Russian ships. The German Emperor began pressing the point that continuance of this operation was entirely at the mercy of the British navy. In fact, he insinuated that his friendly service might have to be terminated unless Russia would agree to some defensive arrangement which offered Germany support in case she faced a hostile Britain as a consequence of permitting the supplying of coal.

The German pressure for a Russian alliance and the vital assistance Germany was giving to the Russian fleet were understood in Paris as a menace to the Franco-Russian Alliance,[20] and served to emphasize again the incompatibility of this alliance for France in any other than the European setting. Under existing

[18] Nicholas to William, Nov. 7, William to Nicholas, Dec. 21, 1904, G.P., xix-1, 310–312, 341; Lee, op.cit., II, 354; William to Nicholas, Nov. 20, 1904, Sergeev, op.cit., pp. 58–59; Savinsky, op.cit., pp. 96–104; Carroll, op.cit., p. 505.

[19] William to Nicholas, Oct. 27, 1904, G.P., xix-1, 303–304; S.B. Fay, "The Kaiser's Secret Negotiations with the Tsar, 1904–1905," American Historical Review, xxiv, Oct. 1918, pp. 62–63; William to Nicholas, Dec. 7, 1904, M.N. Pokrovsky, Perepiska Vilgelma II s Nikolaem II, 1894–1914 gg., Moscow, 1923, p. 85.

[20] Witte to Sheremetev, June 3, 1904, K.A., xvii, 72; Inouye to Komura, No. 219, May 31, 1904, J.F.O.; Nicholas to William, Oct. 29, 1904, G.P., xix-1, 305; Spring Rice to Roosevelt, Dec. 7, 1904, Gwynn, op.cit., I, 439; Anderson, op.cit., pp. 161–162; Paleologue, op.cit., pp. 160–163; Seegar, op.cit., p. 52; Rozental, op.cit., p. 51; de Pressense, op.cit., pp. 24–25.

circumstances, France's interests lay in the observance of as strict a neutrality as possible, allowing no opportunity for the war to spread and seeking diligently for a means of ending the conflict.

Meanwhile, the French government was well aware of the growing German pressures to break the Franco-Russian Alliance and painfully conscious of the strength of the pro-German sentiment in St. Petersburg, both Witte and Bezobrazov being among those sympathetic. After the Dogger Bank affair, this tendency was brought clearly into focus and this question from St. Petersburg was pointedly expressed: What had France to offer to prove her interest in the alliance?

The needs of the Second Pacific Fleet while en route and the distribution of the French possessions between Europe and the Far East suggested the obvious answer.[21] Before the Dogger Bank incident, concrete planning for French assistance to the fleet had been impossible since Russia refused to disclose the precise route. But now Paleologue and French Commander de Saulces de Freycinet were assigned to work out the details of the expedition with the Russian government.

French assistance was so complete and all-encompassing that, in retrospect, it appears to have been all but indispensable. It began with planning the routes through the Mediterranean and around Africa for maximum security and secrecy. Port officials as well as repair and communications facilities were placed at the disposal of the Russians at the French possessions in Africa, Madagascar, and Indochina. Even the attempted secrecy, however, could not conceal the desperate nature of this gamble, though only those who knew the real condition of the fleet understood the futility and the tragedy of it.

[21] Savinsky, *op.cit.*, pp. 96–104; Porter, *op.cit.*, p. 203; Rozental, *op.cit.*, pp. 77ff; Paleologue, *op.cit.*, pp. 127–146.

11. An Impending Deadlock

THE MILITARY victories and defeats which began on New Year's Day 1905, were more decisive than those of the previous year. Yet, taken together, they still lacked anything like the finality of a real victory. At Port Arthur and on the sea, the battles appeared to leave little doubt that a change was taking place in the balance of power in the Far East and, indeed, in the world. The land warfare, on the other hand, was far from having this degree of significance in spite of Japan's victories, since Japan was reaching the end of her capacity to carry on the war.

The question of ultimate victory or defeat remained dependent on the ability of the leaders of each nation to find adequate answers to a host of imponderable problems, basing their findings on the known capacity of their own country to carry on the war, as well as on the known or imagined capacity of their opponent. At the same time, both combatants sought to gain such advantages as they could by concealing from their opponent as much as possible those factors unfavorable to themselves.

Among the innumerable components of this complex equation were: the debilitating revolution in Russia as seen from St. Petersburg and Tokyo; the tendency of some elements in both countries, reenforced by a natural desire for a decisive victory, to overestimate the actual strength of the country; the relative economic and industrial potential of each nation; the accessibility to each belligerent of foreign loans; the available manpower in each country; and the extent to which each could commit its full military power against the external rather than the internal enemy.

The changing evaluations of these factors were reflected in public discussions and diplomatic negotiations. The endeavor to transfer the struggle from the battlefield back to the conference table provided a continuing forum for evaluating the components of this problem, thus furnishing a necessary preliminary to the formal peace conference at Portsmouth. The vital relations between Japan and her allies, Great Britain and the United States, simultaneously reflected the changes wrought by the war. Before the meeting at Portsmouth these changes were formally transmuted into new diplomatic agreements.

The surrender of Port Arthur occurred with an almost un-

natural appropriateness on New Year's Day 1905. In the 240 days
that had elapsed since the Japanese landing in early May, both
sides had made an enormous expenditure in both blood and
treasure.[1] The toll for the Japanese in dead and wounded had
reached 57,780 and for the Russians, 28,200. The capture of 203
Metre Hill on December 5, 1904 alone took a toll of over 13,000
Japanese lives and henceforth it was from this hill that the
Japanese were able to direct their fire with devastating accuracy
into the fortress and toward the Russian Fleet lying close by.

The senior Russian officers at Port Arthur differed as to whether
or not these developments called for surrender. The death on
December 15 of General P.I. Kondratenko seriously weakened
the group that wished to hold out, hoping for the arrival of the
fleet from the Baltic. However, on January 1, 1905, without
further consultation with his staff, General A.M. Stessel the commander, notified General Nogi of his readiness to surrender. The
next day the formal arrangements were made by which the
fortress and all it contained were placed at the disposal of the
Japanese. The fact that this included 24,369 officers and men and
2,500,000 rounds of small arms ammunition seemed to leave a
reasonable doubt as to the need to surrender. General Stessel
has been harshly judged for this act. Even the impartial act of
the German Emperor who conferred the order "Pour le Merite"
on both Stessel and Nogi could not change this view. Stessel was
apparently aware of the unfavorable response his act might
evoke, announcing the painful news to his sovereign in these
words: "Great Sovereign! Forgive! We have done all that was
humanly possible. Judge us, but be merciful. Eleven months of
ceaseless fighting have exhausted our strength."

None of the censure which fell upon General Stessel carried
over to the rest of the Russian forces and they were hailed as
heroes by the Japanese and the whole world. Long before the
actual surrender the two forces had faced each other in hand-
to-hand combat and had even developed a considerable amount
of camaraderie. At the time of the surrender more than half
of the Russian force was incapacitated for actual combat service.
Some said the fort could have held out only a few more days
at best while others thought that such heroes would have been

[1] Maurice, op.cit., pp. 595–596; M.C.T., pp. 444ff; Sorokin, op.cit., pp. 229–240;
S. Tyler, The Japan-Russia War, Philadelphia, 1905, pp. 379–408; B. Burleigh,
Empire of the East or Japan and Russia at War, 1904–5, London, 1905, pp.
403–425; A.I. Sorokin, Oborona Port-Artura, Moscow, 1954, pp. 149–180.

better served had General Kondratenko lived to influence the ultimate outcome.

The wisdom of the long and costly siege of Port Arthur, questioned by many contemporaries, was strongly supported at the time by Admiral Mahan, the renowned American commentator on naval affairs.[2] Writing both during and soon after the siege, he found it definitely a necessity for both sides. The vital importance of this battle to Russia seemed clear since her whole naval power and naval position were involved in the defense of the fortress. The mission of the Baltic Fleet was specifically to rescue both the fortress and the naval units lying in its waters with the hope of ultimately cutting off Japanese access to Manchuria. The other great hope of the Russian commander was to gain time to build up the land forces. The siege played an important part in this, Mahan believed, not only because it required a major part of Japan's limited forces but also because far more Japanese than Russians were engaged at Port Arthur and their losses were greater.

For Japan, Port Arthur was of even greater importance than for Russia. It was axiomatic for Japan that she must retain control of the sea approaches to the mainland. From this point of view, the continuation of the fortress in Russian hands, the survival of a considerable Russian naval force in Far Eastern waters, and the impending arrival of another were factors which Japan could not afford to disregard. Presumably, no land victory could compensate for the reversal Japan might suffer from the successful use of any of these three elements of Russia's sea power or, even worse, the convergence of all three.

To the less critical public in both countries, the fall of the fortress had a different though no less pronounced importance. "Port Arthur has fallen!" were words of tremendous significance to the Japanese and Russians at the front and at home.[3] In fact, the London *Times* expressed this as well as it could have been said in Tokyo: "Port Arthur is more than a fortress. In taking it the Japanese wipe out a bitter memory of unmerited defeat received ten years ago at the hands of the Triple Inter-

[2] A.T. Mahan, "Principles Involved in the War Between Japan and Russia," *National Review*, Sept. 1904, "Retrospect upon the War Between Japan and Russia," *National Review*, May 1906, reprinted in A.T. Mahan, *Naval Administration and Warfare*, Boston, 1908, pp. 87–129, 133–173.

[3] Hori, *op.cit.*, pp. 201–202; *Japan Times*, Jan. 4, 1905; Hayashi to Komura, No. 4, Jan. 3, 1905, *J.F.O.*

vention." While the Japanese press also took account of this prevailing sentiment, the *Nichi Nichi* reminded its readers that the war was by no means over and that the most difficult fighting was yet to be done.

The Russian press reflected two diametrically opposite views of the event.[4] The *Novoe Vremya* stated that the honor of the army and the honor of the people were identical. The army's defeat was, therefore, the people's defeat. This identity of interests was in fact extended to the bureaucracy which, it maintained, was an inseparable part of the nation. The example of Stessel's gallant defense should, therefore, inspire the nation to fight on until complete exhaustion if necessary. The *Nashi Dni* and *Nasha Zhizn*, on the other hand, represented the opposition and took the view that a favorable occasion had been presented for ending the war. *Nashi Dni* expressed the view that since it was the bureaucracy that had started the war, Japan was actually waging war against this bureaucracy rather than the Russian people; the people should recognize that while Manchuria and Korea were of the greatest importance to Japan, for Russia they represented merely questions of colonial policy, foreign to the true interests of the Russian people. *Nasha Zhizn* added that Japan could be expected to accord an honorable peace to Russia as she had already done in the case of the Port Arthur garrison. To his limited readers Lenin took a position that fell somewhat between these views in that it neither supported the government nor desired the end of the fighting. In his article, "The Fall of Port Arthur," in *Vperiod,* he wrote: "It was not the Russian people but the Russian aristocracy which started this colonial war, bringing into the war the old and the new bourgeois world. It was not the Russian people but the autocracy which brought on this shameful defeat. The Russian people are the gainers from the defeat of the autocracy. The capitulation of Port Arthur is the prologue to the capitulation of tsarism."[5]

Lenin's defeatism at this time was aimed very specifically at the tsarist regime of Russia.[6] It has been noted that his views

[4] Hayashi to Komura, No. 14, Jan. 5, No. 16, Jan. 7, No. 18, Jan. 10, 1905, J.F.O.

[5] S.F. Naida, *Voennye Moriaki v Period Pervoi Russkoi Revoliutsii, 1905–1917 gg.,* Moscow, 1955, pp. 20–21.

[6] H. Draper, "The Myth of Lenin's 'Revolutionary Defeatism' (Socialist Reaction to the Russo-Japanese War 1905)," *The New International,* Sept.–Oct. 1953, pp. 255–283. Nov.–Dec. 1953, pp. 313–351, Jan.–Feb. 1954, pp. 39–59; M. Vetoshkin,

were a direct and literal socialist heritage from Marx and Engels who had singled out the tsarist regime as the strongest supporter of reaction everywhere. While socialists and even liberals in Russia shared this general antipathy toward the tsarist government, Lenin's emphasis at that time was on two aspects of defeatism. One was his preference for a Japanese victory because he felt she was more progressive than Russia; the other was the fact that, far from wanting the troops to lay down their arms, he was asking that they turn them against the tsarist regime instead of the Japanese.

Three weeks after the fall of Port Arthur, a mismanaged attempt to present a petition to the Emperor encouraged many more people to share this aversion to the tsarist government.[7] On January 22 (Sunday, January 9 by the Russian calendar), 1905 a procession of workers converged on the Winter Palace from four different points in St. Petersburg and instead of the anticipated reception by the Emperor, the marchers were fired upon by the troops. Soon after this, a selected deputation of workmen was received by the Emperor under favorable circumstances. But the damage had been done. The tsarist government had shown itself to be unmindful of the welfare of the people and left the revolutionaries to expose and emphasize the breach between throne and people.

The petition which the people carried as they approached the Winter Palace on January 22 had been drawn up with the assistance of an Orthodox priest, Father George Gapon.[8] His interests were, at that time at least, in the welfare of the people rather than revolution. The petition he had helped to compose was an appeal against the manager of the Putilov factory who had discharged some workers, and asked for redress and for some general reforms of both an economic and political nature. It was presented in the name of the General Russian Workmen's Association which Gapon had organized with government knowl-

---

Istorii Bolshevistskikh Organizatsii i Revoliutsionnogo Dvizheniia v Sibiri, Moscow, 1947, pp. 65–67; V.E. Poleshchuk, "Revoliutsionnoe Dvizhenie v Manchzhurskoi Armii v 1905 godu," *Istoricheskie Zapiski,* No. 49, 1954, pp. 312–314.

[7] McCormick to Hay, Jan. 31, 1905, W.C. Askew, "An American View of Bloody Sunday," *Russian Review,* xi, 1, Jan. 1952, pp. 38–43; A.M. Pankratova, *Pervaia Russkaia Revoliutsiia 1905–1907 gg.,* Moscow, 1951, pp. 61–68; B.D. Wolfe, *Three Who Made a Revolution,* New York, 1948, pp. 283–286.

[8] G. Gapon, *The Story of My Life,* London, 1905, pp. 257–261; Letter of the Correspondent of the London *Times,* Jan. 28, 1905, *J.F.O.;* Spring Rice to Mrs. Roosevelt, Mar. 13, 1905, Gwynn, *op.cit.,* I, 458.

edge and support. The marchers approached the palace peacefully, carrying ikons and singing "God Save the Tsar."

The shock of this episode is shown in the brief future career
of Father Gapon who had heretofore lived within the law and
carried on his activities under the eye of the police. After the
events of "Bloody Sunday" he fled abroad with the help of the
Socialist Revolutionaries and reached the revolutionary center
in Geneva.[9] One of his first acts was to address a letter to the
Tsar, this time condemning him for his crudely displayed indifference toward the people and calling him a hangman. For a
time Father Gapon became busily engaged in the revolutionary
movement, reading the literature and trying to unite all forces
for more effective action. His newly won prestige seemed at first
to promise some rewards, but before long he came face to face
with the grimmer reality of the diverse programs and objectives
of the liberal and revolutionary groups. He was lionized by the
press and even produced a book about his life which was to
serve as his apologia.

Gapon ultimately tried to carry his revolutionary activities back
into Russia and returned to join the underground. His return
appears to have been associated with a role in a gun-running
project for which a member of the Finnish Party of Active
Resistance, Konni Zilliacus, had received funds from the Japanese
agent, Colonel Akashi.[10] The expedition ended when the British
ship, the "John Grafton," ran aground and blew up off the
Finnish coast. Gapon was soon rightly suspected by the revolu-
tionaires of having reassociated with the government and was
hung in 1906 by Pincus Ruthenberg, the Socialist Revolutionary
who had helped him escape the year before.

The shock that had propelled Father Gapon into the ranks of
the revolutionaries also stimulated the other existing protest
movements, engaged in activities varying from the organization
of parties to elemental protests that were politically pointless.
All these movements suffered from an almost complete absence
of either coordination or cooperation, agreeing neither in their
approach to the hated tsarist regime nor in the goals they
sought.

One of these movements directed its attention to the forma-

[9] Wolfe, op.cit., pp. 302–304.
[10] P.N. Miliukov, Vospominaniia (1859–1917), 2 Vols, New York, 1955, I,
243.

tion of a plan for a constitutional regime.[11] Politically its main support came from the liberal groups. Starting with the zemstvo congress of May 1902 and continuing through two others held in 1903 and 1904, the outlines of a program began to appear. Finally, in the course of four congresses held between the spring and autumn of 1905 there emerged, at least for the liberals, a consensus with respect to their political expectations and a basis for the Constitutional Democratic Party, formed a few months later. This endeavor to form a solid front of all opposition groups behind a political program was a notable failure. Another attempt at forming a solid front was made at a conference held in Paris in late September and early October 1904 at the suggestion of the Polish Socialist Party and of Konni Zilliacus of the Finnish Party of Active Resistance.[12] While the Russian Social Democrats and some of the Marxian parties of the Russian minorities not only refused to send representatives but condemned the whole venture, eight major groups together sent seventeen representatives. These came from three nonsocialist groups, four socialist groups of the populist revolutionary type, and one Marxist party, the Latvian Social Democrats.

The Paris conference found some significant areas of agreement: the abolition of the tsarist regime; the advocacy of a democratic government based on universal suffrage to replace it; the recognition of the right of self-determination for the minorities of the Empire; and a forceful attempt to bring an end to the war such as demonstrations against the calling up of reservists and recruits and, ultimately an insurrection. The conference concluded its work by organizing two bureaus, one in St. Petersburg and one abroad. The latter was placed under the direction of Zilliacus who was to organize a press campaign of public opinion against the tsarist regime and in favor of peace. This attempt to collaborate was unproductive.

Along with these ineffectual programs, there was a more violent expression of opposition from other quarters. The effect of these forceful tactics left Russia with a two-front war: one

[11] G. Fischer, *Russian Liberalism*, Cambridge, 1958, pp. 177–199; D.W. Treadgold, *Lenin and His Rivals*, New York, 1955, pp. 124–137; P.N. Miliukov, *Russia and Its Crisis*, Chicago, 1905, pp. 328ff.
[12] Fischer, *op.cit.*, pp. 168–170; Treadgold, *op.cit.*, pp. 80–82; M.K. Dziewanowski, *The Communist Party of Poland*, Cambridge, 1959, pp. 42–43; Motono to Komura, No. 34, Oct. 23, 1904, *J.F.O.*; Gurko, *op.cit.*, p. 655; K. Zilliacus, *The Russian Revolutionary Movement*, New York, 1905, pp. 345–347; Miliukov, *Vospominaniia*, I, 241–247.

against the Japanese and the other against the Russian people. In the end this fact rendered the government more amenable to meeting the demands of the liberal political programs though its impact on the nation's war-making potential is easier to imagine than to document. At the very least, however, it underminded the prestige of the regime both at home and abroad and shook the self-confidence of the official world of St. Petersburg. Whatever the Japanese contribution to these events may have been, they observed and reported them carefully and in detail.

One aspect of the violent opposition was the terror and assassination aimed at persons in high and powerful positions. In July 1904 Plehve, the minister of interior, who was also associated with the anti-Jewish pogroms, was assassinated. This was planned by two members of the Battle Organization of the Socialist Revolutionary Party, Evno Fishelevich Azev, the notorious practitioner of police socialism, and Boris Victorovich Savinkov, a terrorist in the grand tradition who later philosophized about his craft in fiction. The deed was carried out by E.S. Sazonov, an expelled student and son of a wealthy merchant.

The revolutionary events of January 1905 were followed by other acts of terrorism. It was a period which Andrei Biely has portrayed in his *St. Petersburg*, focusing in his principal character the feverish and frustrating search for truth, the revolutionary plotting, and the incentives for assassination. In February the Socialist Revolutionaries assassinated the Grand Duke Sergei Aleksandrovich, the uncle and brother-in-law of the Emperor. The following June, A.I. Bobrikov, the governor general of Finland, was struck down by Eugene Shauman, the son of a Finnish senator. Even the assassination of the Emperor was planned though finally disapproved by the party.

Rural disturbances were also gathering momentum during the spring of 1905.[13] A new round of disturbances began in early February 1905, about two weeks after the ill-fated march to the Winter Palace. Starting in Kursk Province, the revolutionary disturbance spread general disorder, expressing itself in the pillaging of estates and illegally cutting timber and use of pasture lands. A very serious situation developed by mid-summer—a general strike of agricultural workers.

[13] G.T. Robinson, *Rural Russia under the Old Regime*, New York, 1949, pp. 138ff; Inouye to Komura, No. 110, Mar. 14, No. 355, July 28, 1905, *J.F.O.*; Spring Rice to Mrs. Roosevelt, Mar. 13, 1905, Gwynn, *op.cit.*, I, 456; M.C.R., Jan. 1905, p. 103.

In the course of the next few months both major revolutionary parties, in addition to an independent peasant organization, displayed considerable interest in the rural movement. The Social Democrats, meeting in London and Geneva took account of the possibilities of rural discontent, and in the summer of 1905 the Socialist Revolutionaries were active in organizing this discontent. Under the guidance of revolutionary intellectuals and of the peasants themselves an All-Russian Peasant Union developed that was active for several months, but the discontent was not converted into an effective political weapon against the regime. The peasants' role was to make the countryside unpleasant and unsafe for the landowners and to spread discontent to their relatives in the city and the army.

The strike movement was a more seriously directed and organized expression of discontent.[14] The strike at the Putilov Works which broke out on January 16, 1905 had furnished the issue for the "Bloody Sunday" march to petition the Emperor. Although only the most recent of a series of strikes reaching back through the years of the depression, the petition incident helped to give the movement such momentum that it spread in the course of the next few months and became a menace to the economic life of the country. By February its impact was seriously augmented by a railway strike which also grew in intensity and ultimately encompassed most of the railway network of the country.

The climax of the strike movement was reached in the autumn of 1905, after the treaty had been signed at Portsmouth. It reached its organizational and political culmination in the St. Petersburg Council (Soviet) of Workers' Deputies which assembled on October 26. While all major revolutionary parties were represented, the Council was dominated by the Mensheviks and Leon Trotsky (Lev Davidovich Bronstein) was its outstanding leader. Four days later, on October 30, the Emperor issued the October Manifesto, granting some of the liberal demands. This divided the opposition and cut the political ground from under the St. Petersburg Council which ended its existence a few weeks later.

[14] Pankratova, op.cit., pp. 57–59; I.M. Pushkareva, "Zheleznodorozhniki Rossii —Aktivnye Uchastniki Oktiabrskoi Politicheskoi Stachki 1905 goda," *Voprosy Istorii*, xii, 1958, pp. 153–168; Japanese Consul in Copenhagen, Mar. 17, 1905, Makino to Komura, No. 188, June 24, 1905, *J.F.O.*; *M.C.R.*, Nov. 1904, pp. 10, 140.

The impact abroad of the January 1905 events was profound and widespread.[15] People throughout the world were shocked and indignant at the treatment the Russian people had received at the hands of their government. This provided a golden opportunity for the revolutionaries who found new hope for their programs. In the general indignation against the tsarist regime they had found a popular cause around which they could rally general support. They sponsored protest meetings and street demonstrations in many cities of Europe and America and some governments were alarmed for the security both of the Russian government and their own.

The Ottoman Empire, Germany, and Austria-Hungary were among the nations which feared the impact of the Russian disturbances on their own internal security.[16] The Ottoman Empire, with her immediate proximity to Russia and the rampant nationalism which had already deprived her of important segments of her territory, was eager to insulate her people from the revolutionary infection. The mutiny in the Russian Black Sea fleet in June was especially feared in Constantinople as a direct exposure to the virus of revolution. Germany and Austria-Hungary, particularly the latter because its political stability was so dependent upon the peaceful acquiescence of minorities, were also alert to subversive influences. It was rumored both in Berlin and Vienna that these nations might move military forces eastward if the situation continued to deteriorate. It was assumed that such intervention would serve Russian interests and might not therefore be without its price.

The noncontiguous nations were also affected by the recent troubles and concerned about Russian stability. France, whose own political and financial security was at stake along with that of Russia, suffered a severe jolt to her confidence in the future.[17] This was in part because French politics sharply divided the

[15] Zinoviev (Constantinople) to Lamsdorf, Jan. 24, Krupensky (Rome) report, Feb. 4, Nelidov (Paris) report, Feb. 9, 1905, K.A., (Zalkind), IX, 33–40; Kato (Brussels) to Komura, No. 7, Jan. 26, 1905, J.F.O.; San Francisco Call, Jan. 30, 1905; G.W.F. Hallgarten, Imperialismus vor 1914, 2 Vols., Munich, 1951, I, 433, 452–455; C.E. Schorske, German Social Democracy, 1905–1917, Cambridge, 1955, pp. 36–54.

[16] Mitsuhashi (Copenhagen) to Komura, No. 14, Mar. 31, Makino to Komura, No. 46, Feb. 1, 1905, J.F.O.; Zinoviev, (Constantinople) to Lamsdorf, Jan. 24, 1905, K.A. (Zalkind), IX, 33; K.M.Tsovikian, "Vlianie Russkoi Revoliutsii 1905 g. na Revoliutsionnoe Dvizhenie v Turtsii," Sovetskoe Vostokovedenie, III, 1945, pp. 25–27.

[17] E. Alzona, Some French Contemporary Opinions of the Russian Revolution of 1905, New York, 1921, pp. 30ff; Sternburg to Foreign Minister, July 5, 1905, G.P., XIX-2, 613.

proponents and opponents of the close tie with Russia. Obviously the anti-Russian segment found new support as Russia seemed to plunge on recklessly, shooting its own workers, losing the war, and allowing its very existence as a government to be called into question.

While the prospect of a Russian collapse raised for France a menace to the balance of power in the West, President Roosevelt feared primarily for the balance in the Far East. He feared that even a temporary internal collapse of Russian power might seriously undermine her role as a Japanese rival strong enough to restrain a victorious Japan. For reasons of its own, the German government agreed with this view.

Great Britain's views differed markedly from those of Germany since her national interests were believed to be better served by a concentration of Russian power as close to the German frontier as possible. It was felt in London that the seemingly imminent collapse of the Russian government might eventuate in the restoration of this traditional relationship. Consequently, much to Roosevelt's chagrin, Britain seemed less disturbed than he thought she should have been by the recent rumblings of discontent in Russia.

The fall of Port Arthur and the events of January 22 and after, offered the most hopeful pretext thus far for giving serious thought to a peace settlement. Up to this point in the war, peace had been widely and almost continually discussed both as a rumor and as a serious objective. But before January the course of the war had been indecisive from both points of view and the most that Japan could claim was that while neither antagonist might in fact be winning, she at least appeared to be doing so.

In spite of the inconclusiveness of the peace effort thus far, by January 1905 some guidelines had been established by which peacemaking could proceed when the occasion seemed appropriate. One of these was the firm insistence of both belligerents that they would accept no settlement brought about by a general intervention or one which might lead to a general peace conference.[18] Russian experience with conferences that settled the Crimean war in 1856 and with the Berlin Congress of 1878, and the Japanese experience with the Three Power intervention of 1895 ruled out any group participation. It was understood that the war would have to be brought to an end either by

---

[18] Inouye to Komura, No. 129, Mar. 20, No. 175, Apr. 29, 1904, *J.F.O.;* Nicholas to Edward, Apr. 17, 1904, Lee, *op.cit.,* II, 287–288; Dobrov, *op.cit.,* p. 244.

the decisive defeat of one of the combatants or by direct negotiation, assisted if necessary by the mediation of a third power.
Even the possibility of mediation in any form would be severely
circumscribed by the jealousies implicit in the existing relations
between the great powers.[19] Germany would have been highly
suspicious of any such endeavor by Britian or France since this
might lay the foundation for the dreaded Anglo-Franco-Russian
entente. Mutual suspicion would also have made Germany unacceptable as a mediator to Britain and France.

Japan, as a consequence of her own well-founded suspicions
and special diplomatic objectives, also watched international
developments carefully and critically. Not even her ally, Great
Britain, was immune from her scrutiny, and she watched for the
outcome of the visit of King Edward to Germany in the summer
of 1904. Consultations there might lead to some undesirable joint
action of these two nations or even of these two with France. In
the end, it was apparent that only the United States was sufficiently untainted in the view of both belligerents to qualify for
the delicate role of mediator.

The American-German cooperation which emerged to play a
strong role in the making of peace had its foundation in the
relatively detached role of the United States, the seeming personal compatibility of the heads of the two governments, and in
their basic agreement on postwar policy in the Far East. Both
agreed that Russia should serve as the watchdog over an expansive Japan and shared, at least formally, a common view as to the
future policy in China. When President Roosevelt suggested
they work together in the Far East emphasizing that "I believe
in the open door for the Yangtze just as much as Manchuria,"
the German Emperor commented in the margin, "I too."

The German preoccupation with the Yangtze area, about
which she had concluded an unsatisfying agreement with Britain
in October 1900, became the touchstone of an American-German
rapprochement.[20] They discovered common ground in the early
stages of the war in agreeing on the necessity to preserve the

[19] Sternburg to Foreign Office, Mar. 21, 1904, G.P., xix-1, 112–113; Bülow to
William, Aug. 31, 1904 and annexed Promemoria by Count Pourtales of Aug. 24,
1904, G.P., xix-2, 535–540; Inouye to Komura, No. 170, Apr. 25, No. 230, June
6, 1904, J.F.O.; Betzold to Eckardstein, Feb. 29, 1904, Eckardstein, op.cit., p. 195.
[20] Sternburg to Foreign Office, Feb. 6, Feb. 8, Richthofen to Alvensleben,
Feb. 9, 1904, G.P., xix-1, 99–103; Mühlberg to Bülow, Aug. 4, Bülow to Foreign
Office, Aug. 5, Sternburg to Foreign Office, Sept. 27, Oct. 13, Bülow to Sternburg, Oct. 22, 1904, G.P., xix-2, 531–544 passim.

territorial integrity and the open door in China. Germany was troubled by rumors that Britain intended to seek compensation for her support of Japan by expanding her Yangtze sphere to include contiguous areas of China. She also suspected, particularly after the conclusion of the Anglo-French Entente, that these two nations would coordinate their efforts in preempting Chinese territory.

The United States and Germany began their cooperation by sponsoring a circular note intended to enlist the agreement of the powers in guaranteeing the neutrality of China. Within a few months there had emerged a mutual interest which von Bülow referred to as a "hand in hand" policy. In addition to the assurances as to the general stability, Germany saw in this American partnership a guarantee of the vital Yangtze region which Britain had withheld and hoped that this would serve in the broader sense to modify British ascendancy in East Asia. The idea was so congenial that it was ultimately expanded into a plan for an American-German-Chinese alliance to counteract the Anglo-Franco-Russo-Japanese combination which emerged after the war.

The American government also had something to gain from German support. The cooperative guarantee of the neutrality of China was highly valued in Washington since the other powers were suspected of monopolistic objectives due to their greater financial and territorial stakes in China. Furthermore, without their own concessions American commercial interests were most vulnerable to political instability.

During the war the United States suffered reverses in China which only provided additional reasons to seek solace in general guarantees as well as peace.[21] The Chinese government announced in January 1904 that it would not renew the objectionable immigration treaty concluded ten years before. In December, China canceled the concession to build the Canton-Hankow railway acquired in 1900 by the American China Development Company, and in the spring of 1905 the anti-American boycott broke out,

---

[21] M. Field, "The Chinese Boycott of 1905," Harvard University, Committee on Regional Studies, *Papers on China*, 11, 1957, pp. 63–89; J.W. Foster, "The Chinese Boycott," *The Atlantic Monthly*, xcvii, 1906, pp. 118–127; C.F. Remer, *A Study of Chinese Boycotts*, Baltimore, 1933, pp. 29–34; Chinese Minister to Secretary of State, Dec. 22, 1904, Secretary of State to Chinese Minister, Jan. 4, 1905, Loomis to Coolidge, May 26, 1905, Rockhill to Secretary of State, Aug. 27, 1905, *U.S.F.R.*, 1905, pp. 124–132, 204, 216.

protesting the American attitude toward the Chinese as expressed in the wording and administration of the immigration treaty.

Witte's visit to Europe in the summer of 1904 to negotiate an agreement with Germany was the occasion for the first attempt to mediate the war.[22] Because of his prestige and his association with a group believed to have opposed the war, Witte was apparently thought to be the Russian official most willing and able to influence his government to consider peace. The plan was to bring about a meeting at some neutral place such as Brussels between Witte and Hayashi, the Japanese minister in London. Baron Eckardstein, the German diplomat living in Britain, served as the intermediary between the interested parties. The reason this plan did not succeed has been variously explained. Eckardstein wrote that the assassination of Plehve necessitated Witte's immediate return to Russia, and Witte and Dillon, the latter a close friend of Witte's, agreed substantially that the reason was the absence of instruction from St. Petersburg. The two versions are not, of course, incompatible.

The incident was in some ways characteristic of others that followed the next year. It demonstrated, as later peace efforts would also do, the vital interest of French financial circles in ending the war, as well as the reluctance of the Russian government to face the prospect of a humiliating peace. Even the meager evidence about this first major attempt at mediation reveals that the Russian government was a party to it and the possibility exists that some serious consideration was given to the matter in St. Petersburg.

The Russian awareness at this time of the Japanese peace demands, though difficult to determine, is necessarily a matter of considerable interest. It is known that Japan was considering a set of peace conditions as early as July 1904, and Eckardstein states that the Russian government had before it four basic Japanese demands: a free hand for Japan in Korea; retrocession of Port Arthur to China; placing of the Manchurian railways under international control; and the payment of an indemnity to Japan. In view of the peace conditions then being formulated by the Japanese government, these alleged demands are not only incom-

[22] Eckardstein, op.cit., pp. 76–83; Dillon, Eclipse, p. 296; Witte, op.cit., II, 286–287; Dobrov, op.cit., pp. 215–216; Rutkovsky telegram (to Kokovtsov?), Feb. 25, 1905, K.A., VI, 6–7; K.G., II, 28; L.N. Kutakov, Portsmutskii Mirnyi Dogovor (iz Istorii Otnoshenii Iaponii s Rossiei i SSSR. 1905–1945 gg.), Moscow, 1961, pp. 11ff.

plete and far less severe than the actual ones, but fail to reflect the Japanese determination to acquire the railway and the leased territory of Kuantung. The demand for an indemnity was, however, a very real part of the Japanese thinking and constituted an issue on which the Russian government adamantly refused throughout the war even to negotiate. This question could, therefore, have been the reason for the failure of this initial peace effort.

The Russian decision in this case must also have been influenced by Japan's openly expressed interest in peace.[23] In late June the German press had quoted Baron Suematsu to the effect that Japan would "not hesitate to accept any honorable mediation which may be proposed by a friendly power." The very next day the Russian *Novoe Vremya*, referring to this statement, commented:

". . . it is apparent that Japan is wishing to put an end to the war as it is ruinous to her, and her material resources are not to be compared with those of Russia which are not in a position to feel any disastrous effects. Japan may blame herself for the rashly opened war causing ruin to her finances. . . . When the superior army of Kuropatkin and the combined fleet act together what effect it will have upon them may be, therefore, easily imagined."

By the summer of 1904, therefore, the idea was being expressed that Japan was more eager for peace than Russia. This rested in part on statements to this effect by Russia and in part on some widely accepted views about the two antagonists. There still remained the general image of Russia as the aggressor and of Japan as the defender of an accepted system of control in China. It was also true that Japan was untried in the role of a challenger of a western power and her determination and capacity for modern war were only gradually realized.

A more fundamental reason for Japan's greater willingness to consider peace was her own awareness that the general image of her as the weaker party was, in the fundamental sense, correct. The military force, both in manpower and materiel, which she could commit to the struggle was limited. She had, therefore, to plan for a decision as early as possible. Japan had also to be

[23] Inouye to Komura, No. 248, June 21, No. 250, June 22, 1904, *J.F.O.*

as specific as possible about her objectives and to set the stage diplomatically for their acceptance. It was with this in mind that Suematsu had been sent to Britain and Kaneko to the United States. It was also for this reason that Japan began early to think about acceptable terms for concluding the war and to keep her ear to the ground for signs of a receptive attitude on Russia's part. Though conclusive evidence is unfortunately lacking, it is entirely possible that Japan inspired or even initiated the peace effort of July 1904.

The Japanese pursuit of peace was apparently resumed soon after the fall of Port Arthur.[24] Baron Kaneko and Minister Takahira in Washington, and Baron Suematsu and Minister Hayashi in London seem to have been the driving force in the campaign to restore the conditions for a return to negotiations. President Roosevelt, in consultation with the Japanese representatives, assumed the leading role in organizing European support for ending the war. He carried on his drive directly with the emperors of Germany and Russia in the hope that the former would join in helping to influence the latter.

The uncompleted peace maneuvers of July 1904 were repeated again in London after the Port Arthur disaster. The agent of the Russian minister of finance, Rutkovsky, wrote that he had been approached by intermediaries of the Japanese minister in London. Referring to the proposals of seven months before, the Japanese had emphasized that, while they would demand an indemnity, they would not insist upon it. The minister of finance, Kokovtsov, replied directing Rutkovsky to leave the whole affair to the Russian ambassador and then turned the correspondence over to the Russian foreign minister. This peace movement was a failure largely because Russia was not ready to acknowledge defeat.[25] In spite of the internal disturbances which would seem to have made peace advisable, an military situation was not officially seen as menacing. The defense of Port Arthur had been planned as a means of gaining time to prepare for the decisive struggle of the future and Russia believed that the significant battles yet to come were clearly to be fought far from Russia's own territory.

[24] Kaneko, *Beikoku;* Roosevelt to Meyer, Feb. 6, 1905, Morison and Blum, *op.cit.,* IV, 1115–1116; *N.K.S.,* II, 4–5; Baelz, *op.cit.,* p. 336; Beale, *op.cit.,* pp. 281–283.
[25] Motono to Komura, No. 57, Feb. 27, 1905, *J.F.O.;* MacDonald to Lansdowne, Jan. 12, 1905, *B.D.,* IV, 68.

Another reason for the failure of the first peace campaign of 1905 was the fact that the German Emperor did not at that time give his support to President Roosevelt's efforts.[26] Instead, he was firmly encouraging the Russian desire to fight on in the hope of victory. He understood that internal disturbances might deflect some of Russia's efforts from the war, but strongly advised against seeking a remedy in yielding to reform, warning specifically against listening to Witte and others who were advising reform. The remedy as the German Emperor saw it was to seek victory in the Far East.

The German Emperor had hardly expressed these words when the expected land battle began near Mukden. With the Russian troop accessions of the past few months and the addition of Japanese forces released from the seige of Port Arthur, 300,000 Japanese faced 310,000 Russians. In a two-week's battle ending on March 10, the Japanese won a victory which delivered Mukden entirely into their hands and sent the Russians retreating northward. This was the last of the major land engagements. General Kuropatkin was replaced as commander in chief by General Linievich. Anticipating further retreat, defensive lines were prepared to the northward at Kungchuling and Kuanchengtze, but the expected Japanese advance never came.

The battle of Mukden was scarcely over before a reassessment of the war and of the possibilities for peace began. While this peace movement had its roots in the attempts that had preceded it, from this time on it was far more widespread, better supported by national interests, and in general far more hopeful. The principals began to examine more realistically their capabilities for war. By this time also the diplomatic situation in Europe was developing to the point where the foundations of the Franco-Russian stance in the West were in danger of being completely undermined.

After the battle of Mukden, it was apparent to the Japanese government, particularly the military leaders, that the country was reaching the limits of its striking power in Manchuria.[27] On

---

[26] Shebenko to Nicholas, Jan. 22, William to Nicholas, Feb. 19, 1905, *K.A.* (Sergeiev), ix-1, 62–65.

[27] Hori, *op.cit.*, pp. 205–206; S. Ono, *Gensui Koshaku Oyama Iwao*, Tokyo, 1935, pp. 733–737; MacDonald to Lansdowne, Mar. 24, 1905, *B.D.*, iv, 71; I. Tokutomi, *Koshaku Yamagata Aritomo Den*, 3 Vols., Tokyo, 1933, iii, 674–680; I. Tokutomi, *Koshaku Katsura Taro Den*, 2 Vols., Tokyo, 1917, ii, 242–248; *N.K.S.*, ii, 6.

March 13, Field Marshal Oyama gave notice to the Imperial Headquarters that the next step forward would require a renewed national effort including a significant augmentation of the military forces. His chief of staff, General Kodama, went to Tokyo to insure that a suitable emphasis would be given to the seriousness of the situation.

Paralleling the weakness they found in their own forces, the Japanese commanders had also to take account of the strength of their opponent insofar as they were able to assess it. They could not assume that defeats in South Manchuria would necessarily be sufficient to induce capitulation on the part of a vast empire whose soil had not yet been touched by war. On the contrary, there were many evidences of Russia's determination to continue the struggle. General Linievich, as commander in chief, began preparations for a renewed effort. While Japan was reaching the end of her capacity to replace her losses, both men and materiel were constantly moving eastward over the railway to enhance Russia's fighting strength. The Russian minister of communications, Prince Khilkov, was known to be making progress in improving the transport capacity of the railway. Finally, the approaching Russian Fleet from the Baltic could not be forgotten. The first units of Rozhestvensky's fleet had left Madagascar on March 16 and would arrive in French Indochina on April 14.

Marshal Yamagata and Viscount Ito agreed with Marshal Oyama and joined him in advocating a basic reconsideration of the national policy. On February 12, as Baron Takahashi was leaving for the West to seek another loan, Ito remarked to him that success in his venture would only serve to increase Japan's indebtedness. In Ito's view, even this would not justify allowing the war to continue if it could possibly be terminated.

Prime Minister Katsura and Foreign Minister Komura had initially been unsympathetic toward any hasty efforts to end the war. However, the conclusion of a loan on March 24, 1905 helped to strengthen Japan, at least from the point of view of outsiders unaware of the incapacity of the Japanese army to carry the war beyond Mukden. The loan was in the amount of 30 million pounds at a more favorable rate of 4 and one-half per cent and was again concluded with the help of Mr. Schiff. With this splendid support and before her fatal weaknesses were disclosed, the time seemed appropriate for Japan to end the war. Accordingly, in April the Japanese government decided to seek a favorable peace through American mediation as soon as possible. The Elder Statesmen approved the venture in meetings on April 7 and 17 and a Cabinet conference on April 21 decided upon revised peace terms.

President Roosevelt's readiness to respond to this formal request to mediate had been made clear immediately after the battle of Mukden.[28] On March 11, he telegraphed his congratulations to Kaneko in New York, adding that he hoped to see him before going on a hunting trip in the West. Accordingly, Kaneko visited Roosevelt on March 20 for a general review of the situation. It was on this occasion that Secretary Taft was introduced into the Kaneko-Roosevelt discussions. Secretary Hay's illness had for some time made his conduct of diplomatic affairs almost impossible and he had left for Europe two days before. Subsequently Taft was drawn more and more into the Russo-Japanese affair and would shortly be called upon to relay the Japanese request for mediation to Roosevelt at Glenwood Springs, Colorado.

In the course of the conversation of March 20, Roosevelt disclosed his plans for mediation and, particularly, the progress of his peace discussions with France and Germany. A few days later he had a serious discussion with the Russian ambassador, Count Cassini. He tried to persuade Cassini that it was to Russia's interest to conclude peace before further Japanese victories made the terms more onerous. Roosevelt would have felt encouraged had he known of Cassini's recommendation to Lamsdorf that the President's good offices might be found useful.

The American ambassador in St. Petersburg, George Meyer, found no such cause for optimism. He had sought an audience with the Emperor hoping to encourage acceptance of the President's good offices in bringing the belligerents together. At the audience on April 12 he found that the Empress was also present and saw her as an opponent of his mission since he had already been informed by the British ambassador that she was determined to encourage her husband to carry on the war with the hope of victory. Indeed he sensed her negative effect on her husband during the audience and wrote in his diary that she had "watched him like a cat."

[28] Kaneko, *Beikoku;* Cassini to Lamsdorf, Mar. 31, 1905, Dobrov, *op.cit.,* p. 251; Griscom, *op.cit.,* p. 253; Meyer to Roosevelt, Apr. 13, 1905, M.A. Howe, *George von Lengerke Meyer,* New York, 1919, p. 145; Roosevelt to Sternburg, Mar. 31, 1905, Morison and Blum, *op.cit.,* IV, 1155.

The formal Japanese request for the President's good offices reached Washington during his absence in Colorado,[29] and was relayed to him in a telegram from Taft on April 25. He then notified Taft that he would start home on May 8 instead of a week later, excusing his earlier departure on the grounds of the demands of public business. He also requested Taft to consult the Japanese minister, Takahira, about the possibility of sounding out the Russian ambassador, being careful not to imply that the Japanese had suggested mediation. If Takahira approved, Taft was to discuss with Cassini the possibility of opening direct negotiations between the belligerents.

President Roosevelt was aware that the consent of Russia was the cornerstone of a successful mediation. It was with this in mind that he had sent the American ambassador to make a personal appeal to the Russian Emperor. Roosevelt also brought pressure to bear on Russia from both Paris and Berlin. France had, of course, from the first been eager for peace and needed no persuasion.

Germany, on the other hand, was not ready to urge Russia to make peace.[30] The German Emperor foresaw that ending the war now after all the Russian defeats, might mean the end of the monarchy in Russia and the rise of a popular government; he felt this undesirable in a country with such a low level of literacy. Furthermore, the Emperor expressed the view that should the Japanese take Vladivostok and Sakhalin and destroy the rest of the Russian Fleet, the war would reach a stalemate and end anyway. Undoubtedly the Emperor saw in such an outcome a desirable and secure check on Russian power in the Far East.

The usefulness of France and Germany in the mediation effort was at all times circumscribed not only by their preoccupations with their own interests but also with the tensions between them. This rivalry was reflected in a marginal comment the Emperor made on a dispatch which informed him that Roosevelt had consulted France about mediation before making the same approach to Germany. He wrote sarcastically: "But, of course, he has not consulted the Kaiser who alone can make this possible."[31]

Far from desiring peace at this time, the German Emperor had unfulfilled plans of his own that required maximum Russian discomfiture for their success. He opened a new phase in Franco-

[29] Roosevelt to Taft, Apr. 27, 1905, Morison and Blum, op. cit., IV, 1,165.
[30] Bülow to Sternburg, Mar. 27, 1905, G.P., XIX-2, 583–585.
[31] Sternburg to Foreign Office, Mar. 18, 1905, G.P., XIX-2, 581.

German relations when on March 31, 1905 he landed at Tangier. As defined in Berlin, the Emperor's mission was to defend the open door in Morocco against the intended French monopoly there. In view of the cause of the war in Manchuria as Japan had defined it, this was a principle which neither Japan nor her supporters, Britain and the United States, could treat lightly.

The need was apparent to conserve such strength as Russia still had in order to support France in the impending Moroccan crisis.[32] The Tangier affair was an undisguised test of the Anglo-French Entente and was clearly aimed at breaking it up and reducing France to political inferiority in both Europe and Africa. Carrying out the affair at the moment of Russia's humiliating defeat at Mukden only served to emphasize the helplessness and powerlessness of the Franco-Russian Alliance and, consequently, the danger to French security.

This blow to the Franco-Russian Entente also brought to the fore the problem raised by the eastward movement of the Russian Fleet. This expedition owed its successful passage so largely to French help that France could hardly hope to avoid responsibility for it. Should the Japanese be successful in destroying this last usable vestige of Russian naval power, the consequences to Franco-Japanese relations might be severe. French maritime access to the Far East as well as her territorial possessions there would become hostages to an understandable Japanese desire for revenge. Confronted by both German and Japanese ill-will, France's international position would indeed be severely crippled.

French attempts to bring the belligerents together to renew the search for a basis of agreement were started even before the end of the battle of Mukden. In early March a direct appeal was made to the Russian Emperor, though with no immediate results. During the succeeding weeks the French foreign minister, Delcasse, took a personal hand in pushing the peace movement toward some concrete results. By early April he had assumed a role that suggested the possibility of his carrying on as a mediator. But Japan would not approve of Russia's alliance partner in this role. Instead, Roosevelt was proposed and accepted in Tokyo and from this point on arrangements went forward looking toward direct negotiations between the belligerents.

[32] Paleologue, op.cit., pp. 254–268; Hori, op.cit., pp. 203, 211; Baelz, op.cit., p. 362; T. Dennett, Roosevelt and the Russo-Japanese War, New York, 1925, pp. 174ff; H.F. Pringle, Theodore Roosevelt, A Biography, New York, 1956, p. 269.

12. A Return to Diplomacy

THE WILLINGNESS of the Russian government to seek peace was as half-hearted as its desire to avoid war had appeared. This was in large part because Russia's soil had not been violated nor had her armies been conclusively defeated. It was also because of the presistence in St. Petersburg of the prewar image of Russia as a great power engaged with other great powers in a severe international struggle. In this perspective, Japan's bid for attention to her own wishes appeared as not much more than a temporary annoyance in Russia's path. It was all too natural under such circumstances to assume that, given time to supplement her military forces, the imbalance could be corrected and the full power of Russia's drive in the Far East resumed.

The Russian government found it particularly difficult to accept the actual consequences to her of the war thus far. The predilection to view the early battles as skirmishes preliminary to the main drive that would follow when Russia was adequately prepared had placed the war in an inaccurate perspective. Consequently, there was a tendency for Russia to measure her strength by the number of troops and materiel moving eastward toward Manchuria and to disregard the parallel deterioration of her military position in the Far East. It was understandably difficult to face the fact that Russia's chances of recapturing control of the sea and access to the coasts of the continent were unpromising. Meanwhile, the deterioration of morale which had started with the defeats on land and sea was continuing apace under the impact of economic decline and revolution.

The Japanese naval victory in May 1905 at Tsushima made a profound impression even in St. Petersburg. This was not merely because it was another Russian defeat, but because it was so complete and disastrous. If after this Russia did not admit defeat, she had at least to recognize the wisdom of discussing peace terms.

The diplomatic activity in the capitals of the major powers reflected even more accurately than in St. Petersburg the impact of this battle. International arrangements were carried out at a forced pace to take the fullest advantage of the fluid state of the balance of power and to anticipate the new pattern it was assuming. The Anglo-American-Japanese relationship was re-

affirmed. Simultaneously, Germany made a desperate though unrewarding effort to lay the ghost of encirclement.

The battle of Tsushima Strait was a triumph of careful planning
and precise execution by Vice Admiral Togo Heihachiro and the
Japanese Fleet. Togo waited for his adversary at Masampo on the
Korean coast, a point Russia had in recent years aspired to control. His whereabouts were veiled behind a heavy cloud of
secrecy and silence which, because they were so well preserved,
became a factor in the successful outcome. Along the approaches
from the south, the mountain-tops, promontories, and islands were
alive with observers ready to relay news of the Russian approach.
The seas were divided into squares patrolled by scouting ships
equipped with wireless. Togo would know immediately whether
the Russian ships had chosen to make for Vladivostok through
Tsushima or to encircle the Japanese islands.

At 4:45 a.m. on Saturday morning, May 27, the converted
cruiser, "Shinano Maru" on scouting duty, telegraphed the long-
awaited message: "Enemy's fleet sighted in square 203."[1] This
meant that Admiral Rozhdestvensky was approaching Quelpart
Island on the last leg of his journey and had decided to make
a dash through the strait. There was little to choose for him
between the two alternate routes to Vladivostok. The route east of
Japan presented very difficult coaling operations and the danger
of detection was great. Besides, Admiral Togo could have covered
the distance faster through the Japan Sea route only to trap the
Russian fleet in the strait north of Hokkaido.

The victory which followed in the course of the next twenty-
four hours was complete in every meaningful sense. The Russian
fleet tried to break through just east of Tsushima but was way-
laid by Togo. It was clear from the very first that the Japanese
were outdoing the Russians in the aggressiveness of their tactics
and the deadly accuracy of their guns. Nevertheless, the ordeal
went on for over twenty-four hours until the Russians had nothing
left with which to fight. Almost all of their ships had either been
sunk or captured and Admiral Rozhdestvensky was a captive.

The news of the defeat and victory at Tsushima passed across
the world like an electric shock.[2] The German Emperor wrote
to his fellow monarch in St. Petersburg: "The great stake which

---

[1] Ogasawara, op.cit., p. 334; Brown, op.cit., p. 163.
[2] Willy to Nicky, June 3, 1905, I.D. Levine, The Kaiser's Letters to the Tsar,
London, 1920, pp. 184–185; Roosevelt to Kaneko, May 31, 1905, Morison and
Blum, op.cit., IV, 1198; Griscom, op.cit., pp. 253–254.

he [*i.e.*, Rozhdestvensky] represented in your hand has been played and honorably lost." A note from President Roosevelt to Baron Kaneko in New York stated: "No wonder you are happy! Neither Trafalgar nor the defeat of the Spanish Armada was as complete—as overwhelming." In Tokyo there were singing and dancing in Hibiya Park, streamers flying from the buildings, and the reenactment with fireworks of the burnings of the Russian ships.

The movement to bring the belligerents together for peace discussions was resumed immediately after the battle of Tsushima.[3] President Roosevelt had returned to Washington some days before to find the Japanese attitude very promising. After further preliminary discussions between Roosevelt and Japanese Minister Takahira, Foreign Minister Komura on May 31 formally requested Roosevelt to undertake mediation. He wrote to Takahira:

"You will express to the President the hope of the Japanese government that in actual circumstances of the case and having in view the changed situation resulting from the recent naval battle, he will see his way directly and entirely of his own motion and initiative to invite the two belligerents to come together for the purpose of direct negotiations and you will add that if the President is disposed to undertake the service, the Japanese government will leave it to him to determine the course of procedure and what other Power or Powers, if any, should be consulted in the matter of the suggested invitation."

The Japanese request that Roosevelt undertake mediation "entirely on his own motion and initiative" was understood to mean that Japan was not to be in any way associated with the early stages of the peacemaking endeavor. This would make it possible for her to avoid the stigma of being the first to ask for peace and, at the same time, leave her free to await Russia's response to an invitation before openly acknowledging her own desire for peace.

Roosevelt turned next to the remaining obstacle to a peace conference—the consent of Russia. He urged Russia's acceptance

[3] Roosevelt to Lodge, June 5, 16, 1905, H.C. Lodge, *Selections from the Correspondence of Theodore Roosevelt and Henry Cabot Lodge, 1884–1918*, 2 Vols., New York, 1925, II, 130–131; Komura to Takahira, May 31, 1905, *N.G.M., Nichiro Senso*, v, 231–232.

through three main channels: an interview with Count A.P. Cassini, the Russian ambassador; an appeal to the German Emperor that he join him in urging Russian acceptance; and a direct appeal to the Russian Emperor through the American ambassador in St. Petersburg. Roosevelt emphasized as forcefully as possible that for Russia the war had clearly been a failure and that unless she grasped this opportunity to make peace she might lose all her possessions in eastern Asia. At the same time, he wrote to Lodge that he was not optimistic about prospects of peace. If the Russian Emperor should refuse, he wrote, "then all I can say is that his blood must be on his own head."

The Russian Emperor's decision on the peace question was made under several, almost simultaneous, influences. One of these was the justification for peace that he received from his brother sovereign in Berlin. On June 3 the German Emperor wrote him a long, well-considered communication, reminding him of his longstanding affection for him, and stating plainly that in his opinion the defeat at Tsushima "ends the chances for a decided turn of the scales of the war in your favour."[4] The Japanese were now at liberty, he wrote, to pour unlimited numbers of troops onto the continent and to proceed to the seige of Vladivostok. The Emperor then turned to what he seemed to feel was a more serious aspect of the question—the response of the Russian people to the war and the defeat. "National honour is very good," he wrote in a complete reversal of his stand of only a few weeks before, "but only in case the whole nation is decided to uphold it with all means itself. . ." The Russian soldiers had fought well, but the chances of victory were gone and further sacrifices were not only useless but would in any case be refused by the people. After reminding Nicholas that both Napoleon and Frederick the Great had suffered defeat (did he remember how closely the fates of both had been associated with Russia?), he recommended that Nicholas accept the good offices of President Roosevelt and open peace discussions.

The change in the German Emperor's outlook reflects the reassessment which the Tsushima defeat had brought about.[5] His

[4] William to Nicholas, June 3, 1905, *G.P.*, xix-2, 419–422.
[5] Inouye to Komura, No. 33, Jan. 24, 1905, *J.F.O.*; Roosevelt to Spring Rice, July 24, 1905, Morison and Blum, *op.cit.*, iv, 1285–1286; Spring Rice to Mrs. Roosevelt, Aug. 10, 1905, Gwynn, *op.cit.*, I, 484; K. Mehnert, *Der Einfluss der Russisch-Japanischen Krieges auf die Grosse Politik*, n.p., n.d. (1930?), pp. 15–16.

warning about a prospective siege of Vladivostok can be seen as a realization that his former policy of tying Russia down in the Far East might be carried too far. Excluded from the Pacific, she might again turn her energies westward toward Europe. The same may be said of his reference to the indisposition of the people to continue the war and to the obligation of the sovereign to recognize the necessity of considering their desires in this matter. Clearly the dreaded spectre of revolution had grown too real for his comfort and he earnestly desired peace for his own reasons.

June 3 was also the day on which the sixth national zemstvo congress met and passed resolutions about the war and the need to reorganize the state. Their address to the Emperor, unknowingly reenforcing the two major contentions of William's letter, stated in part:

"Sire, Russia has been drawn into a disastrous war by the criminal abuse of your councillors. Our army is incapable of defeating the enemy, our fleet is annihilated. More menacing than this external danger, civil war is flaming . . . Sire, before it is too late, order immediately the convocation of national representatives who in cooperation with you will solve the vital question of war and peace, settle terms of peace or reject them, thus making this war a national one."[6]

On June 6 a conference of military leaders presided over by Emperor Nicholas was held to consider the crucial question of war or peace.[7] The Emperor directed the attention of the conference to the prospect that the next stage of the war might mean the occupation of Russian territory. He noted that while thus far no Japanese had set foot on Russian soil and not a single bit of Russian soil had been conceded to the enemy, this might well change tomorrow. The destruction of the fleet opened the possibility that Vladivostok, Kamchatka, and Sakhalin might be sacrificed next. Should this occur, it would be much more difficult to undertake peace negotiations. The Emperor, emphasizing the same issues noted in Emperor William's letter and in the zemstvo appeal, suggested that the conference direct its thinking toward four specific questions: first, was it possible, under present internal conditions in Russia, to satisfy the requirements for success

[6] Makino to Komura, No. 172, June 9, 1905, *J.F.O.*
[7] *K.A.*, xxviii, 191ff.

against the Japanese as specified by the commander in chief in Manchuria; second, was it possible, with existing military means, to prevent the Japanese from occupying Sakhalin Island, the mouth of the Amur, and Kamchatka; third, what effect would the success of the Russian armies in northern Manchuria have on peace if Sakhalin, the mouth of the Amur, and Kamchatka were occupied by Japan; and fourth, should steps be taken at once to conclude peace?

The conference approved taking steps toward peace but felt that Russia's bargaining power should be increased by strengthening the military forces. A contingent of 135,000 troops was already en route to Manchuria where they were arriving at the rate of 5,000 each day. Even though 80,000 of these were replacements, they would still augment the fighting forces by 55,000. In addition, it was planned to send four corps as reenforcements. The first of these would be dispatched in mid-June, the second in early July, and the other two in August.

The question of calling up reserves and recruits was discussed at the conference with special reference to the defense requirements of the western frontier. It was not deemed wise to move either reserves or recruits from the western districts of the Empire. It was estimated that about 500,000 recruits could be called up for training during the summer and autumn. Since the Russian and Japanese forces then in Manchuria were approximately equal numerically, these reenforcements could be counted on to give Russia an advantageous balance.

The conference also discussed the Japanese peace conditions which were obviously known with considerable accuracy. It was believed that, among other demands, Japan would require an indemnity equal to the sum of all foreign and domestic loans concluded during the war. This was estimated to be a sum between 600 and 700 million yen. It was assumed at the conference that the Japanese government was aware that Russia would in no case pay an indemnity and consequently, Japan was expected to be very reserved about this demand and willing to discuss alternatives. One possible alternative might be an advantageous commercial agreement or a grant to Japan of the right to receive the payments on the loan to China made at the time of the Boxer uprising.

On the same day as the conference, June 6, the American ambassador was received by the Russian Emperor, his first audience without the watchful presence of either the Empress or Lamsdorf.[8] After noting that both the King of Italy and the Emperor of Germany had advised him to consider peace, the Emperor said:

"You have come at a psychological moment: as yet no foot has been placed on Russian soil; but I realize that at almost any moment they can make an attack on Sakhaline. . . . Therefore it is important that the meeting should take place before that occurs."

The Emperor emphasized the importance of keeping his consent absolutely secret until the Japanese had agreed. In view of the dispute which immediately arose over the question of Russian consent, it is important to realize that the Emperor's message to Meyer was confirmed in a letter from Nicholas to the German Emperor.

The difference between the Emperor and Lamsdorf on the question of peace discussions has been explained as a misunderstanding. In the first place, it has been asserted that the only person who knew about either the letter from Emperor William or Meyer's audience with Emperor Nicholas was the Grand Duke Vladimir Aleksandrovich, the commander in chief of the St. Petersburg Military District. Secondly, the Russian government was apparently unaware of the Japanese negotiations with the United States and Great Britain over the peace issue and had no way of estimating the sincerity of the peace movement.

The lack of cohesion and the factional differences within the Russian government must also be taken into account. It is entirely possible that Lamsdorf knew nothing about the military conference held on June 6. The very fact that on June 7, the same day that Lamsdorf telegraphed Cassini saying that Russia would not then undertake peace discussions, he was still trying to learn from Paris the Japanese terms, indicates Lamsdorf's lack of information and helps explain his reluctance to commit Russia to peace negotiations. Finally, his views might have represented the widespread opposition to peace in official circles.

By the next day, June 8, the problem was sufficiently cleared up to justify Roosevelt in issuing formal invitations to the bel-

[8] Meyer to Roosevelt, June 9, 1905, Howe, op.cit., pp. 160–161; Dobrov, op.cit., pp., 272–274; Nicholas to William, n.d., Bernstein, op.cit., p. 103; Roosevelt to Lodge, June 16, 1905, Lodge, op.cit., II, 141; Galperin, op.cit., p. 17.

ligerents.[9] In identical notes, the President invited them to come together for direct discussions without any intermediary, "in order to see if it is not possible for these representatives of the two powers to agree to terms of peace." He added that he would do everything possible to arrive at a mutually acceptable time and place for the meeting. Japan and Russia responded favorably on June 10 and 12 respectively.

On the very day the Russian Emperor consented to discuss peace, war clouds appeared to be gathering over Paris.[10] For several months, Germany had been exerting pressure in Washington and Paris to have the Moroccan issue committed to a general conference. American help as a mediator was highly valued and was expected to be crucial in preserving the open door in Morocco and, infinitely more important, in preventing the rise after the war of the dreaded Anglo-Franco-Russo-Japanese alliance. The Sultan of Morocco finally consented to the congress on May 28, the day of the Japanese naval victory at Tsushima. With the end of the Russo-Japanese War in sight, haste was necessary if Germany were to achieve one of her major wartime objectives; the climax, or more accurately the anticlimax, was reached on June 6. It was then that President Roosevelt announced that he would not participate in a general conference unless France approved and on the same day, under the severest German pressure, Theophile Delcasse resigned as foreign minister of France.

The German gamble on the Moroccan question was a failure. Both sides had sought American support, Germany with the plea that if her sea power were destroyed over the Moroccan affair the United States would find it difficult to prevent the partition of China by an emergent quadruple alliance. American as well as British support was in effect given to France and with such firm assurances, France accepted the conference in early July. The conference met at Algeciras, Spain in January 1906. A few days before the opening session the German Emperor expressed this gloomy outlook:

"In the first place, we know that England and France will be sure to act together in Morocco. Then, that Fisher is burning

[9] Loomis to Meyer and to Griscom, June 8, 1905, *U.S.F.R.*, 1905, 807–808; *Kampo*, June 12, 1905; *M.H.S.*, XII, 434; Dobrov, *op.cit.*, p. 279.
[10] Beale, *op.cit.*, pp. 356–388; Bülow, *op.cit.*, II, 188; Hale, *op.cit.*, pp. 273–276; Hall, *op.cit.*, pp. 399–404; Spring Rice to Mrs. Roosevelt, Oct. 10, 1905, Gwynn, *op.cit.*, I, 499.

for a chance of destroying our Fleet and Merchant Service. We know that English private capital is being poured into the Paris press for the purpose of working up the French to provoke, and so to provide a *casus foederis*. . . . Most important of all, however, is the fact that England has, in effect, made an offer of armed support to France."[11]

The element in the foreboding outlook which the Emperor did not mention was the role Russia was intending to play at the conference. Russia's dependence on French finance was one of the trump cards which France had easily available. In January 1906 it was well played during the visit to Paris of the Russian minister of finance, Kokovtsov. Russia received a loan of 250 million francs with a promise of more after the settlement of the crisis. In return, the Russian delegates at Algeciras were instructed to support France. Germany's isolation and defeat were assured.

Soon after France had accepted the conference in early July, the German government turned again to the problem of closer Russo-German solidarity. The moment appeared almost as opportune as the occasion of the Dogger Bank incident had been. In early June, Norway had dissolved the union with Sweden and produced a temporary political instability in the north which could not avoid commanding Britain's attention. At the same time, Russia faced military defeat on the one hand and the uncertainties of peace discussions with Japan on the other. It was with these conditions in mind that the German Emperor, during a Baltic cruise in late July, suggested an informal and secret meeting with Emperor Nicholas.[12] Nicholas responded eagerly and exchanged several notes which fixed the rendezvous for Sunday evening, July 23, 1905. Accordingly, shortly before sunset on the appointed day, the German yacht "Hohenzollern" entered Viborg Bay, picked up the waiting pilot at Hochland and soon anchored alongside the Russian Emperor's "Polar Star" near the Björkö and Kavitza Islands.

The next morning the two emperors discussed the questions William had in mind. They considered first the problems that Norwegian independence had created for the Baltic countries and William made it clear that he hoped to settle the Scandinavian

[11] Bülow, *op.cit.*, II, 188–189.
[12] Bernstein, *op.cit.*, pp. 104–109; Fay, *op.cit.*, pp. 66ff; Sontag, *op.cit.*, pp. 287–297; Seegar, *op.cit.*, p. 54.

problems to his own advantage. Then William turned the conversation specifically to Russo-German relations, pulled a prepared treaty from his pocket, and asked the Russian Emperor what he thought of it. It was a defensive treaty similar to the one William had proposed several months before. Nicholas had time to read the brief document four times but no opportunity to consult his ministers. Nevertheless, with the urgent encouragement of the German Emperor, Nicholas signed it.

Under the scrutiny first of Lamsdorf then of Witte, the true meaning of the Björkö agreement became clear. Neither of these ministers entertained any fond attachment for Britain at whom it was purportedly aimed, but they agreed that to ask France to adhere to a secretly concluded Russo-German agreement was tactically unwise. Furthermore, it may be added, in view of Russia's financial needs, it was suicidal. It was decided in St. Petersburg that the treaty had to be annulled. Not until he heard of the instructions of the Russian delegates to the Algeciras conference, however, did the German Emperor realize that the treaty was in fact dead.

Simultaneously, the wartime allies were rethinking their own political strategy. The agreements which were even then tightening the bonds between Japan and her associates, Great Britain and the United States, were also concluded with specific reference to the impending peace settlement and its consequences. Yet the fact that they were secret and lacked the explosive consequences of the German political maneuvers gave them a specific and qualified impact on the peace deliberations. These preconference understandings gave Japan the added self-confidence she needed for her difficult role of reaping at the peace negotiations the full benefits of her incomplete victories. At the same time, such assurances of support undoubtedly encouraged her to avoid making unreasonable demands that might have led to complete failure. Russia, of course, could only guess at the existence and the specific content of these agreements. Accordingly, while she had to bear in mind the possibility that they had been concluded, they were not well known and did not, therefore, merge with world opinion to force Russia to accept a settlement with undignified haste.

Each of the three nations sought through these agreements to gain or preserve some diplomatic advantage from the wartime association, with particular attention to the Japanese victories.

Together, their accomplishments may be said to have been three-fold: recognition of the new balance of power based on Russia and Japan; a reenforcement of the anti-Russian front, a factor which, in the light of recent Russian activities in Central Asia and the consequent possibility that Britain as well as Japan would have to face the prospect of a war of revenge, had assumed a new importance; and the clear fact that considerable encouragement was being given to Russia to concentrate her attention in the west again. In the long run this would have an adverse effect on the German campaign to break down the solidarity of the Entente.

The renewal of the Anglo-Japanese Alliance appears to have become the subject of official discussions as a consequence of two occurrences, each reflecting the interest of one of the partners in the renewal.[13] The first was a despatch in early December 1904 from Sir Charles Hardinge, the British ambassador in St. Petersburg, raising the question as to the possibility of a postwar Russo-Japanese understanding which would leave Britain isolated in the Far East. An inquiry about this brought a categorical denial from Baron Komura, the Japanese foreign minister; he said that such an arrangement would not be contemplated by the Japanese government. The other event was a dinner given by Baron Komura on the very day this inquiry was made. This was in commemoration of the completion of the third successful year of the alliance. On this occasion, Komura had proposed the health of King Edward and had expressed his hope that the alliance "would continue to grow in strength and solidarity." He emphasized the desirability of extending the alliance for a longer period and of giving it "a larger and wider scope."

The renewal was under serious consideration from the latter part of March though its outlines only gradually became clear during the succeeding months.[14] The major problem was the extension of the Japanese guarantees to include India in exchange for the complete freedom of action which Japan desired in Korea. Hayashi strongly supported such an extension on the grounds that it was well worth the security Japan would receive from the renewal. On August 12, two days after Komura had handed

[13] MacDonald to Lansdowne, Feb. 13, Lansdowne to MacDonald, Mar. 24, 1905, B.D., IV, 120–121; Hayashi to Komura, Mar. 24, 1905, N.G.M., XXXVIII-I, 1-2; K.G., II, 162ff.

[14] Cabinet Councils of April 8 and May 24, Komura to Hayashi, May 25, 1905, N.G.M., XXXVIII-I, 7-8, 15–19; Lansdowne to MacDonald, May 17, MacDonald to Lansdowne, May 25. 1905, B.D., IV, 124–128.

the Japanese demands to Witte at Portsmouth, the renewal was signed. It was communicated to Count Lamsdorf on September 8, three days after the conclusion of the Portsmouth treaty, and was published on September 27.

Among the differences between the original agreement and the renewal was the geographical extension of its guarantees from China and Korea to include India. Also, in the 1902 Anglo-Japanese Alliance, Britain had recognized Japan's special rights and interests in Korea whereas the renewal stated that Japan might take such measures of guidance, control, and protection in Korea as she deemed necessary to protect and advance her interests. In 1902 the alliance had been defensive and had required the active participation of both parties only if one were attacked by two other powers; the renewal was both defensive and offensive and required the military cooperation of both parties if either were attacked by even a single other power. Finally, the new agreement was to be valid for ten years instead of five.

The Taft-Katsura agreement was the American counterpart of the Anglo-Japanese Alliance. On the day that discussions of a renewal had begun in London, Hayashi had asked Lord Lansdowne whether he thought it possible that the United States might join the alliance.[15] He had stressed the importance of such cooperation and the interest with which it would be received in Japan. Lansdowne had assured him that, while American policy was identical with that of Britain and was equally friendly toward Japan, the United States was wary of alliances and could not be expected to make so formal a commitment.

While this is in general an accurate statement of American policy, it is so mainly because President Roosevelt was searching for a balance of power in the Far East and thought that he had found it in Japan. To preserve the balance, he felt that there must be not only an equality of military power between Russia and Japan, but a direct confrontation of the two nations on the mainland. This meant giving Japan freedom of action in Korea and leaving Russia some substantial interests in contiguous Manchuria. This would, at the same time, solve the problem of Korea's political instability which, he would have agreed with

[15] Lansdowne to MacDonald, Mar. 24, 1905, *B.D.*, iv, 121; Beale, *op.cit.*, pp. 155–157.

the Russian and Japanese governments, was a disturbing factor in international relations.

By expressing his approval of Japan's Korean policy in an informal and largely noncommittal agreement, President Roosevelt was making an unusually fortunate bargain. For he was exchanging the benefits of honorary membership in the Anglo-Japanese Alliance and a guarantee of America's exposed trans-Pacific possessions for an assurance that Britain was already giving Japan and that he was himself morally committed to give in any case. Roosevelt had been kept informed of the course of the Anglo-Japanese negotiations and was aware of the defensive and offensive cooperation they provided. In fact, it is entirely possible that, through Cecil Spring Rice, Roosevelt was more than a mere observer in these negotiations.

The arrival of Secretary of War Taft in Tokyo on July 25 was a unique opportunity for both the United States and Japan to transact this important arrangement under the cloak of complete secrecy. For even Lloyd Griscom, the American minister in Tokyo, was unaware that Taft was doing anything more than making a courtesy call on his way to the Philippines.

Taft and his imposing party of 75 people were enthusiastically received in Tokyo. The visit was with some reason compared with that of Commodore Perry and President Grant.[16] It included the President's daughter, Alice Roosevelt, as well as a distinguished list of political leaders. The day after his arrival, Taft was received by the Emperor and escorted through his private garden. At a banquet given in his honor by the house of Mitsui, Taft found it impossible to conform to the custom of sitting on the floor and had to use a padded stool.

The conversations of July 27 between Secretary Taft and Prime Minister Katsura, initiated by the latter, out of which the "agreed memorandum" of two days later developed, dealt with the basic problem of Korea and the changes effected by the war. In the end, Katsura gave the strongest assurances that Japan harbored no aggressive designs toward the Philippines, while Taft gave his equally enthusiastic approval for

[16] K.G., II, 45–46, 259–261; Dennett, op.cit., pp. 15–19; Griscom, op.cit., pp. 257–259; Japan Times, July 25, 1905; N.G.M., xxxviii-i, 448-452; R.A. Esthus, "The Taft-Katsura Agreement—Reality or Myth?" Journal of Modern History, xxxi, 1, Mar. 1959, pp. 46–51; R.E. Minger, "Taft's Mission to Japan: A Study in Personal Diplomacy," Pacific Historical Review, xxx, 3, Aug. 1961, pp. 279–283.

the establishment of Japanese sovereignty in Korea to the extent of controlling her foreign relations and thus obviating future trouble. After communicating this exchange to President Roosevelt, Taft was able to telegraph from Manila on August 7 that the President had concurred completely with the views expressed.

An aspect of the balance of power which President Roosevelt could not so easily embody in a diplomatic agreement, however informal, was the military factor. Through the pages of Baron Kaneko's diary and of the President's letters to his close associates, runs the recurrent theme of Roosevelt's deep concern about the future of American naval strength in the Pacific. In the absence of any single convenient solution to the naval problem, Roosevelt had sought alleviation in several different ways; the reduction of the military strength of the two belligerents and his concept of "balanced antagonisms" whereby each would stand guard over the other, were recognized as partial solutions. One cannot avoid seeing another partial solution in the President's constant and earnest encouragement of the Japanese not to demand an indemnity. Had not the Japanese government used the Chinese indemnity of 1895 to prepare for aggressive war?

A further partial solution was found in a reconsideration of and ultimately a new emphasis in American naval policy.[17] Before the outbreak of war, naval plans had been focused on Germany as the prospective opponent and had sought security in the occupation of a naval port on the coast of China. Materiel and equipment had accordingly been assembled at the Cavite naval station in the Phillippines for an advanced base expeditionary force to some place such as the Chusan islands.

The Russo-Japanese war was the signal for a reappraisal of this unrealized program. The Japanese navy, with its home base in the Far East and its obvious effectiveness, loomed as potentially a far greater menace that the Germany navy. This was particularly true since its role in the protection of the national interests was firmly supported by the Anglo-Japanese Alliance, an understanding in the renewal treaty even assuring the allies a favorable naval balance in the Pacific. By 1908 these

[17] W.R. Braisted, The United States Navy in the Pacific, 1897–1909, Austin, 1958, Chs. iii, iv; S.W. Livermore, "The American Naval-Base Policy in the Far East; 1850–1914," Pacific Historical Review, xiii, 2, June, 1944, pp. 116, 129–130; S.W. Livermore, "The American Navy as a Factor in World Politics, 1903–1913," American Historical Review, lxiii, 4, July, 1958, pp. 869–873.

new power alignments had helped to bring into being an American naval policy in the Pacific that, seeking security several thousand miles away from the China coast, centered its principal effort at Pearl Harbor, Hawaii.

One of the imponderables of comparative national strength which must have occupied the thoughts of each of the delegates to the Portsmouth Conference, particularly the Japanese, was the political reliability of the Russian armed forces. It could have been an easy temptation for the Japanese, relying on their excellent covert sources of information as well as the known facts about recent events in Russia, to hope that some striking occurrence would reveal to the world beyond question the complete unreliability of the Russian forces. In fact, however, it was the inability of the Japanese to challenge the Russians in a land battle after March that brought the subject into the open and drew a taunt from the Russians during the Portsmouth Conference.

The outstanding demonstration of political weakness in the Russian fighting forces was the mutiny which occurred on the battleship "Potemkin" on June 27, 1905. The navy had played an even more frustrating role in the war than the army: the main portion of the Pacific fleet had been kept bottled up at Port Arthur until the surrender of the fortress; the Baltic fleet had made the long voyage to the Far East only to suffer the most decisive and humiliating defeat of all; and the Black Sea fleet was completely immobilized by international controls.

Though isolated from the war, the Black Sea fleet was not isolated from either the disturbances within the country or the revolutionary propaganda coming from Sevastopol or Odessa. One of those who brought revolutionary organization to the fleet was Ivan Iakhnovsky, an ex-foundry worker from Kharkov.[18] He joined the Social Democratic Party in 1901 and the navy in 1902. He was assigned to organize revolutionary activities in the Black Sea fleet. Through the instrumentality of the Sevastopol Sailors' Central, revolutionary groups were organized aboard many of the ships and propaganda, inflammatory information, and conspiracy were rife throughout the fleet.

By 1904 it was found necessary to curb the spread of these subversive activities. In January the commander of the Black

[18] A Fedorov, *Revoliutsionnye Vostaniia v Chernomorskom Flote, 1904–1907*, Moscow, 1946, pp. 15–23.

Sea fleet, Vice Admiral Skrydlov, was replaced by Vice Admiral Chukhnin in the hope that sterner measures would be taken. In May, Iakhnovsky was arrested and tried for revolutionary activity. In early November, Admiral Chukhnin tried to prevent the spread of propaganda by confining some sailors to their barracks. The response to this was a mutiny on November 3 in the course of which the sailors broke out of their barracks, demonstrated in the city, and destroyed officers' quarters and barracks.

During late 1904 and the spring of 1905 a mutiny was being planned to effect the entire Black Sea fleet and to take place in June.[19] The leaders prepared a list of demands including: the shortening of the term of military service, a more precisely defined working day, higher pay, and the participation of the sailors in the purchasing of their food supplies. The removal of the disaffected crew of the battleship "Ekaterina II" deprived the movement of one of its best prepared groups and an outstanding leader, Aleksander Petrov. But the planning continued and was given its final form at a meeting held on June 10. The rising would take place during the coming maneuvers at Tendrovsk Bay at a signal from the battleship "Rostislav."

The scheme failed and the mutiny actually took place by accident aboard the battleship "Potemkin" on June 27 and consequently it was poorly planned and premature. It developed out of a protest against the use of some meat which contained maggots. The executive officer, Commander Ippolit Giliarovsky, appeared to be getting the situation under control when Afanasy Matiushenko, a chief petty officer and the representative of the Social Democratic organization, stepped forward and rallied the men against the officers. The mutineers took over; then, realizing their hopeless isolation, unsupported either by other ships or from the shore, they sailed for Constanza, Rumania. The affair was dazzling for the moment but it did not ignite the entire fleet as planned and hoped.

The development of a potentially revolutionary situation in Siberia and Manchuria where the army was concentrated was associated with an unusual combination of circumstances. One of these was the exile system which had provided Siberia with

[19] Fedorov, op.cit., pp. 28–39; C. Feldman, The Revolt of the "Potemkin," London, 1908, pp. 22–31; R. Hough, The Potemkin Mutiny, New York, 1961, pp. 13ff; Naida, op.cit., pp. 12ff.

an imposing list of revolutionary leaders.[20] These included N.N. Baransky, E.M. Iaroslavsky, S.M. Kirov, G.I. Kramolnikov, V.V. Kuibyshev, V.I. Lenin, I.V. Stalin, and I.M. Sverdlov. Their activities had given the towns of Siberia a start in revolutionary organization and planning. The revolutionary work was also aided by the extraordinary dependence of the government on the railway to support the war effort. Most of the industrial workers of Siberia were in some way connected with the railway either as railway workers, mechanics in the repair shops, telegraphers, or coal miners. Thus, the organizational work could be concentrated in a few centers and could exert the maximum impact on transportation.

The organization of these workers had begun to have a significant impact by the summer of 1905. Work stoppages in July and August were effective in impeding the war effort. A telegraphers' strike started on October 28 at Chita and Harbin and spread two days later to Pogranichnaia and Vladivostok.[21] Students and others soon joined the movement in Chita; a crowd carrying red flags tried to reach the arms warehouse but were dispersed. In Harbin one crowd marched on the bank, demanding the cessation of business, while another raised the red flag over the railway station.

Agitation and organizational work were widely carried on among the soldiers and sailors in Manchuria and Vladivostok as well as the prisoners of war in Japan.[22] Thousands of leaflets were distributed bearing such titles as: "Down with the Criminal and Piratical Tsarist Autocracy," "To the Soldiers," "There Is Revolution in Russia," and "The Petersburg Blood Bath," the latter referring to Bloody Sunday.

With the end of the war, the emphasis had to be changed as the return of the troops to their homes became of the greatest importance. The newer recruits were urged to demand that they be sent home first and since both the revolutionaries and the government knew that these recruits were more disaffected than the regular troops and cossacks, sending them home first would have had the effect of spreading the contagion farther and faster as well as delaying the return of the more reliable troops who would have been useful in stamping out revolution. The signifi-

[20] E. Iaroslavsky, *Russo-Iaponskaia Voina; Otnoshenie k Nei Bolshevikov,* Moscow, 1939, p. 27; Vetoshkin, *op.cit.,* pp. 47–51.

[21] *R.-I.V.,* pp. 110–115.

[22] Poleshchuk, *op.cit.,* pp. 309ff.

cance of this revolutionary activity for the peace question could be seen from either of two points of view, both debilitating factors; it could provide an incentive for either the conclusion of peace or the more energetic prosecution of the war. Though fully aware of the campaign of subversion, the responsible heads of the armed forces favored the continuation of the war.[23] This was true of both General Linievich, the commander in chief in Manchuria, and General Kuropatkin. This view was forcefully expressed by General Dobko at the military conference of June 6 which had approved peace discussions as follows:

"As to the conclusion of peace, the return to Russia of an oppressed army which has not won a single victory, will deteriorate rather than improve the internal condition of the country. . . . It will be impossible to prevent the population into which will flow the ranks of a dissatisfied army, without glory or honor, from thinking that the state regime lacks power!"

The Japanese capture of Sakhalin Island in early July was a stern reminder of Russia's lack of a fleet and must have played a considerable part in inclining the Russian government toward peace, and indeed was an eventuality that the Russian Emperor had foreseen when he consented to discuss peace. The day following his approval of a conference, when the Russians appeared to be reneging on this commitment, President Roosevelt had suggested to Japan the seizure of Sakhalin as a means of forcing Russia to give more serious thought to peace. It is an interesting commentary on the obvious, forceful measures still available to Japan that a few days later King Edward suggested that the Japanese occupy Vladivostok as a bargaining point at the Portsmouth Conference.[24]

The idea of seizing Sakhalin Island had been under consideration in Japan for some time.[25] Lieutenant General Nagaoka, who had replaced General Kodama as vice chief of general staff in June 1904, was one of the first high-ranking advocates of the project at that time, neither the army nor the navy

[23] R.-I.V., pp. 98, 102–103, 108; Inouye to Komura, No. 281, June 18, 1905, J.F.O.; K.A., xxviii, 202.

[24] Reid to Roosevelt, June 23, 1905, J.B. Bishop, *Theodore Roosevelt and His Times*, 2 Vols., New York, 1920, i, 396.

[25] J. Shinobu, *Meiji Hiwa Ni Dai Gaiko no Shinso*, Tokyo, 1928, pp. 355–379; S. Ota, *Nichiro Karafuto Gaikosen*, Tokyo, 1941, pp. 234–235; Japan, Karefuto Cho, *Karafuto Enkaku Shi*, Toyohara, 1925, pp, 235–236.

were generally favorable to it. In August 1904, just after the first peace movement, Foreign Minister Komura had emphasized to Nagaoka the importance of occupying Sakhalin as a prod to Russia. The decision to carry out the Sakhalin project was finally adopted by Imperial Headquarters in late March 1905, after the battle of Mukden. The Thirteenth Division was issued orders for this purpose, but the Baltic fleet was still a major concern of the navy and Sakhalin had to wait. Finally, on June 9, after Roosevelt's proposal for the peace conference had been received, the final decision was made to invade Sakhalin and General Nagaoka was informed accordingly. The same order included the occupation of Kamchatka "if circumstances permit."

The occupation of Sakhalin was begun on July 7 when the Thirteenth Division commanded by Major General Haraguchi carried out landings at Korsakov. By August 7, before the Portsmouth Conference had assembled, the occupation was complete and the entire island was in Japanese hands. An article in the *Jiji* gave an interesting commentary on the perspective in which this successful venture was seen:

"Tsushima in the south and Saghalien in the north form the natural challenge gates to the Sea of Japan and the possession in our hands of the one is as important as that of the other. Further, to make the control of that northern gateway really secure in our hands, it is indispensable to hold the littoral country on the opposite continent. Then with Mamiya Strait in our grasp, the blockade of Vladivostok will become a very effective undertaking."[26]

[26] *Japan Times*, July 11, 1905.

THE PORTSMOUTH CONFERENCE
AND A NEW BALANCE OF POWER

13. Mediation and the Conference

THE PORTSMOUTH CONFERENCE, the final arena of the Russo-Japanese War, was confronted with three principal kinds of problems. There were the issues that had been clearly defined in the course of the prewar negotiations and were settled at the conference with little difficulty. Second, there were the peace conditions that Japan had added since the start of the war with a view to reaping the full benefit of her victories, but since victory had been inconclusive, this proved difficult to achieve and almost led to the breakdown of the negotiations. Finally, there were the problems that arose over the actual convocation of the conference. Neither antagonist was completely committed to peace and in addition there were groups in each country determined to obstruct peace if it required too great a sacrifice. This rendered each step of the way extremely tortuous, from the choice of a meeting place to the conclusion of the peace.

The possible meeting place began to be discussed at the same time that the two countries consented to discuss peace. In preliminary conversations with Baron Kaneko, President Roosevelt soon realized that the European capitals, Paris, Berlin, or London, would be unacceptable because of their association with the belligerents during the war.[1] Mukden or Harbin were also ruled out because of their proximity to the battlefields, the scene of recurrent Japanese victories. Kaneko also suggested Shanhaikuan or Chefoo in North China but added that Washington was a thoroughly acceptable choice.

While Japan's first choice would have been a place in the Far East, Russia preferred Europe, particularly the capital of her ally, Paris.[2] Her next choice was The Hague, located in a small neutral state and closely associated with the international arbitration tribunal. Russia nevertheless finally agreed to accept Washington. Sir Percy Sykes wrote that the approval of Washington reminded him of an Indian durbar in which "the Viceroy will meet His Highness in the centre of the carpet."[3]

Even Washington as a conference site had some drawbacks. Most obviously, it suggested the well-known American partisanship for Japan, a feature that might have made it an unfavorable

[1] Kaneko, *Beikoku,* June 8, 1905.
[2] Associated Press message from St. Petersburg, June 17, 1905, Morison and Blum, *op.cit.,* iv, 1231.
[3] Sykes, *op.cit.,* p. 285.

place for Russia. There was also the possibility that, after passing over the European capitals, the choice of Washington might appear to be a shrewd maneuver on Roosevelt's part to associate himself with a generally desired peace. In fact, this was not his purpose since he favored Switzerland and, even more to the point, he had little hope that the conference would succeed.

Since the United States appeared to be generally acceptable to both parties, Roosevelt and Kaneko thought of other localities that would avoid another objection to Washington—the summer heat. The plenipotentiaries would be more likely to endure the long, trying negotiations that might lead to a peace if a comfortable place such as Manchester or Newport were selected. These places, however, were bustling resorts where the negotiations might become too much of a public spectacle and thus prejudice the results. As the search continued, President Roosevelt wrote to the Japanese minister in Washington the specifications of the place he was seeking:

"I am taking steps to try to choose some cool comfortable and retired place for the meeting of the plenipotentiaries, where conditions will be agreeable, and where there will be as much freedom from interruption as possible."[4]

By June 26, Roosevelt's decision was formally announced to both countries, and he was ready to invite them to send plenipotentiaries to Portsmouth, New Hampshire.

Portsmouth provided ideal conditions for the comfort of the delegates. It was remote from the large, crowded cities and furnished restful conditions where the participants could find relief from the daily gruelling ordeal. Situated on a flat plain near the water front, it was backed by wooded country and had the recreation facilities enjoyed by tourists such as tennis courts, golf courses, and a pond for swimming. A letter to the Portsmouth *Daily Chronicle* noted how appropriately selected the region was historically.[5] It was situated in the Piscataqua River valley, a name which meant "the meeting place of waters." It had been a traditional Indian meeting place and the scene of an historic

[4] Roosevelt to Takahira, June 15, 1905, Morison and Blum, *op.cit.*, iv, 1226.
[5] D. Vaughan and T.C. Wilson, *The Peace of Portsmouth*, Portsmouth, 1957, p. 4.

meeting between the settlers and the Indians to end a war—the "Peace of Portsmouth," July 13, 1713. It was suggested that, should the Russo-Japanese negotiations be successful, the document which was signed should be called the Treaty of Piscataqua.

In view of the many uncertainties both at the war front and among the discordant factions in each country, the selection of peace plenipotentiaries was fraught with even more difficulties than the choice of a site. Between the failure to conclude any peace at all and the signing of an unacceptable one it would be difficult for a delegate to choose—either might blacken his name and end his political career.

Prime Minister Katsura had originally hoped to send Viscount Ito, then chairman of the Privy Council, as chief plenipotentiary to the conference with Baron Komura as his colleague.[6] But Ito had declined, feeling that it was more fitting that Katsura should retain responsibility for the war which had been under his guidance as Ito had done in the case of the Sino-Japanese war. The fact that Ito was unsympathetic with Katsura's Russian policy before the outbreak of war gave him additional reason for not wanting to share responsibility for the negotiations which held no guarantee of peace.

It was unquestionably Ito's favorable attitude toward a closer Russo-Japanese accommodation that led Witte to seek to influence the Japanese choice of chief delegate in his favor. Witte went so far as to ask Dr. E.J. Dillon to visit Hayashi, the Japanese minister, in London and request that Ito be urged to go to Portsmouth as chief delegate instead of Komura.[7] But the decision had already been made. Nevertheless, it is an interesting commentary on the mutual confidence in one another which these two statesmen shared that when Ito heard that Witte had been appointed he telegraphed his regrets that he himself would not be there.[8]

When President Roosevelt heard of the selections each country had made he also expressed his regrets that both Witte and Ito could not have been at the conference.[9] Not knowing the actual situation, Roosevelt was confident that, had it been known that Witte was going, Ito would almost certainly have been sent. The President did not seem to have suspected that, had they

[6] Shinobu, op.cit., p. 353.
[7] Dillon, op.cit., p. 301.
[8] Witte, op.cit., i, 358.
[9] Roosevelt to Meyer, July 18, 1905, Morison and Blum, op.cit., iv, 1296.

come, they would undoubtedly have sought precisely what he wanted least—a close Russo-Japanese accord.

Baron Komura Jutaro, the minister of foreign affairs, was the final choice of the Japanese government as chief plenipotentiary. He was of samurai origin, his father having been the owner of a sawmill in Kyushu which he had intended that his son would ultimately inherit and manage. Instead, the lord of the Obi clan to which the family belonged sent him to Nanko Daigaku, the predecessor of Tokyo University, and then to Harvard University from which he graduated in 1878.[10] On his return he served briefly in a judicial capacity and then was transferred to the Foreign Office where he found his life's work. Among his diplomatic posts, he served at Washington, St. Petersburg, Peking, and Seoul. These provided him with the ideal understanding of his duties as foreign minister during the war with Russia and for his assignment to the Portsmouth Conference.

Komura was small and frail in appearance and had a somewhat defferential manner which was, in Dillon's apt phrase, "masked by the opaqueness of the professional diplomat."[11] Yet these outward traits were deceiving to those who did not know him as a man of action. His record both before and during the conference disclose his forcefulness of mind, his ability to probe directly at the essence of a problem, and his impatience with any effort to sidetrack him. At the same time, his long diplomatic experience had taught him to know when the time for compromise had come. At Portsmouth he fought his country's cause with tenacity and almost left the conference when the desired settlement seemed to be out of reach.

Komura was officially appointed chief plenipotentiary on July 3 with Takahira Kogoro, the Japanese minister in Washington, as his colleague.[12] On the same day, he temporarily relinquished to Prime Minister Katsura his office of foreign minister and three days later he received the Imperial Rescript of appointment at an Imperial audience.

On July 8 Komura and his party took official leave for the conference at Shimbashi station in Tokyo.[13] Those on hand for

[10] K.G., I, 1ff; S. Komura, "Jutaro Komura, My Father," Contemporary Japan, I, 4, Mar. 1933, p. 646.
[11] E.J. Dillon, "Sergius Witte and Jutaro Komura," Harper's Weekly, XLIX, 2541, Sept. 2, 1905, p. 1262.
[12] Shinobu, op.cit., p. 369.
[13] Tokyo Asahi, July 9, 1905; M.H.S., XII, 457.

the impressive farewell were estimated at some 5,000 and included: several princes of the Imperial family; Prime Minister Katsura and other members of the cabinet; such elder statesmen as Ito, Inouye, Matsukata, and Yamagata; the Princes Tokugawa, Shimazu, and Kujo; members of both houses of the Diet; military and naval representatives of the Imperial Headquarters; businessmen and representatives of various organizations; various foreign and diplomatic representatives, and others.

As he left Shimbashi, Komura expressed these prophetic words to Prime Minister Katsura: "When I return my popularity will probably be reversed." Three railway cars had been reserved to take Komura and the farewell party to Yokohama. At 4:00 p.m. he departed for America on the Great Northern Steamship Company's ship, the "Minnesota," on which the Japanese flag had been raised in his honor.

How accurately Komura had foreseen his future as a peace plenipotentiary can be seen from his son's description of his return from Yokohama to Tokyo after the conference.[14] It had been rumored that the tracks had been mined and hence, only Komura's older son Kinichi, and a limited number of officials were permitted to go to Yokohama to meet him. Shoji, the younger son, had to wait at Shimbashi and noted that even Katsura, the prime minister, was not among those who received him. Shoji continued:

"At last the train came in and he stepped out on the platform, safe but haggard. His face was ghastly pale, but in his eyes was the familiar spirited look. In a rather loud voice, he began to thank those who had come to welcome him. It was pitiful to see how worn out he was."

Komura's triumphant progress to Portsmouth continued along his route to New York and great popular interest was shown in the plenipotentiary and his mission. When he landed in Seattle on July 19 he was greeted by the mayor while a crowd of citizens estimated at 3,000 had gathered at the dock to receive him. As he passed along the streets under police escort, it was noticeable that the shops had closed and that the streetcars had been temporarily halted. Crowds lined the streets waving hats and handkerchiefs.

[14] S. Komura, op.cit., p. 645.

Komura reached New York on July 25 to find a reception prepared for him befitting the popularity of his cause.[15] At the Waldorf-Astoria Hotel he was interviewed by the press and entertained by the Harvard Club. He had an opportunity of meeting the Japanese people resident in New York at a reception held at the Japan Club. The delegation, which had either come with him or were awaiting him in the United States, included: Takahira Kogoro, Japanese minister to the United States and Komura's colleague as plenipotentiary at Portsmouth; Henry W. Denison, an American who was legal advisor to the Japanese foreign office; Sato Aimaro, Minister Resident and a principal assistant at the conference; Yamaza Enjiro, chief of the political affairs section of the foreign office; Adachi Mineichiro, first secretary of the legation in Washington; Colonel Tachibana Koichiro, military attaché to the legation in Washington, and others amounting to fifteen in all.

The few days which Baron Komura had in New York were occupied in interviews and arrangements preliminary to the conference. Baron Kaneko remained throughout the conference the intermediary in New York. He accompanied Baron Komura on his visit to President Roosevelt at Oyster Bay on July 28 and had also worked out the communications plan by which Komura was able to keep in touch with Roosevelt who remained at Oyster Bay.[16] Consul Uchida Sadazushi of New York City formed the actual link with Komura at Portsmouth, personal messages being carried between them by Uchida's assistant, Sakai Tokutaro.

The selection of a chief plenipotentiary was even more difficult in Russia than in Japan. For while there was general agreement in Tokyo that peace was desirable, the main point of contention being the kind of peace that would be acceptable, in Russia, on the contrary, there were many in high official circles who felt that no peace at all was called for at this point. The course of the war had been so disastrous for Russia that for many the only corrective would be ultimate victory. To be instrumental in ending the war under these conditions would leave one associated with this gigantic failure and, at the same time, guilty of depriving the country of the opportunity for achieving victory. In addition widespread ignorance, even in governmental and

[15] Kaneko, *Nichiro*, pp. 773–775.
[16] Kaneko, *Beikoku*, July 26, 1905.

court circles, of Far Eastern affairs would further obscure the issues.

The most obvious choice for chief plenipotentiary was, of course, Witte. But his relationship to the war was in some respects similar to that of Ito in Japan—his policies had been disregarded and war had followed under other leadership. These two statesmen were equally free to detach themselves from responsibility for the war. Witte might reasonably, therefore, be suspected of eagerness to restore himself to leadership by seeking peace if possible. In addition, the feelings between Witte and the Emperor were such that Witte would be an unlikely choice if anyone else could possibly be found. When Count Lamsdorf recommended Witte for the appointment, the Emperor wrote on the report: "Only not Witte."[17]

Lamsdorf next suggested A.I. Nelidov, the Russian ambassador to France. But Nelidov declined the appointment on the grounds of old age, ill health, and insufficient knowledge of English. The American ambassador in St. Petersburg, George Meyer, noted that this refusal was in his opinion fortunate for Russia because Nelidov was too old and nervous.[18] He added that Nelidov had so completely bungled the matter of the Russian Emperor's failure to return the visit of the King of Italy that he had to give up his post in Rome and was actually persona non grata there.

The next choice considered was N.V. Muraviev, then the Russian ambassador in Rome and a nephew of the renowned governor general of Eastern Siberia under whom Russia had acquired the Amur and Maritime regions.[19] But, after coming to St. Petersburg and discussing the prospects with various persons, including the Emperor, he too declined. He did so on the grounds of his inadequacy to discharge the enormous responsibility he felt the appointment would entail. He felt poorly qualified even to grasp the issues and therefore considered it a hopeless undertaking for him. Furthermore, he felt that the 15,000 ruble allowance he would receive for expenses would be totally inadequate, particularly since he lacked the means to supplement it.

Witte was fully cognizant of this unsuccessful search for an

[17] I.I. Korostovets, *Pre-War Diplomacy*, London, 1920, p. 11.
[18] Meyer to Roosevelt, June 18, 1905, Howe, *op.cit.*, p. 170.
[19] Kokovtsov, *op.cit.*, p. 52.

acceptable chief delegate and of the fact that it was assuming more and more the aspect of a search for a scapegoat. He had himself helped in the search, suggesting such candidates as Lamsdorf, Prince Obolensky, Lamsdorf's assistant, and D.D. Pokotilov, the Russian minister in Peking. But none of these were willing or suited to undertake the mission. Consequently, Witte had little reason to be flattered when the choice finally fell to him. He commented to Kokovtsov: "When a sewer needs to be cleaned, they send Witte; but as soon as work of a cleaner type and nicer kind appears, plenty of other candidates spring up." Nevertheless, he accepted the responsibility and threw himself into the preparations for the assignment. The appointment of Witte was assumed by many in Russia to constitute a gesture favorable to peace. It was so interpreted by those at the Manchurian war front such as General Linievich, the commander in chief, and General Kuropatkin.[20] Nevertheless, though he found the idea of making peace under existing conditions somewhat depressing, Linievich noted in his diary that when it came to making an able defense of Russian interests, Witte was an excellent choice.

Witte was in some ways a contrast to the chief Japanese plenipotentiary. As against the latter's diplomatic experience and acumen, Witte had only his blunt and even gruff manner developed over years of almost unchallenged domination in economic and political affairs. His habit of treating others as juniors and inferiors even emerged at times during the conference when he addressed his opponents across the table in his customary determined and imperious tone. The reserved Komura appeared to be no match for Witte when he chose to exhibit his effusive mode of expression in dramatic outbursts. Nevertheless, when it came to knowledge of the subject, the incisiveness of the arguments, and dogged persistence in pressing a point, the two men were a remarkably good match.

Like Komura, Witte came to the conference provided with a well-selected staff. His colleague as plenipotentiary was Baron R.R. Rosen, a diplomat with extensive experience. He had conducted the unsuccessful prewar negotiations with Japan and just before the conference had replaced Cassini as the Russian minister in Washington. Unlike Witte, Rosen had been considered as potential delegate from the first. Though he seldom spoke in

[20] *R.-I.V.*, pp. 96–98.

the open conference meetings, when he did he exhibited a good grasp of the issues and an ability to supply an understanding of the negotiation process that Witte notably lacked. The relations between Witte and Rosen, according to the latter, were very congenial and the two were apparently in agreement on most issues. Rosen wrote some years later:

"Where we disagreed was in this: I thought that the conclusion of peace after a series of defeats without our army being given a chance to redeem the glory of our arms by a victory which the reinforcements already on the way might have placed within its grasp would hasten the outbreak of the revolution, whereas Witte felt sure that the conclusion of peace as speedily as possible would, by removing one of the principal causes of popular discontent, be helpful in staving off the danger of revolution at least for some time."[21]

Witte's other assistants and advisors included the following: F.F. Martens, a privy councilor, member of the council of the foreign ministry, professor of international law at St. Petersburg University, and an internationally distinguished legal authority; D.D. Pokotilov, the Russian minister to China, talented and well informed about the Far East, and a strong partisan of peace, in the latter capacity a good influence on Rosen; and G.A. Planson, whose experience in the Far East had been gained as head of the diplomatic chancellery of Viceroy Alekseiev and as consul general in Korea, and who was sympathetic to a firm policy in the Far East.

The views that Witte held about the need for peace were strongly supported by his military advisors. Naval Captain A.I. Rusin was a very capable officer whose judgment was respected by his colleagues, including Witte. As a naval attaché in Japan before the war he had estimated the time of the Japanese attack almost to the day; he had just returned from Manchuria where he had served on the staff of General Linievich and, therefore, brought to the conference a recent view of the military realities there. Rusin is said to have exerted an influence on Witte favorable to a conciliatory attitude toward the Japanese.[22] The military advisor, Colonel M.K. Samoilov, formerly the military attaché in Japan, is said to have shared Rusin's views of the military

[21] Rosen, op. cit., I, 268.
[22] Korostavets, op.cit., p. 49.

situation. According to Witte, Samoilov felt that Russia did not have the slightest chance of winning a military victory and, therefore, advocated peace.[23]

One of the two secretaries to the Russian peace mission, I.I. Korostovets, also had experience in Manchuria, having been head of the diplomatic chancellery of the viceroy at the time of the Boxer crisis. Before leaving Russia, Witte had requested him to keep a diary of the conference and all that concerned it, explaining that he wanted a complete chronological account of the event. Korostovets thought that Witte wanted to use this as a basis for an account which he might have intended to write. Witte mentioned this as late as December 1913 when Korostovets was leaving for his post as minister to Persia, but the material was never used by Witte. Korostovets' account later appeared in English under the title, *Pre-War Diplomacy*.

Witte and his party left St. Petersburg on July 19, the day Komura arrived in Seattle. His wife and grandson, L.K. Naryshkin, traveled to France with him and he left Cherbourg on July 27 on the "Kaiser Wilhelm," arriving at Hoboken on August 2. His reception in the United States was enthusiastic—Baron Rosen, newspaper reporters, members of the Slavonic Alliance, and many others being on hand to receive him. He was taken to the St. Regis Hotel on Fifth Avenue, not far from the Waldorf-Astoria where the Japanese delegate was staying.

During the passage to the United States, Witte had prepared carefully for the good impression he intended to make. He was assisted by Dr. E.J. Dillon, a correspondent of the London *Daily News* well acquainted with Russian life and a close friend of Witte. As Witte's advisor during his all-important trip to America, his first duty was to help him prepare the statement he planned to make to the press on arrival. Since Witte knew no English, the statement was read for him by Martens. It was well received and augured well for his relations in a country which he felt was potentially hostile to Russia and to him personally.

In his brief statement Witte emphasized the friendly feeling of the Russian Emperor and people for the United States. He said it was because of the traditional friendship between Russia and America and the confidence felt in this bond that the Emperor had sent plenipotentiaries to the conference at Portsmouth. He had done this without the usual settlement of preliminaries before

[23] Witte, *op.cit.*, I, 362–363.

the meeting in order to show his confidence in the United States. Even though the plenipotentiaries might be unable to find any common ground for peace, Witte hoped this bond would "still remain a memorable event, pregnant, I trust, with beneficent consequences for the great nations of the East and of the West."[24]

It is uncertain how effectively or completely Witte was supplied with information from Russia or elsewhere during the conference. He had, of course, no direct communications with President Roosevelt such as Baron Kaneko furnished for Komura. According to Witte, General Linievich was completely uncooperative in furnishing him information about the situation in Manchuria; his information about the war front presumably came to him indirectly. Count Kokovtsov, the minister of finance whose intelligence was gleaned from a widely scattered network of agents, helped to keep him informed during his absence.[25] He also had frequent telegraphic communications with Count Lamsdorf. If it is true, as has been alleged, that Russia knew the United States diplomatic code, then Witte had a great advantage indeed.[26]

Although President Roosevelt had no intention of becoming a party to the peace negotiations, he had the responsibility of acting as host to the plenipotentiaries and of bringing them together. When the decision was made to hold a conference at Portsmouth, Roosevelt reduced his official commitments to the minimum and devoted as much time as possible to the conference. He also took up his summer residence at Oyster Bay, New York, in order to be ready to receive the delegates on their arrival and to be in as close touch as possible with the negotiations through Kaneko.

One of President Roosevelt's most important and most trying contributions to the peace delegations was his endeavor to bring them together on the difficult issues, particularly that concerning the indemnity. In early June, Roosevelt's discussions with Kaneko turned to the question of moderating the Japanese demands.[27] The President stated that in his view Japan had won a great and historic victory on both land and sea and, therefore, had a right

[24] Korostovets, op.cit., p. 22.
[25] Kokovtsov, op.cit., p. 53; Kokovtsov to Witte, July 25, 1905, K.A., vi, 26.
[26] R.K. Godwin, "Russia and the Portsmouth Peace Conference," American Slavic and East European Review, ix, 4, Dec. 1950, p. 289.
[27] Kaneko, Beikoku, June 8, 1905.

to make some substantial demands. Nevertheless, these demands must be reasonable enough to make them acceptable to Russia and to retain for Japan the sympathy of the other powers. Otherwise, a great opportunity would be lost and Russia would be forced to resume the war. Considering the unquestionable gains she had already made, this would not be to the advantage of Japan.

The President also tried to make peace more palatable to Russia. He had an opportunity to do this when Rosen came to see him in mid-July about the Japanese occupation of Sakhalin.[28] Knowing that at that time Russia was moving toward Manchuria two additional army corps composed of some of her best troops, Rosen had a favorable view of her chances in case of a showdown and thought that the Japanese would not be able to match the Russian increases. Even before Russia had augmented her forces, Japan had made no significant gains since the battle of Mukden in March. Considering the ability and enterprise already exhibited by the Japanese command, this could only be interpreted as evidence of their inability to make any further advances.

The seizure of Sakhalin, Rosen added, was further evidence of Japan's weakness. For the very fact that they had not seen fit to occupy this until the Russians had consented to begin negotiations, showed a lack of strength since they did not risk doing this while the war was still in progress. In the face of such views, Roosevelt's words of caution appeared to hold little attraction.

The arrival of the plenipotentiaries provided Roosevelt with another opportunity to urge moderation on both parties.[29] He knew by that time that the two issues most likely to wreck the conference were those dealing with the Sakhalin and indemnity questions. The President's most recent news from Paris was to the effect that during his brief stop there on his way to America, Witte had said that if Japan were to insist upon an indemnity, his stay in the United States would be brief indeed.

The first of the delegations to be received by the President was the Japanese. Komura and Takahira visited him at Oyster Bay on July 28. A frank discussion was relatively easy with the Japanese because of the school ties with Komura and the frequent comunications throughout the war. Roosevelt tried to impress

---

[28] Rosen, op.cit., ɪ, 260.
[29] Roosevelt to Spring Rice, June 16, 1905, Gwynn, op.cit., I, 473; K.G., ɪɪ, 42–43; Shinobu, op.cit., p. 386; Kaneko, Beikoku, July 28, 1905.

Komura with his fears for the success of the conference, particularly if a breakdown should occur over a Japanese demand that might be considered unreasonable. Roosevelt emphasized to Komura that both nations needed peace and that Japan should by all means retain the sympathies especially of the United States and Great Britain, by recognizing this. He agreed with Komura that Japan had won the right not only to impose reasonable conditions on Russia but also, in the interests of future security, to seek to reduce the aggressive power of Russia. But, unless this were done with moderation it would fail and all the hard-won gains would be lost through a costly prolongation of the war.

After this discussion, the President had further thoughts on the indemnity question and wrote a note about them to Komura in New York by way of Kaneko.[30] He stated that while Witte had indeed ruled out an indemnity, a more recent cable from France quoted him as saying that he might consider paying part of Japan's war expenses. Roosevelt suggested that this might be more easily accomplished if the term "indemnity" were avoided and "reimbursement" used instead since such a substitution would, of course, make no substantial difference to Japan.

Kaneko took this letter to Komura at his hotel and discussed the question with him. It was recognized by both that the indemnity was essential for two reasons. The money was badly needed to help defray the enormous cost of the war. But it also was needed to satisfy those in Japan who were unaware of the true military situation and were demanding not only an indemnity but even the seizure of Vladivostok and its vicinity. It was felt, however, that the substitution of terms could be made without damage to the substance of the demand.

Witte also recognized beforehand the significance of the indemnity issue and, more generally, the importance that access to loans would have for both parties at the conference. With this in mind, he stopped in Paris to learn the attitude of the French government toward the indemnity question and to inquire as to the possibilities of further loans.[31] What he learned was very discouraging—President Emile Loubet and Foreign Minister Maurice Rouvier advised him to be conciliatory. Rouvier told

[30] Kaneko, *Beikoku*, July 29, 1905; Roosevelt to Kaneko, July 29, 1905, Morison and Blum, *op.cit.*, IV, 1293; Kaneko to Roosevelt, July 31, 1905, Dennett, *op.cit.*, pp. 298–299.

[31] Witte, *op.cit.*, I, 363–364.

Witte very frankly that under existing conditions it would be unwise to rely upon the Paris money market for further loans. Rouvier added that in his own opinion it was absolutely necessary for Russia to conclude peace even at the cost of paying an indemnity and added that France would help pay such an indemnity. When Witte replied that, badly as he wanted peace, he would under no circumstances pay an indemnity, Rouvier reminded him of the situation in 1871 when France had accepted the obligation to pay a huge indemnity without any loss of dignity. Witte however, emphasized that the circumstances were very different. If the Japanese army were nearing Moscow, he might be willing to give more serious thought to the matter.

When Witte and Rosen were received by President Roosevelt at Oyster Bay on August 4, the former exhibited no change of mind on this issue.[32] According to his report to Lamsdorf, he made it quite clear to the President that he would countenance no indemnity. He stated that, so far as he was concerned, the peace terms would be based on the actual achievements of the Japanese military forces. He would refuse to take into account any successes they might be expected to achieve in the future or any misfortunes which might be assumed to be in store for Russia. He emphasized that: "If the Japanese will not now adopt our point of view we shall carry on a defensive war to the last extremity, and we shall see who will hold out the longest." It was with reason that Roosevelt despaired of any success at Portsmouth.

Nevertheless, the President proceeded with his scheduled plans. On the following day, August 5, the plenipotentiaries were to start for Portsmouth. According to plan, each delegation arrived at Oyster Bay separately. In the cabin of the presidential yacht, "Mayflower," they were introduced to one another. This was largely a formality since some of them were already acquainted; Komura knew both Witte and Rosen from previous official relationships, while Rosen may have known Takahira in the course of his recent duties in Washington. After the introductions, President Roosevelt addressed the delegates as follows:

"Gentlemen, I propose a toast to which there will be no answer and which I ask you to drink in silence, standing. I drink to the welfare and prosperity of the sovereigns and peoples

---

[32] Korostovets, *op.cit.*, pp. 31–32.

of the two great nations whose representatives have met one another on this ship. It is my most earnest hope and prayer, in the interests of not only these two great powers but also of all civilized mankind, that a just and lasting peace may speedily be concluded between them."[33]

The remaining preparations for departure were brief. A buffet luncheon was served in the salon of the "Mayflower." There were no chairs in the room so that all had to stand, thus avoiding any question of procedure or precedence which might have led to misunderstanding. After lunch all departed for Portsmouth, the Russians on the "Mayflower" and the Japanese on the "Dolphin."

Both parties reached Portsmouth on the morning of August 8 and were received by Admiral William Mead, the commandant of the Kittery navy yard. Each delegation was received separately aboard the vessel on which it had come and then formally piped off. By eleven o'clock the ceremonies were over and all were on the dock. They were then driven in carriages to the courthouse in Portsmouth through lines formed by United States Marines and the New Hampshire National Guardsmen who were serving as a guard of honor. At the courthouse the delegates were greeted by Governor John McLane of New Hampshire and a large crowd of citizens. After this formal reception they were taken to their suites at the Wentworth-on-the-Sea Hotel.

The Wentworth Hotel was located on Newcastle Island, well situated for guarding the delegates, keeping newspaper reporters and other visitors under observation, and maintaining general secrecy. The hotel consisted of three large wooden structures joined together by covered passageways and built to accommodate about 500 persons. During the four weeks of the conference the hotel was a busy place, filled with the delegations of the two countries as well as distinguished guests, including newspaper reporters from several foreign countries and the United States.

The press was represented at the conference by some 120 correspondents, including some of the most famous names in journalism:[34] Dr. George E. Morrison, the Peking correspondent

---

[33] *K.G.*, II, 52–53.
[34] L.E. Van Norman, "The Making of a Modern Treaty of Peace," *The American Monthly Review of Reviews*, XXXII, 4, Oct. 1905, p. 425.

of the London *Times;* Sir Donald Mackenzie Wallace, St. Petersburg correspondent of the London *Times;* Dr. E.J. Dillon of the London *Daily Telegraph;* Salvetore Cortesi, representing several Italian newspapers; Jules Hademann of the Paris *Matin;* Otto Kahn of the *Frankfurter Zeitung;* Camillo Chanfarra of the Buenos Aires *Prensa;* Boris Suvorin of the St. Petersburg *Novoe Vremya;* and K.K. Kawakami of the Tokyo *Asahi.*

The delegates and their staffs lived at the Wentworth as the guests of the United States government. Under the supervision of an assistant secretary of state, Herbert Pierce, everything had been done to make life comfortable for the visitors. Both the principal plenipotentiaries were ill most of the time they were in America but their unhappiness may have been a consequence of the emotional strain and of the unfamiliar food. Komura's situation was aggravated by the fact that he was already ill before coming to the conference.[35] Food was the most common complaint from the delegates. Korostovets recorded a scene that might have occurred at almost any boarding house:

"Lunch was served as usual. Witte took nothing but just walked around the room. He is not well, and has been dieting himself for several days. After this morning's sitting he asked Takahira and Komura if they were well and how they stood the food. They replied that, notwithstanding the lack of variety, they had got used to it, and even tried to enjoy it."

Each day of the meetings the people of Portsmouth might have seen the plenipotentiaries as they were conveyed by automobile from the hotel to the conference site at the Kittery Island naval arsenal in Maine. An upper floor of the Naval store house had been set aside for their use and the meetings were held around a large table in the main hall. On either side of the hall separate conference rooms had been provided for each of the delegations. The whole floor was comfortably furnished for the occasion with rugs, chairs, tables, and electric fans. In the homely phrase of William Dean Howells, the delegates had been furnished with all the comforts of home, that is, of a New England home.[36]

[35] K. Shidehara, *Gaiko Gojunen,* Tokyo, 1951, p. 10.
[36] W.D. Howells, "The Peacemakers at Portsmouth," *Harper's Weekly,* XLIX, 2,540, Aug. 26, 1905, p. 1,244.

Having brought the delegates together and seen to it that they were introduced, President Roosevelt's management of their activities may be said to have been concluded. There was no preexisting arrangement for any actual conference meeting and the next step was up to the delegates, but the problem was amicably worked out on the evening of their arrival.[37] After they had all finished dinner in their private diningroom, Witte addressed a short note to Komura asking whether it would be convenient to plan a preliminary meeting for the next morning, August 9. The waiter brought back Komura's reply approving this and asking what time Witte would suggest. The answer was eleven o'clock in the morning and on this agreeable note the conference was under way.

The next morning the delegates assembled at the Naval store house, known to the Navy as Building 816 and to the hopeful people of the region as the "Peace Building." As they took their places at the conference table, Witte and Komura sat opposite each other with their respective assistants seated on opposite sides as they would be during the next four weeks. Through the days of severe strain that followed, the delegates would be able to observe each other carefully, watching for signs of nervousness or of any declining resistance as the issues became more clearly defined. Korostovets recorded some observations comparing the signs of nervousness on the part of the delegates: Witte began to fidget in his chair, cross his legs, and twist his foot around; Baron Komura maintained a somewhat cooler exterior showing his displeasure by the force with which he knocked the ashes from his cigarette, by hitting the table, and by speaking more shortly and abruptly.

The two second plenipotentiaries had little to say during the conference. Takahira sat smoking one cigarette after another, speaking only when asked something by Komura. Baron Rosen also usually waited for a word from Witte before speaking though he sometimes stepped in at a crucial moment to clear up some obscure point or to offer some tactful suggestion which might cool down heated tempers. At the second or third session of the conference Witte asked for tea and the next day the Japanese did the same, and from then on tea added a relaxing touch to the negotiations.

After the preliminary greetings on the first day, Witte took

[37] Shinobu, *op.cit.*, p. 403.

out his credentials and laid them on the table, asking Komura for his. Komura replied that he had not anticipated using his credentials and so had not brought them but he would be glad to send back to the hotel for them. Witte agreed to examine them later at the hotel. When they were compared it was found that they had both come with about the same powers. Both in practice found it necessary to keep in close touch with their governments for exchanges of views. Nevertheless, it was not quite true, as some of the press reporters noted, that the conference was in fact a parley between St. Petersburg and Tokyo with Oyster Bay as the mouthpiece of both.[38] The plenipotentiaries played a significant role in making the peace treaty.

Another preliminary question settled at the first session was the scheduling of future meetings. It was unclear at that point how long the conference would last and what its outcome would be. But, for as long as necessary it was agreed that the daily sessions would be held from 9:00 to noon and from 3:00 to 5:00 in the afternoon. Between August 9 and 29 there were, in addition to the preliminary session, 10 formal sessions as well as several informal conferences on September 1 and 2 and a final session on September 5 for signing the treaty.

These activities were recorded in a preliminary and 12 regular protocols, 10 of them dealing with the 10 regular sessions, 1 with the informal conferences of September 1 and 2, and 1 with the final meeting of September 5. Each protocol and the accompanying annexes recorded the deliberations and conclusions of the respective session as approved at the succeeding meeting. These protocols constituted the decisions upon which the treaty was ultimately based. The official protocols are in English and French, the latter being practically identical with the former and available in two copies, one not identified with either party to the negotiations and the other constituting the official Russian record. The most complete record is the Japanese and it appears to have been independently composed.

It was agreed at the preliminary session that English and French would be the official languages of the conference and of the conference record.[39] Witte generally spoke French, his remarks being translated into Japanese; toward the end of the conference when he tended more and more to speak in Russian,

[38] Van Norman, op.cit., p. 420; Japan Times, Aug. 24, 1905.
[39] N.K.S., II, 19.

Rosen translated into English for him. Although Komura was able to speak English, he generally spoke Japanese at the conference table, his remarks being translated into French. Komura, however, presented his actual proposals in English accompained by a French translation. The treaty was officially written in English and French, the latter text being accepted in case of question.

One of the most troublesome rules established for the conference was that requiring that the proceedings be kept secret. Witte's disregard of this rule was the source of considerable irritation on the part of the Japanese plenipotentiaries. The writers of the two nations have continued to reflect a strong difference of view on this matter.[40] The view has been expressed on the Japanese side that Witte's success at the conference rests largely on the fact that he cultivated the press to the point of disregarding his promise to preserve secrecy, divulging information which the Japanese were keeping to themselves in good faith. On the Soviet Russian side, it has been said that Komura's request for secrecy was merely a device for forcing Japan's imperialistic demands on Russia.

Witte's attitude toward the question of secrecy must be seen against the backdrop of the Russian objectives and strategy. At the conference held in St. Petersburg on June 6 to decide the question of war or peace, this problem had been discussed. Baron Vladimir Frederichs had expressed the hope that the negotiations would be conducted openly. In this way, if the Japanese conditions should be unacceptable they would be publicly known and would gain public sympathy for Russia. This opinion reflected the reserve with which Russian officialdom regarded peace, particularly if it included an indemnity. Even Witte, who was considered a peace advocate, was unwilling to accept peace if it entailed an indemnity.

A number of precedural details were also agreed upon in advance. One was the agreement not to discuss the origins of the war and this was acceded to wholeheartedly by both parties and may have been largely responsible for the rapid progress of the negotiations. It was also decided to discuss the Japanese demands and the Russian replies article by article. This had been suggested by President Roosevelt as a means of isolating the difficult problems and avoiding a general treatment that might leave the impression of hopelessness.

[40] Shinobu, *op.cit.*, pp. 481–482; Dobrov, *op.cit.*, p. 316.

The adoption of this procedure makes it possible to consider conference meetings in two parts, those before August 17 and those held after this date. During the earlier sessions the questions were discussed that were relatively easy to settle and consideration of the more difficult ones was postponed. By the time the conference came to the difficult problems, both the Russian and the Japanese delegations had a sense of accomplishment and a real incentive for wishing to rescue the gains already made by settling the difficult questions.

14. The Peace Campaign

THE PRESENTATION of the Japanese peace conditions, following the successful assembling of the conference, opened the second and climactic phase of the diplomatic struggle with Russia. Though the Russians already knew in considerable detail the nature of the demands, the final formulation of the two national positions, followed by the verbal duel over them, provided the issues for the conference sessions which were hardly surpassed in dramatic significance by the military events. Yet even the conference discussions, dealing with the most sensitive issues, seem to reflect the fray less vividly than the symptoms of nervous tension, the occasional emotional outbursts, and the illnesses which plagued the principals throughout the conference.

Two groups of conditions created different moods at the conference table: the first group, consisting of the issues more easily settled, appeared to hold promise of peace and consequently stimulated an optimistic outlook; the second group, always hanging menacingly over the conference, emerged to dominate the last days of the proceedings. In the end peace was purchased with agonizing sacrifices from both sides, but especially from the Japanese. These final transactions appeared to be a more accurate gauge of the relative strength of the opponents than the issues already settled.

The peace conditions which Baron Komura presented to Witte at the first regular conference meeting on August 10 were the product of long and careful consideration. From the very beginning Komura saw these terms in their international perspective and discussed them privately with diplomatic representatives in Tokyo, following his established practice of retaining international goodwill in order to assure positive support as well as to ward off any attempt at third power intervention. Baron Komura was able to give a high degree of continuity to the formulation of the proposals. As the foreign minister during the previous attempts to come to an understanding with Russia, including the immediate prewar negotiations, he was acquainted with the difficulties national interests created. After the first successful test of battle in the spring of 1904, he began to elaborate new requirements that went well beyond his original formulations.[1] During June and July 1904, in consultation with Prime Minister Katsura, he worked out a general draft of objectives and specific demands.

Throughout all stages of their planning, Komura and Katsura recognized that the success of the Japanese demands would depend upon the course of the war. But even the plan of July 1904 envisioned the contribution military success would make to the broadening of the demands beyond those made to Russia prior to the war. It dealt with the objectives of the war, the enlargement of Japanese interests, policies relating to China in general as well as Manchuria and Korea, including the specific demands that Japan would make to realize her Korean policies, and finally, it included a set of demands on China.

As approved by the cabinet in August 1904, these plans took the following form. Among those which were a direct projection of the prewar issues was the change from the acceptance of a mere guarantee of the integrity of China to a demand for a more active Japanese sphere of interest in Manchuria. It was stipulated that Russia should be required to turn over to Japan the lease to the Kuantung Peninsula and the railway between Port Arthur and Harbin. The problem of the neutral zone was solved by requiring that Russia withdraw her forces entirely from Manchuria, thus removing the menace to Korea. Japan was to have complete freedom of action in Korea.

A second group of peace conditions proposed in August 1904 was similar to the first in assuming a victorious outcome of the war for Japan and envisioning a broader role on the Asian mainland for Japan than had the prewar demands. One condition would have required Russia to limit her use of the Chinese Eastern Railway to commercial traffic, thus preventing Russian military preparations in the future. Other demands in this second group included: recognition of the principle of equality of commercial and industrial opportunity for all nations; retrocession to China of all occupied territory; the granting of fishing rights along the coast of the Russian Maritime territory; freedom of navigation of the Amur River to Blagoveshchensk; recognition of Blagoveshchensk, Khabarovsk, and Nikolaevsk as commercial ports and of the right of Japan to station consuls in these towns as well as

---

[1] K.G., ii, 27–28; "Foreign Minister Komura's Proposal," July, 1904, N.G.M., xxxvii–xxxviii; Nichiro Senso, v, 59–63; Tokutomi, op.cit., ii, 265–266; Hori, op.cit., pp. 207–208; N.K.S., n, 8–10.

in Vladivostok; the cession to Japan of Sakhalin Island; and the
payment of an indemnity for war expenses.

The final Japanese peace conditions differed from these 1904
conditions in significant ways. Although victory had succeeded
victory during the early months of 1905, the reports from Manchuria about the conditions of the Japanese military effort had
a sobering effect on the peace plans. The final stages of planning
the peace terms began in March under the influence of Marshal
Oyama's urgent requests. By April 8 the plans had reached the
stage of a cabinet approval on two general principles: to hold
and maintain all that had been won thus far and to use them
to press for further gains in the future as opportunity permitted;
and, secondly, to seek the restoration of peace as quickly and
effectively as possible, maintaining friendly relations with foreign
powers in order to prevent any hostile combinations against
Japanese interests and objectives.

The final peace conditions were approved by the Emperor on
July 5, 1905 and handed by him to Komura during his audience
the next day.[2] They represented a more cautious attitude toward
Russia and peace, substantially and tactically, than did the conditions formulated the preceding April. They were intended to
serve as a guide for the plenipotentiaries rather than as a rigid
set of demands. While they were to be used at their discretion
taking full account of the course of the negotiations, it was
apparently assumed that Komura's constant telegraphic contact
with Tokyo would give him the advantage of further consultation. It was from these general proposals that Komura drew up
the conditions which he presented to Witte on August 10.

To facilitate their use by the plenipotentiaries, the conditions
were divided into three categories. The first were given the
highest priority and consisted of those held to be absolutely
necessary because they were indispensable in guaranteeing the
position which Japan had gained in the course of the war. This
category included those dealing with Korea, the evacuation of
the Russian and Japanese military forces from Manchuria, and
the transfer to Japan of the Russian rights in the railway between
Harbin and Port Arthur and in the leased territory of Kuantung.

The second category consisted of conditions considered comparatively necessary. Even though these had a lower priority
than the first, every endeavor was to be made to realize them if

[2] N.K.S., II, 15-16.

circumstances permitted. These included: the payment of an indemnity for war expenditures; the transfer to Japan of the Russian war vessels that had taken refuge in neutral ports because of the war; the cession to Japan of the island of Sakhalin; and the granting to Japan of fishing rights along the coast of the Russian Maritime territory.

The third category was left more fully to the discretion of the plenipotentiaries and depended largely on their judgment. It consisted of the demands that Russia submit to a restriction of her naval strength in the Far East, that the fortifications at Vladivostok be dismantled, and that Vladivostok be made a commercial port.

Comparing the peace conditions of 1904 with those actually handed to Komura, the following emphases appear to characterize the 1905 conditions: a more cautious approach to bargaining that would insure to Japan the most necessary conditions while leaving her free to sacrifice the others if necessary; a lesser concern for the rights of other nations in Manchuria along with a desire to reap all possible benefits for herself; and an apparent disposition to avoid asking for conditions which would be difficult to control in favor of others more accessible and beneficial to her. Specifically, the following changes are noticeable: placing the indemnity and Sakhalin issues in a lower priority, a fact of the greatest interest when it is recalled that in Komura's draft of July 1904 the indemnity was the first of his proposed demands on Russia; the omission of the demands for access to the towns on the Amur River; the elimination of the condition which would have limited the Russian use of the Chinese Eastern Railway (this was reenstated by Komura in the actual conditions); the absence of any stipulation regarding the equality of opportunity in commercial and industrial enterprises in Manchuria or regarding the retrocession of Manchuria to China; and the addition of conditions dealing with the limitation of Russian naval strength, the delivery of interned Russian vessels to Japan, the dismantling of the fortifications at Vladivostok, and the opening of this city as a commercial port.

The instructions which Witte carried to the conference bear some interesting resemblances to those which Komura brought. From opposing points of view both dealt with essentially the same points and agreed substantially on the difficulty or ease with which the various points were likely to be settled. The

Russian instructions were drawn up by the minister of foreign affairs, Count Lamsdorf, with the counsel of other ministers. One of those from whom he sought advice was Count Kokovtsov, the minister of finance.[3] Kokovtsov's letter written in response is significant because it contains views closely resembling those contained in the instructions and because the Emperor made notations on it specifically approving some of these views.

Kokovtsov's letter contains the basic assumption that, as things stood, it was not necessary for Russia to seek a peace at any price; otherwise it would have been unnecessary to furnish detailed instructions for the peace plenipotentiaries. He admitted that from the purely financial point of view peace would be highly desirable, since the war would unquestionably continue to grow more difficult financially. However, Kokovtsov felt that the question of war or peace could not be decided exclusively from a financial standpoint. The vital interests of the nation had to be accorded their due weight in this decision. Accordingly, the coming negotiations should be exploratory only; they should be entered into for the purpose of affording the plenipotentiaries an opportunity to see what the Japanese terms were. There must be definite assurance that the conditions could lead to a just peace and not merely to a settlement which would bring the fighting temporarily to an end without leaving Russia in a more favorable situation than before the war.

The condition which had led to the war was, in Kokovtsov's view, Russia's fear of allowing Japan to establish a foothold on the Asian continent. This was the reason Russia had excluded Japan in 1895 with the help of France and Germany. It was with the same objective that Russia had later seized Port Arthur and carried out other forward policies such as the Yalu timber enterprise. Now, however, Japan has gained a foothold on the mainland. The question was whether she would use her power in such a way as to endanger the security of Russia's possessions in the Far East and of her own communications to and from other areas. If these communications were endangered, the settlement could not be looked upon as a secure and lasting peace. The same would be true if Japan were to maintain her armed forces in the railway area for an extended period after the conclusion of the peace.

[3] Kokovtsov, *op.cit.*, pp. 54–56; Minister of Finance to Minister of Foreign Affairs, June 20, 1905, K.A., VI, 13–17.

Kokovtsov suggested that the indemnity question might be solved by a judicious surrender of railways. He felt that the fortunes of war might make it necessary for Russia to give up the southern branch of the railway to Dalny and Port Arthur, retaining only the trans-Manchurian line to Vladivostok. However, this southern part of the railway should be transferred to China rather than Japan and such a transfer could be made for a redemption price that China could be directed to pay to Japan. Beyond this, the payment of any indemnity to Japan as compensation for war expenses must be considered inadmissible. It is interesting to note that the Emperor underlined the word "inadmissible" and wrote "absolutely" near it.

Two other settlements were suggested in Kokovtsov's letter: one, he held that Japan's predominant interest in Korea would have to be recognized, maintaining, however, no armed forces or fortifications there menacing to the Russian Maritime region. The second maintained that the private rights of Russians as well as the concessions to which Russia was entitled would have to be secured in areas surrendered to Japan.

It is entirely possible that in preparing these observations for the foreign minister, Kokovtsov may have had before him a letter he had recently received from Lieutenant General P.F. Unterberger, governor general of Amur Province and commander of the Amur Military District.[4] Unterberger's views may have been sent to him on request since they dealt with an area that was little known to him though of great official interest. Kokovtsov therefore would consider Unterberger's thoughts seriously.

Unterberger's letter dealt mainly with the bearing of the Japanese peace conditions on the problems of defense and freedom of action in the Russian Far East. Such conditions as the surrender of Sakhalin, the razing of the fortifications of Vladivostok, and the limitation of Russian naval power in Far Eastern waters he considered completely unacceptable, crippling communications and leaving Russia at the mercy of Japan. Unterberger maintained that Russia's military condition did not make it imperative for her to end the war at the cost of an indemnity. He pointed out that such an indemnity would be used by Japan to strengthen her military forces, thus making it easier as time went on for her to coerce Russia whose territories in the Far East were already at such a strategic disadvantage. He dis-

[4] Unterberger to Minister of Finance, June 9, 1905, *K.A.*, vi, 9–12.

counted entirely the alleged need to pay an indemnity in order to prevent Japan from seizing the Russian Far Eastern regions. Even if Japan were able to do this, he argued, the gains would be of negative value to her and surely of no greater economic advantage than the region had been to Russia. Furthermore, Russia would not accept such an occupation as final and the cost to Japan of maintaining such a troubled frontier would be ruinous. He concluded that Russia ought not to pay an indemnity even with a Japanese occupation in prospect.

In contemplating the points of view which entered into the composition of Witte's instructions, the Emperor's comments on Kokovtsov's letter must be included. For, whether or not Witte actually read them, they were unquestionably conveyed to him, perhaps in an audience, before his departure for the conference. The Emperor wrote that he was willing to conclude this war that he had not started provided the conditions did not violate the dignity of the country, for "our army is still intact and I have faith in it." Since Korea was not Russian territory, he was willing to compromise in that part of the settlement. However, he stated emphatically by underlining the word "never" three times that he would never pay an indemnity and would not even consider a limitation of the military forces.

The instructions as finally adopted were clearly based on these or similar views and were approved by the Emperor on July 11, 1905.[5] They fall into two groups, those which specified the concessions which Russia would definitely not make to Japan and the issues on which Russia was prepared to make concessions. Those issues which were held to touch the national dignity so closely that concessions regarding them were held to be inadmissible were: the surrender of any Russian territory; the payment of an indemnity; the dismantlement of the fortifications at Vladivostok; the forfeiture of the right to maintain a military fleet in the Pacific; the acceptance of any other limitation on Russia's freedom of action in the Pacific; and the surrender of the railway line connecting Vladivostok with the rest of Russia.

Yet, even these prohibitions were subject to modifications. Russia would not refuse either to continue the negotiations or to discuss these issues should Japan propose them. On the contrary, alternatives and arguments were provided for the plenipotentiaries to deal with them. In case of a demand for an

[5] Kutakov, op.cit., pp. 19-21.

indemnity, for example, some alternative might be suggested, possibly taking the form of some advantageous concession to Japan of a financial, commercial, or industrial nature. Russian interests, however, must not be directly violated. Tariff privileges on the Siberian or Chinese Eastern railways were also mentioned as substitutes for an indemnity. Should the Japanese demand the surrender of Sakhalin, the plenipotentiaries were to stress the economic and strategic significance of the island for Russia.

Among the demands on which the plenipotentiaries were to be ready to negotiate were those dealing with Manchuria. The instruction approved the surrender to Japan of the leased territory of Kuantung with Port Arthur and Dalny (Darien). They stipulated, however, that inasmuch as China was the original lessor, Japan would have to receive these rights directly from China, Russia protecting herself from any claims against her by retroceding it first to China. The Russian government would be ready to transfer the southern branch of the Manchurian railway up to the boundary of Kirin Province under the same conditions. The railway linking Vladivostok with Siberia through Harbin and the Sungari River shipping line must remain exclusively under Russian control.

Russia was ready to approve a predominant position in Korea for Japan with these limitations: Japan must recognize the independence of Korea; Japan must guarantee that she would neither introduce troops into North Korea nor construct fortifications there; Japan must assure Russia that her ships would have freedom of passage in the Korean strait and that she would build no fortifications along the southern coast of Korea.

The leeway provided for the plenipotentiaries in the instructions may possibly reflect Witte's prestige, influence, or insistence. The minister of foreign affairs told Witte after his appointment as principal plenipotentiary that the existing instructions were not binding on him and he could have new instructions if he wished.[6] The views that he may well have expressed in response to this suggestion are illustrated in an exchange of letters with General Kuropatkin.[7] The general was strongly opposed to concluding peace. His principal argument was contained in this statement:

---

[6] Witte, op.cit., I, 356.
[7] Witte to Kuropatkin, Sept. 1, 1903 [actually 1904], Mar. 12, 1905, Kuropatkin to Witte, June 8, 1905, Witte to Kuropatkin, July 6, 1905, K.A., XIX, 71, 74, 77–80.

"Even now, after the annihilation of Rozhdestvensky's squadron, Russia ought to continue the struggle, and a victory at sea must not concern us particularly, for the Japanese, even before this victory, were already in control of the sea. Our defeat at sea simply shows that we cannot, by order from above, become a sea power and make up our minds to the idea of ruling the waters of the Pacific. But on land, at the present time, we are more firmly established than ever before, and have now a better chance to emerge as the victors from any new bloody encounter. We are fully prepared for action, and I anticipate it with impatience. We should, in my opinion, quickly assume a decisive offensive."

Witte's argument opposing this was Russia's desperate need for peace. Internal disorder was spreading and evidence existed that Russia was in the first stages of revolution. Even before the war, he pointed out, the non-Russian element constituting 44 per cent of the people, detested the Russian government. Now Russians themselves were turning against the government with constitutionalists, revolutionaries, and anarchists appealing to them through propaganda. The government, he wrote, had fallen into complete disrepute with the people. He continued:

"Where they [i.e., the people] formerly disliked the ministers, now they hold them in contempt. Where they formerly did not like the government but continued to reckon with it, now they sneer at it and do so maliciously with the idea of eliminating it."

Witte also made clear in his letters that he saw no merit in Kuropatkin's support for fighting on in the hope of victory. Trying to push Japan back to Port Arthur and the Yalu would at best be an extremely protracted process. And how could Russia take Port Arthur or consolidate her hold on Korea without a fleet? Without a fleet Russia could not even defend herself against Japanese attacks on her coast.

Another of Witte's arguments favoring peace as early as possible was Russia's unfavorable international position. During recent years her policy had alienated not only China and Japan but the western powers as well. With her prestige and credit fallen so low, where would Russia find the loans needed to continue the struggle? Witte had constantly urged accomodation with these nations, both before and during the war, and now with his new appointment as plenipotentiary he intended to achieve this if possible.

In addition to official and court disapproval of his objective at Portsmouth, Witte had also to remember the mood of the Russian press.[8] The conservative *Novoe Vremya* maintained that Russia could not be considered beaten until the Japanese forces had reached the Baltic Sea and occupied St. Petersburg and Kronstadt. Until then she could still recoup her strength, recover from her failures, and maintain her standing as a great power. Some journals advocated that Russia tighten her belt, unite the people under a military dictatorship, suppress the internal disturbances, and prepare to pursue the war in a more unified way. Others, such as *Nasha Zhizn,* were of course amenable to a reasonable settlement.

The pronounced dichotomy of objectives between Witte and these influential persons helps to explain the seemingly indifferent attitude toward the outcome of the negotiations that he assumed during his mission to the United States. However fervently he may have desired peace for his own reasons, he knew only too well the limitations under which it would be acceptable in St. Petersburg. He also knew that the Japanese intended to ask more than he could possibly give for the conclusion of peace and consequently he could lose nothing by appearing unconcerned about the outcome of the conference.

His strategy, planned during his ocean voyage from Europe with the help of Dr. Dillon, expressed his plans in five general propositions.[9] First, he would not disclose a desire for peace but would conduct himself in such a way as to create the impression that if the Emperor had agreed to negotiate, he had done so only because it was the general desire of the whole country that the war be stopped. Secondly, he would conduct himself as became the representative of Russia, that is, as the representative of the greatest of empires temporarily confronted with a rather trivial annoyance.

The three remaining propositions were tactical approaches to winning friends in America: one, he intended to bear in mind the important role of the press in the United States and, accordingly, to be courteous and affable to all its representatives; two, in order to make himself appealing to the people of the United

[8] Inouye to Komura, No. 253, June 19, 1905, *J.F.O.*
[9] Witte, *op.cit.,* I, 373.

States, who are very democratic in outlook and conduct, he would assume a correspondingly simple and democratic bearing, devoid of any haughtiness; and three, he proposed to guide his own conduct to conform with the significant influence of the Jews in America, especially in New York where the press never refers to them in derogatory terms.

Witte put these propositions into practice immediately upon his arrival in the United States by letting it be known that he was not favorable to peace. He informed Melville Stone, director of the Associated Press, that he had no sympathy whatsoever with President Roosevelt's efforts to secure peace at that time.[10] He asserted that the Japanese had passed the peak of their fighting strength and lacked both men and money to continue the struggle and since conditions were now so favorable to Russia, the Emperor should have continued the struggle rather than accept the President's invitation. Regarding the possibility of actually achieving peace, Witte said that he was frankly very dubious and the purpose of his mission was to learn what the Japanese terms were, emphasizing that Russian soil had not been invaded and the country had not been conquered. Hence, if peace required the payment of an indemnity, he wanted it known that Russia would under no conditions pay a single penny.

Dr. Dillon also played his part in expressing the Russian pessimism about the coming negotiations.[11] Since his close relationship to Witte was known, his words were assumed to express the latter's sentiments and he too emphasized that the negotiations were assumed to be preliminary only and that both parties would have to be willing to make all possible concessions. Otherwise, peace would be virtually unobtainable.

The strategy which Witte had devised for the conference, according to Dillon, had as its major objective the ultimate reduction of all outstanding issues between Japan and Russia to a question of money. If peace could appear to depend entirely upon the Japanese demand for an indemnity, Witte felt that Japan's cause would be ruined in the eyes of the world. All arguments grounded on matters of national interest would be completely submerged under such conditions. In the end,

[10] M.E. Stone, "The Portsmouth Conference," *The Saturday Evening Post,* CLXXXVII, 31, Jan. 30, 1915, p. 3.

[11] E.J. Dillon, "The Story of the Peace Negotiations," *The Contemporary Review,* LXXXVIII, Oct. 1905, pp. 466–467.

this maneuver succeeded so well and with such devastating
finesse that one must admire either Witte's shrewdness in
planning or his superb ability to take advantage of the Japanese
miscalculations in strategy.

Another of his plans was tested on the very opening day of
the Portsmouth Conference, August 10, when he was handed
the Japanese peace conditions. He immediately retired with his
staff to their council rooms off the main hall of the "Peace
Building" to prepare his counterproposals.[12] This was intended
to avoid the impression that Russia had once more been caught
unprepared and consequently was perplexed by the Japanese
proposals; telegraphing them back to St. Petersburg would have
meant a delay of as much as two weeks.

The Russians worked through the afternoon and did not complete their task until seven o'clock in the evening. Witte and
the staff worked out the answers while Pokotilov and Shipov
wrote them down and Martens translated them into French.
When the answers were complete, he telegraphed St. Petersburg:
"Today I give an answer to the Japanese terms."

The plan that Witte outlined to his staff envisioned a procedure
for the formal negotiations very similar to the one that Komura
thought advantageous. The advantage to Russia of quickly dis-
posing of the more obvious demands was the impression created
thereby that Russia was willing to comply with reasonable
demands. This would help cast the blame on Japan for insisting
on terms that, by contrast, could be classified as unreasonable.

Korostovets' report of the Russian staff meeting gives every
indication that a frank discussion was held concerning the
realities of Russo-Japanese relations. The military advisors were
of the opinion that, while the Russian armies could hold their
present positions, they were not then in a position to defeat
Japan, and accordingly, some accommodation was necessary.

The foundation of any durable accommodation would require
mutual confidence and Witte admitted that from the experience
of past years Japan had reason to doubt Russia's sincerity.
He mentioned in particular Russia's refusal to accept Ito's compromise proposal in 1901. The uncertainties and antagonisms
which had crystallized since then had in some way to be re-
paired.

[12] Korostovets, op.cit., pp. 53ff; Witte to Kokovtsov, Aug. 10, 12, 1905, K.A.,
VI, 28–29.

The question of the relationship between the indemnity and the problem of security remained. If Russia escaped payment of the indemnity, Japan might expect her to use her resources for a program of military preparation for a war of revenge. If Japan were to receive the indemnity she might (as she had after 1895) use it to increase her own military forces, thus constituting an aggressive factor.

Witte intended, as a substitute for the "unreasonable demands," particularly the indemnity, to propose a mutual guarantee for the security of the interests of the two countries in the Far East. The idea of a reconciliation had been supported by Witte even before the war. Under present conditions it could serve as a test as to whether the "unreasonable" demands were indeed intended to give Japan greater security or whether they had a more aggressive purpose. In any case, if Japan refused to accept this gesture, it would help Russia escape blame should the conference fail.

On August 12, Witte presented the counterproposals to Komura; the plenipotentiaries were now ready to match demands, strategy, wits, and endurance.[13] In view of the instructions each had brought, the two statements of objectives appeared to leave little room for maneuver. However, while each of the plenipotentiaries publicly conveyed the impression that his own statement represented his most liberal concession, neither assumed that his opponent had done so.

Before and during the negotiations with the Japanese, Witte engaged in a campaign of public relations intended to improve the general image of Russia and, hopefully, her chances of success at the conference. A series of articles in the *Algemeine Zeitung* in early July had aimed at restating Russian intentions.[14] Written "by an anonymous Russian close to Witte," it was substantially a defense of Witte, purporting to clear him of complicity in the war. The articles stressed his peaceful intentions and his goodwill toward Japan; the war had come about because a group of adventurers had brought their evil influence to bear on the government and the court.

Witte's specific appeal to the American public was also carefully cultivated with the help of Dillon and Rosen, the latter being an engaging and affable person in contrast to the rough-

---

[13] See Appendix 2 of this study.
[14] Makino to Katsura, No. 37, July 27, 1905, *J.F.O.*

hewn chief plenipotentiary. Even though Witte did not speak English, he was capable of a frank and easy manner and even a folksiness toward the people, and wherever he went he left behind a trail of favorable personal impressions. In an excess of folksiness he is said to have shaken hands with everyone he met including the engineers and firemen on the train and on one occasion he seems to have tried to outdo even President Roosevelt's public graciousness by kissing the conductor.

The Russian attitude toward the Jews was a serious problem in public relations. If it could be justified or explained away, Witte was uniquely suited to do so. His marriage, his business associations, and his positive stand on political rights gave him a degree of personal immunity from identification with the anti-Jewish pogroms that were still endangering the lives and personal security of Russian Jews.

There are two versions of the circumstances which led to the meeting between Witte and a group of Jewish leaders at Portsmouth on August 14, 1905.[15] Either is reasonable and possible. One version is that Adolph Kraus requested the interview through Baron Schlippenbach, the Russian consul general in Chicago. The other is that Witte expressed a desire to meet with some of the American-Jewish leaders and this may have been the inspiration for Kraus's request.

The group that met with Witte included: Jacob Schiff, Oscar Straus, Isaac Seligman, Adolph Lewisohn, and Adolph Kraus. On the Russian side, Baron Rosen and Gregory Willenkin, the latter a Russian Jew and the agent of the Russian minister of finance in Washington, were also present. In the course of the meeting and of a letter that the group later sent to Witte, a very frank exchange of views took place about the conditions under which the Jews lived in Russia.

The American group told the Russians that the issue could not be looked upon as a purely domestic one since the conditions in Russia forced many to emigrate in self-defense and this gave the countries to which they went a natural interest in the matter. Furthermore, emigration was not the solution to a problem which touched the lives of several million people. To Witte's point that granting civil rights to the Jews was difficult because they were

[15] Korostovets, op.cit., pp. 74, 79–80; A. Kraus, Reminiscences and Comments, Chicago, 1925, pp. 155–160; O.S. Straus, Under Four Administrations, Boston, 1922, pp. 189–190; Editorial, "Progress of the World," The American Monthly Review of Reviews, XXXII, 3, Sept. 1905, pp. 264–265.

so prominently identified with movements opposed to the government, the answer was made that if the Jews were given full civil rights they would have no need to join the opposition. Witte conducted this interview with complete frankness and Willenkin later told Korostovets that he had made a very favorable impression on his visitors. Witte, who was also pleased with the interview, wrote to Lamsdorf that he felt he had been able to set the leaders straight on a number of questions on which they were badly informed.[16] He felt that his exchange of views would be of great assistance in the Russo-Japanese competition for the American money market since some of those with whom he had talked had been supporters of Japan and now seemed inclined to assist Russia. It is apparent from the sequel that Witte misinterpreted the response to his statements.

Witte by no means confined his goodwill efforts to the Jewish leaders. On his arrival in New York and again in Boston on his way to Portsmouth, he visited the Jewish sections of these cities.[17] According to his own account, he was well received. He stopped along the street to talk to them in Russian and received some frank responses from them. He learned that while some of them were happy in America and had no love for the Russian system, they did retain considerable love for Russia as their native land and hoped for his success at the conference. They added they would pray to this end.

The effect of the Russian public relations campaign is not easy to assess.[18] A survey of the American press has shown at best a modest success. The New York Times of August 18, 1905, expressed a view that was apparently generally held: the Japanese cause was still believed to be the better cause, and though Russia was judged less harshly, it was now realized that "whichever was victorious we were bound to be the losers." Whereas Russia would have shut the door to American commerce abruptly, Japan, it was believed, would do essentially the same thing by underselling American goods.

The west coast newspapers also gave considerable weight to

[16] Witte to Lamsdorf, Aug. 15, 1905, K.A., vi, 33.
[17] Witte, op.cit., i, 377, 381.
[18] W.B. Thorson, "American Public Opinion and the Portsmuoth Conference," American Historical Review, liii, 3, Apr. 1948, pp. 439–464; W.B. Thorson, "Pacific Northwest Opinion on the Russo-Japanese War of 1904–1905," Pacific Northwest Quarterly, xxv, Oct. 1944, pp. 305–322; R.L. Buell, "The Development of Anti-Japanese Agitation in the United States," Political Science Quarterly, xxxvii, 4, Dec. 1922, pp. 614–620.

the commercial factor. Their opposition to Russia, they wrote, had from the first stemmed from the threat she presented to the commerce of both the western nations and Japan. The Portland *Oregonian* saw a parallel with American interests in the fact that Japan was also fighting "for nothing less than her life . . ." and consequently, a Japanese victory remained the general preference. Even those newspapers that deplored the continuation of Oriental immigration still found that American interests would be served by a Japanese victory.

The opinion reflected in the press remained the same when speculation turned to the question of responsibility in case the war were resumed. Witte had exerted every effort to prepare the American public to accept his view that Japan would be responsible should this occur. Nevertheless, the St. Paul *Pioneer Press* expressed a fairly general opinion that if the war were to continue "no blame can reasonably be attached to Japan . . ." continuing that this might have some advantages since "to 'call' the Russian 'bluff' " might be a guarantee of permanent peace.

Against this pronounced approval of Japan, the strong conviction on the part of both sides that Russia was winning the contest for American approval seems to lack any realistic foundation.[19] In part it must have been a consequence of misunderstood or incomplete press surveys and also it may have been a conclusion drawn from the friendly relations which the Russians experienced with many Americans during their visit. Baron Rosen has described one of these friendly encounters in which he thought he saw evidences of a Caucasian solidarity against the Japanese. A young reporter had said that the original solidarity of American opinion in favor of the Japanese in the war was fast becoming reversed. Rosen replied that he was gratified to hear this and wondered whether this were not because it had been discovered that "after all, we are white." The reporter answered that this was "about the long and short of it."

It can be seen how easy it would have been for both antagonists to exaggerate, the Russians in their favor and the Japanese in their disfavor, the impact on American public opinion of the racial factor. In fact, evidence is entirely lacking that the racial factor had any influence at all on the outcome either of the struggle for public favor or of the outcome of the Portsmouth Conference.

[19] Korostovets, *op.cit.*, pp. 102–103; Kaneko, *Beikoku*, Aug. 27, 1905.

15. The Spoils of War

THE FUNDAMENTAL ISSUES confronting the Portsmouth Conference in August 1905 were those pertaining to Korea and Manchuria—two places long associated with one of the principal fulcrums of power in the Far East and with the sources of discord that led to the Russo-Japanese War. Moreover, Korea and Manchuria were the specific issues over which the military forces had contended and their relative positions might, consequently, be expected to be largely determined by the outcome of the war. At the same time, those two regions were the issues that were least dependent upon the future military prospects of the belligerents, a factor of considerable significance in a struggle so indecisive.

Therefore, these issues were the most easily resolved at the Portsmouth Conference. Witte's rule of thumb that Japan would be entitled to claim whatever her armies had actually conquered facilitated a definite settlement since it assumed two conditions: first, however ready and qualified the Russian forces might be to resume the war, their planning did not necessarily contemplate rolling back the Japanese armies from the places already occupied; and second, the assumption was that the existing Japanese conquests would have to be recognized unless some other counter-force could be brought to bear on the situation. This, in turn, would necessarily be dependent upon the willingness of some other power to express its displeasure with Japan's successfully accomplished expansion in the form of forceful opposition. On purely geographical and juridical grounds, the most likely source of restraint appeared to be China whose rights and interests in Manchuria and Korea were the subjects of the bargaining. Yet, it had to be taken into account that, while China was by no means lacking in incentive to restrain such obvious disregard for her rights, her military strength was clearly unequal to the task.

The discussion of these issues was characterized by a mixture of engaging frankness, ill-disguised endeavors at mutual deception, a specious solicitude for the rights and interests of China, and an unremitting and importunate pursuit of national interests. Russia and Japan had displayed these attitudes before, but a keener rivalry was evident with the resumption of negotiations. Now more evenly matched than before the war, each had to assure itself the margin of security that would prevent the other from asserting a clear hegemony in the Far East. Under such conditions, it would have been difficult to expect them not to disregard the rights of China and the other powers in seeking evey advantage for themselves. At the same time neither cared to endanger the existing gains by treading too blatantly on the rights of others.

The Korean question was to a large extent solved to the satisfaction of the Japanese government even before the meeting of the Portsmouth Conference. Her successful military strategy had left Japan in almost unchallenged control of Korea. Since she had for years disregarded Chinese interests in the country, she could look upon Korean sovereignty as the only ultimate authority with which it would be necessary to have any official transactions. Furthermore, Japan had anticipated the negotiations with Russia by reducing to a considerable extent the independence of Korea and by obtaining approval for this from her associates, the United States and Great Britain. Consequently, Japan confronted Russia at Portsmouth with a largely accomplished fact.

One of the aspects of Japan's prewar Korean policy which most clearly exemplified her long-range and forceful expansion plans was her railway project. This had been associated with her military program and had been openly disclosed to Russia during the prewar negotiations by her demand that the Korean railway be linked to the railway network of Manchuria. In the final preparations to go to war the Japanese government had decided to hasten the railway construction already under way in Korea.

Japan took two significant steps toward realizing her intended permanent domination in Korea as her military forces entered the country in February 1904. She advanced her strategic aims by starting the construction of the Seoul-Uiju railway line through North Korea to the Manchurian line. At the same time she laid the cornerstone of her increasingly broad political control over Korea. On February 17 Viscount Ito reached Seoul to inaugurate the new era.[1] At the audience granted him the next day with the Korean Emperor and in the conversations with Korean officials that followed, he tried to set the standard of a kindly but firm relationship of effective Japanese control.

---

[1] *K.G.*, II, 255ff; Otsu, *op.cit.*, VI, 195; Komura to Takahira, Feb. 25, Griscom to Hay, Mar. 17, 1904, *U.S.F.R.*, pp. 437–438; Tewksbury, *op.cit.*, II, 20–21; Jordan (Seoul) to Lansdowne, May 19, 1904, *B.D.*, IV, 112.

The immediate consequences of this mission were far-reaching. There were return visits of Korean envoys to Japan. There was the severance of all established relations with Russia carried out by Korea's denunciation of her treaties with Russia, including those agreements that granted such special privileges as the timber and mining concessions near the Tiumen and Yalu rivers. Finally, a special protocol was signed on February 23 recognizing the new relationship.

The protocol of February 23 was a first cautious step toward the erasure of Korea as a national state. Article III expressed the view still necessary at this early stage of the war: "The Imperial Government of Japan definitively guarantees the independence and territorial integrity of the Korean Empire." At the same time, it assured Japan the right to intervene in case the Korean Imperial House or the territorial integrity of the country were endangered from either an internal or an external source. To do this, Japan was permitted to occupy such strategic places as were found necessary to discharge this obligation. The protocol also established Japanese political control over the Korean government in two important areas. Concerning internal affairs, Korea was obligated to "place full confidence" in the Japanese government and accept advice from the latter "in regard to improvements in administration." Furthermore, concerning foreign affairs, Korean freedom of action was circumscribed by stipulating that arrangements with third powers that were contrary to the principles of the present protocol were not to be made except by the mutual consent of both Korea and Japan.

By May 1904 the course of the war was favorable enough to warrant taking a further, more audacious step. A Japanese cabinet council met on the 31st to formulate a fundamental policy regarding Korea. The objective was the gradual establishment of protectorate rights over Korea with the ultimate goal of bringing Korea under the sovereign control of Japan. This had to be done in such a way as to avoid arousing, if possible, either internal rebellion or the suspicions or objections of the other powers. This objective was to be carried out by gradually gaining control of the administration as well as the broader areas of Korea life. Japan would seek control over the political, economic, military, and diplomatic affairs of Korea, and would also, as a first step, seek to obtain the direction of all means of communication and of colonization. Undoubtedly with the lessons of a decade before in mind, caution was to be the keynote of the fulfillment of this plan.

This decision was put into operation by a Japanese-Korean treaty of August 22, 1904 that provided for the acceptance of Japanese-appointed advisors to the Korean government.[2] Megata Tanetaro, head of the bureau of revenue of the Japanese ministry of finance, was appointed to the position of financial advisor to the Korean government. He immediately began to take measures looking toward Japanese-Korean economic unity. One of his first steps was the withdrawal of the old-style Korean coins from circulation and the minting of new ones which would correspond with the Japanese currency system.

An advisor to the Japanese imperial household department, Kato Masuo, was appointed to supervise all affairs dealing with the Korean Imperial family. Yet even this did not prevent the Korean Emperor from appealing secretly to the United States in September. The impression seems to have been current in Korean official circles that the United States and other nations could be relied upon to come to the rescue of the country in case of a dire emergency. The Emperor's message was written on this assumption and was transmitted secretly through the counselor of the Korean legation in Washington. Since the American course with respect to Korea was already set, this as well as succeeding appeals were unavailing.

An American advisor to the Japanese legation in Washington, Durham W. Stevens, was appointed by the Japanese government as advisor to the Korean foreign office. Since the Japanese government was convinced that the internal weaknesses of Korea had in recent years been transformed into international incidents through foreign intrigues, foreign affairs was regarded as a highly sensitive aspect of government. The policy adopted was to transfer, as rapidly as conditions permitted, the direction of foreign affairs from Seoul to Tokyo and to isolate Korea from all external relations.

By the summer of 1904, the Japanese policies were already meeting resistance. While the governmental reorganization aroused the upper levels of Korean society, the colonization and other economic measures aroused other groups of the population

[2] K.G., II, 258; Otsu, op.cit., VI, 197; Conroy, op.cit., pp. 450–451; Nelson, op.cit., pp. 254–255; Lansdowne to MacDonald, Sept. 26, 1905, B.D., IV, 112–113; H.B.Hulbert, The Passing of Korea, London, 1906, pp. 208–209; Takahira to Adee, Aug. 30, 1904, U.S.F.R., p. 438.

as well. The Japanese suggested that all uncultivated land and natural resources under Imperial control be opened to their own nationals. Personal property was seized and severe punishments for resistance were meted out by Japanese military courts. Discontent and disorder began to spread and several thousand troops were needed in Seoul to preserve order. The Korean opposition crystallized around the Society for the Promotion of Peace and Safety until it was broken up. Following this, the struggle was carried on by the National Peoples' Society. Independence was giving way to an independence movement.

In March 1905 negotiations were started to place all means of communications under Japanese jurisdiction. It was not necessary to include the telegraph since it was already Japanese owned. But a treaty was concluded on April 1, 1905, in spite of Korean resistance, that gave Japan the desired control over the telephone and postal facilities. This was followed on May 16 by an agreement which permitted Japan complete freedom of navigation in all the coastal and inland waters of Korea.

The renewal of the Anglo-Japanese Alliance in 1905 provided the first of the guarantees Japan desired for her new course in Korea. In the light of succeeding developments, the original treaty, concluded in 1902, appeared completely obsolete since it had guaranteed the independence of Korea. Yet, the very same reason that Japan was to use in 1905 in support of her protectorate plan had already been discussed with Britain in 1901 and 1902.[3] This was her conviction that Korean political weakness was the source of the whole problem. It was this weakness that, in the opinion of the Japanese government, had in the past provided fertile ground for foreign intrigues at Seoul and had eventually led to clashes between nations with interests in Korea.

By mid-1905 the situation had changed favorably enough for the Japanese government to take a more decisive step toward ending the cycle of disturbances over Korea. In the first place, she had by this time fought two wars over the issue and could argue more convincingly than ever in favor of stamping out this source of international disturbance. Even more reassuring, the second of these wars had by then been sufficiently successful to give Japan, in fact, a free hand in Korea. Japan was now interested in a guarantee for her own national security rather than

[3] Hayashi to Sone, Aug. 1, 1901, Hiratsuka, op.cit., I, 9–10; MacDonald to Lansdowne, July 31, 1905, B.D., IV, 158.

merely in the preservation of the old order in Korea. Prime
Minister Katsura was able to state emphatically in late July
1905:

"One of the chief causes of the present war was the habit of
the Emperor of Korea, and of high Korean officials, of intriguing
with Foreign Powers, and of making arrangements and agreements in the most irresponsible manner. This could not be permitted to continue; otherwise . . . the peace of the Far East
would never be assured."

The new treaty with Britain in 1905 changed the emphasis
from the "independence of Korea" to the "paramount interests of
Japan in Korea." These paramount interests were defined as extending to political, military, and economic interests. Britain recognized the right of Japan "to take such measures of guidance,
control, and protection" in Korea as she deemed necessary to
advance these interests. Even before the public announcement
of the new agreement, Russia would already have endorsed
Japan's new position in Korea in these same words.

The treaty left Japan with an obligation regarding Korea that
was somewhat incongruous with the new dispensation. This was
her assurance that she would respect the principle of equal commercial and industrial opportunity in Korea.[4] During the negotiations, Japan had quite logically objected to including in the agreement any reference to other foreign rights. Lansdowne replied
that in case of a violation of treaty rights, Britain would not be
obligated to come to the support of Japan. It became clear as
time passed that the Japanese objection had been an accurate
reflection of her real intention regarding Korea.

The Taft-Katsura memorandum of July 29, 1905 was another
step toward Japanese control over Korea. Roosevelt was cognizant
of the concurrent Anglo-Japanese negotiations and, like the
British, realistically accepted what could not in any case be prevented short of using force. Katsura expressed to Taft in Tokyo
essentially the same sentiments about the international significance of Korean weakness as had been discussed between
Japan and Britain. Taft agreed that Japan's success in the war
entitled her to extend sovereign control over Korea to the extent
of preventing Korea from assuming troublesome international

⁴ Lansdowne to MacDonald, July 1, 14, 18, 19, Aug. 8, 9, Lansdowne to
Hayashi, Aug. 9, 1905, B.D., IV, 143, 146, 150–151, 162–163.

engagements as in the past. It was on this note that the memorandum was concluded.

The Korean question was discussed at the Portsmouth Conference on August 12, significantly the very day on which the new Anglo-Japanese treaty was signed. The Russian counterproposal had already given general approval of the demand in these words:

"Article I does not give rise to any objection. The Imperial government, recognizing that Japan possesses in Korea preponderant political, military and economic interests, are ready to engage neither to obstruct nor interfere with the measures of direction, protection and control which Japan may consider it necessary to take in Korea."

In spite of this seemingly complete agreement, the instructions had in fact some reservations on the part of Russia. The first issue pertained to the sovereignty of Korea; Russia contended that the sovereignty of the country ought to be recognized and that whatever measures were taken by Japan in Korea ought to be taken in full accord with the Korean government. Witte supported his proposal with the following arguments: that the sovereignty of Korea was an international question; that this sovereignty could not and should not be canceled out by a bilateral act on the part of Russia and Japan; that the principle of signing a treaty which violated the sovereignty of another country was one that Russia could not approve; and that unless the sovereignty of Korea were specifically recognized in a treaty, criticism could be expected from other nations.

The Japanese position was essentially this: that at the moment Japan was primarily interested in freedom of action for her program in Korea; that the only question before the conference was the elimination of sources of friction between Japan and Russia; that even if the course Japan was to follow hereafter in pursuing her plans with respect to Korea were to eventuate in international complications, this would be of concern only to Japan; that Japan could not agree to retain Korean sovereignty as it had been heretofore; that, since Japan was already in control of the foreign affairs of Korea, the sovereignty of the country was even then severely qualified; and that, contrary to the views expressed at the conference by Rosen, this issue was not a mere formality but one touching on serious Japanese interests.

A compromise was finally reached on the matter. Instead of either fully recognizing Korean sovereignty in the treaty itself as the Russians had wished or avoiding any mention of it as the Japanese had hoped, it was decided to express the Russian idea in the protocol only. Accordingly, the following statement was embodied in the record:

"The Japanese Plenipotentiaries declare that it is understood that the measures which Japan may find it necessary to take in Korea in the future and which impair the sovereignty of that country will be taken in accord with the Korean Government."[5]

A second issue concerning Korea was the rights that Russia and Russian subjects would enjoy in Korea under the new dispensation. The Russian demand for most favored nation treatment was accepted by Japan after a short discussion. Accordingly, at the next session of the conference this provision was embodied in a statement that, after recognizing the paramount interests of Japan, continued as follows:

"It is understood that Russian subjects will be treated in exactly the same manner as the subjects or citizens of other foreign powers, that is, they shall be on the same footing as the subjects or citizens of the most favored nation."[6]

The third issue was one that had been one of the irritants between the two countries before the war. This was the concern of each nation lest the territory of the other should harbor a military threat to its own security. The freedom of action that Japan had reserved for herself to take such "measures of guidance, protection, and control" in Korea as were deemed necessary, projected this menace in an even more portentous form. In the end, this matter was also the subject of a compromise expressed as follows in the same annex to the protocol that dealt with the most favored nation question:

"It is further understood that, in order to remove all causes of misunderstanding, Japan and Russia will mutually abstain from taking measures on the Russo-Korean frontier, which might menace the security of Russian or Korean territory."

[5] *Protocols,* p. 10.
[6] *N.K.D.H.,* p. 63.

The measures already taken in Korea, reenforced by obtaining the consent of Great Britain, the United States, and Russia, opened the way for Japan to complete the structure of her protectorate.[7] During late September and most of October the final plans were elaborated with the aid of the Japanese minister in Seoul, Hayashi Gonsuke, who was called home for the purpose, and of Komura after his return from Portsmouth. The protectorate plan was approved by a cabinet council on October 27 and then by the Emperor. On November 4, two days before Komura's departure for Peking to secure approval for the new order in Manchuria, Ito left Tokyo for his mission to Seoul to carry the Korean plan into effect.

Ito's mission brought Japanese-Korean relations to a somewhat melodramatic impasse. For this time he had come to gain Korean approval for her own elimination as an independent nation. The Korean Emperor pled with him not to force the issue and some of the ministers of state wept. The prime minister, Han Kyu-sul, firmly refused to give his approval. His opposition was finally overcome by General Hasegawa Yoshimichi, the commander of the Japanese troops who had entered the courtyard and the palace, who, sword in hand, dragged the prime minister unceremoniously out of the room.

In the course of the discussions that took place during these tragic days, the Korean Emperor and his ministers tried in every possible way to avoid taking the steps being forced upon them. When they realized that Japan would insist upon her major demand, they tried to reduce as much as possible the all-inclusiveness and the finality of this step. They succeeded in minor ways. They were able to persuade Ito to remove the words "entirely to herself" from the phrase "Japan shall take over entirely to herself" in an earlier version of the agreement. Also, the Korean desire for some commitment on the part of Japan as to a termination of the protectorate was weakly reflected in a clause which stated that the agreement was "to serve until the moment arrives when it is recognized that Korea has attained national strength . . . "

The climax of the event came in a stormy session lasting from two oclock in the afternoon of November 17 until early the next morning. The treaty dated November 17 was in fact signed at one

[7] K.G., II, 260–270; F.A. McKenzie, The Tragedy of Korea, New York, 1908, pp. 132–137; Takahira to Root, Nov. 23, Root to Griscom, Nov. 24, 1905, U.S.F.R., pp. 612–614; Tewksbury, op.cit., pp. 27–30.

o'clock on the morning of the 18th. A Japanese declaration of November 22 announced the new relationship to the world. The Korean response was emphasized by published protests, by an appeal for help addressed to the United States government, and by the suicide of Prince Min Yong Whan. Two months later the Korean Emperor issued an appeal to the nations stating that his signature on the treaty had been forged and requesting them to establish a joint protectorate over Korea.

The agreement contained three points of particular significance for the future of Japanese-Korean relations. The first, giving Japan complete control over Korean foreign relations, was expressed in Article I as follows:

"The Government of Japan, through the Department of Foreign Affairs at Tokyo, will hereafter have control and direction of the external relations and affairs of Korea, and the diplomatic and consular representatives of Japan will have the [sic] charge of the subjects and interests of Korea in foreign countries."

Secondly, enforcement of this control was to be in the hands of a resident general who was to reside at Seoul and have direct access to the Korean Emperor. This office was first occupied by Ito himself. He was assisted by residents stationed at ports and other places where they were to exercise "the powers and functions hitherto appertaining to Japanese Consuls in Korea." Finally, while the duties of the resident general seemed to be primarily concerned with foreign affairs, Article V stated that "The Government of Japan undertake to maintain the welfare and dignity of the Imperial House of Korea." Clearly, even this agreement contemplated something broader than control over foreign affairs.

The plenipotentiaries at the Portsmouth Conference turned their attention to Manchuria on August 14 and therewith began a discussion of the issue that had first brought the Russo-Japanese antagonism into focus.[8] Article 2 of the Japanese demands concerning the evacuation of Manchuria and the recognition of foreign rights and interests, and Article 3 concerning the recognition of Chinese sovereignty were significantly discussed together. This was done at Witte's suggestion because he felt that any action taken with regard to this question must bind Russia and Japan equally.

[8] *Protocols*, pp. 17–22; *N.K.D.H.*, pp. 64–84.

The Russian occupation of Manchuria had been singled out by Japan in early 1901 as the factor which menaced all other foreign rights and interests in Northeast Asia. This included the territorial integrity of China and Korea as well as foreign interests in both these countries. The issue had later been emphasized by the Anglo-Japanese Alliance, by the joint pressures of the United States and Japan to open new commercial outlets in Manchuria, and by the struggle for the Yalu region.

Komura raised four main points concerning this issue that were discussed at the session of August 14 and at the final sessions of the conference when details of the treaty were under consideration. These points were: one, the simultaneous and scheduled withdrawal of the Japanese and Russian forces from Manchuria; two, the restoration of Manchuria, except for the leased area, to Chinese sovereignty; three, the avoidance of monopolistic use of concessions in Manchuria; and four, the preservation of the principle of the open door in Manchuria.

The second, third, and fourth of these propositions were brought into focus in a discussion of a specific aspect of the relations of foreign states to China: the difference between a monopolistic use of a concession granted by China and a use that recognizes the sovereign rights of China and the rights of other nations to enjoy equality of opportunity. In his counterproposals and at the conference, Witte had maintained that Russia had no exclusive rights which could be considered inconsistent either with the sovereign rights of China or with the principle of equal opportunity. He stated that such rights as Russia had in Manchuria were exclusively those granted by China. Furthermore,

"He was anxious to state precisely, that any right acquired in conformity with the law, in the determined limits, and without restraining others from acquiring similar benefits, ought not to be considered as a privilege or monopoly, but should be recognized as a legal and indisputable right . . . Russia never advanced, supported, or sanctioned any exclusive rights which would involve the idea of monopoly or privilege or would impair the sovereignty of China."

Since Harbin had been introduced into the discussion by Komura as an illustration of a monopoly of rights, Witte replied in defense that this town was situated on an area of land granted by China for the administration and operation of the railway.

Referring to the fiction that the Chinese Eastern Railway was of a private character, Witte stated that because this grant was a private right with which the government could not interfere, it ought to be classified as a concession rather than a special privilege (that is, the Japanese term *tokkyo* as distinguished from *tokken*). Using this grant for the intended purpose, Russia had developed the area and in the course of time a mere village had grown into the existing town of Harbin and such facilities as it now enjoyed had been introduced under the Russian administration.

It was by no means true, Witte maintained, that Russia had intended to reserve the benefits of her success for herself. There was no stipulation in the grant which prevented others from acquiring a similar concession. Also, if the Japanese, as Komura had indicated, had failed to receive equal treatment in Harbin, this was unintentional, and he conjectured that the fault in this case must have lain with the military rather than the municipal authorities. He added his assurances that such a miscarriage of justice would not occur again.

Komura's answer brought his principal argument into clear focus by stating emphatically that Japanese rights in Manchuria must rest upon treaty arrangements with China rather than the goodwill of the Russian government. He felt that Russia occupied a far more extensive area in Harbin than was necessary for the administration of the railway, and asserted that Russia had treated Harbin as though it were a part of her own homeland. Subjecting Japanese citizens to a Russian administration in Manchuria was to disregard Japan's rights under her treaty with China.

This issue was finally the subject of a compromise formulated in words which established complete mutuality between the two countries and which were incorporated into the protocol as follows:

"The Plenipotentiaries of Japan and Russia, with a view to avoid all causes of misunderstanding in the future, declare that the concession for the construction and exploitation of the Chinese Eastern Railway in Manchuria is not inconsistent with the principle of the open door and equal treatment, and that within the limit of the land acquired under such concession, the subjects of His Majesty the Emperor of Japan as well as the subjects or citizens of other foreign powers shall enjoy the same rights and privileges as those of His Majesty the Emperor of Russia."

The policy governing evacuation and restoration of Chinese administration was also dealt with in an annex to the protocol. It was expressed as a mutual obligation in the following words:

"Japan and Russia mutually engage:
1. to evacuate completely and simultaneously [all of] Manchuria except the territory affected by the lease of the Liaotung [*i.e.*, Kuantung] peninsula, in conformity with the provisions of an additional article.
2. to restore entirely and completely to the exclusive administration of China all portions of Manchuria now occupied by Japanese or Russian troops or under their control, with the exception of the above-mentioned territory."

The specific and mutual guarantees of China's rights in Manchuria were extended further in Article 4 of the Japanese demands. This required that both Japan and Russia engage not to obstruct any measures China might take in the development of commerce and industry in Manchuria. Since Russia had enthusiastically endorsed this in the counterproposals, it needed little further discussion.

Nevertheless, the discussion of this article elicited an interesting exchange of views about a question which only a few month before had helped to aggravate relations between the two countries—the opening of centers for foreign commerce. Komura noted Russia's past objections to the opening of certain areas in Manchuria for residence and commerce. Witte answered that this had occurred during a period when Manchuria was very disturbed and had pertained only to certain railway stations, and said that Russia now had no objection to the opening of any ports or places in Manchuria to foreign commerce provided the engagement were reciprocal and applied also to the Kuantung peninsula. Komura agreed to this and stated that Dalny [*i.e.*, Dairen] would be open for foreign commerce.

The demand for the transfer of the lease rights to the Kuantung peninsula raised two objections from Russia. The first was the fact that China had been a party to the lease agreement and would have to be consulted if such a transfer were made.

The other objection was that the private rights of Russian subjects would have to be preserved. The issue was settled by the following statement:

"The Imperial Government of Russia cedes to Japan, subject to the consent of the government of China, the lease of Port Arthur, Talien [*i.e.*, Dairen], and the adjacent territory and territorial waters, as well as all the rights, privileges, concessions and franchises connected with or forming a part of such lease and they also cede to Japan all public works and properties in the territory affected by the above mentioned lease.

"The High Contracting Parties mutually engage to obtain the consent of the Chinese Government mentioned in the above stipulation.

"The Imperial Government of Japan, on their part, give assurances that the property rights of Russian subjects in the territory referred to above shall be perfectly respected."

The disposition of the railway in southern Manchuria, raised in Article 7 of the Japanese demands, was sharply contested by both parties.[9] The first question was to whom the railway should be transferred. In a proposal that suggested the solution mentioned in one of Kokovtsov's letters, Witte outlined the Russian position as follows: that the railway company be directed to transfer a part of the railway to the Chinese government; that the Chinese government be permitted to carry out immediately its right to purchase the railway as provided in the original agreement granting the right of construction; that the Russian government transfer the purchase price to Japan rather than to the company; and that the transferred section of the railway be limited to the area actually occupied by the Japanese army, except that the division point should be a place of some significance for communications.

Komura's answer disclosed the nature of the Japanese interests in Manchuria as already displayed in the course of the dispute with Russia and as it would soon be shown in the negotiations with China. He objected to the Russian plan on the grounds that while it would offer Japan a sum of money it would not provide her with the railway. Witte pointed out that his plan would eliminate both Russian ownership of the railway and Russian

[9] *Protocols*, pp. 35–38; *N.K.D.H.*, pp. 113–138; *K.G.*, ii, 76–79.

influence throughout the southern part of Manchuria. Komura explained that Japan had other than economic motives for wanting control over the railway, and only actual possession could offer Japan the needed assurance that the railway would no longer be a direct obstruction to her interests in that region.

Komura then proceeded to offer a series of proposals based upon the assumption that the railway would be transferred to Japan. These were: that the section of the railway that Japan was demanding was the one from Harbin to Port Arthur, the building of which had been sanctioned by Article VIII of the Port Arthur-Dairen Lease Agreement of 1896; that Japan was demanding all of this branch because it was an important and indispensable part of this lease; that this branch must be transferred with the lease which Russia had already assigned to Japan; and that, even if the lease agreement problem had been different, Japan would still want this section on the grounds that Harbin was a natural division point. He amplified the last point by saying that, just as the Manchurian mainline had been built to connect Vladivostok with Siberia, the branch line had been built to connect Harbin with the leased territory.

Witte took issue with Komura's assertion that the railway was a necessary part of the lease agreement. He said that, even though it was true that the sanction for the railway was contained in Article VIII of the lease, this by no means established the identity of the leased territory and the branch railway. Not only had the railway project been conceived long before the leased territory had become a possibility, but it could have been carried out even if the latter had never been considered. In any case, the purpose of the railway was to reach the sea, not the leased territory. Their appearance in the same document was as fortuitous as the case of a bill of sale which recorded the fact that a man had bought a house and a boat at the same time. Significantly, he compared the situation of Russia in Manchuria with the German position at Kiaochow.

Komura again turned to a point that reflected the realities of the struggle over rival national interests. He said that regardless of the precise differences that this situation might present from the Russian point of view, the point that interested him was the practical consequences to Japanese interests of the construction of the railway southward from Harbin and the occupation of the leased territory. He noted that Japan's experiences during the

past five years would have been very different than they had
been if Russia had gone no farther than the building of the mainline across Manchuria to Vladivostok. It was evident, Komura
continued, that the menace to Japan's interests had arisen from
Russia's association with the branch line and the leased area.
Consequently, it was inevitable that Japan would see these two
problems in the same perspective and demand control over the
sources of both. The parallel between this view and the one
expressed by General Kuropatkin before the outbreak of war
is both striking and interesting with respect to the conditions
under which war might have been averted. For, Kuropatkin's
contention at that time had been that Russia could avert a clash
with Japan by disengaging herself from her indefensible holdings
and commitments in South Manchuria.

In their discussion of the origins of the railway, the plenipotentiaries almost unavoidably made reference to its purpose.
Correcting Komura's statements as to the military and aggressive
objects it served, Witte explained that it had originally been
conceived for peaceful, commercial purposes. Specifically, the
plan had been to project the railway across Manchuria in order
to avoid the difficult terrain of the Amur region and take advantage of a shortcut to Vladivostok.

The military aspect of the railway agreement, Witte explained,
was a consequence of China's reluctance to permit its construction unless Russia would agree to protect China against Japan
and to use the railway for this purpose. Yet, even this aspect of the
agreement was defensive rather than aggressive, and from the
Russian point of view, the railway still remained a commercial
line that served no aggressive object of any kind. He noted that a
railway was not in itself aggressive unless it were used for such
purposes. Illustrating his point, he said that a knife could be used
both to cut paper and to wound a person.

This point was particularly pertinent to Article 8 of the
Japanese demands requiring Russia to make exclusively commercial and industrial uses of the portion of the railways of
Manchuria that she retained. Witte, rather surprisingly, had no
objection to this, noting that Article VIII of the original lease
agreement had stipulated that Russian troops or materials transported over the railway were not to stop in Chinese territory.
Witte disclosed an incentive for his ready concurrence when he
agreed to the restriction on condition that the obligation would

be mutually applied by both Japan and Russia. Komura accepted this for all the railway under Japanese control except that which lay within the leased area.

Since the Russians were unwilling to concede the branch railway on the grounds of its inseparability from the lease agreement, some other principle had to be found. Witte was ready to agree that the portion lying within the leased area might logically be transferred as a part of the lease. As for the rest, he eliminated the possibility of transferring all of it on the grounds that Harbin was a natural division point since Russian experience had shown that it was not. In the first place, it lacked the facilities to fill this requirement and also, as compared with the areas to the south, Harbin was poor both in population and in industrial and commercial advantages.

The negotiations reverted to the formula with which Witte had opened the discussion; the division of the railway at approximately the point reached by the Japanese armies, with a suitable adjustment to make the division point a place with some significance for the railway. Komura at first hesitated to accept this. He pointed to Fakumen on the map, the advance point between Mukden and Changchun reached by the Japanese armies and noted that this was not, in his view, a suitable division point.

Witte suggested that consideration be given to a place with some commercial importance such as Changchun. Komura indicated his preference for a place better suited topographically such as the point between Harbin and Changchun where the railway from the north crossed the Sungari the second time. Finally, Komura agreed to accept Kuanchengtze near Changchun provided the branch line to Kirin were included. Having reached an agreement as to the general area in which the division of the railway was to made, the question was left to be decided more precisely after Witte learned the present status of the branch line to Kirin. Accordingly, the protocol for this session was expressed as follows:

"Russia engages to assign and transfer to Japan, without compensation and subject to the consent of the Chinese Government, the portion of railway between . . . and Port Arthur and all its branches together with all rights, privileges and properties which appertain to it in that region, as well as all coal mines in that region belonging to or worked for the benefit of the railway.

"The High Contracting Parties mutually engage to obtain the consent of the Chinese Government in the above stipulation."

The Japanese demands made in Articles 10 and 11 fell somewhere between those that might be classed as spoils of war and those added as extra demands. While neither pertained to matters that had been a specific cause of irritation between the two countries before the war, they were understandably items that weighed significantly in the balance of power. In the end, neither of these demands was accepted by Russia even though they were used by Japan in the bargaining over the Sakhalin and indemnity questions.

The Russian practice of using neutral ports to protect some of her ships had been an issue since the very beginning of the war. The Russian gunboat "Mandzhur" was the first to come into dispute because it was already in neutral Shanghai harbor at the outbreak of war.[10] In spite of a Japanese demand that she either leave within 24 hours or be interned, it was not until late March 1904 that she was finally taken into custody by the Chinese government. In the course of the war, other Russian vessels sought asylum in neutral ports. Since Japan could do nothing about this without herself committing a violation of neutrality, she chose to seek redress through the peace demands for what she considered had been an undue advantage enjoyed during the war by Russia.

The Japanese demand that Russia surrender to her as lawful prizes all Russian ships that, "in consequence of damage received in battle," had "sought asylum in neutral ports and were there interned . . . ," was refused by Witte. He contended in his counterproposals that it was contrary to the accepted practice of international law; that the demand ran counter to the peaceful and cooperative intentions which pervaded the negotiations; that the material gains to Japan would be slight; and that, in any case, it was incompatible with the dignity of Russia.

When the question was introduced at the afternoon session on August 17, Komura presented the Japanese reply to these objections: Japan's claim was specifically limited to ships that had taken refuge because they had suffered damage in battle; that the principles and precedents of international law permitted a belligerent to exercise his belligerent rights in the

[10] Hershey, *op.cit.*, pp. 188–189.

domain of a neutral country that could not itself perform its own duties; and that Japan had abstained from exercising these rights only because she did not wish to injure the commercial interests of foreign powers and because she intended to raise the question in the negotiations with Russia. Since Witte refused to accept any of these points, the question was tabled for the time being.

The Japanese demand that Russia agree to limit her naval strength in the Far East met the same fate. Witte refused this on the sole grounds that it was incompatible with the national dignity of Russia; nevertheless, he was willing to state for the record that Russia was not thinking of having "in the near future any considerable naval forces in the waters of the Pacific." Komura was unable to move Witte beyond this point. This demand was used along with the interned ships question in bargaining over the Sakhalin and indemnity issues though with no better result.

16. The Crisis: Sakhalin and Indemnity

THE SUCCESS of the Portsmouth Conference depended entirely upon finding a solution to the Sakhalin Island and indemnity issues. Neither was immediately or necessarily related to the specific subjects in dispute before the war; they had been added by Japan as demands after her military campaign appeared to be progressing satisfactorily. As the two antagonists, before and during the conference, disclosed their respective and conflicting views as to a peace settlement, these issues become more than merely "extra demands." They assumed a separate significance as symbols of a decisive as against a bare victory or defeat for Japan and Russia respectively.

In addition to their symbolic role, both nations also recognized in the issues the substance of an effective balance of power and, therewith, the keys to their security in the Far East. To Japan they were a means of adjusting the postwar balance of power in the Far East as favorably to herself as possible. In the case of Sakhalin, the geographical parallel with her continental policies based on Formosa and Korea was obvious. For the possession of Sakhalin would be a strategic factor whether the island constituted a shield for Russia's Siberian coast or a potential springboard for a Japanese advance into Siberia. Likewise, the indemnity, since it was a considerable sum, could be transformed into effective defensive or aggressive strength in the hands of either antagonist.

The Sakhalin issue, raised in Article 5 of the Japanese peace conditions, was discussed at the conference on August 15.[1] While the Russian position had been substantially set forth in Witte's counterproposals, the question was further discussed in the conference session. It was apparent, both from the counterproposals and the discussion, that the two parties were far apart and, consequently, the problem was deferred. On August 23 the issue was revived and from that point on came to be associated with the indemnity question. Together these became the subject of the final bargaining which decided the fate of the Portsmouth Conference.

[1] *Protocols*, pp. 14, 23–27; *N.K.D.H.*, pp. 88–99; Korostovets, *op.cit.*, pp. 78–79; S. Ota, *Nichiro Karafuta Gaikosen*, Tokyo, 1941, pp. 227–234; G. A. Lensen, *The Russian Push Toward Japan*, Princeton, 1959, pp. 425–446, 505–506; J. L. Sutton, "Territorial Claims of Russia and Japan in the Kurile Islands," Center for Japanese Studies, *Occasional Papers*, No. 1, Ann Arbor, 1951, pp. 51–53.

One of the principal issues in dispute with regard to Sakhalin Island was the validity of the respective historical claims. The plenipotentiaries started with a brief exchange about the antiquity of these claims, Komura asserting a seventeenth century origin of Japan's rights and Witte answering that this claim was unrealistic because it had not been made good by actual possession or settlement. The discussion soon turned to the so-called Exchange Treaty of May 7, 1875. This had apportioned the Kuril (Chishima) Archipelago to Japan and Sakhalin to Russia. Both agreed that this settlement had given Russia a valid legal title to Sakhalin.

In the light of the adjustment actually made at the Portsmouth Conference, the dispute which preceded the conclusion of the agreement of 1875 becomes of considerable interest. The attention of the Japanese government had at that time been drawn to the problem by the vigorous Russian policy in the Far East during the 1850's, particularly the occupation and colonization of Sakhalin. In 1862 the Japanese had suggested dividing the island at the 50th parallel but the Russians were unreceptive. A Japanese attempt to establish a better claim to the island by colonization was also unproductive. In the 1870's the Japanese government tried unsuccessfully to enlist the services of the American president as mediator. Finally, inspired by the Russian sale of Alaska, the Japanese proposed, again without any success, to buy out the Russian interests in Sakhalin.

The relations between the two countries were further aggravated when the fishing regulations were changed by Russia in December 1899 in such a way as to limit the number of areas open to Japanese subjects. This would have eliminated 145 to the 269 areas then open for exploitation. The Japanese government retaliated by a law, approved in August 1900, restricting the importation of fish into Japan, a measure that helped to bring about a compromise since it limited the best market then available to Russian fishermen. Again in 1901 and the following year the Russian and Japanese governments respectively took discriminatory and conflicting measures dealing with the problems of access to fisheries. By this time the fishing industry had become far more important to Japan than when the controversy began; instead of the 500 fishermen who had gone to the Sakhalin area in 1876; there were 7,000 by 1904.

The accumulated Japanese resentments of these years were

reflected in a timely book published in May 1905 entitled *The Question of the Conduct of the Occupation of Karafuto* [Sakhalin]. It recalled the bitter conflicts of the preceding decades over Sakhalin and the struggle of the fishermen to carry on their work. In the opinion of the author, Russia had made little effective use of Sakhalin, colonizing it with convicts but neglecting the natural resources while denying them to Japan; Sakhalin was too necessary to the well-being of Japan to countenance this. Now, since the Korean-Manchurian issue had brought about a breach between Russia and Japan, the time was appropriate to settle this question with full attention to Japan's needs.

At the Portsmouth Conference, Witte acknowledged that the Japanese had far more vital fishing and agriculture interests in Sakhalin than did the Russians, asserting, nevertheless, that these interests by no means necessitated Japanese political control and declaring himself prepared to grant Japan fishing rights in and around the island. Against the backdrop of three decades of conflict, it was to be expected that Komura would hesitate to accept this kind of a solution since it had never operated effectively. He stated that the occupation of the island had raised expectations in Japan that could not be satisfied with such an outcome.

The strategic significance of Sakhalin was also discussed by the plenipotentiaries. Komura maintained that the island was geographically a continuation of the Japanese island chain and, consequently, formed a natural part of it and the strategic association was so close that the possession of the island by any other power was bound to constitute a danger to the security of Japan. Furthermore, Komura pointed out that its location so close to the heart of Japan gave it a greater significance than it could possibly have for Russia whose center was far away. This was exemplified by the fact that Russia had used it largely for criminal colonization.

As an instance of Russia's lack of real need for Sakhalin, Komura noted very pointedly the practice of sending criminals there. This issue arose on August 29 when the partition of the island was being discussed. Komura stated that escaped criminals had been a disturbing factor in northern Hokkaido throughout the years when a strait separated their territories, and if the island were partitioned so that the two countries would have contiguous territory, the situation would be far worse unless some steps were taken. Witte responded that this matter was in the jurisdiction of the minister of interior, but he felt sure that if Russia were to continue to maintain penal colonies in Sakhalin, measures would be taken to prevent their being an annoyance to Japan.

The evidences of Russian stewardship in Sakhalin during the preceding half century appeared to bear out the Japanese contention.[2] Criminals had been introduced to Sakhalin in 1859 by Muraviev, the governor general of Eastern Siberia, in order to promote the mining of coal at Dué. Because of the remoteness of the mines and the lack of transportation, the project was soon abandoned, but ten years later the island was declared officially open for the exile of the most incorrigible criminal elements. During the next quarter of a century some 30,000 were sent to the island.

The area with which the Japanese were best acquainted was Korsakov, the former Japanese settlement of Kushunkotan that had been renamed after a governor general of Eastern Siberia. The treaty of 1875 had given the Japanese access to Korsakov in relation particularly to their fishing interests. The population of the settlement had risen from about 272 at the time of Chekhov's visit in the early 1890's to about 1,000 in 1903: 800 criminals; 50 officials and their families; and about 70 Japanese and their families. In addition to the residents, about 400 cossacks and regular troops were stationed at Korsakov.

Witte replied to Komura's assertions about the strategic significance of the island to Japanese security that, far from being strategically unimportant to Russia, Sakhalin was in fact of the greatest importance to the security of the Russian Amur region and its possession by any other power would be more likely to constitute a menace to the national security of Russia than would be the case with respect to Japan. The experience of recent decades had shown, he asserted, that Russia had not in fact used it as a

---

[2] A.P. Chekhov, *Ostrov Sakhalin, 1891–1894, Sochineniia,* x, Moscow, 1948, pp. 71ff; H. DeWindt, *The New Siberia,* London, 1896, pp. 55–135; K. Hefele, "Aus dem Osten. Reisen in Sachalin, Ostrsibirien, der Mandschurei, China und Korea," *Mitteilungen der Deutschen Gesellschaft für Natur- und Völkerkunde Ostasiens,* ix, 2, Tokyo, May 1903, pp. 179–181; C.F. Kleye, "Sakhalin," *Japan Times,* May 30, 1905; Lensen, *op.cit.,* pp. 158ff; S.L. Lutsky, *Ostrov Sakhalin,* Moscow, 1946, pp. 7–8; Malozemoff, *op.cit.,* pp. 10–11; P.F. Unterberger, *Primamurskii Krai, 1906–1910,* in *Zapiski Imperatorskago Russkago Geograficheskago obshchestra,* xiii, St. Petersburg, 1912, pp. 207–211.

base of operations for hostile acts against Japan. Since it was not a menace to Japan, he concluded that it would be better to leave it in Russian hands.

One of the firmest prohibitions Witte had carried with him from St. Petersburg to Portsmouth was that not a single bit of Russian soil was to be surrendered in exchange for peace. Witte is reported to have told Komura in private that while Russia could actually do very well without Sakhalin, it was impossible in principle to make any territorial concession.[3] When Komura asked his permission to enter this statement in the official protocol Witte refused, saying that this remark was made privately and unofficially.

The grounds upon which Witte justified the wisdom of this principle were his interpretations of historical evidence, from which he concluded that the transfer of territory had in the past produced bad relations between nations. Franco-German relations were still disturbed because of the cession of Alsace-Lorraine to Germany in 1871. Bismarck had shown much better judgment in 1866 when he overruled the military men and refused to accept any territorial cessions from Austria, and consequently had been able to conclude his firmest and most lasting alliance. In the case of the Russian occupation of Chinese territory following the rebellion in Sinkiang in the 1870's, Witte added with notable disregard for the realities, Russia herself had followed this policy. It may be added that Russia had indeed returned most of the occupied territory but she had done so under pressure and with the greatest reluctance.

The indemnity question was also a mixture of principle and practical considerations. In the staff discussions of August 10 as well as in his counterproposals, Witte had established the principle on which he intended to take his stand: "Only vanquished countries reimburse expenses of war, but Russia is not vanquished." No significant part of Russian territory had been occupied, he asserted, nor was Russia incapable of producing the means of continuing the war. Even substituting the word "reimbursement" for "indemnity" failed to influence this principle in any way.

In a communication to Lamsdorf on August 14, Witte explained the significance this principle was assuming in the negotiations:

[3] Korostovets, op.cit., p. 78.

"In view of the vast difference between us [*i.e.*, Russia and Japan] over conditions, an agreement cannot be achieved. We must prepare for a continuing, hard war for which it is especially necessary to see to our needs in the foreign money market. Without this the war will be doubly difficult and will completely undermine our finances. The Japanese assume that we cannot get money abroad."

He noted that money would indeed be difficult to get, the most likely places being the United States or France. He was endeavoring, through the press and influential persons, to lay the foundation in the United States for this eventuality.[4]

The discussion of the indemnity issue at the conference may have been somewhat inhibited by the publicity given to it in the public press.[5] *The Nineteenth Century and After* dealt with the subject on the assumption that a reimbursement for war expenses was justified, that it would probably be paid, and that the alternative would be the surrender of a substantial part of the Russian Far East to Japan. On the other hand, a London dispatch quoted in Tokyo expressed the view that: "Press correspondents are unanimous in believing that the rupture of the negotiations is almost unavoidable on account of the Karafuto [*i.e.*, Sakhalin] and indemnity questions."

The dichotomy of views between Japan and Russia about the indemnity issue derived from the same clash over national interests that had generated the war. The feeling was expressed in Japan both privately and publicly that the war had been forced upon her by Russia, that Japan had suffered economically from the war, and that, as a consequence, Russia ought to pay the damages.[6] While the first part of this syllogism had by agreement been eliminated from the conference deliberations because it pertained to the causes of the war, it nevertheless lay at the root of Japanese thinking about the indemnity question.

The second part of this dialectic, that Japan had suffered from the war, was for obvious reasons not stressed at the conference,

[4] *K.A.*, vi, 31.
[5] O. Eltzbacher, "The Collapse of Russia: i, The Indemnity Due Japan," *The Nineteenth Century and After*, LVIII, 341, July 1905, pp. 3–9; *North China Herald*, Aug. 11, 1905; *Japan Times*, Aug. 18, 1905.
[6] *Japan Times*, July 6, 7, Aug. 3, 10, 15, 21–25, 1905; Ogawa, *op.cit.*, pp. 113–129, 234–235; Shinobu *op.cit.*, pp. 380–381, 464–465; *K.G.*, ii, 39, 101–102; Ota, *op.cit.*, pp. 236–237; Dennett, *op.cit.*, p. 299.

the Japanese avoiding it because it emphasized their weakness. The Russians clearly did not know the full extent to which the war had drained the productive manpower and financial strength of Japan, but the Japanese and foreign press disclosed enough to let them know that Japan was in dire need of reimbursement to repair the damage.

Even in Japan two different conclusions were drawn from their own propositions. One was so overwhelmingly important because it was held and shared by some members of the government, by the patriotic societies, and by the press. These important spokesmen for the country held that Russia must pay for the damage for which she was responsible. The other conclusion was that, since Japan was in too weakened a condition to force Russia to pay an indemnity if this became necessary, it was unwise to ask for it. One of the exponents of this latter point of view was General Kodama who is said to have remarked; "The foolish Katsura has decided to claim an indemnity."

It was the latter view, nevertheless, which was responsible for the compromise ultimately reached at Portsmouth. The actual military situation in Manchuria was clarified by a number of visitors to the war front, including General Yamagata on orders from the Emperor,[7] while several influential members of the Diet visited Marshal Oyama. From these sources it became clear to the Japanese government that the seemingly stubborn attitude of the Russians was not held without reason.

The investigations disclosed, in the first place, a manpower situation which was becoming increasingly unfavorable to Japan and which she lacked the means of improving. The victories at Shaho, Liaoyang, and Mukden were indecisive because Japan lacked the preponderance of forces to do better. Following the battle of Mukden the situation had begun to change even more to the detriment of Japan. While the Russians augmented their forces more rapidly than before, the lack of reserves made this impossible for Japan and the opportunity for a decisive Japanese stroke had long passed as the Russians had already discerned.

In the second place, the changes in the troop situation had effected quality as well as quantity. The Japanese had, throughout the active period of the war, estimated that most of the Russian

[7] K.G., II, 109–114; Kuropatkin, op.cit., I, 230–235; Shinobu, op.cit., pp. 464–465.

troops were second line units and the battles through Mukden had borne this out. It was assumed that because of their fear of trouble in the West or some specific commitment to France, they had left their best forces in European Russia. As the peace approached, however, much better units had appeared in Manchuria. General Kuropatkin and others later confirmed this with the observation that with the arrival of the new units in the summer of 1905, General Linievich was able to begin planning for a decisive battle.

A third factor was the recent evidence showing that the earlier Japanese estimates of the capacity of the Russian railways had been mistaken. The Russian minister of communications had undertaken to remedy some of the most obvious defects soon after the start of the war. In addition to the completion of the circum-Baikal link by autumn of 1904, he had built sidings sufficient to produce the effect in places of doubletracking. As a consequence, the further augmentation of troops and the increase of supplies and materiel could go forward increasingly unhindered by transport difficulties.

A fourth factor that influenced the Japanese decision was the relative financial strength of the two antagonists.[8] Japan's national indebtedness had risen sharply in the course of the war from 600 million to 2,400 million yen with an estimated annual interest of over 110 million yen. At the time the crisis was at its height at Portsmouth, Jacob Schiff, a friend of Japan, wrote to Takahira warning him about continuing the war. Russia, he said, would not be able to find any large amounts of foreign money; but she could fall back on her large gold supply or even go off the gold standard. Japan could do neither of these things. While he was always ready to do all he could, Schiff felt that if the war were continued the money markets of the United States, Great Britain, and Germany might be closed to Japan. At best, loans for Japan would rise to around 10 per cent. It has even been conjectured that Roosevelt knew about this and was influenced by it in trying to urge Japan to reach a compromise.

Russia's financial situation was, in fact, hardly any better than that of Japan and Witte knew that he had no financial grounds

[8] Schiff to Takahira, Aug. 25, 1905, Adler, *op.cit.*, I, 231; Dobrov, *op.cit.*, pp. 340–341; Ogawa, *op.cit.*, p. 252; L.M. Gelber, *The Rise of Anglo-American Friendship*, London, 1938, p. 236; Helfferich, *op.cit.*, p. 86.

for treating the negotiations lightly.[9] The cost of the war to Russia was 6,553.8 million rubles, of which more than half went to pay interest on foreign loans. A German loan agreement concluded in the summer of 1904 and worked out during the coming months had given Russia the initial help she needed to undergo the first round of defeats.

The French had tried to use their loan market as a means of encouraging Russia to reach a peaceful settlement with Japan, maintaining the principle that loans were inseparable from peace. In spite of this, a French banking group representative, E. Noetzlin of the Banc de Paris, had reached St. Petersburg on March 1, 1905 to discuss a loan, but, with the further downward course of the Russian military effort beginning with the battle of Mukden, the bankers left St. Petersburg. France had thereafter resumed the policy of making loans conditioned on peace.

The Russian prospects in the summer of 1905 had experienced no improvement since the revolutionary movement had further weakened Russia's claims for financial help. In deciding as to the acceptability of the Japanese peace demands, the Russian government had to weigh her military against her financial potentialities.

Both Witte and Gregory Willenkin, a Jewish financial attaché who had been sent to Washington for the purpose, tried to soften the attitude of the Jewish bankers regarding a loan. Schiff, meanwhile, maintained his attitude of opposition to a loan and encouraged others to do the same. In the end, Witte's endeavor to bypass Schiff by seeking the help of J.P. Morgan was unsuccessful; neither Morgan nor the Russian government found the conditions satisfactory for a loan.

The Russian reason for refusing so adamantly to pay an indemnity appears to have been based upon the same assumptions that had inspired the views of the military leaders of Japan, that is, that Japan lacked the strength to enforce a demand for an indemnity and could ill afford to risk a renewal of the war. Along with this went a conviction that the military situation in Man-

[9] Adler, op.cit., I, 231, II, 128, 133; Bompard, op.cit., p. 121; O. Crisp, "The Russian Liberals and the 1906 Anglo-French Loan to Russia," The Slavonic and East European Review, XXXIX, No. 93, June 1961, pp. 498–499; Feis, op.cit., p. 227; Kokovtsov, op.cit., pp. 63–64; Kokovtsov to Witte, Aug. 16, 18, 1905, K.A., VII, 32–33, 36; Michon, op.cit., pp. 149–162; Romanov, Russia, pp. 323–324, 355; Rozental, op.cit., pp. 39–46; C. Vevier, The United States and China, 1906–1913, New Brunswick, 1955, p. 26.

churia was changing favorably to Russia. This was supported by Russian reports from the front and, unbeknown to the Russians, also by Japanese military reports.[10]

The Russian views on Sakhalin Island and the indemnity were, therefore, founded upon the military realities as they saw them. The indemnity, they felt, need not be paid because in Manchuria, Russia was in a better position militarily than Japan; the Sakhalin issue, however, was negotiable because for the time being Japan's position there was better than Russia's. It is possible that Russia was accepting the reports of her present superiority in Manchuria with an uncritical confidence in the future. If so, it is understandable as a welcomed self-delusion that might furnish the government leaders an opportunity to recover the sense of disdain they had felt for the Japanese at the start of the war and with it some of their self-confidence. In any case, the risk must have seemed worth taking in view of the fact that an indemnity could only strengthen a competitor.

The other reasons given by Witte for his refusal to pay an indemnity, while by no means without significance, must be understood with reference to this situation. His objection on the grounds of the violation of the national honor, with all of its universal appeal, would of necessity have been qualified by Japanese strength if this had been a factor. The same must be said of the contention that Russia could not afford to pay an indemnity.[11] Not only the Russians and the Japanese but Roosevelt as well knew that Russia could in fact have found the money with which to pay an indemnity. It may also be assumed that she would have done so had it been necessary. Under the circumstances, it was more convenient to accept the risk and avoid the expense.

In the light of this unpromising outlook, how could Komura have introduced the indemnity issue with any confidence of success at all? From the exchanges of the preceding months Russian opposition to it was well known and the Japanese government had taken cognizance of this by placing the issue in a lower priority. Komura himself had taken a further step toward compromise when he changed the wording of the demand to

[10] R.-I.V., pp. 169–173; Meyer to Roosevelt, Aug. 1, 1905, Howe, op.cit., p. 189; Unterberger Report, Sept. 17, 1905, K.A., vii, 8–9; Willenkin to Kokovtsov, June 21, 1905, K.A., vi, 18–19; Pavlovich, op.cit., p. 31.

[11] Beale, op.cit., pp. 293, 302; Shipov to Putilov, July 23, 1905, K.A., vi, 24–25; Inouye to Komura, No. 277, June 16, 1905, J.F.O.; Roosevelt to Lodge, June 5, 1905, Lodge, op.cit., ii, 134.

make it more acceptable. Could Komura have assumed that, having come to the conference with full knowledge that the indemnity would be demanded, Russia might at least be ready to negotiate it? If so, the instructions to the Russian plenipotentiaries demonstrate that he was right.

A further hint as to Komura's incentive is found in the role indemnities had played in wars during the years preceding 1905. Over the past decades, China's numerous defeats had eventuated in losses both in money and other valuable assets and Japan had shared such benefits in 1895 and 1900. This Japanese experience as well as an assumption that an indemnity would be necessary, may have been responsible for President Roosevelt's warning them against unreasonable demands. It is clear that Roosevelt would have preferred Japanese elimination of the indemnity demand altogether. Yet, in recognizing Japan's right to exact a price, even in this half-hearted way, he may thereby have given Japan unwarranted encouragement.

The discussion of the indemnity question on August 17 evoked a hostile exchange from the very start. At no time during this or succeeding sessions was there the slightest hint that Russia would accept such a condition. In support of his proposal, Komura made these points: Japan's terms were reasonable both in world opinion and by comparison with terms Japan herself might have expected from a victorious Russia; the payment of an indemnity was a recognition, not of Russia's defeat, but of the normal expectations of a nation in a better position to continue the war; the suggestion of paying an indemnity was a conciliatory gesture in that it offered a way of ending the war without carrying it to the ultimate extreme; an indemnity was a cheaper way out than resuming the war; and by ending the war both parties could return to a more constructive economic way of life.

The Russian responses to the more general points were the following: the payment of an indemnity was appropriate only for a defeated nation and thus inapplicable to Russia; an indemnity would be incompatible with the honor of the country; an indemnity was unrealistic in view of the actual military situation and of Japan's obvious difficulty in pursuing the war; and Russia was able to carry on the war and consequently had no reason even to consider an indemnity.

The Russian answers to the more specific questions raised by Komura's statement were: far from making unreasonable demands, if Russia had been formulating terms for a defeated Japan she would not have considered an indemnity unless the heart of the country were under her control; an early return to a regular economic life was indeed desirable but could be attained more quickly by dropping the demand for an indemnity; far from being moderate, the Japanese terms appeared to be intended to take the fullest advantage of not only actual but even of anticipated successes; the only payment Russia could ever consider would be to reimburse the Japanese government for expenses incurred in caring for Russian prisoners of war, sick, and wounded; and since there appeared to be no possibility of reconciling the two views, a continuation of the war seemed to be the only way out.

On the same day, Witte telegraphed his reaction to St. Petersburg.[12] He stated firmly: "There will be no compromise on the issues of an indemnity for war expenses, the transfer of Sakhalin, limitation of naval power, or the warships detained in neutral ports." He warned that unless there were some conciliatory gesture at the decisive meetings on Monday or Tuesday the conference would probably end. He considered it likely that they would not yield on the Sakhalin and indemnity issues, while making conciliatory gestures in the matter of the interned ships and naval limitations. Restating a view he had held before leaving Russia, he ventured the following judgment of the issue:

"There is no doubt but that for Russia a continuation of the war would be a greater calamity. Although we can still more or less defend ourselves, there is almost no prospect of our conquering Japan. The only hope of a favorable outcome lies in the exhaustion of Japan."

Witte requested that the alternatives of this issue be seriously and carefully examined and a decision made. In Witte's telegram and in the discussions in St. Petersburg, the Sakhalin and indemnity issues were inseparably linked with the national honor. In line with his previous pronouncements, the Emperor settled the issue in a note on the margin of Witte's telegram: "We shall concede neither a single bit of territory nor a single kopek." If Witte had hoped to achieve peace by a compromise on these issues the door appeared to be closed.

At the end of the conference of Thursday August 17, Witte indicated to Komura his conviction that he saw little reason to con-

[12] K.G., II, 85.

tinue the negotiations. Articles 10 and 11, dealing respectively with the problems of interned ships and of the limitation of Russia's Far Eastern naval establishment, had been discussed during the afternoon without any decision. Witte suggested that the remaining issue, the Japanese demand for fishing rights contained in Article 12, might be disposed of the next day. Then, if the conference were adjourned during Saturday and Sunday, the protocol could be prepared and the conference concluded early the next week.

Realizing that the negotiations were in serious danger and that the conference might end in a few days without any satisfactory results, Komura decided upon two courses of action. The first was a compromise. The time had come, he felt, to differentiate between those demands which would be difficult to get in any case and those which were held to be more necessary than the rest. He prepared a compromise proposal in which he would offer to give up the demands regarding the interned ships and the naval limitations, contained respectively in Articles 10 and 11; in exchange, Russia would be asked to reconsider the Sakhalin and indemnity issues. At midnight, August 17–18, he telegraphed this plan to Tokyo.[13]

While Komura's compromise was unsuccessful in resolving the deadlock when it was proposed at the morning session on August 18, it did serve to open the door for serious and, in the end, fruitful discussions. After Komura had presented his plan in the form of an annex to the protocol, Witte suggested that the secretaries leave the conference room in order to allow the plenipotentiaries an opportunity to discuss the vital issues unreservedly.[14] When the secretaries had gone, Witte said that he had already received new instructions from his government regarding the vital Sakhalin and indemnity issues. These, he emphasized, left him little choice but to let the negotiations break down completely. He, however, was personally interested in a successful outcome of the conference and wanted to explore every possible avenue that might lead to success. If any reasonable formula could be found, he would be happy to urge it upon his government.

Witte stated that since his departure from St. Petersburg, the attitude of both government and people had changed in the direction of a reenforcement of the desire to continue the war.

[13] Shinobu, op.cit., p. 427.
[14] ibid., pp. 428–432; K.G., II, 87–101; Kaneko, Beikoku, Aug. 19, 1905.

The indemnity and Sakhalin issues, he pointed out, had stiffened the backs of the proponents of continuing the war and helped to bring about a mood hostile to compromise. The government could not at present disregard public opinion by entering into any compromise on these two issues. Consequently, he could go no further in the indemnity issue than to repeat his offer to reimburse Japan for expenses incurred in caring for Russian prisoners of war and for the sick and wounded.

Witte suggested, however, that the Sakhalin question might be the subject of a compromise by partitioning the island. The northern part, being essential to the security of the Russian Amur region, must remain in Russian hands. This would not in any way be detrimental to Japanese interests since Russia had no intention of using this area in any way strategically inimical to Japan. At the same time, the southern part was of the greatest value to Japan since it was the center of the rich fish resources and the possession of this region would also give Japan control over both sides of the Soya (or La Perouse) Strait. This would require a special agreement guaranteeing Russia freedom to navigate the strait.

Komura responded that when it came to public opinion, the people of Japan enjoyed the franchise and, consequently, their views had to be more assiduously observed than in Russia. He reminded Witte that the Japanese public had waited half a century for the opportunity to resolve the Sakhalin issue in some favorable way. Under present conditions, the Japanese people were demanding not only all of Sakhalin but the Ussuri region and all of the Chinese Eastern Railway as well.

With respect to the proposed compromise, Komura noted that discussion of this issue would have to proceed from the fact that Japan now occupied the island. Consequently, turning the northern part over to Russia would be an act of retrocession for which Japan would require compensation. He suggested the sum of 1,200,000,000 yen, thus making it possible to withdraw the original demand for an indemnity and further suggested a partition along the 50th parallel. Although Witte was very doubtful that his government would consider such an amount, or indeed such a proposal, it was agreed that each would telegraph this compromise plan to his government.

Witte telegraphed this proposal to his government with an urgent request for the most careful consideration and for an immediate, wise, and firm decision.[15] He strongly advocated that, under the circumstances, the question be weighed from the standpoint of world opinion. He felt that while Russia would not be condemned for refusal to accept the demand for an indemnity, this would not be true if the Sakhalin proposal were turned down. The significant facts that had to govern the decision, Witte wrote, were that Japan was in actual possession of the island and that Russia was not at that time able to take it back. Consequently, if Russia wished to shift the blame in case the Portsmouth Conference failed, she would have to recognize this essential fact and could not refuse to come to terms on both these issues. A definite answer was called for that would take both American opinion and President Roosevelt's feelings into consideration.

The procedure to be followed in case of an impending breakdown of the conference had already been formulated by the Japanese representatives and President Roosevelt.[16] In the course of his interviews with the plenipotentiaries at Oyster Bay, the President could see how far apart the antagonists were on the two vital issues, and Witte had frankly said that Russia would refuse any compromise. On the other hand, in conversations with Kaneko even before the arrival of the plenipotentiaries, Roosevelt had been led to believe that Japan proposed to demand a compensation covering the entire cost of the war, a sum over twice as large as the one Komura mentioned to Witte on August 18.

Roosevelt saw the value of a last minute attempt to rescue the conference, not only because he wanted peace but also because he wanted to clear Japan of responsibility for the break. He also suspected that the Russians, or at least Witte, might be more interested in a settlement than it appeared. Witte's adamant refusal to consider compromise seemed to be against such a possibility, as did the fact, known to Roosevelt, that Witte had secretly ordered a special railway carriage to await him in Boston in case he wanted to leave the conference on a moment's notice.[17] Nevertheless, behind this front, Roosevelt told Kaneko, he sus-

[15] Witte to Lamsdorf, Aug. 18, 1905, Dobrov, op.cit., p. 310; Witte to Kokovtsov, Aug. 19, 1905, K.A., VI, 36–37; Witte to Lamsdorf, Aug. 20, 1905, Dillon, Eclipse, p. 308.
[16] Kaneko, Beikoku, Aug. 7, 1905.
[17] E.J. Dillon, "The Story of the Peace Negotiations," The Contemporary Review, LXXXVIII, Oct. 1905, p. 470.

pected a reluctance on Witte's part to let the negotiations fail and stated that he thought his apparently unyielding attitude might be intended to prevent either the Japanese or his own government from suspecting his real hope.

The plan was that when the collapse of the conference appeared imminent, Komura would notify Roosevelt through Kaneko, allowing 48 hours leeway if possible for some action. Upon being notified, Roosevelt would make a personal appeal to the Russian Emperor and, if necessary, to the German Emperor and the President of France as well. The object would be to encourage a more conciliatory attitude on Russia's part. Should the negotiations fail after this, the entire civilized world might conclude that Russia alone was responsible.

A telegram from Komura to Kaneko on August 17 set this plan in motion.[18] Kaneko conferred with Roosevelt the next day at Oyster Bay, explaining the seeming impasse that had been reached the day before. The President was prepared to act on the plan but felt that before sending an appeal to the Russian Emperor he ought as a matter of courtesy to discuss his idea with Witte as the special plenipotentiary of the Emperor. Accordingly, he proposed to telegraph Witte, requesting that Rosen come to Oyster Bay for a personal conference. This idea may have been an outgrowth of a suggestion from Oscar Straus that the President invite the plenipotentiaries to his home.

President Roosevelt had by August 18 received other discomforting news.[19] From Ambassador Meyer came the word that Russia would refuse to conclude peace as long as Japan continued to insist upon an indemnity and Sakhalin. From the German ambassador came another warning of danger in the form of potential intervention in the peace negotiations. The German government was apprehensive about indications from both the press and diplomatic quarters that the British and French might be about ready to extend their "good offices" to the belligerents in view of the possible collapse of the negotiations. This pessimistic German view may have been supported or even stimulated by an Associated Press interview with Witte.

It must have been with considerable anxiety as to the success

[18] Kaneko, *Beikoku*, Aug. 17, 18, 1905.
[19] Dobrov, *op.cit.*, p. 319; Bülow to Sternburg, Aug. 17, Holstein to Sternburg, Aug. 18, 1905, *G.P.*, xix-2, 617–619.

of his diplomatic venture that President Roosevelt undertook to rescue it from collapse. Through Assistant Secretary of State Pierce he first sent this message to Witte:

> "Mr. Witte:
> I wish to request you most urgently to send to me either Baron Rosen or some other person enjoying your confidence in order that he may visit me and convey to you a most confidential message from me."[20]

It must be assumed that Witte consented because Baron Rosen wrote that he was awakened at 2 a.m., on the morning of August 19 by Mr. Pierce with a telegram from President Roosevelt.[21] The President invited him to visit him at Oyster Bay and suggested he take the 7 o'clock train for New York. The "Sylph" would be awaiting him at Bridgeport to take him across the Sound to Oyster Bay in the afternoon. Rosen and Prince Kudashev responded to this invitation and reached Oyster Bay by 4 o'clock in the afternoon.

The discussion between Roosevelt and Rosen was held on a tennis court and lasted about two hours.[22] It was apparently conducted without knowledge of the compromise proposed the day before at Portsmouth. For Roosevelt suggested that of the four disputed conditions three could be disposed of without difficulty if Japan would give up those having to do with the interned ships and the naval limitations and if Russia would recognize the Japanese occupation of Sakhalin as final and conclusive. As for the compensation for war expenses, he suggested submitting it to the arbitration of two persons, feeling this procedure would take some time and thus allow tempers to cool.

Rosen was opposed to both the concessions this would have required of Russia. In urging his solution to the Sakhalin question, the President had remarked by way of illustration that "We Americans are ensconced at Panama and will not leave." This seems to have made a negative impression on Rosen who answered that "Japan is not America and Russia is not Columbia." He also passed off the indemnity proposal by saying that Russia had no need to pay it.

[20] Dobrov, op.cit., pp. 322–323.
[21] Rosen, op.cit., I, 269–270.
[22] K.G., II, 90–91; Dobrov, op.cit., pp. 323–324; Kutakov, op.cit., pp. 62–63.

After the discussion with Roosevelt, Rosen returned to the "Sylph" and drafted a message to Witte. By 2 o'clock the next morning Rosen was back in Bridgeport, one-half hour before train time. While he was having a cup of coffee "an alert-looking gentleman" came in and sat down beside him and "wanted to know all about it." Rosen told him that as an ambassador he was also in the reporting business and could hardly be expected to share with a business rival any exclusive information. The reporter accepted this and left with the thought that since Rosen was in such a cheerful mood he must have had a satisfactory interview with the President.

Official opinion in St. Petersburg appears to have been receptive to the appeal the President intended to make to the Emperor. The credit for this may to a large extent be due to Witte's plea that the negotiations should not be hastily broken off. A note from Lamsdorf to Kokovtsov on August 22 expressed this attitude almost in Witte's own words.[23] In it the foreign minister stated that while there was no further reason to continue discussing the indemnity question, the Sakhalin issue should be kept open. This should be done not only in deference to public opinion in America and especially to President Roosevelt, but because of the fact that the Japanese were in possession of the island. He also noted that the next day at 4 o'clock in the afternoon the American ambassador was scheduled to transmit a personal message from President Roosevelt to the Emperor.

The first appeal from Roosevelt to the Russian Emperor was sent on August 21.[24] On that day Roosevelt received official notice of the compromise discussed at Portsmouth three days before and his appeal to the Emperor was based on this plan, asking that Russia reimburse Japan for returning northern Sakhalin. Copies of Roosevelt's appeal were sent to the Emperor of Germany, the President of France, and Witte, the latter, as requested, forwarding his copy to the Russian Emperor to reenforce the President's appeal. The Emperor wrote in the margin of the message that Russia would make no further concessions.

While Witte protested this decision, he received no satisfaction and was informed that unless the Japanese gave up their extravagant demands the negotiations would be ended.[25] Even

[23] *K.A.*, vi, 38–39.
[24] Dennett, *op.cit.*, pp. 265–267.
[25] Shinobu, *op.cit.*, pp. 435–437.

though Russia was not then in a position to take back Sakhalin, he was informed, there was a great difference between a military occupation of the island that would be considered temporary and a formal cession that would rule out any further action. In a second telegram, Lamsdorf instructed Witte to inform the President of the decision to break off the negotiations, to express appreciation for his assistance, and to suggest that the Russians might in the future meet the Japanese envoys under more favorable circumstances.

A third telegram from Lamsdorf instructed Witte to telegraph the precise date of the final disruption of the negotiation in order that the government might be prepared with a communiqué for the occasion. Witte responded to this with a request for a delay before terminating the conference to allow time for the Emperor's answer to reach the President. He felt sure that the Japanese had exhausted their diplomacy, but that to end the conference at this point would simply help them to enlist stronger American opinion on their side.

While urging the Russians to meet the Japanese demands part way, President Roosevelt resumed his effort to encourage moderation on the Japanese side.[26] He expressed this thought with a new emphasis in letters to Kaneko on August 22 and 23. In the first letter he warned Japan that he had heard public criticism on the grounds that she might continue the war for the sake of a large indemnity and said quite frankly that he considered the price Japan was asking to be unreasonable. While he was urging the Russians to make peace, he felt it equally urgent that Japan should not allow the war to go on for an indemnity. This would cost Japan considerable in public esteem. President Roosevelt's second letter to Kaneko, dated August 23, continued the same theme as the first. He emphasized all the gains Japan had made in Korea and Manchuria. By destroying the Russian navy, Japan had doubled the strength of her own. He could see little reason, after this, for continuing a costly war merely in the hope of getting an indemnity. To underscore his specific argument, he wrote:

"I do not speak of continuing the war rather than give up Sakhalin, which I think would be right; but of continuing the

[26] Roosevelt to Kaneko, Aug. 22, 1905, Lodge, op.cit., ii, 178; Kaneko, Beikoku, Aug. 22, 1905; H. Kamikawa, Japan-American Diplomatic Relations in the Meiji-Taisho Era, Tokyo, 1958, pp. 252ff.

war in order to get a great sum of money from Russia, which I think would be wrong."[27]

The good faith of the President in advising Japan to forego an indemnity is attested by his correspondence with others whom he would have had no reason to misinform. On the same day as his note to Kaneko, he wrote to Henry Durand, the British ambassador, that:

"In my judgment every true friend of Japan should tell it as I have told it, that the opinion of the civilized world will not support it in continuing the war merely for the purpose of extorting money from Russia."[28]

Also on the same day, Roosevelt wrote a letter to Henry White, the American ambassador to Italy, which supports the view that Roosevelt had not "changed his mind," deserting Japan in favor of Russia. In describing his difficulties in bringing the two parties together, he stated that:

"The Russians are the worst, because they stand up with Chinese or Byzantine folly and insist, as Witte has just written me, that Russia will not admit itself vanquished—making it all that I can do not to tell them some straightforward truths in uncomplimentary language. On the other hand, the Japanese have no business to continue the war merely for the sake of getting money . . ."[29]

There is little reason to doubt that behind the President's genuine desire to achieve peace at that moment lay his apprehension about the balance of power. This had been his central purpose in watching the Russo-Japanese developments so closely and a matter that he had discussed with Kaneko during the preceding months. A resumption of the war would have meant gambling on a situation that had already reached a reasonably satisfactory equilibrium. Whether the next stage of the war favored Japan or Russia, an upset balance would result and from the President's standpoint this was decidedly unfavorable.

To Japan, a nation engaged in a desperate gamble for its national security and for status among the great powers, anything less than complete commitment to these causes would al-

[27] Roosevelt to Kaneko, Aug. 23, 1905, Morison and Blum, op.cit., iv, 1312.
[28] Roosevelt to Durand, Aug. 23, 1905, ibid., p. 1310.
[29] Roosevelt to White, Aug. 23, 1905, Bishop, op.cit., i, 408.

most certainly have appeared as benevolent though unhelpful impartiality. Japan had thrown every ounce of her national strength into the balance and her government was pressed by its own interests, by the patriotic groups, as well as by the public expectations that these groups had generated, to derive every possible advantage from the costly war. In satisfaction of this thirst for tangible rewards, the requirements of a balance of power would have been notably meaningless.

It was this difference of outlook that soon brought about a deterioration of American-Japanese relations. As the course of the struggle appeared to have placed within Japan's desperate reach, perhaps for the only time, not just a balance of power but a balance of power favorable to her, the conservative American policy could become a drawback. Kaneko, even after having discussed this policy for months, wrote in his diary that he was surprised and bewildered when he received Roosevelt's note. Thinking that the President only the day before had approved of a sizeable money demand, he could not understand what he referred to as a change of mind.

The conference session of August 23 revealed beyond any further doubt that an indemnity was unattainable for Japan unless she wished to seek it by continuing the war. At that time Komura proposed formally and officially the compromise he had mentioned privately on August 18: the partition of Sakhalin at the 50th parallel; a guarantee of the freedom of navigation in the La Perouse and Tartary straits; the payment by Russia of a compensation of 1,200,000,000 yen for the cession to her of North Sakhalin; and the Japanese withdrawal of the demand for an indemnity. Witte answered categorically that his government could not accept any settlement that entailed the payment of any money reimbursement other than for the care of the Russian prisoners of war and the sick and wounded.

Witte then asked the question that evoked an equally firm refusal from Komura and thus brought the issue into complete focus. If Russia were to transfer all of Sakhalin Island to Japan, would she withdraw the demand for reimbursement? Komura answered that a money reimbursement was indispensable. Korostovets wrote that, fearing the effect of a breakdown of the negotiations on public opinion, Witte had deliberately planned this means of avoiding the blame.[30] For Komura's answer, in

[30] Korostovets, op.cit., pp. 96–97.

spite of Roosevelt's warning, seemed to have made it clear that the Japanese were willing to continue the war for the sake of money.

Two days after this session, on August 25, Kaneko visited Roosevelt at Oyster Bay to learn the reason for the President's "change of mind."[31] Roosevelt reminded Kaneko what a breakdown of the negotiations would, in his view, entail. He thought that Japan would in such a case have to be prepared to continue the war by carrying out the occupation of Harbin and the entire railway in Manchuria as well as Vladivostok and the Maritime region. In the light of their previous conversations, Kaneko could have gathered from this statement either that Roosevelt assumed this to be entirely unfeasible or that he disapproved of it because it would have too disturbing an impact on the balance of power. In any case, Roosevelt left no doubt as to what he thought the outcome of the issue should be: when the crucial moment of decision came Baron Komura should not allow the war to be continued.

The discussion then turned to the appeal that the President had sent to the Russian Emperor. The answer to this the conference session of two days before had already disclosed as negative. Roosevelt described the two-hour conference which Meyer had had with the Russian Emperor on the afternoon of August 23, during the course of which the Emperor had stated firmly that he would go personally to Manchuria and lead the armies against the Japanese before he would compromise on the indemnity issue. It was decided to make a second appeal; Roosevelt called his secretary and, together with Kaneko, composed an appeal along the same lines as the first.[32]

The next scheduled conference session met on the afternoon of August 26. As an augury of its outcome, during the morning Witte had instructed Korostovets to have the hotel bill prepared and to reserve a hotel room in New York preparatory to sailing.[33] At the conference Witte announced that his government had not accepted Komura's proposal of three days before. Komura thereupon asked for a formal reply from the Russian government and for a postponement. Accordingly, the next session was scheduled for the afternoon of August 28.

[31] Kaneko, Beikoku, Aug. 25, 1905.
[32] Roosevelt to Meyer, Aug. 25, 1905, Dennett, op.cit., pp. 272–274.
[33] Shinobu, op.cit., pp. 455–457; K.G., ii, 104–105; Korostovets, op.cit., p. 100.

At the close of the August 26 session, Komura sent two telegrams to Tokyo emphasizing his feeling that the situation was hopeless.[34] The first telegram was largely a report of the private discussion Komura had had with Witte at the conference session just ended. Witte had stated flatly that Russia would under no disguise pay an indemnity for military expenses, but at the same time saw some promise in reaching a compromise over the Sakhalin issue. Witte had emphasized that he himself was ready to do everything possible to reach some compromise. Witte's description of the changing mood in St. Petersburg must have been particularly depressing to Komura. Witte told him that the army was eager to gain the approval of the government to permit a renewal of the war and to vindicate its honor in a victorious battle. This opposition to the conclusion of peace had even gone to the point of objecting to the concessions already made to Japan in respect to Manchuria, and the strength and appeal of the prowar group was impossible for the Russian government to disregard.

Komura's second Tokyo telegram dealt largely with the consequences of the Russian announcement. He contrasted the conciliatory attitude of Japan with the Russian attitude. Neither his own willingness to give up the demands regarding the interned ships and the naval limitations, nor the two appeals by the President to the Russian Emperor had made any impression on this obstinate Russian refusal to be conciliatory. Under the circumstances, further concessions from Japan would amount to a national humiliation and continuation of the war appeared to be the only alternative. At the conference session scheduled for August 28, he proposed to bring the negotiations to an end with a statement assigning full responsibility for the outcome to Russia.

Komura received an answer from Tokyo directing him to secure a postponement of the scheduled August 28 session for 24 hours. In response to this order, Minister Takahira Kogoro and Ochiai Kentaro, a secretary, visited Witte on the evening of August 27 to ask for the delay.[35] Takahira explained that because of the 14-hour time differential, the Japanese delegation was still awaiting orders. Witte answered that while he had no objection

[34] Komura to Katsura, Nos. 104, 105, Aug. 26, 1905, *N.G.N.*, I, 242–244.
[35] Korostovets, *op.cit.*, p. 103; Witte, *op. cit.*, I, 383; *K.G.*, II, 106–108.

to postponing the session until August 29, he wanted this to be the final meeting. Since Russia had no further concessions to make, there was no reason to waste any more time. As the matter stood, there were only two choices: either accept the Russian terms as already defined or end the negotiations.

Komura telegraphed to Tokyo later the same evening his report of the visit. He felt, as he had previously stated, that Witte himself seemed ready to be reasonable, but a party now dominated the Russian government that would rather resume the war than be conciliatory. Consequently, Japan now faced the necessity of either giving up both the indemnity and Sakhalin or continuing the war. Besides this humiliating prospect, it had come to the point where even the original objectives for which Japan had gone to war were far from assured. For the gains in Manchuria needed Chinese consent to be transferred, and obviously without Russian goodwill this could not be achieved.

On the evening of August 27 Roosevelt was also studying the problem which the deadlock in the negotiations had raised. Melville Stone, the general manager of the Associated Press, called at Kaneko's apartment at 8 p.m. with a message from the President, suggesting an appeal to the German Emperor that would urge him to advise the Russian Emperor to reconsider a solution by canceling the indemnity and paying for the return to Russia of North Sakhalin. Kaneko told Stone that he was not authorized to approve such a proposal and would have to refer it to Komura. Stone replied that he would go to the Lotus Club to prepare the message and would await word there from Kaneko.

Stone telephoned Kaneko from the Lotus Club at 1:30 in the morning of August 28 asking him to meet him there.[36] When he arrived, Kaneko was introduced to Baron Hilmar von dem Bussche-Haddenhausen, the German chargé d'affaires who had come down on Stone's invitation from his summer home at Lennox, Massachusettes. The communication which the three composed to the German Emperor contained the following message: it urged the Emperor to encourage the Russian Emperor to accept as a compromise the elimination of the money indemnity

[36] K.G., ii, 121–125; Kaneko, Beikoku, Aug. 27, 1905; Roosevelt to Emperor of Germany, Dennett, op.cit., pp. 275–276; Bussche-Haddenhausen to Foreign Office, Nos. 172, 174, Aug. 28, 1905, G.P., xix-2, 624–626; Roosevelt to Bussche, Aug. 28, 1905, Morison and Blum, op.cit., iv, 1323.

along with the return of North Sakhalin to Russia for a sum to be suggested by a mixed commission. The message, after some delay, was sent to Berlin on August 28.

The delay appeared to be a consequence of a misunderstanding over Kaneko's authority. During the hours that this puzzling obstacle stood in the way, Roosevelt had telegraphed to Bussche-Haddenhausen that while the message might have to be canceled, he was welcome to transmit Roosevelt's idea to the Emperor if he wished. The message ultimately reached Berlin and apparently St. Petersburg as well since Witte received an instruction from St. Petersburg on the morning of the final session, August 29, telling him to expect the Japanese to withdraw the demand for a money indemnity.

Because of the issue which had to be decided before this telegram to Witte could be sent, the delay raised by the question of Kaneko's authority becomes important. On the evening Stone had come to his apartment, Kaneko had telegraphed Komura for approval to proceed with Roosevelt's plan. Not until 1 p.m. the following day, August 28, did Komura reply and then only to say that in view of the Russian Emperor's attitude, nothing could be expected from such a proposal. Meanwhile, Stone had tried to hurry the project along by asking the United Press representative at Portsmouth to inquire about Kaneko's authority to speak for his government. Takahira had answered that Kaneko was not empowered to express any views independently of the plenipotentiaries. Finally, to clear up the perplexing issue, Roosevelt telegraphed directly to Komura asking whether it was true that Kaneko, who had always appeared to have full powers, lacked official authority. To this Komura answered that Kaneko had full authority to speak officially.

Komura's apparent indecision is somewhat more understandable against the backdrop of the changing instructions to which his own plans were subjected in the course of August 27 and 28. During the same evening when Kaneko's telegram of August 27 arrived, Komura was still awaiting the instructions for which he was postponing the session scheduled for the next day. Within the next 24 hours, Komura received three new and different sets of instructions.

The first set of instructions was elaborated in Tokyo during the morning and early afternoon of August 28. The deliberations out of which they developed began at the home of Prime Minister

Katsura in the morning.[37] This meeting was attended by the cabinet ministers and at least three of the elder statesmen (genro): Ito, Yamagata, and Inouye. It was followed by a conference in the presence of the Emperor that lasted until 2 o'clock in the afternoon. The decisions reached were telegraphed to Komura at 8:30 that evening, a time corresponding to 6:30 in the morning of the same day in Portsmouth. The instructions Komura received from Tokyo at that time went a long step beyond the position of some weeks before when the indemnity demand had been reduced to a secondary priority. Komura was categorically directed to give up the indemnity demand. With respect to the territorial demand for Sakhalin, he was to give it up also if the chances of peace were endangered by it. The cardinal point of his new instructions was contained in the words: "we wish to lose no opportunity to achieve peace and you are to be guided by this desire."

Soon after the new instructions had been prepared for transmission, Shidehara Kijuro, then head of the telegraphic section of the foreign office, was visited by Ishii Kikujiro, the head of the commercial bureau of the foreign office.[38] Ishii had just learned from the British minister, Sir Claude MacDonald, the substance of the interview between Meyer, the American ambassador, and the Russian Emperor on August 23. MacDonald had received the information in the form of a copy of a telegram from the British ambassador in St. Petersburg to London and could not give Ishii his copy without special permission. He wanted Japan to know its contents, however, and read it twice to Ishii. The diplomatic report revealed that in his conversation with Meyer the Russian Emperor had consented to the partitioning of Sakhalin, a point obviously missed by the Japanese heretofore. Meyer had successfully overcome the Emperor's three principal objections to this concession. The principle that no Russian territory must be surrendered had been attacked by reminding the Emperor that the southern part of Sakhalin had been in Russian hands for so short a time that it could hardly be called Russian territory any more than Port Arthur.

[37] Y. Kuroki, *Komura Jutaro*, Tokyo, 1941, pp. 358–359; *K.G.*, II, 125–126; Katsura to Komura, No. 69, Aug. 28, 1905, *N.G.M.*, I, 244–245; Kaneko, *Beikoku*, Aug. 28, 1905.

[38] *K.G.*, II, 126–127; Dobrov, *op.cit.*, pp. 142–143; K. Ishii, *Gaiko Yoroku*, Tokyo, 1931, pp. 82–83; Shidehara, *op.cit.*, pp. 15–19; Meyer to Roosevelt, Aug. 25, 1905, Howe, *op.cit.*, pp. 198–200; Lamsdorf to Kokovtsov, Aug. 26, 1905, *K.A.*, VI, 40.

Regarding the problem of having a contiguous frontier with Japan, Meyer reminded the Emperor of the peaceful American-Canadian frontier. Finally, he argued that North Sakhalin was a sufficient shield for Russia's Amur region.

This important bit of information was immediately brought to the attention of Prime Minister Katsura and other ministers. Some, such as the minister of navy, Admiral Yamamoto Gonno-hyoei, were incredulous. In view of the decision to seek peace, the consequences of acting upon misinformation of such a vital nature were fully realized. It is said that Ishii was even reminded that he would be obliged to commit *harakiri* if the information he had passed on were proven wrong and the peace were lost as a consequence.

About four hours after the previous instructions had been dispatched, another telegram was sent to Komura directing him to delay action on the last telegram and await further instructions. The new instructions were sent 35 minutes later: 1:10 a.m. on August 29 in Tokyo and 11:10 a.m. on August 28 in Portsmouth. It was not until 7:30 on the evening of August 28 that Komura transmitted his final answer to Kaneko and President Roosevelt. He must have used the intervening hours to re-plan his strategy for the next conference session. Perhaps he also wanted to leave time for further changes of instructions before committing himself so finally to Roosevelt and the German Emperor.

Witte came to the session of August 29 prepared to accept the breakdown of the negotiations.[39] His last telegram from Lamsdorf had informed him that the Emperor did not even wish "to await Japan's gracious concessions" before breaking up the negotiations. To inform St. Petersburg at the earliest possible moment in case the conference should end, Witte is said to have prepared a signal. It was arranged that when he turned to one of his secretaries and said, "Send for my Russian cigarettes," the latter would casually leave the conference room and return to the Wentworth Hotel where another member of the Russian staff would be waiting to transmit to St. Petersburg a message already coded. In this way the signal would ultimately reach Manchuria where General Linievich would be notified to start the planned offensive against Japan.

[39] Witte, *op.cit.*, I, 390; Korostovets, *op.cit.*, pp. 105–108; Stone, *op.cit.*, pp. 3–4, 48; *Protocols*, pp. 73–78; *N.K.D.H.*, pp. 199, 225–226.

The last session convened at 9:30 on the morning of August 29 as arranged. It was preceded by a private conference between Komura and Witte during which the latter was informed of the surprise that was coming. Then Komura opened the meeting with the announcement that he had as yet received no official answer to the compromise he had proposed on August 23. Witte read a note which formally turned down this compromise. This brief exchange was followed by absolute silence broken only by Witte's nervous habit of tearing up the paper which lay around him. Beside him Rosen smoked his accustomed cigarette.

Komura rose amid the charged silence and in a well-controlled voice made his startling announcement. He first stated that Japan would withdraw the indemnity claim if Russia would recognize her occupation of Sakhalin as an accomplished fact. Witte refused this. Then Komura stated that Japan would return the northern portion of the island if Russia would recognize the 50th parallel as the boundary and if Russia's conditions regarding military measures near the frontier and freedom of navigation of the La Perouse and Tartary straits were accepted as reciprocal. Witte approved this.

The emotional strain under which the conference had labored is best shown in the outburst of congratulations which followed immediately.[40] Witte entered his conference room with the exclamation: "Gentlemen, peace!" The message to St. Petersburg was an expression of the triumph Witte himself was experiencing, but he probably knew that this would not be generally shared at home. To the Japanese delegates who were somewhat dejected, Roosevelt wrote that he was "overjoyed at the news." Though unwanted by some and unsatisfying to many more, peace had come at last.

[40] Roosevelt to Pierce, Aug. 29, 1905, Morison and Blum, op.cit., IV, 1326; Shipov to Minister of Finance, Nos. 61, 62, Aug. 29, 1905, K.A., VII, 41.

17. "Balanced Antagonisms" in Action

THE MOST SIGNIFICANT consequence of the Russo-Japanese War and of the decisions made at the Portsmouth Conference was the emergence of Japan as a continental Asian power. Russia acknowledged this by her readiness to accept those demands already largely assured by the Japanese military victories. In the closing days of the conference, Russia further confirmed her realization of the need to live in harmony with a new and vigorous neighbor by her readiness to cooperate in establishing a common, peaceful frontier. As events were soon to demonstrate, frontier relationships had already become a predominant factor between Russia and Japan.

Beyond the unavoidable and obvious features of an unwonted situation, the two governments nevertheless accepted their new obligations with the greatest reluctance. Dissatisfaction with the war, the peace, or both had left important elements in each country who were unwilling to undertake responsibility for the consequences. The impact was more lasting in St. Petersburg, the capital of defeat and revolution, but was more immediately violent in Tokyo where a more rewarding victory had been anticipated. In spite of this, in the course of the succeeding months and years each government accommodated itself to the new dispensation and to the requirements and restrictions it imposed.

The rise of a new continental power in Asia also had significant consequences for the United States. While mediating the war, in fact as an incentive for his mediation efforts, President Roosevelt had foreseen the likelihood that Japan's new continental base might furnish her with the foundation for a monopoly of power or for a preponderance of power shared with Russia. But he also saw that he lacked any positive means of checking this tendency. The best that could be hoped for was that the preservation of good relations with Japan and the development of a concensus among the powers to contain her expansive impulses might succeed in preserving the balance of power and the security of American interests in the Far East. Yet the peace treaty was hardly more than completed at Portsmouth before Japan's new, independent course was disclosed in her attitude toward the United States.

The issue which had been a symptom of the lack of confidence between Russia and Japan from the very beginning of peace negotiations was the armistice. Japan had avoided granting one for reasons all too easily guessed—her lack of confidence in her own ability to bring Russia to terms without continuing pressure and in Russia's readiness to accede to her demands if pressure were removed.[1] It was felt in Tokyo that any display of magnanimity might be interpreted by Russia as weakness. It might also provide Russia the opportunity to improve her position along the front. All things considered, it was felt that Japan's bargaining position would be better without an armistice.

The settlement of the Sakhalin and indemnity issues on August 29 opened the door for a consideration of an armistice.[2] Witte introduced the subject and with very little discussion the question was settled. By September 1 both governments had agreed to the following terms: an armistice would become effective upon the final signing of the treaty of peace and remain in effect until the definitive conclusion of peace; the relationships between the field armies would be determined by the commanders; during the armistice naval forces were not to bombard territory belonging to or occupied by the other nation; the right of maritime capture in accordance with international law was not to be suspended; reenforcements were not to be dispatched during the armistice; and those already dispatched were not to be sent north of Mukden by Japan or south of Harbin by Russia.

These terms were supplemented by an agreement arrived at by representatives of the field commanders at Shaho station on September 13.[3] Major General Fukushima acted for Marshal Oyama and Major General Oranovsky for General Linievich in elaborating these terms. Following the general rules determined at Portsmouth, the Shaho agreement stipulated: military activity would cease immediately; the demarcation line would be drawn so that the guard posts on both sides of the line would remain in the places they then occupied; and the agreement would come definitively into force on September 18.

The evacuation of the military forces from Manchuria was closely related to the armistice problem and to the issue that

[1] Roosevelt to Meyer, July 7, 1905, Morison and Blum, *op.cit.*, IV, 1263; Shinobu, *op.cit.*, pp. 357–358; *Japan Times*, June 13, Aug. 3, 5, 1905; *K.G.*, II, 19–21.
[2] *N.K.D.H.*, pp. 231–239.
[3] *R.-I.V.*, p. 109; Kuroda, *op.cit.*, p. 407.

had brought the Russo-Japanese conflict into focus over four years before. Accordingly, on August 29, Komura raised three pertinent points for discussion: the mode of evacuation of Manchuria; the determination of the point of demarcation between the respective railway lines in Manchuria; and the protection of the railway lines.[4] He introduced a specific proposal for carrying out the evacuation in three stages, reminiscent of the Sino-Russian agreement of 1902. After further discussions on September 1 and 2, the following formula was adopted:

"The Imperial Governments of Japan and Russia mutually engage to commence the withdrawal of their military forces from the territory of Manchuria simultaneously and immediately after the Treaty of Peace comes into operation, and within a period of eighteen months from that date, the Armies of the two countries shall be completely withdrawn from Manchuria except from the leased territory of the Liao-tung [i.e., Kuantung] Peninsula.

"The forces of the two countries occupying the front positions shall be first withdrawn.

"The High Contracting Parties reserve to themselves the right to maintain guards to protect their respective railway lines in Manchuria. The number of such guards shall not exceed fifteen per kilometre and within that maximum number, the commanders of the Japanese and Russian armies shall, by common accord, fix the number of such guards to be employed as small as possible having in view the actual requirements.

"The Commanders of the Japanese and Russian forces in Manchuria shall agree upon the details of the evacuation in conformity with the above principles, and shall take action by common accord and in any case not later than the period of eighteen months."

These provisions were carried into effect by the agreement reached at a field conference at Szupingchieh on October 30, 1905 again between Major Generals Fukushima and Oranovsky.[5] This specified very precisely the conditions under which the

---

[4] *Protocols,* pp. 66–67, 74–75, 81.
[5] Pokotilov to Minister of Foreign Affairs, Oct. 31, Linievich to Kokovtsov, Nov. 4, 1905, *K.A.,* vii, 27–28; M. Pavlovich, "Vneshniaia Politika Rossii ot Portsmutskago Mira do Nashikh Dnei," L. Martov, *Obshchestvennoe Dvizhenie v Rossii v Nachale XX-go Veka,* iv, Pt. i, 27–28.

evacuation was to be carried out, such as the withdrawal first from the forward positions and from the vicinity of the railway. The terminal dates for the three stages were to be: April 15, 1906, October 15, 1906, and April 15, 1907. The exact location of the troops and the total number then permitted in Manchuria on each of these dates was specified. The schedule was, in fact, closely observed and evacuation was completed within a few days of the date named. After this only railway guards remained: at the ratio specified, 27,000 Russian guards and 14,500 Japanese guards.

The plenipotentiaries were unable to agree on the precise point of demarcation for their respective railways; consequently, the decision was deferred. It was not until the signing of a series of protocols between Russia and Japan on June 13, 1907 that this problem was settled.[6] The result was at best a rather patchy compromise though it may have been as good as could be expected under the circumstances.

In fact, it may be questioned whether even this compromise could have been achieved without the incentives that were by then driving Japan and Russia together. These included the Chinese plans and projects for asserting firmer control in Manchuria, including the appointment of a new viceroy, Hsü Shih-chang, and a new governor at Mukden, Tang Shao-yi, to implement these plans. The danger to Russo-Japanese interests was further emphasized by the arrival the year before in Mukden of a new American consul general, Willard Straight. He became the exponent of a vigorous American policy in Manchuria, coordinated with that of China and, in fact, having as its ultimate objective the reversion of Manchuria to the complete and exclusive control of China.

The effect of the protocols of 1907 was to invest Russia with both actual and legal possession of Kuanchengtze station up to its southern boundary while Japan was to construct her own separate railway terminal at Changchun. In order to make it possible for each to use the other's terminal, the broad-gauge tracks of the Chinese Eastern Railway were to be projected southward to Changchun and tracks of the appropriate gauge for the South Manchurian Railway were to be extended to

---

[6] *U.S.F.R.*, 1907, Pt. 2, pp. 780–783; Japan. Department of Railways, *op.cit.*, pp. 261–267, 274; M. Pavlovich, "Vneshniaia Politika i Russko-Iaponskaia Voina," *op.cit.*, pp. 250–254.

Kuanchengtze. During the next few years, Kuanchengtze relapsed into relative insignificance while the Changchun station, two miles to the south, became the communications center of an increasingly prosperous town. The nucleus was New Town which grew up around the Changchun station toward Kuanchengtze.

The exchange of prisoners of war was also provided for in the last days of the conference.[7] Although an article of the treaty specified that the exchange would be carried out as soon as possible after the signing of the treaty, arrangements had actually been concluded before that event. It was then stipulated that the Japanese prisoners would be delivered at the western frontier of the Russian Empire and the Russian prisoners at Nagasaki, Kobe, and Yokohama. This was supervised by two commissioners, Colonel Oi, military attaché at the Japanese legation in Berlin, for Japan and Colonel Danilov for Russia. The Japanese and Russian prisoners were formally delivered on December 15, 1905 and February 19, 1906 respectively.

The subject of Japanese fishing interests in the Japan, Okhotsk, and Bering Seas which had long been a source of discord between the two countries was introduced in Article 12 of the peace demands. The question was briefly discussed on August 18 and an agreement was embodied in the following statement:

"Russia engages to arrange with Japan for granting to Japanese subjects rights of fishery along the coasts of the Russian possessions in the Japan, Okhotsk, and Bering Seas. It is a matter of course that rights already belonging in that region to Russian and foreign subjects shall remain in force."

Though the Portsmouth treaty embodied the sense of this understanding, it was not until July 15, 1907 that it was finally incorporated into a formal treaty.[8] With its accompanying protocols, this formed a comprehensive statement of Japanese fishery rights for some years.

During the final days of the conference, the Sakhalin compromise was elaborated into an understanding with the following characteristics: the Russian government would cede the southern part of Sakhalin to Japan "in perpetuity and full sovereignty"; the 50th parallel would be the boundary line; the precise demar-

[7] *Protocols,* pp. 76–83ff; Takahashi, *op.cit.,* pp. 142–146; Meyer to Secretary of State, Dec. 18, 1905, *U.S.F.R.,* 1907, p. 800.
[8] *U.S.F.R.,* 1907, pp. 784–790.

cation line would be determined by a commission of delineation representing both parties, the decision of the commission being subject to the approval of the two governments; the rights of Russian subjects would be protected in the area ceded; and no military measures or works were to menace either of the parties from the territory of the other. These provisions were substantially embodied in the treaty.

The commission of delineation carried out its task between 1906 and 1908.[9] The principal members were Colonels Oshima and Lileiev and the findings were embodied in a report signed at Vladivostok on April 10, 1908. This was formally accepted by the two governments in the "Act Delimiting Sakhalin Island between Russia and Japan," signed at Tokyo on August 6, 1908. The treaty approved the demarcation of the 50th parallel boundary by 4 large stone markers located, from east to west, at Narumi, Sakai, Hoshino, and Aboshi. In addition, 17 smaller stone markers had been established and 10-meter zones cleared in the forest on either side of the frontier. Finally, detailed descriptive and cartographic evidence of the commission's work was provided.

The partition of Sakhalin introduced new dispensations on both sides of the boundary. The Japanese government had already taken steps by August 1905 to replace the military government by a civil administration. At that time the new administration was established at Korsakov under General Kumagaya Kiichiro. Finally, by Imperial decree of April 1, 1907, a prefectural-level administration (Karafuto Cho) was inaugurated ultimately responsible to the prime minister. It dealt with internal affairs and police through 7 regional administrations and 2 special agencies (Shutchojo).

The Japanese occupation of Sakhalin had dealt a final blow to the use of the island for the exile of Russian criminals. Reforms had been under consideration by the Russian government even before this event though without any practical outcome. But under the Japanese administration, many of the prisoners escaped from their places of confinement, some crossing the Tartar Strait to the mainland. The ground was prepared for a new regime. When the Russian administration returned

[9] Unterberger, op.cit., pp. 207–211; Japan. Karafuto Cho, Karafuto Enkaku Shi, Toyohara, 1925, pp. 234–240; Japan. Minister of Foreign Affairs, Recueil des Traites et Conventions entre le Japon et les Puissances Estrangeres. 2 Vols., Tokyo, 1936, I, 2528–2536.

to northern Sakhalin, it acted in recognition of the fact that the penal system had been unsuccessful and, consequently, sought to develop a new economic regime for the region. A system of free settlement was inaugurated to replace the dependence on penal colonies to develop the industrial and particularly the agricultural life. In addition to settlers from the mainland, the criminals already there were invited to remain as productive members of a more orderly society.

The drafting of the treaty itself, the final decisions of the Portsmouth Conference, was done by a committee of the two delegations, Denison, assisted by Adachi and Ochiai, acting for Japan and Martens, assisted by Pokotilov and Planson, for Russia. The materials used were the protocols of the conference. They were also guided by the decision that the treaty would, as much as possible, constitute a final and definitive rather than a preliminary settlement. It was to contain all decisions except those specifically excluded during the conference or those that had to be left for determination by special commissions such as the Sakhalin issue. Even in the case of the latter, the general principles applicable to the final outcome were to be embodied in the treaty for the guidance of the commissions.

The ceremony for the signing of the treaty was impressively simple.[10] It was planned for 3:50 on Monday afternoon, September 5. The number of spectators admitted for the occasion was limited. In addition to the delegations, those present included: Admiral William Meade, the commandant of the Navy Yard; Captain Cameron Winslow, aid-de-camp to President Roosevelt and commander of the "Mayflower"; Commander John Gibbons of the "Dolphin;" Assistant Secretary of State Pierce; Governor John MacLane of New Hampshire and his secretary; and some embassy people. A detachment of marines in full dress uniforms was posted at the entrance of the Navy Yard to receive the plenipotentiaries. Witte and Rosen arrived first and were greeted by a flourish of trumpets and by the marines presenting arms, and were met at the door of the "Peace Building" by Assistant Secretary Pierce and Admiral Meade. The Japanese arrived shortly after and were received with the same honors. In the conference hall, the ceremonies were brief. Rosen and Komura made short speeches and official champagne toasts were proposed to the President and the two monarchs.

[10] Korostovets, op.cit., pp. 124–125; Kaneko, Beikoku, Sept. 5, 1905.

By the appointed time, the delegates were seated in their accustomed places at the conference table for the signing. The start of this final act of the Portsmouth Conference was heralded throughout the region by the booming of guns and the sound of whistles and church bells. Witte signed first, using a pen belonging to Dr. Dillon, followed by Rosen, and then by Komura who used a separate pen for each of his signatures from the supply on the table. Finally Takahira signed with a pen he had taken from his own pocket.

All the necessary papers were approved in this same ceremony, meaning that each plenipotentiary signed 12 times: 4 copies of the treaty, 4 supplementary articles, and 4 final protocols. The 4 copies of the treaty (2 each in English and French) were for Russia and Japan.

After the final ceremony, the Russians attended a special service held at Christ Church in Portsmouth. Some thirty local and visiting clergymen were on hand for the occasion representing the Roman Catholic, Protestant, and Russian Orthodox faiths. A Protestant service was followed by an Orthodox service that ended at 6 o'clock in the evening. Seats had been reserved for the Japanese delegates though they did not appear. The Japanese delegation left Portsmouth that evening, the Russians the next morning.

The conclusion of the Portsmouth Treaty was by no means universally welcomed in either Tokyo or St. Petersburg. Under the circumstances, this was to be expected. For the war was not fought for any specific territory or rights. Nor did either side have the force to achieve anything remotely resembling complete security of its gains from the other. Instead, the war was fought for the vaguer goal of achieving the security of national interests and with forces too evenly matched to allow pressing beyond a set of limited objectives. Consequently, a choice had to be made by each country between the attainable and the ideal.

The response to the treaty in Tokyo ranged from dutiful though unenthusiastic acceptance of the inevitable to violent opposition. The main stumbling block to a more favorable treaty, the impotence of the Japanese military forces, was not faced realistically. For security reasons this fact was unquestionably beyond the reach of general public discussion even to those who were conscious of it. Nevertheless, without the knowledge of this essential fact, the heated discussion that ensued was bound

"BALANCED ANTAGONISMS" IN ACTION

to have an air of unreality. The failure to examine the issue on its merits must also have been a source of frustration to those responsible officials who were forced to act within a framework that was largely invisible to their critics.

Among the Japanese newspapers, the semiofficial *Kokumin Shimbum* was the most notably favorable to the Portsmouth Treaty. It contained the following view:

"We Japanese are not a war-like people, and when we fight we do not fight for fighting's sake, but only to attain a certain object. So soon as that object is attained we are always open to peace. Now our object in the present war was to drive Russia out of Manchuria and secure the stability of Korea, those accomplishments being indispensable to our national safety. As a result of our victorious operations we have been successful in negotiating these objects. Indeed we have gained more. Besides establishing our protectorate over Korea and compelling Russia to withdraw from Manchuria, we have obtained the lease of Port Arthur and Talien, the unconditional surrender of a moiety of Saghalien, and fishery rights in the Littorals. The peace secured is, therefore, a glorious as well as a profitable one and the country should rejoice over its restoration."[11]

The *Kokumin* also made the following comment on the opposing view:

"Some say the peace is an ignominious one, because we have failed to carry our demands about an indemnity and the cession of the whole of Saghalien, and we (*Kokumin*) ourselves had our moments of hope that Russia would agree to cede all her territories east of Lake Baikal and pay an indemnity of 3,000 million yen. But these were only visions which our extraordinary victories on land and sea ushered forth, and it would be foolish to rail angrily at the peace terms, which may appear inadequate in comparison with the greatness of our victories . . . On the whole, therefore, the achievements of the plenipotentiaries Baron Komura and Mr. Takahira fully deserves to be called a diplomatic success; while the country knows no words sufficiently expressive to adequately convey the sense of gratitude it feels toward the President of the great Republic."

[11] *Japan Times*, Sept. 1, 1905.

The Tokyo *Asahi* was among the press spokesmen for the opposition. It commented before the riots took place:

"The complete absence of enthusiasm with which the news of the conclusion of peace was received here seems to be conspicuously communicative of how the general public feels about the terms agreed upon, and forms, it may be said, an eloquent prelude to what the popular organs would say thereanent. And there can be no mistaking that their voice is one of intense dissatisfaction . . . those [terms] concerning Korea and Manchuria are what we have acquired by the exercise of our own power, and their recognition cannot necessarily be regarded as a result of the conference. As for the other terms they were the result of concessions largely on Japan's part, and that at the behest of Russia."[12]

Asahi concluded that Japan had essentially made peace on Russia's terms. Having gone this far, the people are ready and willing to experience further sacrifices for a more suitable peace settlement. It concluded:

"What necessity was there then for the Government that they should have submitted to terms dictated by Russia? The Government's action may only be regarded as a deliberate insult to the victorious people!"

A few days later, *Asahi* attributed the riots to the popular dissatisfaction with the treaty.[13] Since the government had betrayed the people, the riots should continue until it resigned. The writer continued:

"Their resignation will prove to the world that, while the politicians in power at present are easy to deal with, the Japanese people possess bones and nerves, and the cunning Russians will think twice before trying again to seduce against us the Koreans and Chinese, who are already evincing signs of flouting at us, as a result of our Government yielding to the ignominious terms of the peace."

It was the misfortune of the Japanese plenipotentiaries that the opposition at home had a specific set of goals and that

[12] *loc.cit.*
[13] *ibid.*, Sept. 6, 1905.

these differed significantly from those reflected in the treaty. These goals also differed from those that the military authorities considered attainable. One of these opposition groups was made up of Professors Tomizu, Takahashi, Terao, Nakamura, Tomii, Kanai, and Onozuka of Tokyo University.[14] Not only did these "Seven Professors," as they come to be known, express their opposition program clearly and effectively, but they also disclosed an unrealistic set of peace conditions to the people before the actual terms were known, thus preparing the public mind for a disappointment.

The minimum terms publicly demanded in June 1905 by the Seven Professors and their associates included: the choice of a place for the negotiations where outside interference would not be an obstructive factor for Japan; no armistice until the conclusion of a treaty; an indemnity of three billion yen; territorial concessions, including Sakhalin, Kamchatka, and the Maritime territory of Russia as well as the entire Russian railway in Manchuria; the surrender of all Russian warships that had escaped and all other ships used for military purposes then east of Singapore; the cession of all mines and other establishments in Manchuria belonging to the Russian government. They also demanded the following as future requirements from Russia: no Russian naval forces to be stationed in the Pacific Ocean or the Japan Sea; the restriction of Russian garrisons east of Lake Baikal; and the prohibition that Russia could not acquire any territorial rights in China without the consent of Japan.

One of the Seven, Professor Tomizu, had a much more radical requirement which he publicized in the pages of Gaiko Jiho. He argued that, for economic, demographic, and strategic reasons, Japan ought to seize effective control of Korea, Manchuria, and the Russian Far East up to Lake Baikal. Unless she pushed her territorial control as far as Lake Baikal, it would not be defensible and the war with Russia would only be renewed later. With Russia suffering internal troubles, the time was appropriate to realize this program rather than to end the war.

The Seven Professors were closely linked with the Association for Those Interested in the Peace Problem (Kowa Mondai Rengo Doshikai) which, in turn, was continuing the work of

[14] *Gaiko Jiho,* Feb. 10, April 10, July 10, 1905, pp. 57–58, 29–57, 63; *Nihon Shimbun,* June 14, 1905, *M.H.S.,* xii, 436.

the Anti-Russian League (Tairo Doshikai).[15] The Association was headed by Kono Hironaka, a Diet member from Fukushima Province, and had as one of its leaders Otake Kanichi, one of the heads of the Anti-Russian League. The Association met at Meijiza on the afternoon of August 17 to pass resolutions opposing the existing trends in the peace negotiations.

On September 4, the day before the peace was signed, the Association carried its opposition a long step further.[16] Bearing a memorial signed by himself and 27 others, Kono went to the Imperial household and requested Baron Hosokawa, chief imperial private secretary, to present it to the Emperor. The memorial condemned the Portsmouth negotiations on the ground that they were not achieving the objective of the war, the preservation of the peace in the Far East. It branded the Japanese plenipotentiaries as criminals against the Emperor, the Japanese people, and future generations. The same day some 30,000 circulars were distributed throughout Tokyo, describing the sacrifices in men and money that the victories thus far had cost and calling the peace terms a humiliation before all the nations of the world. All patriots, young and old, were urged to come to a meeting to be held at 1 o'clock the next afternoon in Hibiya Park to hear a discussion of the Imperial wish for eternal peace.

The police tried unsuccessfully to postpone the September 5 meeting on the grounds that the peace had not yet been concluded and that the effect of such a demonstration would be internationally unfortunate; a peremptory police order forbidding the meeting was ignored. The police then tried to obstruct the proceedings by detaining some of the leading members of the Association and by barricading the entrances to Hibiya Park, but this only aroused the municipal authorities who had jurisdiction over the park.

The crowd began to gather near the park about noon and when the police tried to obstruct their entry, they responded with a shower of stones, with cries of "banzai," and then by charging the barricades. The estimated 350 policemen apparently made no further attempt to prevent the meeting that took place at about 2 o'clock near signs marked "Mass Meeting" [Kokumin Daikai]. Many of the people displayed the national flag, and after

---

[15] *Tokyo Asahi,* Aug. 18, 1905, *M.H.S.,* XII, 470.
[16] *Tokyo Asahi,* Sept. 5, 6, 1905, *M.H.S.,* XII, 484; *Japan Times,* Sept. 5, 6, 1905; Ota, *op.cit.,* pp. 263–264.

a ceremonial display of fireworks, Kono read a resolution asking that the peace treaty be annulled. The resolution was wildly acclaimed and other speeches completed the affair.

After the meeting, the crowd, headed by a band and singing the national anthem in doleful tones, moved in the direction of the Imperial Palace. At this point another open battle occurred with the police accompanied by flying fists and stones and by the cries and uproar of the people, all surrounded by a huge cloud of dust. Shaking off the police, a part of the group approached the offices of the *Kokumin Shimbun,* a paper that had defended the government position regarding the treaty, and destroyed the company's furniture and presses. Because of a rumor that the *Kokumin Shimbun* was being printed there, the *Shueisha* suffered the same fate.

Another group moved toward the official residence of the home minister, again encountering the firm resistance of the police. Later, a rumor was circulated that Prime Minister Katsura was inside and five men rushed toward the house with drawn swords but were stopped by the police, one of the men being killed instantly and the other four captured. Although an attempt to set the house on fire was frustrated, the residence of the home minister's secretary was fired with kerosene-soaked rags. The arrival of two companies of Imperial Guards ended this phase of the attack.

During the night and the next day, September 6, the crowds turned on the streetcars and the police boxes. Some streetcar employees had expressed satisfaction when one of the would-be incendiaries had fallen from the wall of the home minister's residence and in retaliation, cars were set on fire with kerosene and the offices of the company burned. Throughout the night and day police boxes were burned, starting at Shiba, until nearly all were said to have been destroyed. By evening the people were attacking the larger police stations such as those at Nihonbashi and Kanda and the police were unsuccessful in stemming this seemingly elemental assault. A press statement gave this summary of the situation:

"Yesterday Tokyo was the scene of bloodshed, fire and fighting. Never in the history of the Meiji era has the popular indignation been given vent to in such a terrible manner as in the last twenty-four hours."

The climax of this popular orgy was almost unique in Meiji history. Marshal Law was invoked on September 7 by Imperial Ordinances, introducing control by military forces and police, censorship of newspapers, journals, and the mail, as well as other restrictions. The Ordinances were to remain in force until November 29. Some of the newspapers greeted this new turn of affairs with a continued note of resistance. *Jiji* called it "a disgrace to the nation and will leave a most deplorable stain on the illustrious name of the Emperor." It pointed out that the government should have frankly admitted its error and disavowed the Portsmouth Treaty.

The socialists, whose brethren had played so conspicuous a part in the Russian uprisings, were unable to add their force to this protest in any way comparable to the Association that had organized the spectacular riots. The socialist antiwar program undertaken even before the outbreak of the conflict, had died down long before the Portsmouth Conference met.[17] It had begun rather spectacularly on October 8, 1903, the date when the Russian withdrawal from Manchuria was to have been completed. On that date two members of the staff of the *Yorozu Choho*, Kotoku Denjiro and Sakai Toshihiko, resigned in protest against the prowar policy the newspaper had just adopted. The same day the socialists passed a resolution opposing a conflict with Russia. Kotoku and Sakai turned to the organization of the Commoners' Society (Heiminsha) and began to publish the Commoners' Newspaper (*Heimin Shimbun*) with Sakai as editor and opened a campaign to turn the people against the war.

During the war the Japanese socialists clearly expressed their sympathy for their Russian brethren, issuing a proclamation to this effect on March 13, 1904 that was reprinted abroad. The sentiment it expressed was answered in the pages of the Russian Social Democratic *Iskra*. In August 1904, Katayama Sen was elected first vice president at the Sixth Congress of the Second International at Amsterdam. He and the second vice president, George Plekhanov, spectacularly shook hands on the platform of the congress.

These initial efforts were, however, notably unproductive of any significant results. Katayama Sen, the best-known leader, had

[17] H. Kublin, "The Japanese Socialists and the Russo-Japanese War," *Journal of Modern History*, XXII, 4, Dec. 1950, pp. 322–339; Y. Matsushita, *Hansen Undo Shi*, Tokyo, 1954, pp. 11ff.

left Japan in late 1903 and did not return until early 1906. Before the end of 1904 the socialist effort through journalism had passed the peak of its influence, and, in March 1905, Kotoku and Nishikawa were given prison sentences. Kotoku was released in time to witness the riotous protests against the treaty and to ponder over the future.

It is clear that the leadership of the expansionists was organized, vocal, and able to express itself through public protest. For the immediate future, its opposition to the governmental policies would probably continue to be expressed through appeals to sentiments of strong patriotism and loyalty to the Emperor. It drew its support from persons of various walks of life including Prince Konoe Atsumaru, Toyama Mitsuru, the noted nationalist and expansionist organizer of patriotic societies such as the Genyosha, members of the Diet and the Kenseikai, such as Shimmuchi Tomotsune, the Seven Professors, and many others. These people influenced the government to be alert for opportunities to expand its already considerable gains on the continent.

This outburst against the treaty already included a factor that soon emerged as a major one in the international relations of Japan—an expression of indignation against the United States. On the evening of the initial attacks by the crowd, a member of the American legation in Tokyo, Huntington Wilson, was dining with "a cabinet minister," perhaps the home minister.[18] Although his host tried at first to distract his attention from the dangers, he eventually became aware of what was going on. Wilson soon learned that the American legation had also been singled out as a point of attack by the rioters. The closest thing to an actual attack on an individual American, Mr. Wilson wrote, was the overturning of the rickshaw in which Mr. Schwerin, vice president of the Pacific Mail Steamship Company, was riding. Guards were sent to the legation grounds and before long some 400 troops were guarding the area and a permanent military detachment remained there throughout the period of martial law.

The sentiment disclosed toward the United States during the riots was to have a vital bearing on the plan then being formulated by the American financier, Mr. E.H. Harriman. Harriman had been encouraged to look upon Manchuria as a field for invest-

[18] F.M.H. Wilson, *Memoirs of an Ex-Diplomat*, Boston, 1945, pp. 116–117.

ment by the American-Japanese financial relationships during the war when Mr. Schiff had taken the initiative in floating loans for Japan.[19] It was assumed that Japan would need further financial assistance in the reconstruction and development of Manchuria. Lloyd Griscom, the American minister in Tokyo, had urged Harriman to come to Japan in person and survey the situation.

These prospects fitted admirably into Mr. Harriman's existing interests in the Far East. His Pacific Mail Steamship Company connecting the western coast of the United States with the Far East was an expression of this interest and furnished an incentive for further business expansion in the western Pacific. He was drawn, accordingly, by a desire to promote business in a region where opportunities appeared to lie at hand. Specifically, he proposed to do this by establishing a round-the-world transportation system based upon his American railway interests and the Pacific Mail Steamship Company, projected westward by means of the railways of Manchuria and Russia to reach the Baltic ports. From there another steamship line would complete the circuit.

It was with this purpose in mind that Harriman left New York for Japan on August 10, the day the plenipotentiaries held their first meeting at Portsmouth. His party included Mrs. Harriman, their sons Averell and Roland, Mr. and Mrs. Robert Goelet, Mr. R.P. Schwerin, and Dr. W.G. Lyle, Harriman's personal physician. Departing from San Francisco on the 16th aboard the "Siberia," he reached Yokohama on the 31st as the Portsmouth Conference was winding up its affairs. He was met on the ship by representatives of the leading banking circles and housed at the Grand Hotel.

During the next six weeks, Harriman was busily occupied in surveying the situation in Manchuria and in working out the details of an understanding in Tokyo. When he finally left Japan on October 16, he had every reason to assume that his proposal would be accepted. If it had been, he would have found himself a partner with the Japanese government in a syndicate to rebuild, operate, and expand the railways of South Manchuria. The partnership would have been equal except in the case of a war between Japan on one side and either China or Russia on the other. Under either of these conditions, the railway would have been completely at the disposal of the Japanese government.

[19] K.G., II, 204–213; G. Kennan, E.H. Harriman's Far Eastern Plans, New York, 1917, pp. 3–47 passim.

This optimistic mood did not survive Harriman's return trip. When he reached San Francisco, the Japanese consul met him with a message from Tokyo suspending the proposed agreement for the time being. In New York in mid-January 1906 he received a message from Soeda Juichi, the president of the Japan Industrial Bank and official agent of communications between the partners of the proposed syndicate. The message in effect terminated the agreement. Mr. Schiff tried unsuccessfully to revive the project during his visit to Japan in the spring of 1906.

The reason for this turn of events is easier to explain than to understand. When Komura returned to Tokyo from Portsmouth in mid-October, he is said to have been astonished and to have wondered how the syndicate project could ever have been approved by the Japanese government. His opposition was based on two principal grounds: one, it was inconsistent with Article VI of the Portsmouth Treaty which required Chinese consent for all transactions concerning the Manchurian rights Japan had received at Portsmouth; and two, the Japanese people had already expressed their dissatisfaction with the treaty and the failure to receive an indemnity, and this situation would only be aggravated if it were learned that the government had delivered a large share of the limited gains to the Americans.

The message Soeda Juichi sent to Harriman in January was based on Komura's first point and upon the results of the Sino-Japanese agreement just concluded at Peking. He wrote that it had been found necessary to follow the terms of the original grant to Russia and to operate the railway exclusively under a Sino-Japanese partnership. Harriman must have wondered as he read this: if this were indeed the reason, why didn't Prime Minister Katsura know about it?

Years later Baron Kaneko published a sidelight on the Harriman episode about which judgment must be suspended until further substantiated.[20] He wrote that after the Portsmouth Treaty had been concluded he was visited by Montgomery Roosevelt, a cousin of the President, who said he had come to suggest an alternative to the Harriman plan and that his alternative proposal was approved by President Roosevelt. He urged Japan to retain full control of the Manchurian railway and said that if Japan would buy steel and rolling stock from American

[20] Kaneko, "A Japanese 'Monroe Doctrine' and Manchuria," *op.cit.*, pp. 177–179.

factories, he would help them to get loans of 30 to 40 million yen at 5 and one-half per cent from five New York banks.

Kaneko continued that when Komura reached New York on his way home he was very dejected at having failed to receive an indemnity and only half of Sakhalin. He said that Japan would need a great deal of money to repair the damage in Manchuria and asked Kaneko to help find it among New York bankers. When Kaneko told him of the Roosevelt plan he was reportedly delighted and said that this would help him to face his government in spite of the treaty. Later loans, on a far more modest scale, and purchases of American steel and rolling stock were said to have followed from this proposal. Nevertheless, the question remains: assuming this story to be accurate, does it supply the reason Komura was able so quickly to change the accepted policy of the Japanese government?

The reception of the Portsmouth Treaty in Russia was much more of a social than a national matter.[21] The people had never accepted the war as a national event as the Japanese people had. Also unlike Japan the issues and even the very locale of the war were largely beyond the comprehension of most of the Russian people. As Baron Rosen wrote later, the people bore it with as much patience as possible because they had to, and when it was over they were scarcely aware, outside of their own unwonted share in it, what it was that had come to an end.

The scene in St. Petersburg at the time of the peace, as described by an observant British visitor, forms a complete contrast to Tokyo, then engulfed in riots. He characterized the popular mood as "appathetic and indifferent" toward the peace. Seeing the streets decorated with flags, he inquired about it only to learn that the flags were in honor of the visit of the Shah of Persia rather than the peace. At a gathering of several thousand people for an illustrated lecture on the war, a picture of Admiral Makarov was loudly cheered, one of General Linievich drew faint applause, and one of General Kuropatkin drew no cheers at all. A comment by the lecturer that if the peace had been put off, General Linievich could have beaten the Japanese soundly was received with "stolid indifference."

It is entirely in character that the widespread disturbances that

[21] Rosen, op.cit., i, 279; Dillon, "Story," op.cit., p. 462; W.T. Stead, "How St. Petersburg Received the News of Peace," The American Monthly Review of Reviews, xxxii, 4, Oct. 1905, pp. 426–427.

had been absorbing the Russian people for some months before the announcement of the peace were not primarily related to the war. While the revolutionaries made full use of both the war and the peace in planning their strategy, the slogans that they used relied largely for their cogency upon social and political maladjustments that had only been accentuated by the war. Even the subversive activities focused on the troops at or near the war front, only used the dislocations of the war or the peace as a means of achieving their long-range political purposes.

The other strata of Russian society varied considerably in their appraisal of the peace.[22] The liberal and conservative press, with some exceptions, accepted it although they considered it a hard one. In spite of the loss of half of Sakhalin, for which Witte was latter to be called "Count Half-Sakhalin," they generally gave Witte credit for retaining part of it. The industrial interests were pleased with the peace.

Even some members of the Imperial family, including the Emperor, were said to have been guardedly pleased with the peace. The Grand Duke Aleksander Mikailovich is reported to have said enthusiastically: "What a clever fellow Witte is." Nevertheless, the obvious reluctance with which the Emperor bestowed the title of "count" upon Witte for his service at Portsmouth probably reflected both the prevailing mood of the court as well as the Emperor's own personal feelings toward the former minister of finance.

The reception of the peace among the upper ranks of the bureaucracy was conditioned either by their responsibilities for the security of the national interests or by their concern for their own fortunes, or both. A dominant conception current among them was that Russia had been forced into the war. This view was a corollary of the assumptions that the national interests required a controlling interest in Northeast Asia and that, given time, this could have been achieved without war. These assumptions were reenforced by the low appraisal of Japan's fighting strength prevalent before the war.

There were two general points of view as to the peace that followed directly from these assumptions.[23] One was to welcome the peace and use the opportunity for the rehabilitation of the

[22] Putilov to Shipov, Sept. 1, 1905, K.A., vi, 43–44; Korostovets, op.cit., pp. 110, 154; Seegar, op.cit., pp. 129–130.

[23] Witte to Kuropatkin, Mar. 12, 1905, K.A., xix, 74; Unterberger, op.cit., p. 340.

country; this had long been Witte's view. The other was to delay the peace in the hope that one more battle would turn the tide. Either of these views would necessarily accept with many qualifications a peace that brought defeat.

This mood was aptly expressed some time later by General Unterberger, the governor general of the Amur. The general noted that neither side had been satisfied with the outcome of the war. Japan had by no means achieved her objective—to drive Russia back from the Pacific Ocean and exact a large indemnity. Russia, on her part, had been left with the feeling that the outcome had been an unfortunate coincidence of circumstances rather than a consequence of a genuine test of strength between the two nations.

The mutual dissastisfaction in Japan and Russia with respect to the Portsmouth Treaty could have led to either of two eventualities: a war of revenge or a stable balance of power. The course of the war and of the peace negotiations had shown that, while both of these were indeed latent in the situation, the stability of the balance of power was, for the time being at least, the more likely development. In this sense, it appeared that the expectations of both Great Britain and the United States might be fulfilled. A British memorandum of March 1901, in discussing the benefit of helping Japan to gain control of the Liaotung Peninsula, enunciated a policy that was to be expressed many times by President Roosevelt:

"Its possession by Japan would be a guarantee that there would be no reconciliation between Russia and Japan. This would be an advantage to England and Europe. The yellow danger would be kept in check by Russia and the Russian danger by Japan."[24]

[24] Bertie "Memorandum," Mar. 11, 1901, *B.D.*, II, 43.

18. China and the New Balance of Power

THE JAPANESE CAMPAIGN for a satisfactory peace had finally to be carried from Portsmouth to Peking. The immediate and indispensable objective was to obtain Chinese approval for the transfer of the rights in Manchuria already granted by Russia at Portsmouth. Beyond the restricted scope of the specific rights lay the less easily definable requirements of national security. These could be satisfied to some extent by requiring China to institute reforms in Manchuria and thereby insure peace and order and, consequently, security for foreign interests. Under the prevailing international conditions, however, it would have been almost inconceivable that Japan would not seek further security in the expansion of her continental interests.

Demands such as those Japan contemplated, which tended to enlarge the rights and interests of only one of the powers, would almost inevitably encounter opposition from two principal sources. The most immediately ominous one was the jealous watchfulness with which the western nations regarded the balance of power. The other, potentially far more significant, was the increasingly self-conscious solicitude with which China was seeking to insure her own national security through the liquidation of adverse foreign influences within her territory.

Japan's deftness in steering a safe course between these two rocky shoals and establishing a secure base for a continental empire was an achievement of the greatest significance. It conferred upon her the benefits of being the only one of the foreign powers with interests in China which had its center in the Far East. Furthermore, she derived such prestige from being the only Asian nation which had defeated a western power that many Asians overlooked her expansive ambitions and saw in her the best available leader of the struggle against western imperialism. Her shrewd use of these advantages enabled her to establish a new balance of power in the Far East by assuming a position from which she could take full advantage of the weaknesses of both her foreign rivals and of China, eventually playing one against the other and, to some extent, controlling them.

The peace plans approved by the Japanese cabinet in August

1904 included demands to be made of both Russia and China.[1] Those to be presented to China included the following basic requirements: nonalienation of Manchuria; the maintenance of complete peace and order in Manchuria; reform of the administrative, police, and military systems in order to carry out the foregoing; recognition of the Russian cession to Japan of the railway between Changchun and Port Arthur; and recognition of the Russian cession of the lease rights to the Kuantung Peninsula.

The following were also to be required of China in the interest of a much enlarged sphere of activity for Japan in the general area of Manchuria: a concession to build a railway from the right bank of the Yalu to Liaoyang and another to Kirin; freedom to carry on fishing along the coast of Fengtien Province in Manchuria; cession of forestry and mining rights in the Yalu and Hun river valleys; freedom of navigation in the Liao, Sungari, and Yalu rivers; opening of the following Manchurian towns to all nations: Fenghuangcheng, Liaoyang, Tiehling, Tungchiangtze, Kuanchengtze, Harbin, Kirin, Hunchun, Sanhsing, Tsitsihar, Hailar, and Aigun.

After the fall of Port Arthur the planning for peace was pursued even more seriously than before. The Japanese minister in Peking, Uchida, was called home for consultations on the peace conditions.[2] In the course of the next few months there emerged a set of proposals supplementing those intended for the conference with Russia. After the Portsmouth Conference these were given their final form and approved by a cabinet council on October 27, 1905.

With these instructions in hand, Komura once more turned over the office of foreign minister to Prime Minister Katsura and departed for Peking for the final battle for peace. In spite of his poor physical condition, he felt the need to complete his task and, if possible, to save the Katsura cabinet, already endangered by the unpopular Portsmouth Treaty. It was none too soon. The Katsura cabinet fell on January 7, 1906, five days after Komura had once more resumed his post in the cabinet.

Komura left Japan on November 6, 1905, this time aboard a warship from Yokosuka. He reached Peking on November 12 and was housed at the Grande Hotel des Wagon Lits. On the

[1] *K.G.*, ii, 27-28; "Foreign Minister Komura's Proposal," July 1904, *N.G.M.*, xxxvii-xxxviii, *Nichiro Senso*, v, 59-63; Tokutomi, *op.cit.*, ii, 265-266; Hori, *op.cit.*, pp. 207-208; *N.K.S.*, ii, 8-10.
[2] *K.G.*, ii, 216ff.

16th he and Uchida, the minister to China who was serving as his plenipotentiary colleague, were received in audience by the Emperor of China. On November 17 the first formal session of the conference was held with the Chinese plenipotentiaries: Prince Ching, the Chief Grand Councilor and Presiding Minister for Foreign Affairs; Yuan Shih-kai, the viceroy of Chihli Province; and Chü Hung-chi, the Minister for Foreign Affairs. The conference lasted five weeks, the sessions ending on December 22 when the treaty was concluded.

The task which Komura proposed to accomplish in Peking was fraught with many pitfalls and difficulties. During the conference at Portsmouth, Witte had more than once reminded him that the concessions Russia was making in Manchuria were invalid without Chinese approval. The Russian government, following up this opportunity to checkmate its determined rival, watched closely the course Japan followed and even tried to learn from Yuan Shih-kai the details of the Peking negotiations pertaining to the railway.[3]

Although Russia may have seen little possibility of preventing China's approval of the transaction already made at Portsmouth, further complications could arise if Japan were to permit the rights in the railway to be redeemed by China. For this would require a sizeable loan which might, in turn, lead to intervention in Manchuria on the part of the lender. Furthermore, Prince Ching was informed that if Japan were to receive any concessions over and above those transferred, Russia would have some demands of her own to make.

Needless to say, Japan found diplomatic support particularly from the United States and Great Britain, as vital for this part of her program as any other. At the close of the Portsmouth Conference, Komura used the occasion of his farewell visit to President Roosevelt on September 9 to discuss the matter.[4] He informed the President that there were certain fundamental demands, such as those pertaining to the leased territory and the railway, which Japan would require of China. To accept less by returning these to China would be interpreted by Russia as a sign of weakness and would almost certainly invite a war of revenge.

[3] Davydov to the Director of the Chancellery of the Ministry of Finance, Sept. 22, 1905, *K.A.*, vii, 10–11; *K.G.*, ii, 227.
[4] *K.G.*, ii, 218.

Roosevelt agreed with Komura's views. Since Japan had expended lives and money to wrest these from Russia, he felt it unreasonable that China should refuse to grant them. Komura thereupon requested, and Roosevelt agreed, that the American minister in Peking should be informed of Roosevelt's views in order to avoid misunderstandings in the future. The same precaution was taken to assure British support.

Another formidable impediment for Japan was the attitude of the Chinese government and of some elements in China, especially the officials and the gentry.[5] This was a time when China was planning and instituting fundamental reforms. The examinations system itself had been abolished on September 2, only three days before the signing of the Portsmouth treaty. The reforms included the centralization and strengthening of the governmental administration and the railway network. In fact, administrative centralization and railway construction became inseparably intertwined as one of the major issues in the drive for internal reconditioning. Among the objectives of this program was the reduction, and prospectively the elimination, of foreign control over railways. The refusal of further railway concessions and even the withdrawal of existing concessions were contemplated.

Such a program, while clearly at odds with the existing interests as well as the expectations of the foreign powers, was, nevertheless, already being accepted. Britain had made a gesture toward recognizing this trend in the Sino-British agreement signed July 3, 1905. Referred to as a redemption arrangement, this had retroceded some concessions to China, meanwhile leaving the British in virtual control until all financial obligations had been met.[6] This transaction included both railway and mining property.

In view of her new course and of British acquiescence, it appeared unlikely that China would willingly grant Japan new rights in Manchuria. She might even be expected to resist the transfer of the Russian rights. In fact, China had already expressed her desire to have a part in the Portsmouth settlements.

[5] A. Feuerwerker, *China's Early Industrialization,* Cambridge, 1958, pp. 67ff; S-y Teng and J.K. Fairbank, *China's Response to the West,* Cambridge, 1954, pp. 195–218.

[6] E.T.Z. Sun, *Chinese Railways and British Interests, 1898–1911,* New York, 1954, p. 128; Denison to Griscom, Jan. 1906, Kennan, *op.cit.,* p. 34; MacMurray, *op.cit.,* I, 506–515.

She had also served notice that she was contemplating claims for damages against both belligerents and that she intended to restrict Japan's new position in Manchuria to the original Sino-Russian treaty rights.

Conversely, these expressions of intentions indicate that China was conscious of the dangers she would encounter in allowing Japan to acquire too great a stake in Manchuria. As the victor in the war it could be anticipated that Japan would press for all she could get, including the same monopolistic role Russia had played. At the same time, the other powers would also be watching jealously for such a possibility and might require compensation if Japan were too liberally rewarded.

The opening session of the Peking conference was devoted to procedural and preliminary matters.[7] The proceedings were to be conducted in secrecy. The languages of the conference were to be Chinese and Japanese. Protocols were to be drawn up in both languages at the close of each session. The existing record of this conference is considerably longer than that for the Portsmouth Conference and provides fuller reports of the discussions.

After the formalities were over, Komura made a short speech. He described the origins and opening of the recent war and the sacrifices in men and money it had cost Japan. The sacrifices were made, he emphasized, not only for the self-defense of Japan, but also for the sake of the general peace of the Far East. In the peace just concluded with Russia certain settlements had been made regarding Manchuria. Since China had an interest in these, he had come to discuss them.

Komura characterized the Japanese proposals as having three objectives. The first was to corroborate the cessions Russia had made to Japan in Manchuria. The second was to encourage the Chinese to strengthen their administration in Manchuria in order to afford protection for the lives and property of foreign nationals. It was hoped that this would prevent the occurrence of international disorders in the future. Finally, Komura expressed the hope that in the future Manchuria would be a place where commercial enterprise would be allowed to proceed freely. Prince Ching's response was politely formal and appeared to approve these sentiments.

[7] *M.K.N.K.D.H.*, pp. 2ff.

The Peking negotiations displayed graphically the actual disparity in outlook between China and Japan. The former was endeavoring to promote a "rights recovery" program in an international atmosphere which gave the great powers reason to disregard the claims of the politically infirm in order to survive. The latter was trying to rise to great power status under the same circumstances.

The presentation of these two sets of propositions at the beginning of the conference brought into sharp focus the striking dichotomy between the expansive ambitions of Japan and the assertive national self-consciousness of China. The immediate result of their juxtaposition was a Japanese victory which was recorded in three documents signed on December 22, 1905.[8] The first was the basic treaty which transferred to Japan the rights in Manchuria granted by Russia at Portsmouth. The second was an "Additional Agreement" which approved some of Japan's own demands of China. The third document was a special protocol dealing with certain aspects of Sino-Japanese relations in Manchuria which was at first kept secret, perhaps because it was feared that the infringement of China's integrity which it sanctioned might precipitate similar demands from the other powers.

In their counterproposals, the Chinese plenipotentiaries had expressed the willingness of their government to transfer to Japan, with certain conditions, the southern branch of the railway and the leased territory. Yuan Shih-kai, who actually conducted most of the discussions for the Chinese government, explained in the course of the negotiations that the conditions were inspired by a desire to establish a genuine partnership with Japan in the hope that the peace might be a durable one.[9]

Yuan drew a distinction between the old and the new eras as he visualized them or, perhaps more accurately, as he wished Komura and Uchida to visualize them. He explained that in the course of her tenure in Manchuria Russia had committed many aggressive acts which included overstepping both the spirit and the letter of the agreements concluded with China. On the other hand, in her declaration of war Japan had set the tone for a new regime by expressing her interest in the preservation of

[8] Appendix 2, of this study.
[9] *M.K.N.K.D.H.*, pp. 61–77.

perpetual peace. It was in this spirit that China wished to grasp the opportunity to reconsider the leases and to place them on the basis of mutuality.

Among the suggested changes was a revision in the terms of the lease for the naval port of Port Arthur. With her center so far from the Pacific, the Chinese plenipotentiaries conceded that Russia had need of a naval port nearer to her Far Eastern possessions. Japan, on the contrary, was located nearby and had several naval ports in her homeland. Accordingly, her need for Port Arthur was not as great as Russia's. It was suggested that Japan share its use with China and that a portion of it be set aside as a commercial port for general use by the nationals of all countries. In view of the success which Port Arthur had enjoyed before the war as a commercial port and of the current Chinese "rights recovery" program, this proposal was of the greatest significance for the future.

China's other proposed conditions for approving the transfer of the leased territory to Japan had the same objective of increasing her own share of control and would have seriously reduced the economic and strategic value of the territory for Japan. Her proposals included the following: the recognition of Chinese sovereignty and legal jurisdiction in the leased territory and the prohibition of any foreign official there bearing the title of military governor; the use of Dairen as a wholly commercial port and the establishment there of a branch of the Chinese Imperial Maritime Customs Service; and Chinese control over the movement of Japanese military forces into and out of the leased territory of Kuantung.

Komura and Uchida responded very brusquely and unsympathetically to these proposals, referring to them as "inconsequential matters." Their answer was, in effect, that Japan had risked her very national existence to unseat the aggressive Russians in South Manchuria. Accordingly, she was not prepared to accept any qualifications of the prize she had won. They insisted that the rights received from Russia at Portsmouth be unconditionally approved and that if these needed any modification, later negotiations could deal with this problem. These rights in the leased territory and the railway to Kuanchengtze were given Chinese approval in the principal treaty signed between China and Japan on December 22, 1905.

The main treaty was followed by the "Additional Agreement"

which defined some of the relationships between China and
Japan in Manchuria. Among these was the problem of the Mukden-Antung railway.[10] This line had been hastily constructed
by Japan for military use during the war and formed a vital link
in the larger Japanese plan to join together the Korean and Manchurian railway systems. With the completion of the Seoul-Uiju
line and the use of the Mukden-Antung line, Japan would have
easy access to the potentialities of the region for which her
armies had just fought. It was a part of her plan which had in
the past been so highly valued that she had pressed it unrelent-
ingly upon Russia during the prewar negotiations.

The issue was equally important to China, and her plenipotentiaries fought valiantly to avoid this concession. Especially
at this moment in her internal development it would have been
important to avoid the establishment of another foreign enterprise
of such permanent significance upon her soil. The Chinese
plenipotentiaries proposed either demolishing the line or selling
it to China. They also proposed a minimum five-year term of use
for Japan. But they finally compromised by accepting an extension of Japanese use for a specific term of years, fixing the
terminal date of 1924. Under the circumstances of the First
World War and a renewal of Japanese pressure, this was extended to 2007, one hundred and two years from the time of the
Peking conference.

One of the issues in this part of the settlement on which China
scored some measure of success was with respect to the demand
for the opening for commerce, industry, and residence of certain
towns in Manchuria.[11] In her counterproposal, China had agreed
to open these places but wished to do so at a time and under
conditions to be decided by her own government. While Komura
left no doubt in the minds of the Chinese plenipotentiaries as to
the importance he attached to this demand, he was quite willing
to allow China a share in elaborating the details as long as the
substance was granted.

It was decided that China would open these places as soon as
possible after the evacuation of the Japanese and Russian forces.
In fact, during 1906 and 1907 all the towns named in the agreement except Manchuli were opened. But the growing monopolization of Manchuria by Japan and Russia in the course of

---

[10] *ibid.*, pp. 161, 332–333; Hosie, *op.cit.*, p. 165.
[11] *M.K.N.K.D.H.*, pp. 31–33, 57–58.

these years seriously compromised the value of the "open door" for any but these two nations.

The return of Chinese property seized or occupied since the outbreak of war was an issue which China herself raised and on which she scored at least a partial and formal victory.[12] While the Japanese plenipotentiaries directed their remarks toward property, the seizure and use of which was associated with war and was therefore excused by the international rules of land warfare, Yuan emphasized his special interest in other classifications of seized property. He referred particularly to the cutting of timber and to the destruction of homes which had been committed even after the conclusion of the Portsmouth agreement.

The Japanese plenipotentiaries were reluctant to commit their government to the broad claims which Yuan's point suggested. They assured him that both the foreign office and the armed forces were investigating the issues raised by the wrong use of property for nonmilitary purposes and that in time steps would be taken to remedy this. In spite of Yuan's warning that these incidents were irritating to the Chinese people and were arousing anti-Japanese feeling, Japan would go no further than to give assurances that these cases would be taken care of without any open, official commitment. The public treaty assurances were confined to property appropriated for military use.

The "Additional Agreement" also dealt with the question of the withdrawal of the Japanese and Russian forces, the use of railway guards, and Chinese responsibility for peace and order after the withdrawal. The discussion centered around Japan's uneasiness regarding Russian intentions and her consequent need for vigilance on the one hand and, on the other, China's distrust of both Japan and Russia and her desire to eliminate all foreign forces, even railway guards. Komura advised the Chinese that he considered the elimination of railway guards impractical not only because Russia was unwilling to go this far but also because he felt the security of the railways was important in case hostilities were renewed. Nevertheless, Japan would withdraw her guards if Russia would do the same. The agreement contained their final conclusions about these problems.

During this discussion, Yuan questioned Uchida's assertion that a military occupant was by international practice entitled to retain political control even after the end of the war. Komura stated

[12] ibid., pp. 240–255.

firmly that this control would continue in the occupied zone until the withdrawal was complete. In these areas Japan had the right to refuse foreign nations permission to station consuls and to prevent the travel of foreigners there in spite of rights established by treaty with China. Within a few weeks, the application of this principle to the advantage of Japan's commercial and political control would inspire an American protest.

A third group of issues was provided for in a second supplementary agreement, known as a protocol, which was signed at the same time as the others but was at first classified as secret. Like the "Additional Agreement," it dealt with matters which pertained to the relations of the two countries in Manchuria. But the control over the region which it committed into the hands of Japan was far more thoroughgoing. Its provisions fell into the following categories; the restoration of Chinese administrative authority in Manchuria; the present and future control of railways other than the mainline; and a miscellaneous group of special privileges granted by the Chinese government.

One of these questions concerned a proposed railway between Changchun or Kuanchengtze and Kirin. This railway had been given serious thought by Witte in 1902 when he was seeking every means of strengthening the Russian grip on Manchuria preparatory to evacuation and his own grip on the Russian stake as a defense against his enemies.[13] Since "evacuation" would in effect mean concentration of Russian forces in the leased territory and the railway zone, the extension of the latter to Kirin appeared to be a suitable way of maintaining troops at this vital point. It was with this objective in mind that the Russians had hoped to locate the railway station "on the height commanding the city." But the railway was not built, and at the Portsmouth Conference Witte gave Russian approval to the construction of the line by Japan.

In pressing China for the right to build and control the branch line to Kirin, Japan relied largely on the Russian menace and on her own corresponding interest in defense to support her claim.[14] She maintained that had Russia remained in occupation of Manchuria she would have monopolized it and the question of any other rights there would not even have arisen. At enormous cost in lives and treasure, Japan had retrieved part of the region.

[13] Romanov, *Russia*, pp. 286–287; *N.K.D.H.*, p. 135; Protocols, p. 67.
[14] *M.K.N.K.D.H.*, pp. 95–158, 193–207, 326–328, 373–392, 400–411.

Consequently, she had earned the right to a share in determining the vital question of defense.

The Japanese plenipotentiaries asserted that the war had disclosed Japan's inferiority to Russia in numbers of troops. Consequently, other factors, especially transportation, were bound to assume a crucial importance. Had Russia entered the war with adequate transport facilities, it is entirely possible that Japan might have lost. At present Russian plans called for improving the capacity of her railways by double-tracking them. Since a war of revenge must be considered an ever-present possibility, Japan could not avoid the necessity of matching Russia by developing her own readiness. Otherwise the defeat she had just escaped would overtake both her and China in the future.

Prince Ching and Yuan responded that the integrity of Manchuria was basically a Chinese problem. The mere fact of the war did not automatically entitle Japan and Russia to remain indefinitely the arbiters of a matter so vital to China's interests. While China was not ready to assume the entire responsibility within the next five years, she would certainly be prepared to do so before the end of a decade. In the meantime, China did not want to be left out at this crucial point in the determination of the future of Manchuria.

The control of the Kirin railway, the Chinese plenipotentiaries concluded, must be in the hands of China. Russian approval of the assumption of this responsibility was meaningless because Russia had no such right to bestow. On the other hand, it had been agreed at Portsmouth that the railways of Manchuria would be used for commercial, not military, purposes. China did not want to extend a privilege to Japan which would only prompt Russia to demand an equivalent grant.

China, nevertheless, expressed her readiness to apply to this railway the same formula used with respect to some of the railway agreements with Britain: Chinese control and, as much as possible, financing; application for Japanese loans when needed. It was a victory for China that the final protocol contained essentially this formula. A loan was later negotiated with Japan and the line to Kirin was opened for traffic in October 1912 though it fell under Japanese control five years later.[15]

In the case of the Mukden-Hsinmintun line, built during the

[15] P.H. Clyde, *International Rivalries in Manchuria, 1689–1922*, Columbus, 1928, p. 206.

war for military use by Japan, China's bid for control appears to have been aided by the relationship of the project to Britain, the ally of Japan.[16] Supported by an expert whom the Chinese negotiators called in for the occasion, they contended that a loan agreement concluded between the Chinese government and a British corporation in 1898 had contemplated the building of this line. In the end, the Japanese accepted this explanation and agreed that the line would be sold to China. They insisted, nevertheless, that the sale of the sector of the line lying east of the Liao River should be aided with a Japanese loan. By 1909 this transaction had been completed.

In the second of their supplementary demands the Japanese expressed a desire to control future railway construction in Manchuria by requiring prior consultation between China and Japan. The Chinese, on their part, were understandably reluctant to accept any such limitation on their own freedom of action.[17] When Uchida mentioned a rumor that Russia had demanded a concession to construct a line northward to Fakumen, Yuan denied that such a grant was contemplated. He added that no railways would be built in South Manchuria which would effect adversely Japan's existing railway rights.

The protocol embodied a much-disputed Chinese assurance that she would not construct any railways which would injure Japan's existing railway interests. Still, the Chinese found it difficult to accept such an obvious limitation on their own rights in Manchuria. By 1907 they were preparing to build a railway northward from Hsinmintun to Fakumen with the expectation of projecting it into the fertile plain beyond, at least to Tsitsihar. The question was further complicated by the fact that a British company was associated with the project, thus raising again the delicate question of Japan's relation with her alliance partner. It was also complicated within the next two years by the activities of Tang Shao-yi and Willard Straight and by the Knox neutralization plan which combined to carry the Russo-Japanese rapprochement a significant step further.

The first two articles of the Japanese demands had raised the basic question of China's integrity, the Chinese plenipotentiaries asserted, by requiring China to carry out reforms

---

[16] *M.K.N.K.D.H.*, pp. 169–180; MacMurray, *op.cit.*, I, 173–177; Clyde, *op.cit.*, pp. 205–206.
[17] *M.K.N.K.D.H.*, pp. 287–290.

specifically for the protection of foreign lives and property. The Chinese looked upon this as an affront to the national dignity. Furthermore, it was feared that carrying out reforms under foreign command might give rise to a whole set of new evils. What would then prevent Russia from demanding desired administrative changes in Mongolia and Sinkiang or Great Britain and Germany from doing the same in the Yangtze region or Shantung respectively. The secret protocol resolved this by stating simply that China would herself take adequate measures of reform.

The remainder of the provisions of the secret protocol, while highly favorable to the enhancement of Japanese power, left China a significant share of the honors. Japan received Chinese approval, subject to Russian concurrence, for her navigation of the Sungari River. She also retained considerable control over the conditions under which the towns of Manchuria would be opened for commerce, over the movement of Chinese troops in some regions of Manchuria, and over the disposal of both customs revenues and taxes at Yinkow.

The victories which the Chinese plenipotentiaries gained at the conference table are to some extent attributable to the cogency and forcefulness of their arguments. At the same time, they had the full benefit of Japan's anxiety lest a disclosure of the secret discussions alert Russia and the other powers to the enormous gains she was making at China's expense and to the detriment of the general balance of power. It was undoubtedly to a great extent because of this latter circumstance that China was able to retain some control over the mineral wealth of Fengtien Province, to receive Japanese approval for her participation in future Russo-Japanese negotiations regarding connecting railway services, and that there would be some relief in the matter of the property confiscated for nonmilitary purposes. She also obtained Japanese consent to an early resumption of administrative control at Yinkow.

The conclusion of these negotiations marked the inception of a new era in the history of the Far East. Heretofore, the course of events there had been determined to an overwhelming degree in the capitals of Europe. Out of this political inertness, Japan had won for herself a place among the dominant powers and had done it in a way least subject to dispute—in an ordeal by battle. This entitled her to a new sense of self-confidence which was itself bound to constitute a new and dynamic factor in world politics.

Japan had already, at the Portsmouth Conference, demonstrated her skill in transmuting the newly won power into diplomatic leverage. In the coming years, this would give her an increasingly more imposing stature, not only in Peking and St. Petersburg but also in the other major capitals of the world. Moreover, the very fact that she was the first Asian nation to accomplish this feat in contemporary times not only made her case exceptional but made it a striking contrast to that of China which continued to suffer defeat.

Having exposed the systematic and aggressive nature of her continental plans, Japan would accelerate her advances more openly and determinedly during the coming years.[18] Her manifold program of advancing her interests, as disclosed by the end of 1905, included: the building of railways and the parallel development of Manchuria; the stimulation of Chinese insurgency in Manchuria, a program which had been encouraged by Japan's sponsorship during the war of Chang Tso-lin as the leader of an outlaw band harassing the Russians; the promotion of close, subversive relations with Inner and Outer Mongolia; and projection of vigorous commercial and espionage activities into Siberia east of Lake Baikal.

By contrast with Japan, the prestige and self-confidence of Russia were lowered. Both her external and internal weaknesses had been exposed for all to see, particularly her own leaders and people. As a consequence, her international credit suffered and her diplomatic stature was diminished.[19] The insecurities which beset her encompassed the whole range of her foreign policy including her relations with France and her troublesome frontiers in Eastern Europe and in the Far East. In the years after the war, she sought and found security in ties with Great Britain and Japan, the relationship both these nations had eagerly sought before the war.

The changes in Japan and Russia were reflected in a new

[18] H.L. Boorman, et al., *Moscow-Peking Axis: Strengths and Strains*, New York, 1957, p. 145; Harrison, *Peace or War East of Lake Baikal?*, Yokohama, 1910, pp. 127, 212, 228–229, 242; *M.C.R.*, Mar. 1904, p. 818; R. Rupen, "Mongolian Nationalism," *Journal of the Royal Central Asian Society*, XLV, Pt. II, Apr. 1958, p. 173; Unterberger, *op.cit.*, pp. 343–344.

[19] Pavlovich, "Vneshniaia Politika i, Russo-Iaponskaya Voina," *op.cit.*, p. 224; A. Tardieu, *France and the Alliances*, New York, 1908, pp. 223–240.

relationship between the two countries. Japan was now a far more significant rival than before the war. Her energetic developmental program had been projected into Korea and Manchuria where commercial advance was shown in the rapid rise of Dairen to the detriment of Vladivostok. At the same time, Russia's difficulty in marshalling her strength on a distant frontier was remedied only slowly and incompletely by double-tracking the Siberian railway, by building of the Amur line and by entrenching herself more firmly in the railway zone of Manchuria. Even though this rivalry continued, after 1907 the two formed a solid front against other competitors, particularly China and the United States.

The Japanese victory also made a significant impact on Asia and the rest of the world. The people of Asia were impressed with Japan's success in wielding military and political power to the detriment of an Occidental nation. Furthermore, Japan's forceful challenge to Russian expansion had already been responsible for major changes in the power configuration of Europe itself. By the time the First World War broke out, Japan would be a full-fledged member of the European alliance system.

The Russo-Japanese war had also written another chapter in the history of sea power which the world could read with profit.[20] In the first place, it had emphasized its limitations. Had Russia been ready and able to engage Japan's armies after the halt at Mukden, how would sea power have operated to save the situation? In fact, of course, this did not occur and Japan had survived the test of battle to become one of the principal naval powers of the world. To the United States she was to become more troublesome in this respect than Germany had been.

Finally, Roosevelt's role in helping to create this situation became a factor of major consequence. Those who praised him for it did so to a great extent on the grounds that he had performed a humanitarian act by stopping the war.[21] Messages of congratulations were received from the Emperors of Japan and Russia and many others. He received the Nobel Peace Prize as well as a gift from the French Parliamentary Group of International Arbitration and Conciliation of the *Memoires*

---

[20] R. Machray, "The Collapse of Russia: v Great Britain, Germany, and Sea Power," *The Nineteenth Century and After*, LVIII, 341, July 1905, pp. 51–52.

[21] Beale, *op.cit.*, p. 307; Bishop, *op.cit.*, I, 413–423.

of the Duke of Sully which contained a project for international peace under the name of "Great Design of Henry IV."

Some of Roosevelt's critics, on the other hand, accused him of being instrumental in stopping the war too soon.[22] Mark Twain, Frank Cobb of the *New York World,* and the Minneapolis Norwegian journal *Vor Tid,* held that this had unfortunately saved Russia from defeat. Others, such as John Hays Hammond, General Leonard Wood, and Professor John W. Burgess of Columbia University, felt that this had been unduly helpful to Japan. There were others who asserted that Roosevelt should have insisted upon a place at the conference table for both China and Korea.

In fact, it is clear that the best Roosevelt could hope for was that a balance of power might be struck. He was in no position to do any more than persuade the principals to accept a course of action in which they could see some advantages. His reasons and arguments had to appeal to them both. With all his endeavors to avoid the indemnity and Sakhalin issues nothing was done about them until Japan and Russia decided, for reasons of their own, to act. To have imagined that it lay within his power to rescue China or Korea from the consequences of the war or to give them a place at the conference table would, to say the least, have been an overestimation of his role.

In view of the rapid deterioration of American-Japanese relations after the Portsmouth Conference, what can be said of President Roosevelt's success as a mediator? Could he have pursued any other course which would have given greater assurances of solidarity with Japan after the war? Under the circumstances, it is difficult to see more than three choices open to the United States: active support of the objectives of either Japan or Russia in the hope that this might help to support the open door; passive acquiescence in the outcome of the struggle in the hope that good will or a balance of power might leave American interests unharmed; or active military intervention in support of American interests against one of the principals.

Since Roosevelt, like most others in Washington who knew the situation, was cognizant of the impossibility of using mili-

---

[22] Beale, *op.cit.,* pp. 311–312, 459; J. Bigelow, *Peace Given as the World Giveth or the Portsmouth Treaty and Its First Year's Fruits,* New York, 1907, pp. 3-10, 17; "Roosevelt as Russia's Helper," *The American Monthly Review of Reviews,* xxxii, 4, Oct. 1905, p. 475.

tary force to support a strong policy, some form of acquiescence seemed the only alternative. In the prevailing outlook of the times, a decision in favor of active moral support of Japan appeared to be the most promising course. One might even say that any other choice would have been even worse for American interests than the one made. In any case, the policy of "balanced antagonisms" was undoubtedly as trustworthy as any system which has to be based on an accommodation between the conflicting national interests of other independent and ambitious powers.

APPENDICES

APPENDIX 1

Russo-Japanese Diplomatic Exchanges 1901–1904

A. Exchanges during the mission to St. Petersburg of Viscount Ito Hirobumi:[1]

Japanese proposals

1. Mutual guaranteee of the independence of Korea.

2. Mutual undertaking not to use any part of Korean territory for strategic purposes against one another.

3. Mutual undertaking not to resort to any military measures along the Korean coast which could endanger free passage through the Korean strait.

4. Recognition by Russia of freedom of action for Japan in Korea in regard to political, industrial, and commercial affairs, and the exclusive right of Japan to help Korea by advice and assistance in carrying out the obligations of well organized governments, including military activities necessary for suppressing uprisings and other disorders that would obstruct peaceful relations between Japan and Russia.

5. The present agreement replaces all preceding ones.

Russian counterproposals

1. Mutual guarantee of the independence of Korea.

2. Mutual undertaking (or Japan undertakes) not to use any part of Korean territory for strategic purposes.

3. Mutual undertaking (or Japan undertakes) not to resort to any military measures along the Korean coast which would endanger free passage through the Korean strait.

4. Recognition by Russia of freedom of action for Japan in Korea in regard to industry and commerce, and likewise sole preferential right by preliminary agreement with Russia, to help Korea with advisors in order to help her fulfill the obligations of a well-ordered state, such help to include those military matters necessary to suppress uprisings and other disorders that would obstruct peaceful relations between Japan and Russia.

5. Japan undertakes, in the case of the last preceding point, to send to Korea only the most necessary numbers of troops and to withdraw them as soon as they have fulfilled their duty. It is further stipulated that the Japanese forces shall in no case penetrate into a zone on the Russian frontier to be defined.

6. On the other side, Japan recognizes the predominant right of Russia in all border regions of the Chinese Empire along the Russian frontier and undertakes not to interfere with Russia's freedom of action in these regions.

7. The present agreement replaces all preceding ones.

[1] K.A., LXIII, 46; Hori, *op.cit.*, pp. 49–50.

B. Japanese proposals made to Russia in 1902:[2]

August proposals

1. Mutual guarantee of the independence and territorial integrity of the two empires of China and Korea.

2. Mutual guarantee not to use any part of Korean territory for military or strategic purposes.

3. Recognizing the preponderance of Japan's interests in Korea, Russia guarantees not to interfere either with the affairs of Korea or with the actions of Japan affecting the peaceful interests of that country and to recognize specifically the following rights of Japan to be exercised in the Korean Empire:

A. Freedom of action in promoting commercial and industrial interests.

B. Giving advice and help to Korea in fulfilling the obligations of a good government.

C. Dispatching such numbers of troops as may be necessary when rebellion or any internal disorders threaten the peaceful relationship of Japan with Korea, with the understanding that they are to be withdrawn immediately upon the accomplishment of the mission.

D. Maintenance of the guard and police forces already established to protect the telegraph and railway lines.

4. Japan will recognize formally the leased concession to Port Arthur and Talienwan as communicated by Russia to the Japanese government in 1898, as well as Russian freedom of action in protecting her railway rights and interests in Manchuria.

November proposals

1. A declaration of support for the principles of the territorial integrity of China and Korea and of equal opportunity with respect to them in commercial and industrial enterprises for all nations.

2. Both Japan and Russia will recognize their existing rights in Korea and Manchuria and may take measures necessary to protect these.

3. In the protection of these rights, Japan and Russia recognize their mutual right to send troops to suppress any local disturbance that might lead to international complications.

4. Russia recognizes the exclusive right of Japan to give advice and assistance, including military assistance, for the purpose of carrying out reforms in the Korean government.

[2] Kurino to Russian Foreign Minister, Aug. 4, 1902, *Obzor*, p. 78; *K.G.*, I, 298–299.

5. All existing arrangements between Japan and Russia concerning Korea are hereby terminated and no longer binding.

5. Russia will not object to connecting a Korean railway with the Chinese Eastern Railway and the Newchwang Railway.

C. Exchanges between August 1903 and February 1904:

I. THE FIRST EXCHANGE:[3]

Japanese proposals of August 12, 1903

1. Mutual engagement to respect the independence and territorial integrity of the Chinese and Korean empires and to support in these countries the principle of the equality of rights of all nations in commercial and industrial relations.

2. Mutual recognition of the dominant interests of Japan in Korea and those special interests of Russia in railway enterprises in Manchuria and of the right of Japan in Korea and of Russia in Manchuria to take measures necessary to maintain their respective interests as defined above, subject, however, to the reservations noted in Article I of the present agreement.

3. Mutual undertaking on the part of both Russia and Japan not to obstruct the development of those industrial and commercial enterprises of Japan in Korea and of Russia in Manchuria which are not inconsistent with the stipulations of Article I of this agreement.

A supplementary undertaking by Russia not to oppose the possible projection of the Korean railway into South Manchuria and its juncture there with the Chinese Eastern and Shanhaikwan-Newchwang railways.

4. Mutual recognition that should it be found necessary for Japan to send troops to Korea or for Russia to send troops to Manchuria either

Russian counterproposals of October 3, 1903

1. Mutual engagement to respect the independence and territorial integrity of the Korean Empire.

2. Recognition by Russia of Japan's preponderating interests in Korea and of the right of Japan to give advice and assistance to Korea tending to improve the civil administration of the Empire without infringing the stipulations of Article I.

3. Engagement on the part of Russia not to impede the commercial and industrial undertakings of Japan in Korea, nor to oppose any measures taken in order to protect them so long as such measures do not infringe upon the stipulations of Article I.

4. Recognition of the right of Japan to send for the same purpose troops to Korea, with the knowledge of Russia, but their number shall not

---

[3] *R.-I.V.*, pp. 159–160; *K.G.*, I, 334–335; Komura to Kurino, Oct. 5, 1903, *N.G.M.*, XXXVI-I, 22–23; *Correspondence*, pp. 22–24; *Obzor*, pp. 22–28.

to protect the interests defined in Article II or to suppress any insurrection or disorder capable of causing international complications, the number of troops sent shall not exceed the number actually required, and the forces shall be withdrawn as soon as the mission for which they were sent shall have been accomplished.

5. Recognition on the part of Russia of the exclusive right of Japan to give advice in the interest of reform and good government in Korea, including necessary military assistance.

exceed that actually required and Japan shall engage to recall such troops as soon as their mission is accomplished.

5. Mutual engagement not to use any part of the territory of Korea for strategic purposes nor to undertake on the coast of Korea any military works capable of menacing the freedom of navigation in the Straits of Korea.

6. Mutual engagement to consider that part of the territory of Korea lying to the north of the 39th parallel as a neutral zone into which neither of the contracting parties shall introduce troops.

7. Recognition by Japan of Manchuria and its littorals as in all respects outside her sphere of interest.

6. This agreement to supercede all previous ones concluded between Japan and Russia concerning Korea.

8. This agreement to supercede all previous ones concluded between Russia and Japan concerning Korea.

II. THE SECOND EXCHANGE:[4]

Japanese proposals of October 30, 1903

1. Mutual engagement to respect the independence and territorial integrity of the Chinese and Korean empires.

2. Recognition by Russia of Japan's preponderating interests in Korea and of the right of Japan to give to

Russian counterproposals of December 11, 1903

1. Mutual engagement to respect the independence and territorial integrity of the Korean Empire.

2. Recognition by Russia of Japan's preponderating interests in Korea and of the right of Japan to assist

[4] *Correspondence,* pp. 28–29, 41–42; *K.G.,* I, 340–341, 344–345, *N.G.M.,* xxxvi-i, 27–28, 36.

Korea advice and assistance, including military assistance, tending to improve the administration of the Korean Empire.

3. Engagement on the part of Russia not to impede the development of the commercial and industrial activities of Japan in Korea, nor to oppose any measures taken for the purpose of protecting those interests.

4. Recognition by Russia of the right of Japan to send troops to Korea for the purpose mentioned in the preceding article or for the purpose of suppressing insurrection or disorder capable of creating international complications.

5. Engagement on the part of Japan not to establish on the coasts of Korea any military works which might menace the freedom of navigation in the Korean Strait.

6. Mutual engagement to establish a neutral zone on the Korean-Manchurian frontier extending 50 kilometers on each side, into which neutral zone neither of the contracting parties shall introduce troops without the consent of the other.

7. Recognition by Japan that Manchuria is outside her sphere of special interest and recognition by Russia that Korea is outside her sphere of special interest.

8. Recognition by Japan of Russia's special interests in Manchuria and of the right of Russia to take such measures as may be necessary for the protection of those interests.

9. Engagement on the part of Japan not to interfere with the commercial and residential rights and immunities belonging to Russia by virtue of her treaty engagements with Korea and engagement on the part of Russia not to interfere with the

Korea with advice tending to improve the civil administration.

3. Engagement on the part of Russia not to oppose the development of the industrial and commercial activities of Japan in Korea, nor the adoption of measures for the protection of those interests.

4. Recognition by Russia of the right of Japan to send troops to Korea for the purpose mentioned in the preceding article or for the purpose of suppressing insurrections or disorders capable of creating international complications.

5. Mutual engagement not to make use of any part of Korean territory for strategic purposes and not to establish on the Korean coast any military works which might menace the freedom of navigation in the Korean Strait.

6. Mutual engagement to consider the territory north of the 39th parallel as a neutral zone, within the limits of which neither of the contracting parties shall introduce troops.

commercial and residential rights and immunities belonging to Japan by virtue of her treaty engagements with China.

10. Mutual engagement not to impede the connection of the Korean railway with the Chinese Eastern Railway when those railways shall have been extended to the Yalu.

11. This agreement shall supplant all previous agreements between Japan and Russia regarding Korea.

7. Mutual engagement not to impede the connection of the Korean and Chinese Eastern railways when these railways shall have been extended to the Yalu.

8. Abrogation of all previous agreements between Russia and Japan regarding Korea.

III. THE THIRD EXCHANGE:[5]

Japanese proposals of December 21, 1903

The Imperial government have examined with great care and attention the new Russian counterproposals of the 11th instant. They regret to find that the Imperial Russian government did not see their way in those proposals to give to the compass of the suggested understanding the same territorial extension as was deemed essential by Japan. The Imperial government, in their original invitation to the Imperial Russian government in August last, endeavored to make it entirely clear that they desired, with a view to removing from their relations with the Imperial Russian government every cause for future misunderstanding, to bring within the purview of the proposed arrangement all those regions in the Far East where the interests of the two empires meet, and they cannot bring themselves to the conviction that a full realization of that desire can be expected if a large and important portion of those regions is wholly excluded from consideration. Accordingly, the Imperial government feel constrained to ask the Imperial Russian government to reconsider

Russian counterproposals of January 6, 1904

[5] Komura to Kurino, Dec. 21, 1903, Jan. 7, 1904, *Correspondence,* pp. 42–43, 46–47; *N.G.M.,* xxxvi-i, 36–37, xxxvii-i, 13–14; *K.G.,* i, 346, 349.

their position on the subject, and they hope that the Russian government will be able to see their way to arrive at a satisfactory solution to the question. The Imperial government also find it necessary to ask for the following amendments to the new Russian counterproposals:

1. Article 2 to read: Recognition by Russia of Japan's preponderating interests in Korea and of the right of Japan to give Korea advice and assistance tending to improve the administration of the Korean Empire.

2. Article 5 to read: Mutual engagement not to undertake on the Korean coast any military works capable of menacing the freedom of navigation in the Korean Strait, and

3. Article 6 to be suppressed.

As the principal parts of these amendments cannot be said to be in excess of the modifications which were agreed to *ad referendum* at Tokyo, and as the Imperial government consider those changes indispensable, it is hoped that they will receive the ready agreement of the Imperial Russian government.

Having no objection to the amendments to Article 2 of the Russian counterproposals as proposed by the Imperial Japanese government, the Imperial government considers it necessary:

1. To maintain the original wording of Article 5 which had already been agreed to by the Imperial Japanese government, that is to say, "mutual engagement not to use any part of the territory of Korea for strategic purposes, nor to undertake on the coasts of Korea any military works capable of menacing the freedom of navigation in the Korean Strait."

2. To maintain Article 6 concerning a neutral zone (this for the very purpose which the Imperial Japanese government has likewise in view, that is to say, to eliminate everything that might lead to misunderstandings in the future; a similar zone, for example, exists between the Russian and British possessions in Central Asia).

In case the above conditions are agreed to, the Imperial government would be prepared to include in the projected agreement an article of the following tenor:

"Recognition by Japan of Manchuria and her littoral as being outside her sphere of interests, while Russia within the limits of that province, will not impede Japan, nor other powers in the enjoyment of the rights and privileges acquired by them under existing treaties with China, exclusive of the establishment of settlements."

IV. THE FOURTH EXCHANGE:

Japanese proposals of
January 13, 1904[6]

The Imperial Government, in order to arrive at a pacific solution of the pending questions, and to firmly establish the basis of good relations between Japan and Russia, and in addition with a view to protect the rights and interests of Japan, have given most careful and serious consideration to the reply of the Imperial Russian Government which was delivered by His Excellency Baron Rosen of the 6th instant. They have finally come to the conclusion that the following modifications are necessary, *i.e.*:

1. Suppression of the first clause of Article 5 of the Russian Counterproposals (presented to the Japanese Government through Baron Rosen December 11th), that is to say, "not to use any part of Korean territory for strategical purposes."
2. Suppressing of the whole Article (6) concerning establishment of a neutral zone.

Russian counterproposals of
February 3, 1904[7]

(As transmitted to Admiral Alekseiev)

1. Mutual guarantee to respect the independence and territorial integrity of the Korean Empire.
2. Recognition by Russia of the predominant interests of Japan in Korea and the right of Japan to give Korea advice and help directed toward regulating the administration of the Korean Empire.
3. A guarantee by Russia not to interfere with the development of the industrial and commercial activity of Japan in Korea or with the right of Japan to take measures for protecting these interests.
4. Recognition by Russia of the right of Japan to send troops to Korea for the purposes stated in the preceding article, and for the suppression of uprisings or disturbances which might lead to international complications.
5. Mutual guarantee not to use any part of Korean territory for strategic purposes, and not to take any military measures with reference to the Korean coast capable of threatening the freedom of navigation in the Korean Strait.

[6] *K.G.*, I, 252–253; Komura to Kurino, Jan. 13, 1904, *N.G.M.*, xxxvii-i, 32–34; same in *Correspondence*, pp. 47–49.
[7] Lamsdorf to Alekseiev, Feb. 3, 1904, *Obzor*, p. 86, and *R.-I.V.*, pp., 51–52.

3. The Russian proposals concerning Manchuria to be agreed to with the following modifications:

A. Recognition by Japan of Manchuria and its littoral as being outside her sphere of interest and an engagement on the part of Russia to respect the territorial integrity of China in Manchuria.

B. Russia within the limits of Manchuria will not impede either Japan or other powers in the enjoyment of rights and privileges acquired by them under the existing treaties with China.

C. Recognition by Russia that Korea is outside her sphere of interest.

4. Addition of an article to the following effect:

Recognition by Japan of Russia's special interests in Manchuria and of the right of Russia to take measures for the protection of those interests.

The grounds for these amendments having been frequently and fully explained on previous occasions, the Imperial Government do not think it necessary to repeat the explanations. It is sufficient here to express their earnest hope for reconsideration by the Imperial Russian Government.

It should be further remarked that the suppression of the clause excluding the establishment of settlements in Manchuria is desired because it conflicts with stipulations of the new commercial treaty between Japan and China. In this respect, however, Japan will be satisfied if she receives equal treatment with another power which has already acquired similar rights in regard to settlements in Manchuria. The statement in the Russian reply that the Japanese government have agreed to the original wording of Article 5 of the Russian counterpro-

6. Russia will respect all rights and privileges obtained by Japan as well as other powers by treaty with China, while Japan on her part will recognize Manchuria as outside her sphere of interest.

7. Mutual guarantee not to prevent the joining of the Korean and Chinese Eastern railways when these railways reach the Yalu.

8. Abrogation of all previous agreements between Russia and Japan.

posals is erroneous, no such agreement ever having been expressed by
the Imperial Government.

The above-mentioned amendments
being proposed by the Imperial
Government entirely in the spirit of
conciliation, it is expected that they
will be received with the same spirit
at the hands of the Imperial Russian
Government; and the Imperial Government further hope for an early
reply from the Imperial Russian
Government, since further delay in
the solution of the question will be
extremely disadvantageous to the
two countries.

APPENDIX 2

Issues Discussed at the Portsmouth and Peking Conferences

A. The Russo-Japanese issues discussed at the Portsmouth Conference:[1]

Japanese peace conditions presented August 10, 1905

1. Russia, acknowledging that Japan possesses in Korea paramount political, military and economical interests, to engage not to obstruct or interfere with any measures of guidance, protection and control which Japan finds it necessary to take in Korea.

Russian counterproposals presented August 12, 1905

1. Article 1 does not give rise to any objection. The Imperial government, recognizing that Japan possesses in Korea preponderant political, military and economic interests, are ready to engage neither to obstruct nor interfere with the measures of direction, protection, and control which Japan may consider it necessary to take in Korea. It is a matter of course that Russia and Russian subjects will enjoy all rights which belong or will belong to other foreign Powers and their subjects or citizens. Also it is understood that the execution by Japan of the above-mentioned measures will not impair the sovereign rights of the Emperor of Korea. In that which concerns particularly military measures Japan, in order to remove all causes of misunderstanding, will abstain from taking measures which might threaten the security of the Russian territory bordering upon Korea.

2. Engagement on the part of Russia to evacuate Manchuria completely within a period to be specified and to relinquish all territorial advantages and all preferential and exclusive concessions and franchises in that region in impairment of Chinese sovereignty or inconsistent with the principle of equal opportunity.

2. The Imperial government are ready to accept the first part of this article and are disposed to withdraw their troops from Manchuria simultaneously with the withdrawal of the Japanese troops. The details and terms of the evacuation might be decided afterwards. As to the last part of this article, the Imperial government are ready to declare that they have no claims to territorial privileges, exclusive concessions, or facilities of such a nature as to menace the sovereign rights

[1] *Protocols*, pp. 5–6, 13–15.

of the Empire of China or to be incompatible with the principle of equality of rights. The Imperial government are disposed to give in that respect the necessary guarantees. This fundamental principle once established, the plenipotentiaries of Russia propose to the plenipotentiaries of Japan to make precise the desire of the Japanese government regarding this part of Article 2 and they declare that the Imperial government are disposed to eliminate everything likely to bring prejudice to the interests of Japan or other Powers. The only Russian private enterprise in Manchuria having a public character is the Chinese Eastern Railway. The examination of the question connected with this railway is especially dealt with in other articles.

3. Japan shall engage to restore to China, subject to the guarantees of reform and improved administration, all portions of Manchuria which are in her occupation, saving only the regions affected by the lease of the Liao-tung Peninsula.

3. The Imperial government are ready to accept this article but it is a matter of course that Russia and Russian subjects conserve in these portions of Manchuria all rights which belong or will belong in those regions to other foreign Powers and their subjects or citizens. As to the regions affected by the lease of the Liao-tung Peninsula, Russia is disposed to cede to Japan her rights in the regions in question. However, considering the sovereign rights of China in those regions and the treaties concluded with the Chinese government on the subject, such cession cannot be made otherwise than by virtue of an understanding with the latter.

4. Japan and Russia reciprocally to engage not to obstruct any general measures common to all countries which China may take for the development of the commerce and industries in Manchuria.

4. Acceding entirely to the principles laid down in this article the Imperial government declare that if this stipulation had not been inserted in the conditions proposed by Japan, Russia would have deemed it her duty to propose it herself.

5. Sakhalin and all islands appertaining thereto and all public works and properties are to be ceded to Japan.

5. The ancient rights of Russia on the Island of Sakhalin existed already at an epoch when Japan did not possess or at least did not exercise any rights of proprietorship on the greater part of the island; on the other hand, Sakhalin is only the natural continuation of the Russian possessions in Asia, as it is separated from the continent by a very shallow strait only 7 versts wide. Owing to these considerations, Russia would be unable to consent to a cession of this island, but she is at the same time quite disposed to grant to Japan the rights of wide exploitation of sea fisheries and other commercial enterprises in the island. The conditions of such exploitation can be made the subject of a special arrangement.

6. The lease of Port Arthur, Talien and adjacent territory and territorial waters together with all rights, privileges, concessions and franchises acquired by Russia from China, in connection with or as a part of such lease and all public works and properties to be transferred and assigned to Japan.

6. The Imperial government would have no objection to this article; but considering the sovereign rights of China on the territories specified, Russia could not cede her rights to Japan without a previous agreement with China. It is a matter of course that the rights of private individuals in the whole region affected by the lease concluded between Russia and China should remain intact.

7. Russia to assign and transfer to Japan free of all claims and encumbrances, the railway between Harbin and Port Arthur and all its branches together with all rights, privileges and properties appertaining thereto, and all coal mines belonging to or worked for the benefit of the railway.

7. The Imperial government accept in principle this article, on condition, however, that they are to part with only that portion of the railway which is at present occupied in fact by Japanese troops. The terminal station of the portion to be ceded under these conditions should be determined by common accord. It is, however, indispensable to keep in view that it is to a private company that the concession for construction and operation of the line was granted by China which conserves the sovereign rights in respect thereto and that military occupation

should not in any way impair the rights of that company. The Imperial government of Russia are ready to undertake to arrange with the said company while authorizing the Chinese government to exercise from this moment the right to purchase the line in question. The purchase-money accuring to the company would be ceded to Japan.

8. Russia to retain and work the Trans-Manchurian railway, subject to the terms and conditions of the concession under which it was constructed, and subject also to the condition that it is to be employed exclusively for commercial and industrial purposes.

8. This article raises no objection. The Railway Company will strictly conform—concerning the exploitation of the main line as well as that portion of the South Manchurian branch which will remain in its possession—to the terms of the Act of Concession of August 27th (September 8th), paragraph 8 of which stipulates that Russian troops and war materials which are transported by the line shall make no stop in Chinese territory.

9. Russia to reimburse to Japan the actual expenses of the war. The amount as well as the time and manner of such reimbursement to be agreed upon.

9. Russia is unable to consent to the stipulations contained in this article. Only vanquished countries reimburse expenses of war, but Russia is not vanquished. A country would be unable to recognize itself as such, while its territory has hardly been attacked by the enemy. Even if Japan had taken the whole of the Maritime Provinces of Amur, the vital force of Russia would be in nowise impaired, and she will continue the struggle. Only when victorious Japanese armies had invaded the territory of Russia, would the nation understand that the question of reimbursement of war expenses could be brought forth. The plenipotentiaries of Russia believe it to be their duty to call the attention of the plenipotentiaries of Japan to the fact that, even at the Congress of Paris which took place after the fall of Sevastopol, the allies did not think it possible to raise the question of

reimbursement of war expenses. Such expenses are reimbursed only by countries which have no longer the means of continuing war. Such is in no way the case with Russia. While refusing to reimburse the war expenses, the Imperial government will recognize as equitable to indemnify Japan for such expenses as she may have incurred, not for the war itself and to the prejudice of Russia, but for the welfare of those Russians who suffered from the act of war, such as expenses for the maintenance of prisoners of war, and for the care of the sick and other persons.

10. All Russian ships of war which, in consequence of damage received in battle, sought asylum in neutral ports and were there interned, to be surrendered to Japan as lawful prizes.

10. Russia is unable to consent to this demand. It appears difficult to find out, in the practice of international relations, precedents which serve to support such a demand. Besides, this demand is hardly in accord with the pacific intentions with which the two negotiating parties are animated. The material advantages to be acquired by Japan, if Russian vessels remaining in neutral ports should be assigned to her, would be comparatively very slight. Moreover, the consent to such a clause would be incompatible with the dignity of Russia.

11. Russia to engage to limit her naval strength in the waters of the Extreme East.

11. Russia is unable to consent to such an engagement imposed by a foreign Power, because it would be equally incompatible with her dignity. The Imperial government believe themselves, however, to be in a position to declare that it is not in their mind to keep in the near future any considerable naval forces in the waters of the Pacific.

12. Russia to grant to Japanese subjects full fishery rights along the coasts and in the bays, harbors, inlets and rivers of her possessions in the Japan, Okhotsk and Behring Seas.

12. Russia will be ready to arrange with Japan for granting to Japanese subjects rights of fishery on the coasts of the Japan, Okhotsk and Behring Seas. These rights, however, can only be extended to the coasts

of those seas themselves without touching inlets and rivers. It is a matter of course that the rights already appertaining in that region to Russian or foreign subjects will remain in force.

B. The Sino-Japanese issues discussed at the Peking Conference:[2]

The Japanese demands

1. At the time fixed in Article III of the Russo-Japanese peace for the withdrawal of the military forces of Russia and Japan from Manchuria, the Chinese government shall immediately establish the administrative organs necessary to preserve peace and order in the areas from which the withdrawals have been made.

2. The Chinese government shall establish an effective administration in Manchuria and shall undertake administrative reforms in that area with the object of giving suitable and effective protection to the lives and property of foreign residents there.

3. The Chinese government shall take all measures necessary to afford complete protection for the graves of the Japanese military forces who died in Manchuria and for the war memorial erected there for them.

4. The Chinese government shall under no guise whatsoever, without the approval of Japan, alienate any part of Manchuria to another country or permit occupation by another country.

5. The Chinese government shall open the following cities in Manchuria to foreigners for commerce, industry, and residence under the same conditions as pertain to open markets elsewhere in China:

In Shengching [Fengtien] province: Fenghuangcheng, Liaoyang,

The Chinese counterproposals

1. Articles 1, 2, 4, and 10 of the principal Japanese demands are to be eliminated.

2. Articles 3 and 11 are approved.

3. Article 5 is to be changed to state that China will herself open the various places named in the article, and the details concerning the opening shall be decided by the Chinese government.

[2] *M.K.N.K.D.H.*, pp. 15, 206, 208; *K.G.*, II, 223–227.

Hsinmintun, Tiehling, Tungchi-angtze, Fakumen.

In Kirin province: Changchun (Kuanchengtze), Kirin, Harbin, Ninguta (or Ninganfu), Hunchun, Sanhsing.

In Heilungchiang province: Tsit-shihar, Hailar, Aigun, Manchuli.

6. The Chinese government shall agree to all the concessions made by Russia to Japan in Articles V and VI of the Russo-Japanese peace treaty.

4. Regarding Article 6, it concerns an important article [of the Portsmouth treaty] and in this agreement shall be given special consideration; the following revision is proposed:

The Chinese government will approve the cessions made by Russia to Japan in Articles V and VI of the Russo-Japanese agreement on the following conditions:

A. The Chinese government will accept the transfer and lease to Japan of the Port Arthur and Talien-wan [Dairen] region which was leased to Russia.

B. An area is to be set aside as a commercial center for the various nations and Dairen is to be entirely converted into a commercial center and a customs house is to be established by China. Legal causes of Japanese residents of the leased territory against Chinese are to be heard by a mixed Sino-Japanese court. Chinchoucheng and the neutral zone in the northern sector of the Port Arthur-Dairen leased territory are to be under Chinese jurisdiction as before.

C. Since the lease agreement concluded between China and Russia was for 25 years, Russia has already reduced it and only 18 years of the lease remain.

D. Port Arthur shall be a naval port to be used jointly by Japan and China and special regulations established for its use.

E. The Japanese government shall recognize that Chinese sovereignty in the leased territory is absolutely not to be infringed and the title of military governor general is not to be used.

F. Japanese military forces stationed within the leased territory are not to be sent outside of it without the permission of China.

G. A special agreement shall be concluded on the basis of the Sino-Russian lease agreement.

H. The Chinese government will approve the transfer to Japan of the Changchun (Kuanchengtze)-Port Arthur railway and the rights pertaining thereto which have been granted to Russia.

All rights enjoyed by China in accordance with the Chinese Eastern Railway agreement concluded between China and Russia shall remain in force. However, regulations pertaining to joint management and control by China and Japan shall be elaborated in a separate agreement and the number of years during which Russia has enjoyed the use of the railway shall be subtracted from the total required by agreement to elapse before China may take possession of the railway.

I. When it is decided by Japan and Russia to consider, under Article VIII of the Russo-Japanese peace treaty, the establishment of a connection between their respective sectors of the railway, the Chinese government shall participate officially.

7. The Chinese government shall agree to the maintenance and use by Japan of the railways constructed between Antunghsien and Mukden and between Mukden and Hsinmintun; the Chinese government has no objection to the extension in the

5. Article 7 shall be revised as follows:

A. At the expiration of a five-year period from the signing of this agreement, during which the Japanese government shall have the use of it, the Mukden-Antung railway

future of the Changchun-Port Arthur line to Kirin.

8. The Chinese government shall grant to Japan the right to cut timber in a specified zone of the Yalu River valley along the Korean frontier.

9. The Chinese government shall agree to freedom of navigation on the Liao, Yalu, and Sungari rivers and their tributaries.

10. The Chinese government shall grant to Japanese subjects fishing rights on the coast of Shengching [Fengtien] province.

11. Most-favored-nation treatment shall be mutually granted for commerce on the Manchuria-Korea frontier.

shall be either completely removed or sold to China.

B. The Mukden-Hsinmintun railway shall at this time be transferred to the Chinese government with suitable compensation.

C. The Changchun-Kirin railway shall be built by China alone, and in case foreign capital is used, application for this shall be made first to the Japanese government.

D. Since the Tashihchiao-Kuanko line was constructed as a temporary line to aid in the building of the mainline, it shall, in accordance with the existing agreement, be removed.

6. With respect to Article 8, Japan and China shall establish a joint company which shall demarcate the timber areas and the Chinese and Japanese shareholders shall have complete equality of rights in the company; the details concerning the establishment and management of other companies shall be determined in a separate agreement.

7. Regarding navigation on the Liao, Yalu, and Sungari rivers mentioned in Article 9, the Chinese regulations for internal river navigation shall apply.

In addition to these basic conditions, each government made supplementary proposals.

The Japanese proposals

1. In order to promote and facilitate communications and transportation, the Japanese and Chinese governments shall, as soon as possible, conclude a special treaty which shall

The Chinese proposals

1. Within one year after the signing of the peace treaty, all Japanese forces are to be withdrawn from Manchuria; China shall send troops to protect the railway and their

establish regulations for connecting the South Manchurian Railway and the railways of China.

2. Because of the need to guarantee the advantages of railways in South Manchuria, the Japanese and Chinese governments shall consult beforehand regarding the construction of railways in that area.

3. The Chinese government acknowledges the Japanese telegraph establishments along the Port Arthur-Chefoo and Niuchiatun-Yinkow railways; and hereby approves the addition of a line along the telegraph poles of the Chinese line from Yinkow to Peking.

4. Materials needed for the South Manchuria Railway as well as supplies for the railway guard detachment shall be exempt from all kinds of taxes and likin.

5. In order to promote the development of agriculture and commerce in Manchuria, the Chinese government shall permit the export of various cereals from that region.

6. With respect to the agreements in the main treaty and the special treaty, the Chinese government shall accord to Japan the same treatment as the most-favored-nation.

number shall be in the proportion of five for every Chinese *li* (one third of a mile).

2. Japanese officials and other citizens shall return immediately lands and other public and private Chinese properties.

3. China may send suitable military forces to preserve order and tranquility even if Japanese troop withdrawal has not yet been completed.

4. Minerals belonging to the railways in Fengtien Province shall be the subject of a special agreement.

5. The question of the demarcation of the residential areas in the commercial centers in Fengtien Province already opened or opened by treaty shall be made by the local Chinese administration.

6. The Chinese regional officials formerly resident in Yinkow, shall immediately return to their posts and shall be completely free to exercise their accustomed official functions.

7. Taxes collected in Fengtien by the Japanese military administration shall be returned to the local Chinese administration and shall be used to defray the expenses of local reforms.

APPENDIX 3
Chronology

1875

May 7 Russo-Japanese Exchange Treaty

1891

May 31 Trans-Siberian Railway construction began

1892–1903

Sergei Iulievich Witte minister of finance

1895

Apr. 23 Three Power (Russia, Germany, France) intervention notes to Japan

Dec. 5 Russo-Chinese Bank organized

(late 1895) Japanese armament plan drawn up

1896

Grand Duke Aleksander Nikolaevich advocated military preparedness to match Japan

May 14 Weber-Komura agreement

June 9 Lobanov-Yamagata agreement

Sept. 8 Contract signed for construction and operation of Chinese Eastern Railway

Sept. 9 Briner concession (North Korea) signed

1897

Dec. Russia seized Port Arthur

1898

Mar. 12 Vonliarliarsky-Bezobrazov memorandum on use of Briner concession

Mar. 27 Russian lease to Kuantung Territory signed

Apr. 25 Rosen-Nishi agreement

Apr. 26 Sino-Japanese nonalienation agreement regarding Fukien Province

May 24 Briner concession option acquired under Imperial Russian patronage

1900

Mar. Admiral Alfred T. Mahan article on Russian threat

June 10 Boxers enter Peking in force; international force sent from Tientsin

June 18 East Asian Development Company (Bezobrazov) approved by Russian Emperor; Foreign Minister Muraviev note to Admiral Alekseiev regarding Russian policy in China

July 9 Russian military forces entered Manchuria

1900

July 14–17	Sino-Russian crisis around Blagoveshchensk
Aug. 4	Russian forces occupied Newchwang
Aug. 25	Russian government circular note regarding policy in China
Oct. 16	Anglo-German "Yangtze" agreement
Nov. 26	Tseng-Alekseiev agreement (Manchuria)

1901

Jan. 3	*Times* disclosure of Tseng-Alekseiev agreement
Jan. 7	Russia proposed neutralization of Korea to Japan
Feb. 8	Russia presented conditions to China for withdrawal from Manchuria
Feb. 28	Chinese edict asked support of the powers in opposing Russia
Apr. 6	Russian policy regarding China announced in *Journal de St. Petersbourg*
July	North-South railway service completed in Manchuria
Nov. 25	Ito reached St. Petersburg for negotiations

1902

Jan. 30	Anglo-Japanese Alliance signed
Feb. 2	East Asian Development Company dissolution forced by Witte
Feb.	United States protested Russo-Chinese Bank monopolization of Manchuria
Mar. 16, 20	Franco-Russian declarations in response to Anglo-Japanese Alliance
Mar. 17	Lvov's projected Sino-Russian lumber concession
Apr. 8	Sino-Russian agreement defining terms of military evacuation of Manchuria
June 28	Triple Alliance renewed
June 30	Franco-Italian agreement
July	Witte organized Manchurian Mining Company
Oct.	Witte visited Far East
Oct. 8	Completion of first stage of evacuation of Manchuria
Nov. 9	First Russian government conference at Yalta regarding Far Eastern problems
Nov.	Bezobrazov went to Manchuria

1903

Jan.	Bezobrazov granted 2,000,000 rubles for special use
Jan. 24	Second Russian government conference regarding Far Eastern problems
Feb. 7	Third Russian government conference regarding Far Eastern problems
Mar. 1	Kuropatkin and Russian Emperor discussed reenforcements for Manchuria
Apr. 1	Sino-Japanese timber company formed

1903

Apr.   8 Fourth Russian government conference regarding Far
          Eastern problems; second stage of evacuation of
          Manchuria not completed
Apr.   Bezobrazov returned from Manchuria
Apr. 18 Russia presented conditions to China for withdrawal
          from Manchuria
Apr. 19 Russian anti-Jewish pogrom at Kishinev
Apr. 22 China refused Russian conditions for withdrawal from
          Manchuria
Apr. 28 Kuropatkin departed for the Far East
May   15 Emperor's order to Alekseiev regarding reenforcement
          of Manchuria; Bezobrazov appointed state secretary
May   20 Fifth Russian government conference regarding Far
          Eastern problems
June 12 Kuropatkin reached Japan
June 13 Russian Lumber Company of the Far East (Bezobra-
          zov) organized
June 23 Japanese government conference regarding negotiations
          with Russia
June 29 Bezobrazov reached Port Arthur
June 30 Kuropatkin reached Port Arthur
July 1–10 Port Arthur conferences (16 sessions)
July 28 Japanese government sounded out Russian government
          regarding the opening of negotiations
July 31 Kurino conveyed *note verbale* to Lamsdorf
Aug. 12 Russo-Japanese negotiations opened with presentation
          of the first Japanese proposals; Viceroyalty of the Far
          East created
Aug. 14 Russian government conference regarding presenta-
          tion to China of conditions for evacuation of Man-
          churia
Aug. 23 Lamsdorf suggested moving the center of negotiations
          from St. Petersburg to Tokyo
Aug. 24 d'Amade report regarding Russian menace
Aug. 28 Witte dismissed as minister of finance
Sept. 6 Russia presented the five demands to China
Sept. 9 Komura accepted transfer of negotiations from St.
          Petersburg to Tokyo
Sept. 15 China refused the five Russian demands
Sept. 23 Rosen left Tokyo for conference at Port Arthur regard-
          ing Japanese demands
Oct.   3 Rosen returned to Tokyo, presented first Russian coun-
          terproposals to Komura
Oct.   4 Austro-Russian agreement
Oct.   8 Scheduled completion of Russian evacuation of Man-
          churia; failure to complete evacuation protested by
          Japanese socialists; Alekseiev held military review

1903

at Port Arthur; United States and Japan signed treaties with China which called for opening of towns in Manchuria (Mukden, Tatungko, and Antung)

(late) Oct.   Lamsdorf visited Paris

Oct. 30   Second Japanese proposals presented to Russian government

Dec. 11   Second Russian counterproposals presented to Japanese government

Dec. 21   Third Japanese proposals presented to Russian government

Dec. 26   Alekksiev message to Emperor views situation as hopeless

Dec. 28   Russian government conference regarding the negotiations

Dec.   Japanese government asked for British loan

1904

Jan. 6   Third Russian counterproposals presented to Japanese government

Jan. 12   Japanese government conference regarding negotiations and war

Jan. 13   Fourth Japanese proposals presented to Russian government

Jan. 21   Korean appeal for recognition of a neutral status

Jan. 22   Komura announced to Japanese diplomats that last proposals are to be considered an irreducible minimum

Jan. 28   Russian government conference regarding the negotiations

Feb. 2   Russian Emperor approved final counterproposals

Feb. 3   Fourth Russian counterproposals transmitted to Alekseive

Feb. 4–5   Fourth Russian counterproposals transmitted to Japan

Feb. 4   Japanese government conference approved breaking off negotiations; Ito and Kaneko confer regarding Kaneko mission to the United States

Feb. 6   Japanese Combined Fleet departed Sasebo naval base

Feb. 7   Fourth Russian counterproposals may have reached Rosen in Tokyo

Feb. 8   Japanese fleets reached Chemulpo (Inchon) and Port Arthur

Feb. 10   Japanese declaration of war

Feb. 11   Rosen departed Tokyo; Kurino departed St. Petersburg

Feb. 12   Chinese declaration of neutrality

Feb. 17   Ito mission to Seoul

Feb. 18, 22   Russian declarations labeling Japanese attack treacherous

1904

Feb. 22, Mar. 2	Japanese defense of attack procedure
Feb. 23	Japanese-Korean protocol regarding control in Korea
Mar. 26	First Kaneko meeting with Roosevelt in Washington
Apr.	Battle of Yalu
Apr. 8	Anglo-French Entente formed
May 5	Japanese forces land in northern Kuantung peninsula
May 11, 12	First Japanese foreign war loans
May 31	Japanese government formulated Korean policy
July	Japanese government approved first peace conditions; first peace efforts made
July 28	Russo-German commercial agreement renewed; Plehve assassinated
Aug. 20	Nogi began first general assault on Port Arthur
Aug. 22	Japanese-Korean treaty
Aug. 24	Battle of Liaoyang began; Russian government decision to send Baltic fleet to Pacific
Sept. 30–Oct. 8	Conference of Russian opposition groups at Paris
Oct. 4	Battle of Shaho began
Oct. 15	Austro-Russian agreement
Oct. 21–22	Dogger Bank incident
Oct. 26	Russian fleet bottled up at Vigo harbor
Oct. 28	Anglo-Russian war crisis ended
Nov.	Second Japanese foreign war loan
Dec. 22–Feb. 25 (1905)	International commission on Dogger Bank incident met in Paris

1905

Jan. 1	Stessel prepared to surrender Port Arthur
Jan.	Seoul-Fusan railway line completed
Jan. 16	Strike at Putilov Works in St. Petersburg
Jan. 22	Bloody Sunday
(early) Feb.	New rural disturbances began in Russia
Feb. 25	International commission on Dogger Bank issue completed work
Mar. 1	E. Noetzlin of Banc de Paris reached St. Petersburg, loan negotiation unsuccessful
Mar. 9	Russian ambassador in London paid 65,000 pounds for Dogger Bank claim
Mar. 10	Battle of Mukden concluded
Mar. 13	Oyama notified Imperial Headquarters of difficulty of continuing war
Mar. 16	First units of Russian fleet reach Madagascar
Mar. 20	Secretary of War Taft entered Roosevelt-Kaneko discussions instead of Hay; Roosevelt broached peace plans
Mar. 24	Third Japanese foreign war loan
Mar. 31	German Emperor landed at Tangier

1905

Apr.	1	Japanese-Korean treaty
Apr.	8	Japanese government approved general principles of peace terms
Apr.	12	Meyer audience with Russian Emperor regarding Roosevelt peace proposal
Apr.	21	Japanese government approved peace terms
Apr.	25	Japanese government made preliminary proposal of Roosevelt mediation
May 27–28		Battle of Tsushima
May	31	Japanese government formally requested Roosevelt mediation
June	3	Russian Zemstvo sixth national congress
June	6	Conference of Russian military leaders with Emperor; Meyer audience with Emperor; Roosevelt announced he would not participate in a Moroccan conference unless France approved
June	8	Roosevelt issued formal invitations to belligerents to a conference
June	10	Japan formally accepted Roosevelt invitation
June	12	Russia formally accepted Roosevelt invitation
June	27	"Potemkin" mutiny
July	3	Komura appointed principal Japanese plenipotentiary
July	5	Japanese Emperor approved peace conditions
July	6	Komura received peace conditions at Imperial audience
July	7	Roosevelt-Kaneko first discussion of an Asian Monroe Doctrine
July 7–Aug. 7		Japanese occupied Sakhalin
July	8	Komura left Japan for Portsmouth
July	11	Russian Emperor approved Russian peace conditions
July	19	Komura reached Seattle; Witte left Russia for Portsmouth
July 23–24		German and Russian emperors met at Björkö
July	25	Taft reached Tokyo; Komura reached New York
July	27	Taft-Katsura conversations; Witte left Cherbourg
July	28	Komura and Kaneko visited Roosevelt
Aug.	2	Witte reached Hoboken
Aug.	4	Witte and Rosen visited Roosevelt
Aug.	5	Japanese and Russian plenipotentiaries left New York for Portsmouth
Aug.	7	Taft telegraphed Katsura of Roosevelt concurrence in conversations
Aug.	8	Japanese and Russian plenipotentiaries reached Portsmouth
Aug.	9	(Wed.) Preliminary meeting of the conference
Aug.	10	(Thurs.) First regular meeting of the conference at which Japanese peace conditions presented (Protocol No. 1); Harriman left New York for Japan

1905

Aug. 12   (Sat.) Second regular meeting of the conference at
          which Russian counterproposals presented (Protocol
          No. 2); Anglo-Japanese Alliance renewed
Aug. 14   (Mon.) Third regular meeting of the conference (Pro-
          tocol No. 3); Witte conference with Jewish leaders
Aug. 15   (Tues.) Fourth regular meeting of the conference
          (Protocol No. 4)
Aug. 16   (Wed.) Fifth regular meeting of the conference (Pro-
          tocol No. 5)
Aug. 17   (Thurs.) Sixth regular meeting of the conference
          (Protocol No. 6); Komura telegram to Kaneko acti-
          vated plan for Roosevelt intervention; Japanese Anti-
          Russian Society met to oppose peace
Aug. 18   (Fri.) Seventh regular meeting of the conference
          (Protocol No. 7)
Aug. 19   (Sat.) Rosen visit to Roosevelt
Aug. 21   Roosevelt's first appeal to Russian Emperor
Aug. 23   (Wed.) Eighth regular meeting of the conference
          (Protocol No. 8); Roosevelt's second appeal to
          Russian Emperor
Aug. 26   (Sat.) Ninth regular meeting of the conference (Pro-
          tocol No. 9)
Aug. 27–28   Roosevelt prepared appeal to German Emperor
Aug. 28–29   Japanese government formulated new policy regarding
          crisis
Aug. 29   (Tues.) Tenth regular meeting of the conference
          (Protocol No. 10)
Aug. 31   Harriman reached Japan
Sept. 1–2   (Thurs., Fri.) Special meetings of the conference
          (Protocol No. 11)
Sept. 4   Japanese Anti-Russian Society protested peace to Em-
          peror and in public demonstrations
Sept. 5   (Mon.) Final meeting of the conference (Protocol
          No. 12)
Sept. 7–Nov. 29   Martial law in Tokyo
Sept. 8   Anglo-Japanese Alliance renewal announced to Lams-
          dorf
Sept. 10   Roosevelt-Kaneko farewell luncheon at which Asian
          Monroe Doctrine discussed
Sept. 13   Armistice agreement reached in Manchuria
Sept. 27   Anglo-Japanese Alliance published
Oct. 26   St. Petersburg Council (Soviet) of Workers' Deputies
          convened
Oct. 27   Japanese government approved policies regarding
          Korean protectorate and conditions for conference
          with Chinese government
Oct. 28   Telegraphers strike in Manchuria, spread to adjacent
          regions

1905

Oct.	30	October Manifesto; evacuation agreement reached in Manchuria
Nov.	4	Ito mission to Korea
Nov.	6	Komura departed Japan for conference with Chinese government
Nov.	12	Komura reached Peking
Nov.	17	Japanese-Korean protectorate treaty
Nov. 17–Dec.	22	Sino-Japanese negotiations
Dec.	15	Japanese prisoners of war formally turned over to Japanese government
Dec.	22	Sino-Japanese agreement

1906

Feb.	19	Russian prisoners of war formally turned over to Russian government
Apr.		Seoul-Uiju railway line completed

1907

Apr.	1	Prefectural-level administration established in Japanese Sakhalin
June	13	Russo-Japanese railway demarcation line agreement reached
July	15	Russo-Japanese fisheries agreement

1908

Apr.	10	Russo-Japanese report on partition of Sakhalin
Aug.	6	Russo-Japanese agreement on partition of Sakhalin

BIBLIOGRAPHY AND INDEX

BIBLIOGRAPHY

Adachi Kinnosuke, "Japan's Elder Statesmen and the Peace," *The American Monthly Review of Reviews* (New York, xxxii, 4, Oct. 1905, pp. 430–432.

Adler, Cyrus, *Jacob H. Schiff*. 2 Vols. New York, 1928.

——, *The Voice of America on Kishineff*, Philadelphia, 1904.

Akagi, Roy H., *Japan's Foreign Relations, 1542–1936. A Short History*. Tokyo, 1936.

Akashi Motojiro, *Rakka Ryusui* (Falling Blossoms and Flowing Waters). Foreign Office manuscript, 1938.

Albertini, Luigi, *The Origins of the War of 1914*. 3 Vols. London, 1952.

Albrecht-Carrié, Rene, *A Diplomatic History of Europe Since the Congress of Vienna*. New York, 1958.

Aldanov, Mark, "Count Witte," *The Russian Review*, i, 1, Nov. 1941, pp. 56–64.

Alzona, Encarnacion, *Some French Contemporary Opinions of the Russian Revolution of 1905*. New York, 1921.

Anderson, Eugene N., *The First Moroccan Crisis, 1904–1906*. Chicago, 1930.

"Another View on the Strategy of the Russo-Japanese War," *The China Weekly Review* (Shanghai), lxx, 2, Sept. 8, 1934, pp. 49–50.

Asakawa Kanichi, *The Russo-Japanese Conflict: Its Causes and Issues*. Boston, 1904.

——, *The Russo-Japanese War: Collected Articles and Documents*. n.p., n.d.

Askew, William C., "An American View of Bloody Sunday," *Russian Review* (New York), xi, 1, Jan. 1952, pp. 35–43.

Aubert, *Der Russisch-Japanische Krieg, 1904–1905*. 2 Vols. Berlin, 1909.

Baelz, Toku (ed.), *Awakening Japan: The Diary of a German Doctor: Erwin Baelz*. New York, 1932.

Baker, Dwight C., "Germany and the Far East 1895–1908." Ph.D. Dissertation, University of California, Berkeley, 1927.

Beale, Howard K., *Theodore Roosevelt and the Rise of America to World Power*. Baltimore, 1956.

Bee, Minge C., "Origins of German Far Eastern Policy," *The Chinese Social and Political Science Review* (Peking), xxi, 1, Apr. 1937, pp. 65–97.

Beresford, Charles W., *The Break-Up of China*. New York, 1899.

Bernstein, Herman (Foreword by Theodore Roosevelt), *The Willy-Nicky Correspondence. Being the Secret and Intimate Telegrams Exchanged Between the Kaiser and the Tsar*. New York, 1918.

deBesabrassow, A.M., "Les Premieres Causes de l'Effondrement de la Russie. Le Conflit Russo-Japonais," *Le Correspondent* (Paris), Vol. 291, 1923, pp. 577–615.

Beveridge, Albert J., *The Russian Advance.* New York, 1904.

Bigelow, John, *Peace Given as the World Giveth or the Portsmouth Treaty and Its First Year's Fruits.* New York, 1907.

Bing, E.J. (ed.), *The Secret Letters of the Last Tsar Being the Confidential Correspondence between Nicholas II and His Mother, Dowager Empress Maria Feodorovna.* New York, 1938.

Birkenhead, Frederick E.S., *International Law as Interpreted during the Russo-Japanese War.* Boston, 1905.

Bishop, Joseph B., *Theodore Roosevelt and His Time.* 2 Vols. New York, 1920.

Blakeslee, George, "The Japanese Monroe Doctrine," *Foreign Affairs* (New York), xɪ, 4, July, 1933, pp. 671–681.

Blum, John M., *The Republican Roosevelt.* Cambridge, 1954.

Bompard, Maurice, *Mon Ambassade en Russie (1903–1908).* Paris, 1937.

Boorman, H.L., *et al., Moscow-Peking Axis: Strengths and Strains.* New York, 1957.

Bornhak, Konrad, *Die Kriegsschuld: Deutschlands Weltpolitik, 1890–1914.* Berlin, 1929.

Boulger, Demetrius C., "The Collapse of Russia: ɪv, Germany and Belgium," *The Nineteenth Century and After* (London), ʟvɪɪɪ, 341, July, 1905, pp. 43–50.

Braisted, William R., *The United States Navy in the Pacific, 1897–1909.* Austin, 1958.

Brown, Arthur J., *The Mastery of the Far East; The Story of Korea's Transformation and Japan's Rise to Supremacy in the Orient.* New York, 1919.

Brown, Delmer, M., *Nationalism in Japan; an Introductory Historical Analysis.* Berkeley, 1955.

Buell, Raymond L., "The Development of Anti-Japanese Agitation in the United States," *Political Science Quarterly,* xxxvɪɪ, 4, Dec. 1922, pp. 605–638.

Bullard, Arthur, *The Russian Pendulum. Autocracy-Democracy-Bolshevism.* New York, 1919.

von Bülow, Prince, *Memoirs.* 4 Vols. London, 1931.

Burleigh, Bennet, *Empire of the East or Japan and Russia at War, 1904–5.* London, 1905.

Burtsev, Vladimir L., *Tsar i Vneshniaia Politika; Vinovniki Russko-Iaponskoi Voiny po Tainym Dokumentam: Tainaia Zapiska Gr. Lamsdorfa i Malinovaia Kniga* (The Tsar and Foreign Policy; the Perpetrators of the Russo-Japanese War in Secret Documents: Secret Memorandum of Count Lamsdorf and the Crimson Book). Berlin, 1910.

Cameron, Rondo E., *France and the Economic Development of Europe, 1800–1914.* Princeton, 1961.

Carroll, E. Malcolm, *Germany and the Great Powers 1866–1914*. New York, 1938.

Cassell's History of the Russo-Japanese War. 5 Vols. London, n.d.

Chang Chung-fu, *The Anglo-Japanese Alliance*. Baltimore, 1931.

Chekhov, Anton P., *Ostrov Sakhalin, 1891–1894* (Sakhalin Island, 1891–1894). *Sochineniia*, x, Moscow, 1948.

China. Treaties, *Translation of the Minutes of the Negotiations for the Conclusion of the Treaty and Agreement of 1905 between China and Japan*. n.p., 1932.

Chinese Eastern Railway Company, *North Manchuria and the Chinese Eastern Railway*. Harbin, 1924.

Christie, Dugald, *Thirty Years in Moukden. 1883–1913. Being the Experiences and Recollections of Dugald Christie, C.M.G., F.R.C.S., F.R.C.P.* London, 1914.

Churchill, R.P., *The Anglo-Russian Convention of 1907*. Cedar Rapids, 1939.

Clark, Grover, *Economic Rivalries in China*. New Haven, 1932.

Clyde, Paul H., *International Rivalries in Manchuria, 1689–1922*. Columbus, 1926.

Collum, C., "Prince Katsura," *The Contemporary Review* (New York), CIV, Nov. 1913, pp. 656–662.

Conroy, Hilary, *The Japanese Seizure of Korea, 1868–1910*. Philadelphia, 1960.

Cortissoz, Royal, *The Life of Whitelaw Reid*. 2 Vols. London, 1921.

Crisp, Olga, "The Russian Liberals and the 1906 Anglo-French Loan to Russia," *The Slavonic and East European Review* (London), XXXIX, 93, June 1961, pp. 497–511.

Crist, David S., "Russia's Far Eastern Policy in the Making," *Journal of Modern History* (Chicago), XIV, 3, Sept. 1942, pp. 317–341.

——, "Russia's Manchurian Policy; 1895–1905." Ph.D. dissertation, University of Michigan, Ann Arbor, 1940.

"The Deer Island Episode," *Korean Repository* (Seoul), v, Mar. 1898, pp. 109–113.

Dennett, Tyler, "Early American Policy in Korea, 1883–7," *Political Science Quarterly* (Boston), XXXVIII, Mar. 1923, pp. 82–103.

——, "President Roosevelt's Secret Pact with Japan," *Current History* (New York), XXI, Oct. 1924, pp. 15–21.

——, *Roosevelt and the Russo-Japanese War*. New York, 1925.

Dennis, A.L.P., *Adventures in American Diplomacy 1896–1906*. New York, 1928.

——, "The Anglo-Japanese Alliance," D.P. Barrow, E. Landon, F.M. Russell (eds.), *University of California Publications in International Relations*, Vol. I, 1923–1929, Berkeley, 1934, pp. 1–111.

Denny, O., *China and Korea*, Shanghai, 1888.

Deutsch, Leo, *Sixteen Years in Siberia*. London, 1905.

De Windt, Harry, *The New Siberia; Being an account of a visit to the penal island of Sakhalin, and political prison and mines of the trans-Baikal district.* London, 1896.

Dickins, F.V., "A Japanese Official's Narrative of His Journey Across Karafuto (Sagalin) in 1854. With Commentary by a Later Japanese Traveller in Those Parts," The Japan Society, London, *Transactions and Proceedings*, iv, 1895–8, Dec. 11, 1895, pp. 19–48.

Dickinson, G. Lowes, *The International Anarchy 1904–1914.* London, 1937.

Dillon, E.J., *The Eclipse of Russia.* New York, 1918.

————, "The Official Narrative of the Peace Conference," *Harper's Weekly* (New York), xlix, 2543, Sept. 16, 1905, pp. 1334–1337.

————, "The Peace Conference at Portsmouth, N.H.," *Harper's Weekly* (New York), xlix, 2540, Aug. 26, 1905, pp. 1222–1224.

————, "Progress of the Russian Revolution," *The American Monthly Review of Reviews* (New York), xxxii, 2, Aug. 1905, pp. 197–202.

————, "Sergius Witte," *The American Monthly Review of Reviews* (New York), xxxii, 3, Sept. 1905, pp. 292–295.

————, "Sergius Witte and Jutaro Komura," *Harper's Weekly* (New York), xlix, 2541, Sept. 2, 1905, pp. 1262–1264, 1279.

————, "The Story of the Peace Negotiations," *The Contemporary Review* (New York), lxxxviii, Oct. 1905, pp. 457–478.

————, "What the Peace of Portsmouth Means to Russia," *Harper's Weekly* (New York), xlix, 2543, Sept. 16, 1905, pp. 1337, 1351.

Dobrov, Alexander S., *Dalnevostochnaia Politika S Sh A v Period Russko-Iaponskoi Voiny* (The Far Eastern Policy of the U.S.A. in the Period of the Russo-Japanese War). Moscow, 1952.

Dobrynin, A., "S Sh A i Nezavisimost Korei (1904–1905 gg)" (The U.S.A. and the Independence of Korea (1904–1905)), *Izvestiia Akademii Nauk, Seriia Istorii i Filosofii*, No. 4, 1947, pp. 342–354.

Draper, Hal, "The Myth of Lenin's 'Revolutionary Defeatism,'" *The New International* (New York), Sept.–Oct. 1953, pp. 255–283; Nov.–Dec. 1953; pp. 313–351; Jan.–Feb. 1954, pp. 39–59.

Duffy, Thomas Glenn, "Russia's Balkan Policy 1894–1905," Ph.D. dissertation, Clark University, Worcester, 1959.

Dugdale, Blanche E.C., *Arthur James Balfour; First Earl of Balfour.* 2 Vols. New York, 1937.

Dziewanowski, Marian K., *The Communist Party of Poland; An Outline of History.* Cambridge, 1959.

————, "The Revolution of 1905 in Poland," *Journal of Central European Affairs* (Boulder), xii, 3, Oct. 1952, pp. 259–275.

Eastlake, F.W. and Y. Yamada, *Heroic Japan; A History of the War Between China and Japan.* London, 1897.

von Eckardstein, Hermann, *Die Isolierung Deutschlands* (*III Band der Lebenserrinerungen und Politischen Denkwürdigkeiten*). Leipzig, 1921.

Edwards, E.W., "The Japanese Alliance and the Anglo-French Agreement of 1904," *History* (London), XLII, 144, Feb. 1957, pp. 19–27.

Eisele, Leona W., *A Digest of the Krasnyi Arkhiv—Red Archives—Vols. 31–106*. Ann Arbor, 1955.

Eltzbacher, O., "The Collapse of Russia: I, The Indemnity Due Japan," *The Nineteenth Century and After* (London), LVIII, 341, July, 1905, pp. 1–21.

Erukhimovich, I., "Nakanune Russko-Iaponskoi Voiny (Dekabr 1900g.-Ianvar 1902g.)" (On the Eve of the Russo-Japanese War, December 1900–January 1902), *Krasnyi Arkhiv* (Moscow), LXIII, 1934, pp. 3–54.

Esthus, Raymond A., "The Taft-Katsura Agreement—Reality or Myth?" *Journal of Modern History* (Chicago), XXXI, 1, Mar. 1959, pp. 46–51.

Fay, Sidney B., "The Kaiser's Secret Negotiations with the Tsar, 1904–1905," *American Historical Review* (New York), XXIV, 1, Oct. 1918, pp. 48–72.

Fedorov, A., *Revoliutsionnye Vostaniia v Chernomorskom Flote, 1904–1907* (The Revolutionary Rising in the Black Sea Fleet, 1904–1907). Moscow, 1946.

Feis, Herbert, *Europe the World's Banker, 1870–1914*. New Haven, 1930.

Feldmann, Constantine, *The Revolt of the "Potemkin."* London, 1908.

Feuerwerker, Albert, *China's Early Industrialization; Sheng Hsuan-huai (1844–1916) and Mandarin Enterprise*. Cambridge, 1958.

Field, Margaret, "The Chinese Boycott of 1905," Harvard University, Committee on Regional Studies, *Papers on China*, II, 1957, pp. 63–98.

Fischer, George, *Russian Liberalism, from Gentry to Intelligentsia*. Cambridge, 1958.

Florinsky, Michael T., *Russia: A History and an Interpretation*. 2 Vols. New York, 1955.

Ford, Harold P., "Russian Far Eastern Diplomacy, Count Witte, and the Penetration of China, 1895–1904," Ph.D. dissertation, University of Chicago, Chicago, 1950.

Ford, W.C., "The Economy of Russia," *Political Science Quarterly* (Boston), XVII, Mar. 1902, pp. 99–124.

Foster, John W., "The Chinese Boycott," *The Atlantic Monthly* (Boston), XCVII, 1906, pp. 118–127.

France. Ministry of Foreign Affairs, *Documents Diplomatiques Francais (1871–1914), 2ᵉ Serie (1901–1911)*. 14 Vols. Paris, 1930–1955.

Franke, Otto, *Die Grossmächte in Ostasien von 1894 bis 1914.* Braunschweig, 1923.

Fraser, Lovat, *India Under Curzon and After.* London, 1911.

Fujisawa Rikitaro, "Roosevelt and Manchuria," *Contemporary Japan* (Tokyo), I, 3, Dec. 1932, pp. 363–371.

Galperin, A., *Anglo-Iaponskii Soiuz, 1902–1921* (The Anglo-Japanese Alliance, 1902–1921). Moscow, 1947.

——, "Koreiskii Vopros v Mezhdunarodnykh Otnosheniiakh Naka-nune Anneksii Korei Iaponiei (1905–1910)" (The Korean Problem in International Relations on the Eve of the Annexation of Korea by Japan, 1905–1910), *Voprosy Istorii* (Moscow), Feb. 1951, pp. 12–30.

Gapon, George, *The Story of My Life.* London, 1905.

Gelber, L.M., *The Rise of Anglo-American Friendship.* London, 1938.

Gippius, A.I., *O Prichinakh Nashei Voiny s Iaponiei. C. Prilozheniiami (Dokumenty)* (Concerning the Causes of Our War with Japan. With Appendices (Documents)). St. Petersburg, 1905.

Glinsky, B.B., *Prolog Russko-Iaponskoi Voiny. Materialy iz Arkhiva Grafa S. Iu. Witte* (The Prologue to the Russo-Japanese War. Materials from the Archives of Count S.I. Witte). Petrograd, 1916.

Godwin, Robert K., "Russia and the Portsmouth Peace Conference," *American Slavic and East European Review* (New York), IX, 4, Dec. 1950, pp. 279–291.

Goerlitz, Walter, *History of the German General Staff.* New York, 1954.

Gooch, George P., *Recent Revelations of European Diplomacy.* London, 1940.

—— and Harold Temperley (eds.), *British Documents on the Origins of the War, 1898–1914.* 11 Vols. London, 1927–1938.

—— and A.W. Ward (eds.), *The Cambridge History of British Foreign Policy: 1783–1919.* 3 Vols. New York, 1923.

Great Britain. Parliamentary Papers, "Blue Books," *China No. 2 (1904): Correspondence Respecting the Russian Occupation of Manchuria and Newchwang.* London, Feb. 1904.

Grimm, E.D., "Kitaiskii Vopros ot Simonosekskogo Mira do Mirovoi Voiny (1895–1914)" (The Chinese Problem from the Peace of Shimonoseki to the World War, 1895–1914), *Novyi Vostok* (Moscow), No. 6, 1924, pp. 43–62.

Griscom, Lloyd C., *Diplomatically Speaking.* Boston, 1940.

Griswold, A.W., *The Far Eastern Policy of the United States.* New York, 1938.

Gull, E.M., "A Visit to Mongolia," *Journal of the Royal Central Asian Society* (London), Pt. I, 1914, pp. 3–13.

Gurko, Vladimir I., *Features and Figures of the Past: Government and Opinion in the Reign of Nicholas II*. Stanford, 1939.

Gwynn, Stephen, *The Letters and Friendships of Sir Cecil Spring Rice*. 2 Vols. Boston and New York, 1929.

Haimson, Leopold H., *The Russian Marxists and the Origins of Bolshevism*. Cambridge, 1955.

Hale, Oron J., *Publicity and Diplomacy; with Special Reference to England and Germany, 1890–1914*. New York, 1940.

Hall, Luella J., "The Abortive German-American-Chinese Entente of 1907–8," *Journal of Modern History* (Chicago), I, 2, June 1929, pp. 219–235.

———, "A Partnership in Peacemaking: Theodore Roosevelt and Wilhelm II," *Pacific Historical Review* (Berkeley), XIII, 4, Dec. 1944, pp. 390–411.

Hall, William E., *A Treatise on International Law*. London, 1938.

Hallgarten, George W.F., *Imperialismus vor 1914*. 2 Vols. Munich, 1951.

Ito Masanori, *Kato Takaakira*. 2 Vols. Tokyo, 1929.

———, *Kokubo Shi* (A History of National Defense). Tokyo, 1941.

Hamada Kengi, *Prince Ito*, Tokyo, 1936.

Hamilton, Ian, *A Staff Officer's Scrap-Book during the Russo-Japanese War*. 2 Vols. London, 1905–1907.

Hammond, John H., *The Autobiography of John Hays Hammond*. 2 Vols. New York, 1935.

Hargreaves, Reginald, *Red Sun Rising: the Siege of Port Arthur*, Philadelphia, 1962.

Harrington, Fred H., *God, Mammon and the Japanese; Dr. Horace N. Allen and Korean-American Relations, 1884–1905*. Madison, 1944.

Harrison, Austin F., "The Collapse of Russia: III Germany and Morocco," *The Nineteenth Century and After* (London), LVIII, No. 341, July 1905, pp. 34–42.

Harrison, E.J., *Peace or War East of Baikal?* Yokohama, 1910.

Hatada Takashi, *Chosen Shi* (A History of Korea). Tokyo, 1952.

Hauser, Oswald, *Deutschland und der Englisch-Russische Gegensatz, 1900–1914*. Berlin, 1958.

Hayes, Carleton J., *A Generation of Materialism, 1871–1900*. New York, 1941.

Hefele, K., "Aus dem Osten. Reisen in Sachalin, Ostsibirien, der Mandschurei, China und Korea," *Mitteilungen der Deutschen Gesellschaft für Natur- und Völkerkunde Ostasiens*, IX, No. 2, Tokyo, May, 1903, pp. 169–272.

Helfferich, Karl, *Das Geld im Russisch-Japanischen Krieges*. Berlin, 1906.

Hershey, Amos S., *The International Law and Diplomacy of the Russo-Japanese War.* New York, 1906.

Hiratsuka Atsushi, "Nichiei Domei to Nichiro Kyosho" (The Anglo-Japanese Alliance and the Russo-Japanese Understanding), *Ito Hirobumi Hiroku.* 2 Vols. Tokyo, 1929, I, pp. 1–58 (back of volume).

Höcker, Gustav, *Russland und Japan im Kampf um die Macht in Ostasien.* Leipzig, n.d.

Hoetzsch, Otto, *Russland: Eine Einführung auf Grunde seiner Geschichte von 1904 bis 1912.* Berlin, 1913.

Hofstadter, Richard, *Social Darwinism in American Thought (1860–1915).* Philadelphia, 1945.

von Hohenzollern, Karl, Prinz, *Meine Erlebnisse während des Russisch-Japanischen Krieges, 1904–1905.* Berlin, 1912.

Hori Makoto, Nichiro Senso Zengo (*The Russo-Japanese War, Its Prelude and Aftermath*). Tokyo, 1940.

Hosie, Alexander, *Manchuria; Its People, Resources and Recent History.* Boston, 1910.

Hough, Richard, *The Fleet That Had to Die.* New York, 1958.

———, *The Potemkin Mutiny.* New York, 1961.

Howe, M.A. DeWolfe, *George von Lengerke Meyer.* New York, 1919.

Howells, W.D., "The Peacemakers at Portsmouth," *Harper's Weekly,* (New York), XLIX, No. 2540, Aug. 26, 1905, pp. 1225, 1244.

Hsü Shuhsi, *China and Her Political Entity (A Study of China's Foreign Relations with Reference to Korea, Manchuria and Mongolia).* New York, 1926.

Hulbert, Homer B., *History of Korea.* 2 Vols. New York, 1962.

———, *The Passing of Korea.* London, 1906.

Hummel, Arthur W., *Eminent Chinese of the Ch'ing Period.* 2 Vols. Washington, 1943.

Iaroslavsky, Emelian, *Russko-Iaponskaia Voina i Otnoshenie k Nei Bolshevikov* (The Russo-Japanese War and the Relation of the Bolsheviks to It). Moscow, 1939.

Illiustrirovannaia Khronika Russko-Iaponskoi Voiny (Illustrated Chronicle of the Russo-Japanese War). No. 1–50, n.p., 1904–1905.

Ishii Kikujiro, *Gaiko Yoroku* (Diplomatic Reminiscence). Tokyo, 1931.

Itakura Takuzō, *Kokusai Funsō Shikō* (Historical Reflections on International Disturbances). Tokyo, 1935.

Jansen, Marius B., *The Japanese and Sun Yat-sen.* Cambridge, 1954.

———, "Opportunists in South China during the Boxer Rebellion," *Pacific Historical Review* (Berkeley), XX, 3, Aug. 1951, pp. 241–250.

Japan Chronicle. Tokyo, 1904–1905.

Japan. Department of Railways, *An Official Guide to Eastern Asia. I Chosen & Manchuria, Siberia.* Tokyo, 1920.

Japan. Foreign Office, *Diplomatic Correspondence*.

———, "Kirokuka Kimitsu-gakari; (1904–1905)" (Secret Records—1904–1905).

———, *Komura Gaikoshi* (A History of Komura's Diplomacy). 2 Vols. Tokyo, 1953.

———, *Manshu ni Kansuru Nisshin Kōshō Dampan Hikki* (November 17–December 18, 1905) (Record of the Sino-Japanese Negotiations Concerning Manchuria).

———, "Nichiro Kosho Shi" (A History of the Russo-Japanese Negotiations). 2 Vols. Foreign Office Circulation.

———, "Nichiro Kowa Dampan Hikki; Tsuki Ryokoku Zenken lin Hiseishiki Kaiken Yoroku" (August 9–September 5, 1905) (Record of the Russo-Japanese Peace; including the Informal Discussions of the Plenipotentiaries of the Two Nations).

———, *Nihon Gaiko Monjo* (Japanese Diplomatic Documents). Vol. xxxiii-xl, Tokyo, 1956–1960.

———, *Nihon Gaiko Nempyo narabi Shuyo Monjo* (Japanese Diplomatic Chronology and Principle Documents). 2 Vols. Tokyo, 1955.

———, "Protocoles de La Conference de la Paix entre le Japon et la Russie." Foreign Office Circulation.

———, "Protocols of the Peace Conference between Japan and Russia." Foreign Office Circulation.

———, *Recueil des Traites et Conventions entre le Japon et les Puissances Etrangeres*. Vol. i. Tokyo, 1936.

———, Yamamoto Gonnohyoei, *Yamamoto Haku Jitsureki Dan* (The Career of Baron Yamamoto). n.d., Foreign Office Circulation.

Japan. Imperial Diet, *Correspondence Regarding the Negotiations between Japan and Russia (1903–1904)*. (translation) Presented to the Imperial Diet, March 1904, Washington, 1904.

Japan. Imperial Japanese Commission to the Louisiana Purchase Exposition, *Japan at the Beginning of the 20th Century*. Tokyo, 1904.

Japan. Karafuto Cho, *Karafuto Enkaku Shi* (History of the Development of Karafuto). Toyohara, Karafuto, 1925.

Japan Times. Tokyo, 1904–1905.

Joseph, Philip, *Foreign Diplomacy in China, 1894–1900*. London, 1928.

Kai Miwa and P.B. Yampolsky, *Political Chronology of Japan, 1885–1957*. New York, 1957.

Kamikawa Hikomatsu, *Japan-American Diplomatic Relations in the Meiji-Taisho Era*. Tokyo, 1958.

———, *Kindai Kokusai Seijishi* (A History of Recent International Affairs). 4 Vols. Tokyo, 1953.

Kaneko Kentaro, "American Millions for Japan's War," *World's Work* (New York), x, May 1905, pp. 6124–6126.

———, "A 'Japanese Monroe Doctrine' and Manchuria," *Contemporary Japan* (Tokyo), I, 2, Sept. 1932, pp. 175–184.

———, *Beikoku Daitoryo Kaiken Shimatsu* (An Account of Interviews with the President of the United States). Foreign Office manuscript, July 9, 1907.

———, *Nichiro Seneki Beikoku Tairyuki* (Record of a Sojourn in the United States during the Russo-Japanese War). Foreign Office manuscript, Dec. 26, 1906.

———, *Nichiro Seneki Hiroku* (Secret Record of the Russo-Japanese Campaign). Tokyo, 1930.

Kantorovich, Anatolii, *Amerika v Borbe za Kitai* (America in the Struggle for China). Moscow, 1935.

Karpenko, Z., *Grazhdanskaia Voina v Dalnevostochnom Krae (1918–1922)* (The Civil War in the Far Eastern Region, 1918–1922). Khabarovsk, 1934.

Katkov, George, "German Foreign Office Documents on Financial Support to the Bolsheviks in 1917," *International Affairs* (London), XXXII, 2, Apr. 1956, pp. 181–189.

Kawai, Kazuo, "Anglo-German Rivalry in the Yangtse Region 1895–1902," *Pacific Historical Review* (Berkeley), VIII, 4, Dec. 1939, pp. 413–433.

Kemp. E.G., *The Face of Manchuria, Korea and Russian Turkestan*. London, 1910.

Kennan, George, *E.H. Harriman's Far Eastern Plans*. New York, 1917.

———, (trans.), "The Military and Political Memoirs of General Kuropatkin," *McClure's Magazine* (New York), XXXI, 5, Sept. 1908, pp. 483–499; XXXII, 1, Nov. 1908, pp. 213–222; XXXII, 3, Jan. 1909, pp. 237–246.

Khodorov, A.E., "Manchzhurskaia Problema" (The Manchurian Problem), *Novyi Vostok* (Moscow), No. 2, 1922, pp. 560–567.

Kobayashi Hiroshi, *Shosetsu Nihon Rekishi* (An Account of Japanese History). 3 Vols. Tokyo, 1929.

Kobayashi Ushisaburo, *War and Armament Taxes of Japan*. New York, 1923.

Kokovtsov, Vladimir N., *Out of My Past*. Stanford, 1935.

Komori, Tokuji, *Akashi Motojiro*. 2 Vols. Tokyo, 1928.

Komura, Shoji, "Jutaro Komura, My Father," *Contemporary Japan* (Tokyo), I, 4, Mar. 1933, pp. 641–649.

Korostovetz, J.J., *Pre-War Diplomacy; the Russo-Japanese Problem; Treaty Signed at Portsmouth, U.S.A. (Diary of J.J. Korostovetz, Secretary to Count Witte at the Peace Conference at Portsmouth)*. London, 1920.

———, *Rossiia na Dalnem Vostoke* (Russia in the Far East). Peking, 1922.

von Korostowetz, Wladimir (Vladimir Konstantinovich Korostovets), *Graf Witte, der Steuermann in der Not*. Berlin, 1929.

———, "Memoirs of Witte," *Contemporary Review*, CLXXXIV, Aug. 1953, pp. 85–89.

Kraus, Adolph, *Reminiscences and Comments*. Chicago, 1925.

Krausse, Alexis, *Russia in Asia; A Record and a Study*. London, 1900.

Krupenski, Kurt, *Russland und Japan; Ihre Beziehungen bis zum Frieden von Portsmouth*. Königsberg, 1940.

Kublin, Hyman, "The Japanese Socialists and the Russo-Japanese War," *Journal of Modern History* (Chicago), XXII, 4, Dec. 1950, pp. 322–339.

Kuroda Koshiro, *Gensui Terauchi Hakushaku Den* (Biography of Marshal Count Terauchi). Tokyo, 1920.

Kuroha Shigeru, *Sekaishijo yori Mitaru Nichiro Senso* (The Russo-Japanese War Viewed from a World Standpoint). Tokyo, 1960.

Kuroki Yukichi, *Komura Jutaro*. Tokyo, 1941.

Kuropatkin, Aleksei N., *The Russian Army and the Japanese War*. 2 Vols. New York, 1909.

Kutakov, L.N., *Portsmutskii Mirnyi Dogovor (Iz Istorii Otnoshenii Iaponii s Rossiei i SSSR. 1905–1945 gg.)* (The Portsmouth Peace Treaty (from the History of the Relations of Japan with Russia and the USSR, 1905–1945)). Moscow, 1961.

Ladd, George T., *In Korea with Marquis Ito*. London, 1908.

Lambton, Ann K.S., "Secret Societies and the Persian Revolution of 1905–6," St. Antony's Papers, No. 4, *Middle Eastern Affairs* (New York), No. 1, 1959, pp. 43–60.

Laney, Frank M., "The Military Implementation of the Franco-Russian Alliance, 1890–1914," Ph.D. dissertation, University of Virginia, 1954.

Langer, William L., *The Diplomacy of Imperialism, 1890–1902*. 2 Vols. New York, 1935.

Lattimore, Owen, "Chinese Colonization in Manchuria," *The Geographical Review*, XXII, 2, Apr. 1932, pp. 177–195.

von Laue, Theodore H., "Count Witte and the Industrial Development of Russia." m.s., n.d.

———, "High Cost and the Gamble of the Witte System: a Chapter in the Industrialization of Imperial Russia," *Journal of Economic History*, XIII, 4, 1953, pp. 425–448.

———, "Count Witte and the Russian Revolution of 1905," *The American Slavic and East European Review* (New York), XVII, 1, Feb. 1958, pp. 25–46.

———, "Problems of Modernization," Ivo J. Lederer, *Russian Foreign Policy; Essays in Historical Perspective*. New Haven, 1962, pp. 69–108.

————, "Secret Memorandum on the Industrialization of Imperial Russia," *Journal of Modern History*, xxvi, 4, Mar. 1954, pp. 60–74.

Lee, Sidney, *King Edward VII—a Biography*. 2 Vols. London, 1925–1927.

Lensen, George A., "The Attempt on the Life of Nicholas II in Japan," *The Russian Review* (New York), xx, 3, July 1961, pp. 232–253.

————, *The Russian Push Toward Japan*. Princeton, 1959.

Lepsius, Johannes, *et al.* (eds), *Die Grosse Politik der Europäischen Kabinette 1871–1914. Sammlung der Diplomatischen Akten der Auswärtigen Amptes*. 54 Vols. Berlin, 1922–1927.

Levine, Isaac D., *The Kaiser's Letters to the Tsar*. London, 1920.

Li Tieh-Tseng, *The Historical Status of Tibet*. New York, 1956.

Little, Frances [Mrs. Fannie (Caldwell) Macaulay], *The Lady of the Decoration*. New York, 1907.

Livermore, Seward W., "The American Naval-Base Policy in the Far East, 1850–1914," *Pacific Historical Review* (Berkeley), xiii, 2, June 1944, pp. 113–135.

————, "The American Navy as a Factor in World Politics, 1903–1913," *American Historical Review* (New York), lxiii, 4, July 1958, pp. 863–879.

Lodge, Henry C. (ed.), *Selections from the Correspondence of Theodore Roosevelt and Henry Cabot Lodge, 1884–1918*. 2 Vols. New York, 1925.

Ludwig, Emil, *Wilhelm Hohenzollern: the Last of the Kaisers*. New York, 1927.

Lutsky, S.L., *Ostrov Sakhalin* (Sakhalin Island). Moscow, 1946.

Lvov, F.A., *Likhodei Biurokraticheskago Samovlastiia kak Neposredstvennye Vinovniki Pervoi Russko-Iaponskoi Voiny* (The Criminals of Bureaucratic Wilfulness as the Direct Instigators of the Russo-Japanese War). St. Petersburg, 1906.

McCormick, Frederic, *The Tragedy of Russia in Pacific Asia*. 2 Vols. New York, 1909.

McCune, George M., "The Exchange of Envoys between Korea and Japan during the Tokugawa Period," *The Far Eastern Quarterly* (Ann Arbor), v, 3, May 1946, pp. 308–325.

McCune, Shannon, *Korea's Heritage: A Regional and Social Geography*. Tokyo, 1956.

MacKenzie, F.A., *The Tragedy of Korea*. London, 1908.

MacKinder, Halford J., "The Geographical Pivot of History," *The Geographical Journal* (London), xxiii, 4, Apr. 1904, pp. 421–444.

MacMurray, John V.A., *Treaties and Agreements with and concerning China, 1894–1919*. 2 Vols. New York, 1921.

McWilliams, C.F., "What Russia Has to Pay For," *Harper's Weekly* (New York), xlix, 2545, Sept. 30, 1905, pp. 1406–1409.

Machray, Robert, "The Collapse of Russia: v, Great Britain, Germany, and Sea Power," *The Nineteenth Century and After* (London), LVIII, 341, July 1905, pp. 51–61.

Madison, Frank, "The Russians in Manchuria," *Harper's Weekly* (New York), XLVIII, 2469, Apr. 16, 1904, pp. 582–584.

Mahan, Alfred T., *Naval Administration and Warfare*. Boston, 1908.

——, "Principles Involved in the War between Japan and Russia," from *National Review*, Sept. 1904, reprinted in A.T. Mahan, *Naval Administration and Warfare*, Boston, 1908, pp. 87–129.

——, *The Problem of Asia*. Boston, 1900.

——, "Retrospect upon the War between Japan and Russia," from *National Review*, May 1906, reprinted in A.T. Mahan, *Naval Administration and Warfare*, Boston, 1908, pp. 133–173.

——, "The Value of the Pacific Cruise of the United States Fleet, 1908," A.T. Mahan, *Naval Administration and Warfare*, Boston, 1908, pp. 307–353.

Malozemoff, Andrew, *Russian Far Eastern Policy 1881–1904*. Berkeley, 1958.

Marder, Arthur J., *The Anatomy of British Sea Power*. New York, 1940.

Matsushita Yoshio, *Hansen Undo Shi* (History of the Anti-War Movement). Tokyo, 1954.

Maurice, F.B., "The Russo-Japanese War," *The Cambridge Modern History*, Cambridge, 1910, XII, 576–601.

Mavor, James, *An Economic History of Russia*. 2 Vols. London, Toronto, New York, 1925.

May, Ernest, R., "The Far Eastern Policy of the United States in the Period of the Russo-Japanese War: A Russian View," *American Historical Review* (New York), LXII, 2, Jan. 1957, pp. 345–351.

Mehnert, Klaus, *Der Einfluss der Russisch-Japanischen Krieges auf die Grosse Politik*. n.p., n.d. (1930?).

Michelson, Alexander M., *et al.*, *Russian Public Finance during the War*. New Haven, 1928.

Michon, Georges, *The Franco-Russian Alliance, 1891–1917*. New York, 1929.

Military Correspondent of the Times [Charles A'Court Repington], *The War in the Far East 1904–1905*. New York, 1905.

Millard, Thomas F., "The Fruits of Japan's Victory," *Scribner's Magazine* (New York), XXXVIII, 2, Aug. 1905, pp. 240–251.

Milyoukov, Paul [Pavel Nikolaevich Miliukov], *Russia and Its Crisis*. Chicago, 1905.

Minger, Ralph E., "Taft's Mission to Japan: A Study in Personal Diplomacy," *Pacific Historical Review* (Berkeley), XXX, 3, Aug. 1961, pp. 279–294.

Minrath, Paul, *Das Englisch-Japanische Bündniss von 1902. Die Grundlegung der Ententepolitik im Fernosten*. Stuttgart, 1933.

Mookerjee, J. N., *A Poem on the Russo-Japanese War, 1904–1905*. 4 parts. Calcutta, 1904–1905.

Morison, Elting E., *et al.*, *The Letters of Theodore Roosevelt*. 8 Vols. Cambridge, 1951.

Moritzen, Julius, "Denmark the Buffer State of the North," *The American Monthly Review of Reviews* (New York), xxxii, 3, Sept. 1905, pp. 305–309.

Morse, Hosea B., *The International Relations of the Chinese Empire*. 3 Vols. London, 1910.

———, *The Trade and Administration of China*. London, 1921.

Mowry, George E., *The Era of Theodore Roosevelt, 1900–1912*. New York, 1958.

Nagayama Yasumasa (ed.) *Shimbun Shusei Meiji Hennen Shi* (A History of the Meiji Press). 15 Vols. Tokyo, 1934–1940.

Naida, S.F., *Voennye Moriaki v Period Pervoi Russkoi Revoliutsii, 1905–1907 gg.* (The Sailors of the Fleet in the Period of the First Russian Revolution, 1905–1907). Moscow, 1955.

Nelson, M. Frederick, *Korea and the Old Orders in Eastern Asia*. Baton Rouge, 1946.

Newton, L., *Lord Lansdowne. A Biography*. London, 1929.

Nikolaevsky, B., "Russia, Japan, and the Pan-Asiatic Movement to 1925," *The Far Eastern Quarterly* (Ann Arbor), viii, 3, May 1949, pp. 259–295.

Nish, I.N., "Japan's Indecision during the Boxer Disturbances," *Journal of Asian Studies* (Chicago), xx, 4, Aug. 1961, pp. 449–461.

Noland, Aaron, *The Founding of the French Socialist Party (1893–1905)*. Cambridge, 1956.

Norman, E. Herbert. "The Genyosha: A Study in the Origins of Japanese Imperialism," *Pacific Affairs* (New York), xvii, 3, Sept. 1944, pp. 261–284.

The North-China Herald and Supreme Court and Consular Gazette. Shanghai, 1904–1905.

Novikoff-Priboy, A.S., *Tsushima*. New York, 1937.

Ogasawara Nagayo, *Life of Admiral Togo*. Tokyo, 1934.

Ogawa Gotaro, *Expenditures of the Russo-Japanese War*. New York, 1923.

Ogg, Frederic A., "European Alliances and the War," *The American Monthly Review of Reviews* (New York), xxxii, 3, Sept. 1905, pp. 295–301.

Okuma Shigenobu, "My Views on Chinese Questions," *The Sun Trade Journal* (Tokyo), xi, 1, Jan. 1, 1905, pp. 5–10.

Ono Giichi, *War and Armament Expenditures of Japan*. New York, 1922.

Ono Sanenobu, *Gensui Koshaku Oyama Iwao* (Marshal Marquis Oyama Iwao). Tokyo, 1935.

Oppenheim, L.F., *International Law: A Treatise*. 2 Vols. London, 1952.

Ota Saburo, *Nichiro Karafuto Gaikosen* (The Russo-Japanese Diplomatic Struggle for Sakhalin). Tokyo, 1941.

Otsu Junichiro, *Dainihon Kenseishi* (History of Constitutional Government of Greater Japan). Tokyo, 1927.

Oudendyk, W.J., "Russia and China," *Journal of the Royal Central Asian Society* (London), xxii, 3, July 1935, pp. 369–402.

Oukhtomsky, E. (E.E. Ukhtomsky), "A Russian View of American Sympathy," *Harper's Weekly* (New York), xlviii, May 28, 1904, p. 826.

Oyama Hisashi, *Expenditures of the Russo-Japanese War*. New York, 1923.

Paleologue, Georges M., *Un Grand Tournant de la Politique Mondiale (1904–1906)*. Paris, 1934.

Palmer, Frederick, *With Kuroki in Manchuria*. New York, 1906.

Pankratova, A.M., *Pervaia Russkaia Revoliutsiia 1905–1907 gg.* (The First Russian Revolution, 1905–1907). Moscow, 1951.

——— (ed.), *Pervaia Russkaia Revoliutsiia 1905–1907 gg. i. Mezhdunarodnoe Revoliutsionnoe Dvizhenie* (The First Russian Revolution, 1905–1907 and the International Revolutionary Movement). Moscow, 1955.

Pavlovich, Mikhail, "Iaponskii Imperialism na Dalnem Vostoke" (Japanese Imperialism in the Far East), *Novyi Vostok* (Moscow), No. 2, 1922, pp. 3–57.

———, "Tikho-Okeanskaia Problema" (The Pacific Problems), *Novyi Vostok* (Moscow), No. 1, 1922, pp. 16–33.

———, "Vneshniaia Politika i Russko-Iaponskaia Voina" (Foreign Policy and the Russo-Japanese War), L. Martov, *et al.*, *Obshchestvennoe Dvizhenie v Rossii v Nachale XX-go Veka*. St. Petersburg, 1910, ii, Pt. i, pp. 1–32.

———, "Vneshniaia Politika Rossii ot Portsmutskago Mira do Nashikh Dnei" (The Foreign Policy of Russia from the Portsmouth Peace to the Present), L. Martov, *et al.*, *Obshchestvennoe Dvizhenie v Rossii v Nachale XX-go Veka*. St. Petersburg, 1910, iv, Pt. i, pp. 223–278.

"The Peace and After," *The American Monthly Review of Reviews* (New York), xxxii, 5, Nov. 1905, pp. 598–600.

"The Peace of Portsmouth and Its Consequences," *Harper's Weekly* (New York), xlix, 2543, Sept. 16, 1905, p. 1332.

Pelcovits, Nathan A., *Old China Hands and the Foreign Office*. New York, 1948.

Petrov, Victor P., "Manchuria as an Objective of Russian Foreign Policy," Ph.D. dissertation, The American University, Washington, D.C., 1954.

Pierce, Richard A., *Russian Central Asia, 1867–1917*. Berkeley, 1960.

Pokrovsky, M.N. (ed.), *Dnevnik A.N. Kuropatkina* (The Diary of A.N. Kuropatkin). n.p., 1923.

———, "Dnevnik A.N. Kuropatkina, Nov. 17, 1902–Feb. 7, 1904, Oct. 23–Dec. 23, 1905, Dec. 23, 1905–Mar. 12, 1906" (The Diary of A.N. Kuropatkin), *Krasnyi Arkhiv* (Moscow), II, 1922, pp. 5–117; VII, 1924, pp. 55–69; VIII, 1925, pp. 70–100.

———, *Perepiska Vilgelma II s Nikolaem II, 1894–1914 gg.* (Correspondence of William II and Nicholas II). Moscow, 1923.

———, *Vneshniaia Politika Rossii v XX Veke* (Foreign Policy of Russia in the Twentieth Century). Moscow, 1926.

Poleshchuk, V.E., "Revoliutsionnoe Dvizhenie v Manchzhurskoi Armii v 1905 godu" (The Revolutionary Movement in the Manchurian Army in 1905), *Istoricheskie Zapiski* (Moscow), No. 49, 1954, pp. 301–351.

Politovsky, Evgenii S., *From Libau to Tsushima. A Narrative of the Voyage of Admiral Rojdestvensky's Fleet to the Eastern Seas*. London, 1906.

Pooley, A.M. (ed.), *The Secret Memoirs of Count Tadasu Hayashi*. New York, 1915.

Popov, A., "Anglo-Russkoe Soglashenie o Razdele Kitaia 1899 g." (The Anglo-Russian Agreement on the Partition of China in 1899), *Krasnyi Arkhiv* (Moscow), XXV, 1927, pp. 111–134.

———, "Bokserskoe Vosstanie" (The Boxer Uprising), *Krasnyi Arkhiv* (Moscow), XIV, 1926, pp. 1–49.

———, "Pervye Shagi Russkogo Imperializma na Dalnem Vostoke (1888–1903 gg.)" (The First Steps of Russian Imperialism in the Far East, 1888–1903), *Krasnyi Arkhiv* (Moscow), LII, 1932, pp. 34–124.

———, "V Shtabe Adm. E.I. Alekseeva (Iz Dnevnika E.A. Plansona)" (With the Staff of Admiral E.I. Alexeiev (From the diary of E.A. Planson)), *Krasnyi Arkiv* (Moscow), XLI–XLII, 1930, pp. 148–204.

Porter, Charles W., *The Career of Theophile Delcassé*. Philadelphia, 1936.

Potemkin, V.P. (ed.), *Istoriia Diplomatii* (A History of Diplomacy). 3 Vols. Moscow, 1945.

Pratt, Edwin A., *The Rise of Rail-Power in War and Conquest 1833–1914*. London, 1915.

Presseisen, Ernest L., "Roots of Japanese Imperialism: A Memorandum of General Le Gendre," *Journal of Modern History* (Chicago), XXIX, 2, June 1957, pp. 108–111.

dePressensé, Francis, "The Collapse of Russia: II, The Fall of M. Delcassé and the Anglo-French 'Entente,'" *The Nineteenth Century and after* (London), LVIII, 341, July 1905, pp. 22–23.

Price, Earnest B., *The Russo-Japanese Treaties of 1907–1916 Concerning Manchuria and Mongolia*. Baltimore, 1933.

Pringle, Henry F., *Theodore Roosevelt: A Biography*. New York, 1956.

Potter, E.B. (ed.), *The United States and World Sea Power*. Englewood Cliffs, 1955.

"The Progress of the World," *The American Monthly Review of Reviews* (New York), XXXII, 3, Sept. 1905, pp. 259–266.

Pushkareva, I.M., "Zheleznodorozhniki Rossii-Aktivnye Uchastniki Oktiabrskoi Politicheskoi Stachki 1905 goda" (Russian Railwaymen-Active Participants in the October Political Strike of 1905), *Voprosy Istorii* (Moscow), XII, 1958, pp. 152–169.

Rasmussen, O.D., *The Reconquest of Asia*, London, 1934.

Reinsch, Paul S., *World Politics at the End of the Nineteenth Century*. New York, 1908.

Remer, Charles F., *Foreign Investments in China*. New York, 1933.

——, *A Study of Chinese Boycotts*. Baltimore, 1933.

Renouvin, Pierre, *La Question d'Extreme-Orient 1840–1940*. Paris, 1946.

"The Riots in the Russian Oil Fields," *The American Monthly Review of Reviews* (New York), XXXII, 5, Nov. 1905, pp. 605–606.

Robinson, Geroid T., *Rural Russia under the Old Regime*. New York, 1949.

Rockhill, William W., *Treaties and Conventions with or concerning China and Korea, 1894–1904*. Washington, 1904.

Romanov, Boris A. (ed.), "Bezobrazovskii Kruzhok Letom 1904 g." (The Bezobrazov Circle in the Summer of 1904), *Krasnyi Arkhiv* (Moscow), XVII, 1926, pp. 70–80.

—— (ed.), "Konets Russko-Iaponskoi Voiny; Voennoe Soveshchanie 24 Maia 1905 g. v Tsarskom Selo" (The End of the Russo-Japanese War; Military Conference of 24 May, 1905 at Tsarskoe Selo), *Krasnyi Arkhiv* (Moscow), XXVIII, 1927, pp. 182–204.

——, "Diplomaticheskoe Razviazyvanie Russko-Iaponskoi Voiny 1904–1905" (The Diplomatic Unleashing of the Russo-Japanese War 1904–1905), *Istoricheskie Zapiski* (Moscow), No. 8, 1940, pp. 37–67.

——, "Kontsessiia na Ialu" (The Concession on the Yalu), *Russkoe Proshloe* (Moscow), No. 1, 1923, pp. 87–108.

——, *Ocherki Diplomaticheskoi Istorii Russko-Iaponskoi Voiny, 1895–1907* (A Survey of the Diplomatic History of the Russo-Japanese War, 1895–1907). Moscow, 1947.

——— (ed.), "Portsmut. Perepiska S. Iu. Witte i Drugikh Lits" (Portsmouth. Correspondence of S.I. Witte with Other Persons), *Krasnyi Arkhiv* (Moscow), vi, 1924, pp. 3–47, vii, 1924, pp. 3–31.

———, *Russia in Manchuria* (1892–1906). Ann Arbor, 1952.

———, "Witte i Kontsessiia na Reke Ialu" (Witte and the Concession on the Yalu River), S.F. Platonov, *Sbornik v Chest,* Petrograd, 1922, pp. 425–459.

———, "Witte Nakanune Russko-Iaponskoi Voiny" (Witte on the Eve of the Russo-Japanese War), *Rossiia i Zapad* (Petrograd), No. 1, 1923, pp. 140–167.

"Roosevelt as Russia's Helper," *The American Monthly Review of Reviews* (New York), xxxii, 4, Oct. 1905, p. 475.

Rosen, Oscar, "German-Japanese Relations, 1894–1902: A Study of European Imperialism in the Far East," Ph.D. dissertation, University of Wisconsin, Madison, 1956.

Rosen, Roman R., *Forty Years of Diplomacy.* 2 Vols. London, 1922.

Rozental, E.M., *Diplomaticheskaia Istoriia Russko Frantsuzkogo Soiuza v Nachale XX Veka* (Diplomatic History of the Russo-French Alliance at the Beginning of the Twentieth Century). Moscow, 1960.

Rupen, Robert A., "Mongolian Nationalism," *Journal of the Royal Central Asian Society* (London), xlv, Pt. ii, Apr. 1958, pp. 157–178.

Russia. Ministry of Foreign Affairs, *Obzor Snoshenii s Iaponieiu po Koreiskom Delam s 1895 goda* (Survey of Relations with Japan concerning Korean Affairs since 1895). St. Petersburg, 1906.

———, *Protokoly Portsmutskoi Mirnoi Konferentsii i Tekst Dogovora mezhdu Rossieiu i Iaponieiu Zakliuchennago v Portsmut 23 Avgusta (5 Sentiabria) 1905 goda* (Protocols of the Portsmouth Peace Conference and the Text of the Treaty Concluded between Russia and Japan at Portsmouth on August 23/September 5, 1905). St. Petersburg, 1906.

———, *Sbornik Dogovorov i Diplomticheskikh Dokumentov po Delam Daliago Vostoka, 1895–1905 gg.* (Collection of Treaties and Diplomatic Documents on Affairs of the Far East, 1895–1905). St. Petersburg, 1906.

Russia. Pereselencheskoe Upravlenie Glavnago Upravleniia Zemleustroistva i Zemledeliia, *Aziatskaia Rossiia* (Asiatic Russia). 3 Vols. St. Petersburg, 1914.

"Russia and Japanese Finances," *The American Monthly Review of Reviews* (New York), xxxii, 3, Sept. 1905, pp. 381–382.

"Russia in Manchuria," *Harper's Weekly* (New York), xlvii, 2420, May 9, 1903, p. 772.

"The Russians in Manchuria," *Harper's Weekly* (New York), xlvii, 2405, Jan. 24, 1903, p. 141.

Saeki Heizo (ed.), *Kato Takaakira Den* (Biography of Kato Taka-akira). Tokyo, 1928.

Savinsky, A.A., *Recollections of a Russian Diplomat*. London, 1928.

"Jacob H. Schiff the Pioneer of American Foreign Financing," *The Annalist* (New York), xvi, 404, Oct. 11, 1920, pp. 452–454.

Schorske, Carl E., *German Social Democracy, 1905–1917, The Development of the Great Schism*. Cambridge, 1955.

Schurer, H., "The Russian Revolution of 1905 and the Origins of German Communism," *The Slavonic and East European Review* (London), xxxix, 93, June 1961, pp. 459–471.

Seegar, Charles L. (trans. and ed.), *The Memoirs of Alexander Iswolsky: Formerly Russian Minister of Foreign Affairs and Ambassador to France*. London, 1920.

Sergeiev, A.A. (ed.), "Vilgelm II o Russko-Iaponskoi Voine i Revoliutsii 1905 goda" (Wilhelm II concerning the Russo-Japanese War and the Revolution of 1905), *Krasnyi Arkhiv* (Moscow), ix, 1925, pp. 56–65.

Seton Watson, Hugh, *The Decline of Imperial Russia*. New York, 1952.

Shelking, Evgenii N., *Recollections of a Russian Diplomat; the Suicide of Monarchies (William II and Nicholas II)*. New York, 1918.

Shidehara Kijuro, *Gaiko Gojunen* (Fifty Years of Diplomacy). Tokyo, 1951.

Shinobu Jumpei, *Meiji Hiwa Ni dai Gaiko Shinso* (Two Principal Diplomatic Episodes of the Meiji Period). Tokyo, 1928.

Shinobu Seisaburo and Haruichi Nakayama (eds.), *Nichiro Senso Shi no Kenkyu* (A Study of the History of the Russo-Japanese War). Tokyo, 1959.

Shitei Tsunamasa, *Sensoshi Gaikan* (An Outline of Military History). Tokyo, 1943.

Shostak, I.F. and I.G. Pozdniakov, "Proklamatsiia Iaponskikh Sotsialistov" (Proclamation of the Japanese Socialists), *Sovetskoe Vostokovedenie* (Moscow), iii, 1958, pp. 120–121.

Sidorov, Arkadii L., *Russko-Iaponskaia Voina, 1904–1905 gg.* (The Russo-Japanese War, 1904–1905). Moscow, 1939.

Slonimsky, L., "Pravyia Partii i Patriotizm" (The Right Party and Patriotism), *Vestnik Evropy* (St. Petersburg), iv, 1907, pp. 724–732.

Sokolsky, George E., *The Story of the Chinese Eastern Railway*. Shanghai, 1929.

Sontag, Raymond J., "German Foreign Policy, 1904–1906," *American Historical Review* (New York), xxxiii, 2, Jan. 1928, pp. 278–301.

Sorokin, A.I., *Oborona Port-Artura. Russko-Iaponskaia Voina, 1904–1905 gg.* (The Defense of Port Arthur. The Russo-Japanese War, 1904–1905). Moscow, 1954.

——, *Russko-Iaponskaia Voina, 1904–1905 gg.* (The Russo-Japanese War, 1904–1905). Moscow, 1956.

Speransky, A.F., "Materialy k Istorii Interventsii" (Materials for the History of the Intervention), *Novyi Vostok* (Moscow), No. 2, 1922, pp. 591–603.

Spinks, Charles N., "The Background of the Anglo-Japanese Alliance," *Pacific Historical Review* (Berkeley), VIII, 3, Sept. 1939, pp. 317–339.

——, "Origins of Japanese Interests in Manchuria," *The Far Eastern Quarterly* (Ann Arbor), II, 3, May 1943, pp. 259–271.

——, "The Termination of the Anglo-Japanese Alliance," *Pacific Historical Review* (Berkeley), VI, 4, 1937, pp. 321–340.

Stead, William T., "How St. Petersburg Received the News of Peace," *The American Monthly Review of Reviews* (New York), XXXII, 4, Oct. 1905, pp. 426–429.

von Steinmann, Friedrich, *Russlands Politik im Fernen Osten und der Staatssekretär Bezobrazov; Ein Beitrag zur Vorgeschichte des russisch-japanischen Krieges.* Leipzig, 1931.

Steiner, Zara S., "Great Britain and the Creation of the Anglo-Japanese Alliance," *Journal of Modern History* (Chicago), XXXI, 1, Mar. 1959, pp. 27–36.

Stone, Melville E., "The Portsmouth Conference [Roosevelt's mediation efforts with Japan, Aug. 19, 1905]," *The Saturday Evening Post* (Philadelphia), Vol. 187, No. 31, Jan. 30, 1915, pp. 3–4, 48.

——, *Fifty Years a Journalist.* New York, 1921.

Stopalov, G. (ed.), "Perepiska S. Iu. Witte i A.N. Kuropatkina v 1904–1905 gg." (Correspondence of S.I. Witte and A.N. Kuropatkin in 1904–1905), *Krasnyi Arkhiv* (Moscow), XIX, 1927, pp. 64–82.

Straus, Oscar S., *Under Four Administrations.* Boston, 1922.

Sugawara Takamitsu, "Japanese Interests in Korea and the Yalu Issue 1903–1904," M.A. thesis, University of Hawaii, Honolulu, 1963.

Sumner, B.H., "Tsardom and Imperialism in the Far East and Middle East, 1880–1914," *Proceedings of the British Academy* (London), XXVII, 1941, pp. 25–65.

Sun E-tu Zen [Sun I-tu Jen], *Chinese Railways and British Interests 1898–1911.* New York, 1954.

Sutton, Joseph L., "Territorial Claims of Russia and Japan in the Kurile Islands," Center for Japanese Studies, Ann Arbor, *Occasional Papers*, No. 1, 1951, pp. 35–61.

Suyematsu Kencho, *The Risen Sun.* New York, 1905.

——, "Russia and Japan," *Asiatic Quarterly Review* (London), XXXVII–XXXVIII, July 1904, pp. 1–27.

Sykes, Percy, *The Right Honourable Sir Mortimer Durand.* London, 1926.

Takahashi Sakue, *International Law Applied to the Russo-Japanese War*. New York, 1908.

Takeuchi Tatsuji, *War and Diplomacy in the Japanese Empire*. New York, 1935.

Tan, Chester C. (Ch'un-lin T'an), *The Boxer Catastrophe*. New York, 1955.

Tardieu, Andre, *France and the Alliances*. New York, 1908.

——, *Questions Diplomatiques de L'Année 1904*. Paris, 1905.

Tarle, Evgenii V., *Imperatory Vilgelm II i Nikolai II v 1904–1907 gg.* (The Emperors William II and Nicholas II in 1904–1907). Petrograd, 1917.

deTaube, Michael, *La Politique Russe d'avant-guerre et la Fin de l'Empire des Tsars (1904–1917)* (*Memoires*). Paris, 1928.

Teng, S-y and J.K. Fairbank, *China's Response to the West*. Cambridge, 1954.

von Tettau, E., *Achtzehn Monate mit Russlands Heeren in der Mandschurei*. 2 Vols. Berlin, 1907–1908.

Tewksbury, Donald G. (comp.), *Source Materials on Korean Politics and Ideologies*. New York, 1950.

Thayer, William R., *The Life and Letters of John Hay*. 2 Vols. Boston and New York, 1919.

Thorson, Winston B., "American Public Opinion and the Portsmouth Peace Conference," *American Historical Review* (New York), LIII, 3, Apr. 1948, pp. 439–464.

——, "Pacific Northwest Opinion on the Russo-Japanese War of 1904–1905," *Pacific Northwest Quarterly* (Seattle), xxv, Oct. 1944, pp. 305–322.

Togo Kichitaro (trans. by J. Takakusu), *The Naval Battles of the Russo-Japanese War*. Tokyo, 1907.

Tokutomi Iichiro, *Japanese-American Relations*. New York, 1922.

—— (ed.), *Kōshaku Katsura Taro Den* (Biography of Marquis Katsura Taro). 2 Vols. Tokyo, 1917.

—— (ed.), *Kōshaku Yamagata Aritomo Den* (Biography of Marquis Yamagata Aritomo). 3 Vols. Tokyo, 1933.

Tolstoi, Lyof N., *Bethink Yourselves!* New York, n.d.

Tomizu Hiroshihito, "Kōwa no Jiki Hatashite Itaritaru ya" (Is the Peace Opportune?), *Gaiko Jiho* (Tokyo), No. 92, July 10, 1905, pp. 61–65.

——, "Sekai no Taisei to Nichiro Senso no Ketsumatsu" (World Trends and the Termination of the Russo-Japanese War), *Gaiko Jiho* (Tokyo), No. 89, Apr. 10, 1905, pp. 29–67.

——, "Senso no Keizoku" (Continuation of the War), *Gaiko Jiho* (Tokyo), No. 87, Feb. 10, 1905, pp. 57–58.

Tompkins, Stuart R., "Witte as Minister of Finance, 1892–1903," *The Slavonic and East European Review* (London), XI, Apr. 1933, pp. 590–606.

Torgashev, P.I., *Avantiura na Dalnem Vostoke* (Adventure in the Far East). Moscow, 1907.

Townsend, M.E., and Cyrus H. Peake, *European Colonial Expansion since 1871.* Chicago, 1941.

Treadgold, Donald W., *Lenin and His Rivals.* New York, 1955.

Trubetzkoi, G., *Russland Als Grossmacht.* Stuttgart, 1913.

Tsiang, T.F., "Sino-Japanese Diplomatic Relations, 1870–1894," *The Chinese Social and Political Science Review* (Peking), XVII, 1, Apr. 1933, pp. 1–106.

Tsovikian, K.M., "Vliianie Russkoi Revoliutsii 1905 g. na Revoliutsionnoe Dvizhenie v Turtsii" (The Influence of the Russian Revolution of 1905 on the Revolutionary Movement in Turkey), *Sovetskoe Vostokovedenie* (Moscow), III, 1945, pp. 15–35.

Turley, Robert and C.T. Collyer, "Southern Manchuria and Korea," *The Geographical Journal* (London), XXIII, 4, Apr. 1904, pp. 473–492.

Tyler, Sidney, *The Japan-Russia War.* Philadelphia, 1905.

Ueda Toshio, "Nichiro Senso to Ruzuverto" (The Russo-Japanese War and Roosevelt), in Ueda Toshio, *Tsutsunde Kanreki wo Shukushi Kamikawa Sensei ni Sasagu,* Tokyo, 1956, pp. 109–174.

Ukhtomskii, E., "Russia Will Crush Japan," *Independent* (New York), LVI, 2899, June 23, 1904, pp. 1418–1420.

Union of Soviet Socialist Republics. Central Archives, *Krasnyi Arkhiv* (Red Archives). 106 issues in 73 vols. Moscow, 1922–1941.

———, *Russko-Iaponskaia Voina; iz Dnevnikov A.N. Kuropatkina i N.P. Linievicha* (The Russo-Japanese War; from the Diaries of A.N. Kuropatkin and N.P. Linievich) (Foreword by M.N. Pokrovsky). Leningrad, 1925.

United States. Department of Commerce and Labor. Bureau of Statistics, *Monthy Consular Reports 1903–1905.* Washington, 1903–1905.

United States. Department of State, *Papers Relating to the Foreign Relations of the United States—1903–1905.* Washington, 1904–1906.

United States. National Archives. Microfilm Publications, *Despatches from United States Ministers to China 1843–1906.* Washington, 1953.

———, *Despatches from Foreign Legations Japan 1858–1906.* Washington, 1953.

———, *Despatches from United States Ministers to Russia 1808–1906.* Washington, 1953.

United States. War Department. Office of the Chief of Staff, *Reports of Military Observers Attached to the Armies in Manchuria during the Russo-Japanese War.* Pts. II, III. Washington, 1906.

Unterberger, P.F., "Priamurskii Krai, 1906–1910" (The Amur Region, 1906–1910), *Zapiski Imperatorskago Russkago Geograficheskago Obshchestva* (St. Petersburg), xiii, ed. by V.V. Morachevskii, 1912.

Vagts, Alfred, *Deutschland und die Vereinigten Staaten in der Weltpolitik.* 2 Vols. New York, 1935.

Vambery, Arminius, "The Reaction of the Russian Defeat upon the Moslem World in Asia" (Digest of Arminius Vambery's article in *Deutsche Revue*), *The American Monthly Review of Reviews* (New York), xxx, 2, Aug. 1905, pp. 240–242.

Van Norman, Louis E., "The Making of a Modern Treaty of Peace," *The American Monthly Review of Reviews* (New York), xxxii, 4, Oct. 1905, pp. 418–425.

Varg, Paul A., "The Foreign Policy of Japan and the Boxer Revolt," *Pacific Historical Review* (Berkeley), xv, 3, Sept. 1946, pp. 279–285.

———, *Open Door Diplomat: The Life of W.W. Rockhill.* Urbana, 1952.

Vaughan, Dorothy and Thomas C. Wilson (eds.), *The Peace of Portsmouth.* Portsmouth, 1957.

Vetoshkin, M., *Iz Istorii Bolshevistskikh Organizatsii i Revoliutsionnogo Dvizheniia v Sibiri* (From the History of the Bolshevik Organizations in the Revolutionary Movement in Siberia). Moscow, 1947.

Vevier, Charles, *The United States and China, 1906–1913; A Study of Finance and Diplomacy.* New Brunswick, 1955.

Viallate, Achille, *Economic Imperialism and International Relations during the Last Fifty Years.* New York, 1923.

Volonter. Rossiiskaia Sotsialdemokraticheskaia Rabochaia Partiia, *Russko-Iaponskaia Voina; Prichiny, Khod i Posledstviia. (God Voiny) (Izdanie "Iskra")* (The Russo-Japanese War; the Causes, Course and Consequences. A Year of War. An "Iskra" Publication). Geneva, 1905.

Vonliarliarsky, Vladimir M., *Moi Vospominaniia, 1852–1939 gg.* (My Memoirs, 1852–1939). Berlin, 1939.

——— (actually unsigned, merely attributed to him), "Why Russia Went to War with Japan: The Story of the Yalu Concession," *Fortnightly Review* (London), No. dxxi New Series, May 2, 1910, pp. 816–831, No. dxxii New Series, June 1, 1910, pp. 1030–1044.

Votinov, A., *Iaponskii Shpionazh v Russko-Iaponskuiu Voiny 1904–1905 gg.* (Japanese Espionage in the Russo-Japanese War 1904–1905). Moscow, 1939.

Vucinich, Wayne S., *Serbia between East and West: The Events of 1903–1908.* Stanford, 1954.

Watanabe Ikujiro, *Nisshin Nichiro Senso Shiwa* (Historical Discussions of the Sino-Japanese and Russo-Japanese Wars). Tokyo, 1937.

Weale, B.L. Putnam [Bertram Lenox Simpson], *Manchu and Muscovite*. London, 1907.

Weber, B.G., and S.R. Dimant (eds.), "Russian Documents Relating to the Sino-Japanese War, 1894–1895," *The Chinese Social and Political Science Review* (Peking), xvii, 3, Oct. 1933, pp. 480–515; 4, Jan. 1934, pp. 632–670.

Weigh, K.S., *Russo-Chinese Diplomacy*. Shanghai, 1928.

Weressajew, W. (Vikenti Vikentevich Smidovich), *Meine Erlebnisse im Russisch-Japanischen Krieg*. Stuttgart, 1909.

Whigham, Henry J., *Manchuria and Korea*. London, 1904.

White, John A., *The Siberian Intervention*. Princeton, 1950.

Whitney, Henry N., "British Foreign Policy and the Russo-Japanese War," Ph.D. dissertation, University of Pennsylvania, Philadelphia, 1948.

Who's Who in America 1903–1905. Chicago, n.d.

"Why America is in Manchuria to stay," *Harper's Weekly* (New York), xlvii, 2421, May 16, 1903, p. 786.

Williams, Benjamin H., *Economic Foreign Policy of the United States*. New York, 1929.

Wilson, F.M. Huntington, *Memoirs of an Ex-Diplomat*. Boston, 1945.

"Graf Witte v Borbe s Revoliutsiei. Doklad Gr. Witte Nikolaiu II v Dekabre 1905—Ianvare 1906 g." (Count Witte in the Struggle with the Revolution. Report of Count Witte to Nicholas II in December 1905–January 1906), *Byloe* (Petrograd), No. 3 (31), Mar. 1918, pp. 3–10.

Witte, Sergei I., "Russia's Work in Manchuria," *Harper's Weekly* (New York), xlviii, 2468, Apr. 9, 1904, pp. 544–545.

————, *Vospominaniia. Tsarstvovanie Nikolaia II* (Memoirs. The Reign of Nicholas II). 2 Vols. Berlin, 1922.

————, *Vospominaniia* (Memoirs). 3 Vols. Moscow, 1960.

————, *Vynuzhdennyia Raziasneniia po Povodu Otcheta Gen. Ad. Kuropatkina o Voine s Iaponiei* (Necessary Clarifications of General Kuropatkin's Account of the War with Japan). Moscow, 1911.

Wolfe, Bertram D., *Three Who Made a Revolution*. New York, 1948.

Wright, Mary, "The Adaptability of Ch'ing Diplomacy: the Case of Korea," *Journal of Asian Studies* (Chicago), xvii, 3, May 1958, pp. 363–381.

Wright, Stanley F., *Hart and the Chinese Customs*. Belfast, 1950.

Yakobson, Sergius, "Russia and Africa," *The Slavonic and East European Review* (London), xvii, Apr. 1939, pp. 623–637; xix, 1939–40, pp. 158–174.

Yano Jinichi, *Nisshin Ekigo Shina Gaikō Shi* (Diplomatic History of China since the Sino-Japanese War). Kyoto, 1937.

Young, C. Walter, *Japan's Special Position in Manchuria; Its Assertion, Legal Interpretation and Present Meaning.* Baltimore, 1931.

Zabriskie, Edward H., *American-Russian Rivalry in the Far East; A Study in Diplomacy and Power Politics 1895–1914.* Philadelphia, 1946.

Zalkind, S. (ed.), "Otrazhenie Sobytii 1905 g. za Granitsei" (The Events of 1905 as Reflected Abroad), *Krasnyi Arkhiv* (Moscow), ix, 1925, pp. 32–55.

Zetland, Lawrence [Earl of Ronaldshay], *The Life of Lord Curzon.* 3 Vols. London, 1927.

Zhukov, E., *Mezhdunarodnye Otnoshenia na Dalnem Vostoke, 1870– 1945* (International Relations in the Far East, 1870–1945). Moscow, 1951.

Zilliacus, Konni, *The Russian Revolutionary Movement.* New York, 1905.

Index

Abaza, Aleksei Mikailovich, Rear Admiral, 36, 113, 127
Akashi Motojiro, Colonel; military attaché at St. Petersburg, then Stockholm, 140–141, 190
Albert, Matvei Osipovich, 37
Aleksei Aleksandrovich, Grand Duke, 18, 37, 42, 74, 144, 328
Aleksei Aleksandrovich, Grand Duke, General Admiral, titular head of the Navy, 37, 54, 113–114
Alekseiev, Evgenii Ivanovich, Admiral; viceroy and commander in chief, Russian Far East, 6–7, 65, 67, 72, 103–106, 112–113, 129, 130, 148, 151–152, 165, 356
Algeciras conference, 213–215
Allgemeine Zeitung, 151, 259
American-Chinese relations, 57, 89–91, 97–98, 106, 197–198, 313
American-German relations, 196–197
American-Japanese relations, 57, 83, 89–91, 97–98, 106, 302
American-Russian relations, 97, 118
Anglo-French Entente, 116–117, 172–176, 178, 181, 205
Anglo-German relations, 175, 177
Anglo-Japanese Alliance, 1902, 9, 25, 57, 83–85, 88–94, 96–97, 125, 173
Anglo-Japanese Alliance, 1905, 216–217, 267–268
Anglo-Russian agreement, 1899, 87
Anglo-Russian negotiations, 1903–1904, 27, 173
Anti-Russian League (Tairo Doshikai), 95–96, 321
Anti-Semitism, 13–14, 36–37, 57–58, 168–169, 192, 260–261
Antung, 44, 91, 106, 150
Armistice, 311
Arthur, William, Lieutenant, 21
Asahi, 242, 319
"Asia for the Asians" policy, 115–116, 121
Association for Those Interested in the Peace Problem (Kowa Mondai Rengo Doshikai), 320–321
Azev, Evno Fishelevich, 138, 192

Baelz, Irwin, quoted, 120–121, 177
Baikal, Lake, 146–147, 320
Balashev, Ivan Petrovich, 41–42
Balfour, Arthur James, British Prime Minister, 116–117
Benckendorff, Count Aleksander Konstantinovich, Russian ambassador to Great Britain, 27, 180

Beveridge, Albert, United States Senator, 12, 72
Bezobrazov, Aleksander Mikhailovich, 24–46, 62, 109, 127, 150
"Bezobrazov circle," 36, 55, 65, 68
Bezobrazov, Manchurian tour, 42–46
Biely, Andrei, 192
Björkö meeting, 214–215
Black Dragon Society (Kokuruykai), 95
Black Ocean Society (Genyosha), 95, 324
Blagoveshchensk, 5, 248
"Bloody Sunday," 189–190, 193, 222
Boer War, 2, 177
Border region—Sino-Russian, 8, 35, 87, 286, 342–343, 349
Boxer Rebellion, 2, 4–5, 7, 10, 24, 41, 48, 90, 94, 109
Briner, Iulius Ivanovich, timber concession, 32–34, 40
von Bülow, Bernhard, Chancellor of Germany, 172, 197
Burgess, John W., 161, 345
von dem Bussche-Haddenhausen, Baron Hilmar, 305–306

Cambon, Paul, French ambassador to Great Britain, 174
"Captain Rybnikov," 139
Cassini, Count A.P., Russian ambassador to the United States, 203–204, 212, 234
Changchun, 279, 313–314, 339
Chang Tso-lin, 343
Chefoo, 124
Chekhov, Anton D., 285
Chemulpo, 148
Chihli province, 21
China, 83, 123, 255, 292
China, integrity, 341
China, Japanese policy regarding, 115–116
China-rights recovery, 333–334
China, Russian policy, 6, 9, 52, 54, 56, 59, 69–70, 104
China, United States and Japan treaties regarding Manchuria, 57, 91, 106–107
Chinese Eastern Railway, 8, 18–19, 22, 24, 28, 248, 250, 254, 313, 354, 360, 362, 366
Chinese Haikuan Bank, 23
Chinese Imperial Maritime Customs Service, 22, 69, 336
Ching, Prince, 56–57, 332, 340

405

Daiichi Bank, 78
Dalny (Talien, Dairen), 18, 21–22, 24, 152, 275, 336, 344
Delcassé, Theophile, French minister of foreign affairs, 124–127, 174, 176, 181, 213
Denison, Henry W., 232, 316
Dmowski, Roman, 141–142
Dogger Bank, 179, 182–184, 214
Dillon, Edward, 141, 229–230, 236, 242, 256–257, 259

East Asian Development Company, 40–41

von Eckardstein, Baron Hermann, 84, 198
Edward VII, King of England, 196, 223
Egypt, relation to Britain, 84

Fenghuangcheng, 44, 70, 150, 152
Fengtien province, 20, 70, 331, 342, 368
Fisher, Sir John, Admiral, First Sea Lord, 180, 213
Fishery rights, 283–284, 314, 363–364, 367
France, 92
France, mediation efforts, 124–127
Franco-Japanese relations, 205
Franco-Russian alliance, 94, 178, 183–184, 205
Franco-Russian declarations of March 1902, 9
Fukien-Japanese interest, 80–91, 101
Fukushima, Yasumasa, General, 139, 311
Fushun mines, 45, 63

Gaiko Jiho, 320
Gamecock Fleet, 179
Gapon, Father George (Georgii Apollonovich), 141, 189–190
Germany, 92–94, 117, 161, 170–171, 174–178, 196, 213, 277, 286, 297
Giers, N.K., Russian minister of foreign affairs, quoted, 76
Ginsburg, Baron Moise Haimovich, 55
Gurko, V.I., quoted, 38

Harbin, 18, 20–21, 41, 65, 222, 227, 248, 273–274, 277, 279, 311, 361
Hardinge, Sir Charles, British ambassador to Russia, 216
Harriman, E. H., 325–327
Hart, Sir Henry, 23, 24
Hay, John, United States Secretary of State, 118–119, 158, 161, 203

Hayashi, Tadasu, Baron, Japanese minister to Great Britain, 82–84, 88–89, 116, 135, 142, 216–217
Heilungchiang province, 20, 70
Horvath, Dmitri Leonidovich, Colonel; general manager of the Chinese Eastern Railway and administrator of the leased territory in Manchuria from 1902, 67
Howells, William Dean, quoted, 242
Hsinmintun-Fakumen Railway, 341
Hsü Shih-chang, 313

Indemnity, demand, 295, 302, 362; issue at the Portsmouth Conference, 282–309, 362
India, 3, 216
Ishii Kikujiro, 307
Ito Hirobumi, Viscount, 77, 101, 156, 202, 229, 258, 307; Korea, 264, 271–272; Negotiations in St. Petersburg, 84–88, 97, 108, 174
Iugovich, A.I., Chief engineer of the Chinese Eastern Railway, 67
Izvolsky, Aleksander Petrovich, 12

Japan, conferences regarding Russia, 101–102, 109, 114–116, 121, 128; diplomacy regarding Russia, 81–94, 96–100, 104, 114–119, 128; 301; foreign loans, 117–118, 167–169, 202–203, 327; intelligence service, 136–142; interests in Korea, 76–81, 92, 100–101; Korean protectorate, 264–272; military preparedness, 135–136; military strength in 1905, 201–203, 317; public relations, 245–246, 261–262; railways in Korea, 79
Japanese Emperor, 249, 321, 344
Japanese-Korean relations, 76–81
Japanese-Russian negotiations, 102; first exchange, 102–108; second exchange, 108–111; third exchange, 112–121; fourth exchange, 121–130
Japanese socialists, 323–324
Jews in America, 257, 260–261, 290
Jiji Shimpo, 135, 323
Jodko, Witold, 142
"John Grafton," 190

Kaneko Kentaro, Baron, 156–159, 203, 219, 227, 237, 239, 296–297, 300–303, 305–306, 308, 326–327
Katayama Sen, 323–324
Katsura Taro, Viscount, Japanese prime minister, 66–67, 84–85, 100–101, 218, 229–231, 268–269, 288, 307–308, 322, 326, 331

von Ketteler, Baron Klemens, German minister to China, 6

Khilkov, Prince Mikhail Ivanovich, Russian minister of communications, 202

Kirin province, 20, 70, 254, 279, 339

Kishinev pogrom, 57–58, 168

Kittery navy yard, 241–243

Kodama Gentaro, General, 140, 149, 202, 223, 288

Kokovtsov, Vladimir Nikolaevich, Russian minister of finance, 13, 237, 251–252, 276; views regarding peace, 251–252

Kokumin Shimbun, 318, 322

Komura Jutaro, Baron, Japanese minister of foreign affairs; plenipotentiary to Portsmouth and Peking conferences, 56–57, 66, 88–89, 96, 100–101, 103, 105, 107–109, 120, 124–127, 140, 157, 206, 216, 224, 229, 248–249, 326–327; Peking conference, 331–337; Portsmouth conference, 229–231, 234, 243–247, 249, 258, 273, 275–281, 284–286, 291–297, 302–306, 308–309, 312, 316

Kondaratenko, Roman Isidorovich, General, 186–187

Kono Hironaka, 321–322

Korea, 26, 32–35, 39–40, 51–53, 55, 60–62, 68, 71, 78, 86, 123–124, 218; issue at Portsmouth conference, 253, 264–272; Japanese development, 78; Japanese railways, 79; Japanese timber concession, 80; neutral zone, 86–87, 108–110, 122, 130, 349, 352–353, 355–356; neutralization policy, 81, 123–124; United States policy, 91

Korostovets, I.I., 25, 236, 242, 258, 302–303

Korsakov (Sakhalin), 224, 285, 315

Kraus, Adolph, 260

Kuanchengtze, 21, 24, 279, 313–314, 336, 339

Kuantung (Liaotung) peninsula, 18, 21, 25, 56, 60, 71–72, 77–78, 82, 151–152, 248, 254, 275–276, 312, 331, 360, 365

Kuroki, Tamemoto, General, 149–150, 153

Kuropatkin, Aleksei Nikolaevich, General; war minister, 1, 38, 46–50, 62, 86, 109, 113, 143, 148, 150–153, 170, 223, 234, 254–255, 289, 327; Far Eastern tour, 58–60, 63–75; Japan visit, 64–67, 101; views, 46–49, 56, 86, 113, 146

Kurino Shinichiro, Japanese minister to Russia, 64, 88, 102–103, 122, 127, 130–131, 140

Lamsdorf, Vladimir Nikolaevich, Russian minister of foreign affairs, 36, 52, 86–87, 92, 103, 114, 124, 212, 234, 251, 299–300, 308

Lansdowne, Lord, British secretary of state for foreign affairs, 84, 99, 180, 182, 217

Lenin, Vladimir Ilich, 188, 222

Lessar, P.M., Russian minister to China, 51–52, 67

Li Hung-chang, viceroy of Chihli, 4, 19, 76–77

Liao River, 20, 22, 45

Linievich, N.P., Lieutenant General, commander in Manchuria, 7, 148, 202, 223, 234–235, 289, 308, 311, 327

Livadia palace (Yalta), 42, 50–51

Lobanov-Rostovsky, Prince A.B., Russian minister of foreign affairs, 39

Lodge, Henry Cabot, United States Senator, 162

Lvov, Fedor Aleksandrovich, 43, 46

MacArthur, Arthur, General, 166

MacDonald, Sir Claude, British minister to Japan, 307

McLane, John, Governor of New Hampshire, 241, 316

Madritov, A.S., Lieutenant Colonel, 43, 46

Mahan, Alfred Thayer, Admiral, writer, 3, 159–160, 187

Makarov, S.O., Vice Admiral, 148–149, 178, 327

Manchuria, 16 (map), 20, 136 (map); bubonic plague, 22–23; issue at the Portsmouth conference, 273–280; Japanese interests, 251–262; Japanese troop withdrawal, 337–339, 364, 366; open commercial cities, 331, 337, 364–365; Russian interests, 18–30, 38–54, 59, 92, 97, 99–100, 102, 114–116, 351–362; Russian occupation, 3–5, 92; Russian troop withdrawal, 10, 53–54, 61, 68–71, 98, 311–313; 337; Sino-Russian agreements, 7–10, 53, 68, 81–82, 91, 104, 106, 323

Manchurian Mining Company, 25, 41, 63

Manchurian railway issue at Portsmouth conference, 276–280, 313–314

March, Payton C., Captain, 166
Martens, Fedor Fedorovich, Professor of International Law, St. Petersburg University, 235–236, 258, 316
Matiunin, Nikolai Gavrilovich, Russian diplomat, 32, 34
Mead, William, Admiral, U.S. Navy, 241, 316
von Mendelssohn-Bartoldi, Ernst, 172
Meyer, George von Lengerke, United States ambassador to Russia, 203, 211–212, 233, 297, 303, 307–308
Miliukov, Pavel Nikolaevich, 141
"Monroe Doctrine" for Asia, 163
Morgan, J.P., 290
Morocco issue, 205, 213–214
Morrison, George E., 241
Mukden, 20, 24, 43, 91, 106–107, 148, 227, 279, 311; battle, 201–202, 205, 224, 288, 290
Mukden-Antung Railway, 337, 366
Mukden-Hsinmintun Railway, 340–341, 366–367
Muraviev, Mikhail Nikolaevich, Russian minister of foreign affairs, 6, 35

Neprozhnev, N.I., Russian privy councilor, 40
Neue Freie Presse, 119
Neutrality, 166–167
New York Times, 119, 261
Newchang (Yinow), 22–24, 70, 342
"New Course," conference concerning 1902–1903, first conference, 50–52; second conference, 52; third conference, 52–54, fourth conference 54–56, fifth conference, 60–63
Nikolai Nikolaevich, Grand Duke, 35
Nicholas II, Emperor of Russia, 14, 28, 65, 74, 107, 165, 182, 193, 203, 209, 211–215, 233, 257, 299, 302–304, 307, 316, 344
The Nineteenth Century and After, 287
Nitobe Inazo, Bushido, 158
Nogi Maresuke, General, 149, 152, 186
North China Herald, 119, 126
Novoe Vremva, 31, 188, 199, 242, 256
Novyi Krai, Russian Port Arthur newspaper, 45, 143
Nozu Michitsura, General, 149

Ochiai Kentaro, 304
Oku Yasukata, General, 149
Oriental Consolidated Mining Company, 79–80

Oriental immigration, 162
Ottoman Empire, 194
Oyama Iwao, Marshal, Japanese commander in chief in Manchuria, 101, 149, 153, 202, 249, 288, 311

Pacific Mail Steamship Company, 324–325
Pavlov, A.I., Russian minister to Korea, 51–52, 67, 104
Peace proposals, 198–201
Pearl Harbor naval base, 220
Peirce, Herbert H.D., United States assistant secretary of state 242, 316
Peking Conference, Additional Agreement, 336–339; Chinese property claims, 338; peace conditions, 330–335; special supplementary protocol, 339; treaty, 334–336
Peking-Hankow Railway, 20
Philippines, 218–219
Pilsudsky, Joseph, 138, 142
Planson, G.A., 235
Plekhanov, G.V., 323
Pleske, Eduard Dmitrievich, Russian minister of finance, 74, 113
Plehve, Viacheslav Konstantinovich, Russian minister of interior, 37–38, 74, 113, 172, 192
Pokotilov, D.D., head of Russo-Chinese Bank in China and representative of Chinese Eastern Railway in China; then Russian minister to China and member of Russian delegation to Portsmouth conference, 67, 234, 258
Pokrovsky, M.N., quoted, 18
Port Arthur (Lüshun), 18–19, 21, 24, 33, 59, 68, 70, 77, 93, 99–100, 103, 139, 143, 149, 150–151, 153, 177, 185, 248, 251, 255, 307, 336, 361, 365–366
Port Arthur Conferences, 67–75, 104
Port Arthur surrender, 186–189, 195, 331
Port Nikolai (see Yongampo)
Portsmouth, New Hamphsire, 228–229
Portsmouth Conference, 223, 227–230, 244–246, 257; interned ships, 280–281, 363; peace conditions, 247–249, 258–259, 359–364; Russian naval strength in the Pacific, 281, 363, 294, 300, 363
Portsmouth Treaty, 316–317, 326, 333, 364; reception, 317–329

"Potemkin" mutiny, 220–221
Prisoners of war, 222, 314

Rockhill, William W., 90, 160
Roosevelt, Theodore, President of the United States, 90, 156–157, 159, 181, 195, 208, 217, 219, 296, 316, 326–327, 332–333; mediation, 203–204, 208–209, 212–213, 227, 229, 232, 237–240, 243, 257, 297, 301, 303–306, 308, 344–346; views, 159, 301
Rosen, Baron Roman Romanovich, Russian minister to Japan; ambassador to the United States; plenipotentiary to the Portsmouth Conference, 52, 58, 89, 91–92, 105–108, 120, 129–131, 234–236, 240, 259, 262, 298–299, 309, 316, 327, 356
Rosen-Nishi agreement, 78, 82, 100
Rothstein, A.I., 25, 34, 168
Rozhdestvensky, Zinovii Petrovich, Vice Admiral, 179, 181–182, 202, 207
Rusin, Aleksander Ivanovich, Naval Captain, 235
Russia, Baltic fleet, 145, 177–182, 187, 224; Black Sea fleet, 145, 194, 220–221; China policy, 6; conferences regarding Japanese negotiations, 113–114, 129; expansion, 3–4; Far Eastern outlook, 144–145; foreign economic competition, 27–28; foreign loans, 171–172, 214, 261, 289–290; interests in Korea, 349–359; military preparedness, 100, 143–147; military strength, 211, 291, 294; "new course" conferences 1902–1903, first conference, 50–52; second conference, 52; third conference, 52–54; fourth conference, 54–56; fifth conference; 60–63; Pacific fleet, 145; revolution of 1905, 189–195, 220–222
Russian conference on peace proposals, 210–211
Russian Far East, 28–29, 31, 33, 48, 72, 77, 114, 138, 248, 250, 278, 287, 295, 320, 362
Russian Lumber Company of the Far East, 62–63
Russo-Chinese Bank, 8, 19–20, 22, 25, 34–35, 42, 67, 70, 90, 97
Russo-Chinese Joint Stock Lumber Company, 46
Russo-German commercial treaty re-renewed, 172
Russo-German relations, 92–94

Russo-Japanese conflict, mediation efforts, 123–127; negotiations, 1903–1904, 102, first exchange, 102–108, second exchange, 108–111, third exchange, 112–121, fourth exchange, 121–130; relations broken, 128–130, 164–165; war; danger foreseen, 119–120, 123–124, 126; military engagements, 149–153; naval engagements, 148–149; sea power, 344; significance, 219–220, 310, 342–344; United States naval policy, 219, 261–262, 310
Russo-Korean Bank, 34

Sakhalin Island, 210–211, 223–224, 238, 250; Russo-Japanese claims, 283, 285; issue at the Portsmouth conference, 282–309, 311, 314, 320, 361; partition, 314–316
Schiff, Jacob H., 168–169, 202, 260, 289–290, 325–326
von Schlieffen, Count Alfred, plan, 176
Seoul, 32, 79, 104, 110, 123–124, 149
Seoul-Fusan Railway, 79, 81
Seoul-Uiju Railway, 79, 81, 109, 264, 337
Sergei Aleksandrovich, Grand Duke, 192
"Seven Professors" (Japan), 320–321, 324
Shidehara Kijuro, 307
Siberia, 16 (map), 18, 36, 139
Sino-Russian agreements, 7, 9–10, 18, 82, 96–98, 312; negotiations, 104
Skrydlov, Nikolai Illirionovich, Vice Admiral, 149
South Manchuria Railway, 313, 362, 368
Special Committee for Far Eastern Affairs, 72
Stackelberg, G.K., Lieutenant General, 153
Stalin, Iosif Vissarionovich (Dzhugashvili), 222
Stark, O.A., Vice Admiral, 148
Stessel, Anatolii Mikhailovich, General; commandant of the fort at Port Arthur, 68, 186
Stockholm, 131, 140
Stone, Melville, 257, 305
St. Petersburg, 42, 58, 82, 103, 131, 172, 189, 192, 256, 190, 194, 304, 327; Council (Soviet) of Workers' Deputies, 193
Straight, Willard, 313, 341
Suematsu Kencho, Baron, 156–157, 199–200
Sungari River, 20, 254, 342

Taft, William Howard, United States secretary of war, 203–204, 217–219

Taft-Katsura agreement, 217–219, 268–269

Taiwan, 101

Takahashi Korekiyo, 168–169, 202

Takahira Kogoro, Japanese minister to the United States, 118, 204, 208, 230, 232, 238, 240, 304, 306

Tanaka, Giichi, Colonel, later General and Japanese prime minister, 65

Tang Shao-yi, 313, 341

Tangier, 205

Tatungko, 106

Terauchi Masatake, General, Japanese minister of war, 65, 101

Three Power (Russia, France, Germany) intervention 1895, 93, 98, 156, 178, 195, 251

Times (London), 81, 119, 242

Togo Heiharchiro, Vice Admiral, 148

Tokyo riots 1905, 321–322, 324

Transbaikal region, 72, 221–222

Trans-Siberian Railway, 16, 146–147, 254, 289

Triple Alliance, 174–175, 178, 187

Trotsky, Leon (Lev Davidovich Bronstein), 193

Tseng Ch'i, Chinese governor general in Manchuria, 7

Tseng-Alekseiev agreement, 7, 9, 81–82

Tsushima, 224; naval battle, 206–209, 213

Uchida Yasuya, Japanese minister to China, 45, 331, 335, 341

Ueno Park (Tokyo) demonstrations, 95

Uiju, 33, 44, 150

Ukhtomsky, Prince Esper Esperevich, 19

Unterberger, Pavel Fedorovich, Lieutenant General; governor general of Amur Province, 252–253, 329

Uriu, Sotokichi, Rear Admiral, 148

Utsonomiya, Taro, Lieutenant Colonel, 140

United States, 57, 89–91, 93, 97–98, 159

Vanity Fair, 177

Viceroy of the Russian Far East (Admiral Alekseiev, 72–73

Vladivostok, 20, 22, 27, 32–33, 99–100, 145, 204, 207, 210, 222–224, 239, 250, 252, 254, 278, 315, 344

Vogak, Konstantin Ippolitovich, Major General, 60, 62, 65, 67

Volunteer Fleet, 37

Vonliarliarsky, Aleksander Mikhailovich, 35, 40, 42

Vorontsov-Dashkov, Count I.I., 36–37, 40

Vyshnegradsky, I.A., Russian minister of finance, 12

Wallace, Sir Donald MacKenzie, 242

Washington, D.C., 227–228

Weber, Carl, Russian minister to Korea, 32

Wentworth-on-the-Sea Hotel, 241, 308

William II, Emperor of Germany, 160, 178, 182–183, 186, 204, 207, 209–210, 213–215, 299, 308, 316

Willenkin, Gregory, 260–261

Witte, Matilda Ivanova (Lisanevich), wife of Sergei Iulievich Witte, 13, 24

Witte, Sergei Iulievich, minister of finance, plenipotentiary at Portsmouth conference, 35–36, 127, 328, 332, 339; antecedents, 11; Asia, 15, 16; career, 13–15; dismissal as minister of finance, 73–75; Manchuria, 4, 172; Manchurian interests, 16, 19–30, 143; opposition to, 32–49; personality, 12; Portsmouth conference, 229, 233–237, 240, 243–247, 249, 255, 257–259, 261, 273, 275–281, 284, 286, 291–300, 302–304, 306, 308–309, 311, 316; public relations, 255–262; trip to Manchuria, 25–30; views, 13–15, 18–19, 26–30, 61, 113, 152

Yalu timber concession, 32–33, 41, 43, 45, 55–56, 61–64, 71, 79, 105, 251

Yamagata Aritomo, Marshal, 202, 288, 307

Yamamoto Gonnohyoei, Admiral, Japanese minister of navy, 101, 308

"Yellow peril," 115–116, 121, 156, 158

Yinkow (see Newchwang)

Yongampo (Korea), 33, 44, 104

Yuan Shih-kai, Viceroy of Chihli Province, 332, 335, 338, 340

Zasulich, Mikhail Ivanovich, Lieutenant General, 148, 150

Zemstvo, 210

Zilliacus, Konni, 141, 190–191